AP
OF
ANCISCO
WEBSTER ST.
MARIETTE ST.
SPARKS ST.
LARKIN ST.
HIDE ST.
LEAVENWORTH
JONES ST.
RUSSIAN HILL
TAYLOR ST.
MASON ST.
POWELL ST.
STOCKTON ST.
DUPONT ST.
KEARNEY ST.
MONTGOMERY ST.
SANSOM ST.
BATTERY
FRONT
DAVIS
DRUMM ST.
PUBLIC
SQUARE
SPRING VALLEY
BELLEVUE
CALIFORNIA
CALIFORNIA ST.
SACRAMENTO
CLAY
WASHINGTON
JACKSON
PACIFIC
BROADWAY
VALLEJO
GREEN
UNION
FILBERT
GREENWICH
LOMBARD
CHESNUT
FRANCISCO
NORTH BEACH
BAY
NORTH POINT
BUSH
PINE
SUTTER
STEUART ST.
EAST ST.
CLARK'S POINT
NORTH POINT
1
2
3
4
5
6
SAN FRANCISCO
SCALE.
0 1 2 3 4 5 6 7 8 9 10

William Tecumseh Sherman:
Gold Rush Banker

WILLIAM TECUMSEH SHERMAN

From a full-length portrait painted by Col. Samuel Lockett, about 1859.

Courtesy of Louisiana State University

William Tecumseh Sherman: Gold Rush Banker

BY DWIGHT L. CLARKE

CALIFORNIA HISTORICAL SOCIETY
San Francisco 1969

Other books by Dwight L. Clarke

Stephen Watts Kearny, Soldier of the West

The Original Journals of Henry Smith Turner
(With Introduction and Biographical Chapter by Dwight L. Clarke)

Special Publication No. 45
Library of Congress Card No. 70-92033

Designed by Adrian Wilson

Printed in the United States of America

Distributed by Lane Magazine & Book Company, Menlo Park, California 94025
Society members should order directly from the Society

To My Good Friends
and Favorite Bankers,

JOSEPH H. ROSENBERG
of Los Angeles

and

EMMETT G. SOLOMON
of San Francisco

Preface

"William Tecumseh Sherman, a banker?" Many people have asked that question. Naturally, Sherman is remembered primarily as one of America's great military commanders. The average American recalls his four-letter definition of war and his advance from Atlanta to the sea—to the accompaniment of flying flags and bands playing "Marching through Georgia." He knows who Sherman was, but surprise, even incredulity, greets the statement that this same man could ever have engaged in so incongruous a calling as banking.

Sherman was forty-one when the Civil War began. He had graduated from West Point the summer after he was twenty. Certainly this restless, energetic figure did not live in a vacuum during the two decades prior to the Civil War. The stormy years devoted to the banking business in pioneer San Francisco occupied the longest span of that ante-bellum period. Those banking years were the most hectic and crisis-laden of his life up to 1861.

Yet Sherman used only forty-seven pages of his two-volume *Memoirs* to tell about them. Small wonder that the writers who have dealt with his career have paid such scant attention to the years from 1853 to 1858. Two of the earlier biographers devoted four and five pages to this period. Two others gave it only a few lines. Some ignored it completely. B. H. Liddell-Hart was more generous; his full-length book has fourteen pages about the California experience. Lloyd Lewis in his interesting volume of more than six hundred pages, filled only a dozen with a summary of the banking episode.

Writers whose subject matter was limited to certain campaigns or restricted periods either disregarded his stay in California altogether or dismissed it with a word—more than once an incorrect word! One book about the march across Georgia connected Sherman's stay in San Francisco with the "collapse" of a bank! Any more inaccurate description of an orderly, voluntary withdrawal from business with all creditors paid in full is hard to imagine. A recent biography of another pioneer San Franciscan quotes a letter Sherman wrote expressing his opinion about the 1856 Vigilance Committee, and identifies its writer as a merchant!

One might ask why at this late date the story of Sherman's banking experiences merits retelling at greater length. Several answers suggest themselves.

Despite the wealth of diaries, letters, and writings of California pioneers, we find surprisingly few firsthand accounts of the conduct of banking in the decade following the discovery of gold. Melodramatic events like San Francisco's early fires have been vividly recounted by eyewitnesses. Both partisans and opponents of the Vigilance Committee fully described those stirring happenings. But search for detailed histories of any of the numerous banking houses follows a barren lode on which the prospector usually searches in vain.

The economy of the Gold Rush was one of the strangest in all history. Banking services were essential to its operation. In the centuries of our recorded knowledge of finance, we can find no greater contrast than that between the sophisticated, automated institution of banking today and its primitive California predecessor of a little more than a century ago. Banking then was a laissez-faire organism so unrestricted and unregulated that its authentic records qualify as artifacts for museum study. Both concept and methodology were unbelievably primitive by present-day standards. However, the number of pioneer banking houses, in proportion to the population served, compares very favorably with that of our age. That is one more evidence of the fiercely competitive spirit of the 1850s.

Californians are now so accustomed to huge branch banking systems, with deposits and loans totaling billions of dollars, that the balance sheets of Gold Rush bankers seem pygmy-like. Their figures command somewhat greater respect if viewed in relation to other statistics of their time. Early San Francisco, with some 50,000 inhabitants, would by present-day standards require fewer banking houses than were actually serving it during the Gold Rush. The entire population of California in 1855 was no greater than today's totals in many local centers. We might also remember that in 1850 the entire United States contained only slightly more inhabitants than California does in the 1960s.

Apart from any urge to correct errors, there is another cogent reason for evoking Sherman as a banker. Few of his contemporaries among pioneer California bankers were as deeply rooted in the Gold Rush.

He had been present when the messenger bearing the news of Marshall's discovery brought the first specimens of gold to Colonel Mason at Monterey. With such knowledge of geology as he possessed, Sherman had scrutinized the nuggets, tested one between his teeth and proved its malleability with a hammer. He assured the incredulous Mason that this was indeed gold! He was one of the small group who had ridden posthaste with the governor to Coloma to verify this astounding news. He had assisted Mason in writing the famous official report about Marshall's find that Lieutenant Loeser carried East with the specimens to President Polk—the bearer of tidings that rocked the world and literally ushered in a new era in human affairs.

Yes, Sherman was part of the Gold Rush. It was in his blood, influenced his thought and inspired his vision. Its effect on many men was to drive them crazy. Sherman too was stirred but quickly reacted to take cool and clear-eyed stock of the feverish and distorted environment into which he was suddenly hurled. In the next few years, he came to know men of the Gold Rush by the hundreds and noted how so many of them cracked under its abnormal strains. This hard school of experience may well have played a part in maturing Sherman's judgment of men and their mettle.

I did not deliberately seek to recreate Sherman's banking career. Occasionally researchers who explore musty records have their task enlivened by stumbling upon something of far greater interest than the data originally sought. The thrill of such serendipity can be fully understood only by those who have experienced it. The story of William Tecumseh Sherman, banker, is a case in point.

A few years ago, I made use of some unpublished journals of Maj. Henry Smith Turner. They seemed worthy of publication. Part of the task of editing them was the preparation of a biography of Turner. This called for considerable research; and in that process, I encountered references to "a great batch of letters" between Turner and his lifelong friend, William T. Sherman, a source likely to add to my knowledge of Turner's life. The "great batch" proved quite elusive. I have not found all of them yet, but after long search I discovered in the New York Public Library photostats of more than two hundred letters, written by Sherman to Turner. A far smaller lot of Turner's replies are in the Library of Congress and in the Missouri Historical Society in St. Louis.

Piecing them together enabled me to fill in many gaps in the story of Turner himself. More importantly, the letters contained a nearly complete account of the bank established in San Francisco by Lucas, Turner & Co. in 1853.

Sherman, stationed in San Francisco, had conscientiously written to Turner in St. Louis by every mail steamer during the long periods when the two partners were separated. These letters were virtually a day-by-day account of what had transpired in the bank. The building of deposits, the loans and discounts made, profits and losses, matters concerning quarters, personnel, expenses, and relations with competitors, public officials, and the community in general were told in surprising detail.

Most of these letters have never been published, although marks on some of the manuscripts lead me to suspect that excerpts were taken and perhaps used, maybe by more than one writer. Certainly the originals were never designed for publication. Sherman invariably wrote to Turner—and indirectly to the firm's senior partner, James H. Lucas—with one eye on the clock because of the inexorable closing hour for the steamer mail. It was important to report happenings up to the very last moment. I feel certain that Sherman almost never reread what he had written. In the voluminous material I have read, I cannot recall seeing more than one or two corrections.

Sherman possessed some talent for writing; his *Memoirs* attest that. Naturally, these are more polished than the hastily written business letters, yet even the latter are breezily phrased with a sardonic vein of humor frequently revealed. Sherman often repeated himself and the steamer letters contain many awkwardly worded passages and small errors of tense, number, and an occasional grammatical slip.

Some of the repetition was intentional, to guard against mail lost in transit. More than once, two steamers of different lines left within hours of each other; a letter of Sherman's went on each ship.

It must be emphasized that these were business letters. The personal news frequently included was incidental. There was scarcely any of the social gossip contained in much of the pioneers' correspondence. So we do not read that Sherman witnessed Edwin Booth's performance of *Hamlet* or heard Elise Biscaccianti sing in concert. As residents of San Francisco in their day, he and Mrs. Sherman probably attended such performances. Although nearly everyone in the city flocked to see Lola Montez, if Sherman did, he failed to note it in his letters.

He was undoubtedly aware of his shortcomings as a letter writer. Late in life he wrote that he admired brevity and longed to develop a terse style of writing. Whatever their imperfections, the letters in this collection tell a vivid, sometimes exciting, sometimes harrowing account of the daily life of a banker in the

San Francisco of Gold Rush days. I have not read anything else like them.

In using these letters as the basis for the narrative, I have quoted many passages, employing ellipses to indicate omission of immaterial content or repetitive matter. At times, a summary seemed better than actual quotation. Occasionally, I have supplied punctuation but have been sparing of corrections.

Certainly, any full reproduction of the letters even with editing, seems unwarranted. The repetitions involved would destroy the interest for most readers.

A comparison of this steamer mail with the pages of the *Memoirs* dealing with the same period is interesting. Even though the composition of the *Memoirs* is better, the letters tell a more vivid and exciting story. When Sherman wrote his autobiography twenty years after his California experiences, the perspective of time had planed down some episodes and blurred or entirely blotted out others. The sheer immediacy of a letter written while the subject discussed is still an unfinished story, while the success or failure of a proposed course is still in doubt, preserves an air of suspense that the greatest art cannot rival. As the banker wrote, profits and losses hung in the balance, lawsuits had not as yet come to trial, the very integrity of many men was still a question.

Few other men have written of their experiences in the frenetic runs on San Francisco banks in the 1850s. Sherman's letters told fully of his near involvement in the run on Page, Bacon & Co. and the subsequent one on Lucas, Turner & Co. His command of the situation when his own bank's existence hung in jeopardy, with no help obtainable from the outside world, revealed qualities of the generalship for which he later became famous. Coolness, courage, ingenuity, and boldness to improvise were all exhibited by Sherman on that Black Friday.

Two important exceptions to these general comments on the letters to Turner are to be noted. I refer to Sherman's long accounts of his relations with the Vigilance Committee contained in Chapters 22 and 23. It is quite evident that these two letters were more carefully prepared. Their writer even feared that untoward events could make them a posthumous defense of his own position! Because the documents are of major historic interest and have been previously published with important and unexplained deletions, they are reproduced in full so far as was possible from the damaged manuscript available.

These letters leave with a reader a sense of the integrity of their writer, which shines on every page and with it his detestation of sanctimonious hypocrisy and the parade of piety.

One concludes the reading of this collection with both amazement and admiration for men who for years could overcome the handicaps of great distance and slow, uncertain communication while coordinating the management of a complicated business with harmony and mutual respect. The key to their success lay of course in the implicit confidence they had in each other. Their opinions differed; they argued heatedly more than once but never with rancor. In a letter of June 30, 1854, Sherman expressed the hope that their business connection might continue for life. While Fate ruled otherwise, both men, to the end of their partnership and throughout the friendship of later life, carried on in that spirit.

Each knew the disappointments and tragedies of the Gold Rush as well as its glamour. It is not surprising to find Sherman writing more than once that he hated, yet loved, this land of California. That was no mere ambivalent whimsy and Turner understood him.

Acknowledgments

I am grateful to many persons who have aided me in various ways in the research for this book.

It is appropriate that the list should commence with the New York Public Library and its Keeper of Manuscripts, Robert W. Hill, and his staff, since this institution possessed the original photostats of the Eleanor Sherman Fitch Collection of Sherman Letters. Mr. C. Morrison Fitch, a nephew and the executor of Miss Fitch, graciously allowed the Library to make the set of photostats with which I have worked. I also appreciate the time that he and his brother, Mr. T. S. Fitch, and his sister, Mrs. Frank E. Richardson, Jr., spent examining my manuscript.

Thanks go also to Mrs. Joseph H. Colquitt and Miss Julia Minnigerode of Washington, D.C.; both are granddaughters of Henry Smith Turner. From their correspondence when I was preparing his Journals and Letters for publication, I was led indirectly to the discovery of the Fitch Collection. I am also indebted to Miss Minnigerode for the portrait of her grandfather.

The Missouri Historical Society of St. Louis and its Archivist, Mrs. Frances H. Stadler, have been helpful with some Turner letters and Sherman's important account of the 1856 Vigilante movement, and they also supplied the portrait of James H. Lucas.

Mr. David C. Mearns, Chief of the Manuscript Division of the Library of Congress, and his staff diligently sought out little-known Turner correspondence that filled in important gaps in the story of Lucas, Turner & Co.

The Bancroft Library supplied many rare old newspapers, and its staff (especially John Barr Tompkins and Miss Irene Moran) and Everett Moore, Director of Research at UCLA Library were of material aid in my long search for early pre-Civil War photographs of William T. Sherman. Miss Gertrude C. Creswell located the portrait of her grandfather, B. R. Nisbet.

I am indebted to the Louisiana State University for the picture of William Tecumseh Sherman, made from the full-length portrait painted by Col. Samuel Lockett, about 1859. The painter was a member of the faculty of the Louisiana Seminary and Military Academy (predecessor of Louisiana State University) during Sherman's term of service there as superintendent. Lockett was undoubtedly the officer mentioned in the following paragraph in Lloyd Lewis' biography of Sherman:

> It was the 25th of May [1863] . . . after the assault on Vicksburg. Federal dead between the lines . . . were making the air so unbearable that Confederates . . . requested that they be buried. Under a white flag soldiers threw dirt on late comrades, while . . . Sherman and a Confederate officer sat on a log. The Southerner, Captain S. H. Lockett, had come out to gather information, but had become so fascinated by Sherman's conversation that he had forgotten his mission. "Intentionally or not," said Lockett afterward, "his civility prevented me from seeing many points . . . I was very anxious to examine." *

I suspect that the two former colleagues were reminiscing about their days at the Seminary, including recollections of the portrait painting. Lewis probably did not know of their previous association.

Thanks also are due the National Collection of Fine Arts, Smithsonian Institution for the photograph of George P. A. Healy's portrait of Mrs. William Tecumseh Sherman.

Considerable space would be needed to recount all the help

* Lloyd Lewis, *Sherman, Fighting Prophet* (New York: Harcourt, Brace & Company, 1932), pp. 284–285.

given me by my good friend George L. Harding of Berkeley. This included valued material on Sherman's relations with the Vigilance Committee and his knowledge of the Lucas-Turner Building and of early San Francisco.

Another good friend, Dr. C. Albert Shumate, of San Francisco, uncovered a hitherto unidentified photograph of Sherman's Harrison Street home on Rincon Hill and made other valued comments.

My thanks also go to Mrs. Helen S. Giffen, Librarian of the Society of California Pioneers. She drew on her knowledge of Montgomery Street's history and provided me with most interesting photographs of the Lucas-Turner Building in the interval between its heyday as a bank and the 1906 holocaust.

May I also acknowledge the courtesy of Mr. Dale M. Walwark and other officials of the Transamerica Corporation, who supplied the picture of Montgomery Street north of Washington, a few weeks after the April, 1906, earthquake and fire.

My friend, Dr. John H. Kemble of Pomona College, an outstanding authority on Pacific Coast maritime history, sent me the very unusual story of the steamer *America* and supplied helpful leads on the early San Francisco banks.

James de T. Abajian, Librarian of the California Historical Society, aided with names and dates about a wide variety of subjects.

Others who responded graciously to questions were Charles A. Fracchia and Rev. John J. McGloin of the University of San Francisco; my friends William W. Clary and Everett Hager of Los Angeles, and Fred I. Green, of Reno, Nevada; Allen R. Ottley, Librarian of the California Section of the California State Library, and W. K. Davis, Jr., Chief of Archives in the Secretary of State's Office, both of Sacramento; Wallace H. Meyer, Vice-President of Crocker-Citizens' National Bank of San Francisco; R. C. Gillingham, author of *Rancho San Pedro;* and Russell Read, University Research Librarian, UCLA, Los Angeles. I also conferred with Miss Irene Simpson of the Wells Fargo History Room, San Francisco; and she supplied me with the interesting memorandum of James A. Lawrence, of Gardnerville, Nevada, present owner of the Lucas-Turner Building. Mr. Lawrence graciously gave permission to quote any portion of same. Miss Catherine Mon helped me on research work at the Huntington Library and on other tasks. Robert A. Weinstein aided me with his expert knowledge of photographs of San Francisco during the Gold Rush.

I would like to mention the pleasant young lady who typed my manuscript, Mrs. Joyce Warren. Miss Ellen R. Seacat, for the tedious task of preparing the manuscript for the printer, deserves hearty commendation.

It is my earnest hope that I have not omitted anyone. To all these go my sincere thanks.

In conclusion I find words quite inadequate to record the never failing encouragement and co-operation of my dear wife, Edna Marie. Her help, which ranged from the drudgery of proofreading to weighing the readers' probable interest in each chapter, could be neither duplicated nor sufficiently praised.

Contents

Illustrations

Part One:
The Golden Mirage

I

Probably no community in the world ever experienced such startling changes and rapid growth as did San Francisco during the early years of the Gold Rush. When Commander John B. Montgomery raised the Stars and Stripes over Yerba Buena's plaza in July, 1846, it is estimated that the hamlet's population was a little more than 200. American sovereignty was in itself a stimulant. Lieutenant William T. Sherman, passing through Yerba Buena in the summer of 1847, commented that the population was about 400, of whom Kanakas from the Sandwich Islands formed the bulk. A school census taken only a few weeks after James Marshall discovered gold at Coloma showed the new town of San Francisco had 812 inhabitants. The discovery of gold set immigration in motion. At the beginning of 1849 population was 2,000; sixty days later, 3,000. By July, there were 5,000; in August, 6,000. By the close of that astonishing year, 1849, there were between 25,000 and 30,000 people in the lusty, roaring city that San Francisco had now become. Even this rapid growth kept accelerating. A census taken in 1852 gave a total of 36,151. At the end of December, the same authority showed 42,000. In 1853, San Francisco had grown to nearly 50,000 inhabitants—sixty times as large as it had been a little more than five years earlier.[1]

Equally amazing was the growth of California itself. While no formal census was ever taken during the Mexican period, a leading authority estimated that the inhabitants of California in 1848, excluding the Indians, numbered only about 14,000. By the end of 1849, that total had swelled to 100,000. Three years later, the population was 326,000; and at the close of 1852, the residents of California were twenty-three times as numerous as they had been less than five years before.[2] A historian who specialized in the cartography of the region was amply justified in commenting on the "feverish activity in the course of which every nook and cranny of the western country was visited and examined. . . . Never before in history had man so rapidly overrun so vast an unoccupied country." [3]

Almost overnight, a huge demand developed for goods of every description. During the early years, nearly everything had to be imported. Very few of the immigrants planned to produce anything other than gold. Until they learned the hard facts and uncertainties of life in the mines, even those with previous farming experience seldom gave any thought to the agricultural possibilities of their new home land.

Previous to Marshall's discovery, a few hardy American pioneers had begun the cultivation of a little acreage, principally in the Sacramento Valley, but this had been subsistence farming. The scanty population of the Mexican era produced barely enough foodstuffs for its own consumption; certain staples had always been imported. The chief article of commerce, cattle, had been valued only for hides and tallow. It was not merely a jest that hides were called "California bank notes"; they were generally valued in trade at from $1.50 to $2.00. Meat had been a by-product of the livestock industry, not noted for its quality nor considered as an article of any economic importance. Therefore, the arrival of thousands of gold seekers more nearly resembled a horde of locusts than an opportunity for commercial advantage.

Very few of the newcomers had traveled to California with the intention of entering trade or manufacture. A handful were farsighted enough to bring salable merchandise. Others quickly decided that there were greater opportunities for fortune in catering to the needs of the miners than in working with pick and pan in the placers. Some engaged in ventures similar to their former occupations. Many boldly opened stores, saloons, restaurants, and hotels or started stage and express lines, even though these were unfamiliar undertakings. Men daring enough to cut loose from all former ties and to risk the hazards of travel across the plains or in makeshift craft on the high seas were little deterred by the uncertainties of new and strange callings. Bancroft's *Pioneer Register* lists only some of these Argonauts. The autographed membership rosters in the Society of California Pioneers also constitute an incomplete roll. Yet both record a numerous company of persons who in a very few years undertook such a variety of occupations as would scarcely ever have engaged one individual's attention in any other milieu.[4]

All this was inherent in the unique environment of Gold Rush California, with the restlessness and zest for adventure of its youthful population. Essential to the production and marketing of goods and services is a circulating medium of exchange and a safe repository for that medium. In the era that came to such an abrupt end in January, 1848, there was little or no coin in circulation anywhere in the area outside Monterey, San Francisco, San Diego, and Los Angeles. Some barter was practiced; and payments of debt, as previously noted, were frequently made in cattle and hides. Soon after Marshall's fateful discovery, gold dust itself became the most common circulating medium, being accepted at $16 an ounce. Coin was so scarce and the need for it so great to pay customhouse duties that gold dust was frequently offered at $10 and even $8 an ounce.[5]

The most elementary function of a bank—as a place for the safekeeping of coin, gold dust, or other valuables—was in the beginning often provided by saloons and mercantile establishments that owned strong and supposedly burglar-proof safes. Their owners frequently did not welcome the responsibility thrust upon them. More than one banker began his career by this involuntary route. Some early custodians of wealth employed even more primitive methods of safeguarding the valuables left with them.[6]

A second inevitable need for banks grew out of the very nature of wholesale and retail trade itself after 1848. When virtually every commodity had to be transported long distances, importers and merchants had need for some process whereby they could pay for cargoes. The long delay between the shipment of goods from the eastern states and their availability for resale to the ultimate consumer was in itself an obstacle. Even if a merchant possessed sufficient coin or gold dust, he had to have a channel through which he could pay the shipper. When, as was very often the case, credit was required by the western importer, that further complicated the transaction.

Legend to the contrary, not all the miners were roistering and improvident. Many of those upon whom fortune smiled preferred to employ either a bank or an express company to remit substantial sums to their former homes. Like Nature, economics abhors a vacuum; therefore, it was most necessary that someone in San Francisco perform banking functions from the very beginning.

Authorities are not agreed as to which was the first bank established in San Francisco. Robert A. Parker, subsequently proprietor of the famous Parker House, ran a store in an adobe building on Dupont Street in 1848 "and very possibly conducted a little primitive banking" along with his other business prior to April, 1848. Others claim that the first banking establishment was the Miners Bank, presumably opened toward the end of 1848 by Dr. Stephen A. Wright. By September 1849, Wright and Company did an exchange and brokerage business that involved some banking at the corner of Kearny and Washington Streets. Shortly thereafter, Wright and some partners announced themselves as bankers with a capital of $200,000. In 1854, this bank changed its name to the Miners Exchange and Savings Bank, located at the northeast corner of Montgomery and Sacramento Streets. A little later, it moved to new quarters at the northwest corner of Montgomery and Jackson Streets.[7]

Another authority, writing as early as 1855, claims that Naglee and Sinton established San Francisco's first regular bank on June 9, 1849. While it seems surprising that persons so close to the happenings could differ about such details, one must remember that the headlong rush of events by 1855 made the "days of '49" seem veritably another age. Conflagrations had destroyed records as well as landmarks. Life was fluid and ever-changing to a degree seldom experienced anywhere else. Whether Parker or Wright or Naglee and Sinton opened the first bank cannot be asserted too positively; but certainly by the close of 1849, four other banks were doing business: Burgoyne & Co., B. Davidson, Thomas G. Wells (later to become Wells & Co.), and James King of William.[8] Some of these earliest bankers for a time apparently prospered as amazingly as the most fortunate of the placer miners.[9]

Three more banking firms opened for business in 1850, D. J. Tallant (Tallant & Wilde) in February, and Page, Bacon & Co. and F. Argenti & Co. in June.[10] The next few years saw a number of other banks bidding for business.

It will be noted that all these early banking houses were operated either by individuals or partnerships. No incorporated banks were to appear on the scene until as late as 1862 (and then only mutual and stock savings banks). This was because of the decided aversion felt by most pioneer Californians to corporations and especially to banks and banking.

From the very beginnings of statehood, Californians were advocates of "hard money," a tradition that rejected the "greenbacks" of Civil War days and survived to very modern times. Most of the pioneers retained painful memories of the panic of 1837 in the East, which had been caused in part by the unrestricted and unregulated issuance of bank notes that circulated freely as a medium of exchange. When the issuing bank closed its doors, the holders of such notes suddenly found themselves with "money" that had no value.

The convention that met in Colton Hall at Monterey in September and October, 1849, to draft a constitution for California overwhelmingly reflected these prejudices. Hours were consumed in denunciation of banks and banking as something inherently evil.[11] These debates produced two prohibitory actions. The first decreed that

> the Legislature shall have no power to pass any act granting any charter for banking purposes but associations may be formed under general laws for the deposit of gold and silver but no

association shall make, issue, or put in circulation any bill, check, ticket, certificate, promissory note or other paper or the paper of any bank to circulate as money.[12]

As if this did not state the delegates' views strongly enough, they adopted still another prohibition:

> The Legislature of this State shall prohibit by law any person or persons, association, company or corporation from exercising the privilege of banking or creating paper to circulate as money.[13]

Hubert Howe Bancroft describes the 1849 convention as not lacking in talent and composed of a curious mixture of men of refinement and the more unkempt products of the frontier. "Fourteen were lawyers, twelve farmers, seven merchants. The remainder were engineers, bankers, physicians, and printers." [14] Despite this statement, a review of the names does not disclose any bankers, and the listing of one delegate as a banker in another account seems entirely erroneous.[15]

A modern critic of the proceedings at Monterey cites as one defect of the 1849 constitution that it was "dumb" on the subject of finance.[16] Before we think with too much condescension of the 1849 constitution makers, we would do well to study the financial delusions and vagaries of some of our present-day statesmen. We might then recognize that mankind is sometimes very slow to learn painful lessons. Some men never learn them.

It seemed more simple to the budding lawmakers at Monterey to legislate against the symptoms they dreaded than by study to determine the basic principles of banking and the useful services it could render to the people of California under proper controls. It was easier to outlaw a malady than to practice prophylaxis.

Therefore, the 1849 constitution padlocked two doors of California's financial structure and left two others wide open. By its silence, the document made it perfectly legal, easy in fact, for any individual or partnership without any license or permit to buy a safe, furnish an office, paint "Bank" on the windows, and invite the public to entrust its financial business to the new establishment. Neither more nor less formality was involved than opening a butcher shop or a hardware store. Moreover, once the new bank was operating, the constitution made no provision for the later regulation, supervision, or examination of its affairs. For nearly three decades, banking in California was to offer a perfect example of unrestricted laissez-faire.

It is not too surprising then to read that one of the first banks to open, that of Henry M. Naglee, suspended payment on September 7, 1850. There was a great run on all banks at this time.[17] On October 3, 1851, Wells & Co. failed. A commentator wrote: "When the place and the speculative spirit of the people are borne in mind it is high testimony to the general stability of the banking interest, that only two of their establishments have become bankrupt." [18] In the afterlight of the next few years, this writer must have recognized that his remarks were quite premature.

At least one voice was raised at an early date in favor of a more enlightened attitude and especially to warn of the dire necessity for some type of public supervision of banking. This was an editorial expression by James King of William, soon to achieve a tragic fame. Writing in the *Evening Bulletin* on December 31, 1855, he said: "We need Chartered Banks, with or without a paper currency. We must have corporations for banking, just as we have corporations for merchandising, mining, or mechanical purposes . . . subject to such regulation and inspection as the legislature may direct." [19]

2

By 1849, California not only had attracted an ever-growing stream of gold hunters but also had captured the imagination of rich and poor throughout the civilized world. Profits from the sales of goods and services were said to be in keeping with the richness of the placer mines. St. Louis had from its earliest days been a gateway to the West; now the fabulous news from the Pacific coast spelled opportunity in capital letters to many merchants and financiers in that Missouri city. The St. Louis banking house of Page & Bacon had been one of the first to open a branch in San Francisco in 1850. Their neighbors and competitors, Lucas & Simonds,[20] paid ever-increasing attention to this bold venture. Responsible business houses in California were reliably reported to be paying 3% interest a month for loans. It was easy to credit the reports that the new house of Page, Bacon & Co. was a success. Lucas & Simonds may well have felt a little envious. Its resources compared favorably with Page & Bacon's, so why could not Lucas & Simonds share in the greater prosperity of the Golden West?

The senior partner of the firm was James H. Lucas, owner of much valuable real estate in St. Louis and a member of a well-known local family. Other partners were Capt. John Simonds and, a little later, Henry L. Patterson, both of St. Louis. Mr. Lucas' interest in San Francisco as a possible site for a branch of his bank was probably first aroused by a young man named Benjamin R. Nisbet, originally of St. Louis, who was employed as a teller by Page, Bacon & Co. at their branch in California.

Apparently, he was ambitious to improve his station in life and was sure that the expanding commerce of San Francisco allowed ample room for another firm financed in St. Louis. If he could interest Mr. Lucas, he might hope for a junior partnership. Lucas was favorably impressed by Nisbet but felt he was too young to be entrusted with the management of so important a venture at such a great distance from its owners.[21]

Mr. Lucas' niece, Julia Hunt Turner, was the wife of Maj. Henry Smith Turner, who had served as an aide to Gen. Stephen Watts Kearny in the long march of the Army of the West from Fort Leavenworth to conquer New Mexico and California in the War with Mexico. He had fought in the battles of San Pasqual, the San Gabriel, and the Plains of the Mesa. He had served as Kearny's adjutant during all his stay in California. His six-month tour of duty there had involved considerable travel through the territory; and he had resided for brief periods in San Diego, Los Angeles, and Monterey. After the close of the war, Turner resigned from the army and rejoined his family in St. Louis where he became assistant United States treasurer. Major Turner was a natural source of additional information about California. Mr. Lucas proposed that he go out to San Francisco as a partner, to open and to manage the branch of Lucas & Simond's bank.[22] Turner agreed that the field was inviting but was loath to leave St. Louis. His chief reason for resigning his military commission was the extreme homesickness he had suffered in the long absence from his family during the war. He was a devoted husband and father. San Francisco seemed very remote and inaccessible. Still, he felt the opportunity offered by Mr. Lucas too inviting to decline, so eventually he hit upon a method whereby he could become a part of the new enterprise yet not be indefinitely separated from his family.

Shortly after Turner's arrival at Monterey in February, 1847, he had made the acquaintance of Lt. William T. Sherman of the 3rd Artillery. After enduring the long grueling march from Missouri to California and the rigors of battle, Turner was almost destitute of shirts and underwear. Sherman, having traveled by sea, had an ample reserve and generously supplied Turner's deficiencies. This homely incident was the beginning of a warm friendship. As he reviewed what the San Francisco post would require, it occurred to Turner that Captain Sherman, as was now his rank, would be the ideal man for the place.

The captain in September, 1852, had gone to New Orleans for the commissary department of the army. Turner had to travel to New York, not only to take ship for California, but also to appoint bank correspondents for the San Francisco bank. He arranged his trip by way of New Orleans in order to explain the situation to his friend Sherman. On meeting him, Turner showed the captain the articles of co-partnership of Lucas, Turner & Co. Sherman was astonished to find his own name included as one of the partners. Turner proposed that Sherman secure a leave of absence from the army and follow him to California. There he could assist Turner in getting the bank in operation; and as soon as its affairs were running smoothly, Turner would rejoin his family in St. Louis. Nisbet could be relied upon to conduct the details of the business, but Sherman would be the senior partner in San Francisco to whom the St. Louis owners would look for the major decisions. Captain Sherman could use his six-month leave of absence to familiarize himself with the firm's problems and to decide if he wished to leave the army and become a banker.

Major Turner left New Orleans for New York before Sherman had reached a decision. He sailed for Nicaragua on the S.S. *Ohio* on January 20, 1853, and wrote Sherman the day before he left, to express the hope that the captain would follow him in about a month. If Sherman decided to accept Mr. Lucas' offer, Turner felt it would be helpful for Sherman to spend a few days with the firm in St. Louis.

Turner had visited prospective correspondents in New York and wrote Sherman about the reception given him: "I find the Wall St. people wonderful, attentive and polite. The fact is Page & Bacon's great success in California have [*sic*] opened their eyes somewhat and they doubtless begin to think that Western people have some sagacity." [23]

Shortly after Turner left New Orleans, Lucas came down from St. Louis to continue the discussion with Captain Sherman. He promised the latter a liberal salary and expenses, as well as an eighth interest as a partner. Sherman was impressed by Mr. Lucas' personality and proposals. Before the financier returned to St. Louis, the captain agreed to ask for the necessary leave of absence and to join Major Turner in San Francisco.[24]

Comparatively few of San Francisco's pioneer bankers had had much previous experience in banking. Sherman was no exception. In all other respects, Lucas and Turner could hardly have found a man better qualified to manage a new bank in California. Sherman's military service there had lasted almost three years—a period covering the Mexican War, the American annexation, Marshall's earthshaking discovery, and the earlier stages of the Gold Rush. He was, therefore, well acquainted with all of the army and navy officers who had served in California during the period. Many of them had remained there after the war and, if not still in uniform, were active in all manner of enterprises. As an aide to Colonel R. B. Mason,[25] Sherman had attended the constitutional convention in Monterey as an observer and had come to know many of the California rancheros as well as lately arrived Americans who were interested in the politics of the new land. Many of these acquaintances would prove to be valuable contacts and sources of information in the conduct of a bank.

Captain Sherman had also had abundant opportunity to know the land itself. Because Monterey had been his headquarters, he was most familiar with that vicinity, but he had also spent a little time in Southern California. He had made official trips to Yerba Buena, Sausalito, San Rafael, Bodega, Sonoma, Napa, Benicia, San Jose, and the New Almaden quicksilver mines.

The most important of all Sherman's travels in California had been his visits in 1848 to Sutter's Fort and the gold fields with Colonel Mason. Except for the miners themselves, Sherman and Mason were undoubtedly among the very first visitors to California's gold region. Before they could finish their tour of the mines, they were called back to Monterey by news of the conclusion of peace with Mexico.[26]

Sherman and Mason visited the mines again that fall and inspected other gold camps on the Stanislaus River and at Sonora. During the second trip, Sherman embarked on a commercial venture with some fellow officers and for a short time was a partner in a store at Coloma. A few months later, this business was liquidated at a satisfactory profit. In similar fashion, Sherman engaged in what would today be termed "moonlighting"; he did some surveying of new townsites and ranch lands in the Sacramento Valley. Living had become so astronomically costly in California that army officers, who received only $70 per month, had to augment their salaries to maintain existence. Sherman by this same enterprise acquired both town lots and ranch lands on which he realized a good profit. Letters he wrote during this period vividly depict life in the mining camps. One of them reports his own very brief experience as a miner: ". . . went to work. But the success was not great and I determined to move." [27] Another tells more formally of the difficulty of preventing desertions from the army by men who were excited by tales of sudden wealth in the mines. Ship captains facing a similar hazard either dared not dock their vessels or lay in harbor without crews to man their ships.[28]

In letters written to his brother John during this period, Sherman disclosed that he had really become infected with the ebullient optimism of the miners.

> We saw enough to make us entertain the only fear that the gold will be found in such quantities as seriously to diminish its value as a circulating medium. . . . About 4,000 persons at work and amount of gold obtained daily cannot fall short of $30,000. to $50,000 . . . we [employees of government] are the sufferers. All prices have so advanced that we cannot possibly exist on our pay. . . .

He wrote John that, in Colonel Mason's opinion, $10,000 of miscellaneous merchandise as priced in the East would quickly

JAMES H. LUCAS
Courtesy of Missouri Historical Society

bring $100,000 in California. "I have seen blankets worth $1 or $2 in New York sell for $50." In his enthusiasm, he recommended to his brother that the latter at once ship out a cargo of goods most in demand. Clothing of any sort, if ready-made in various sizes, would be most salable. On the other hand, bolts of cloth were of little value in California—"no one has time to make it up . . . no doubt five or six million dollars already extracted. Men are now getting from $300. to $500. a month and $1. an hour is the usual price of labor."

Among the same letters is one dated August 25, 1848, to some friend in St. Louis (probably Major Turner), which states that rooms at Sutter's Fort were bringing $100 a month and one indifferent house was renting for $500 a month. Horses recently worth $15 or $20 were now selling for $75 to $100.[29]

All these varied scenes and experiences had left a vivid impression on Sherman's alert mind. Even more important to the success of the new banking house were the captain's hard common sense and his innate integrity. Here James Lucas had been forced to rely on Major Turner's estimate of his friend's character. Turner was either a shrewd judge of men or the St. Louis financiers were exceedingly fortunate.

3

Henry Turner reached San Francisco early in 1853. He secured temporary quarters for the bank on the east side of Montgomery between California and Sacramento Streets; the monthly rental was $600. Immediately across the street, in the new granite Parrott Building, were Page, Bacon & Co. and Adams & Co. On hand to assist Turner in opening the bank was B. R. Nisbet. They employed James Reilly to serve as teller.[30]

Turner found living quarters at the house of a Mrs. Ross on Clay Street near Powell. A fellow lodger there was another old army friend of Turner's and Sherman's—Brig. Gen. E. A. Hitchcock, then in command of the Department of California.[31]

In the meantime, Captain Sherman had been granted his six-month leave of absence. His wife, two children, and a nursemaid had joined him in New Orleans just a short time before. Now he had to send them back to their former home in Lancaster, Ohio. In early March, 1853, after winding up his military and personal affairs, Sherman took passage on a steamer for Nicaragua. In seven days, he reached Greytown and crossed to the Pacific by way of the San Juan River and Lake Nicaragua. At San Juan del Sur he reembarked on the S.S. *Lewis* for California.

Had Sherman been superstitious, he might have felt that the manner of his arrival in San Francisco augured ill for his career as a banker. The *Lewis* made a very slow passage northward; its arrival was scheduled for the nineteenth day out of San Juan del Sur. At four o'clock in the morning of April 9, the last day of the voyage, Sherman was awakened by a heavy bump, after which the engines immediately stopped. Then the vessel struck again and more alarmingly. When Sherman ran on deck, the night was pitch dark and a heavy fog enveloped the *Lewis*. The sea was comparatively calm, but the stricken craft rose and fell with the heave of the ocean and continued to bump and quiver on the reef that had snared it.

A few hours later, the morning light revealed that they had been wrecked about a mile from a beach. The *Lewis*' boats took all the passengers and crew ashore—in all, some 385 persons. The vessel was lying on the bottom and was rapidly breaking up under the pounding of the waves.

Sherman walked along the shore until he came to a camp where laborers were loading a small schooner with lumber for San Francisco. He learned that he was at Bolinas Bay about eighteen miles northwest of the Golden Gate. In the dense fog, the *Lewis* had overrun the entrance to the harbor and had piled up on Duxbury Reef, which lies to the west of Bolinas Bay.[32]

The schooner's captain agreed to take Sherman and a companion as passengers, and early in the afternoon they hoisted sail and started on this second voyage. A stiff breeze was blowing, but the fog had lifted. In a couple of hours, they were entering San Francisco Bay. Things went well until they encountered a strong ebb tide flowing out of the Golden Gate. The nose of the schooner dived into the oncoming waves, and the small craft went over on her side and began to drift out to sea. Sherman found himself in the water but swam around to the stern, climbed onto the keel, and clambered to safety on the side of the schooner. Because of the lumber cargo lashed on the deck, he was satisfied that the vessel could not sink "but thought two shipwrecks in one day not a good beginning for a new peaceful career." Nobody had drowned, and a passing sailboat undertook to succor the capsized schooner. Meanwhile, a man in a rowboat appeared opportunely and agreed to land the two dripping passengers at nearby Fort Point. Here Sherman was on familiar ground and quickly walked to the Presidio, where he secured a horse to ride into the city. That evening, he located Major Turner and engaged lodging at Mrs. Ross's. The friends had their meals at restaurants downtown, mostly at Martin's, a French café at the southeast corner of California and Montgomery Streets.

The steamship company, on learning of the *Lewis* disaster, had promptly sent other vessels to rescue the marooned passengers at Bolinas Bay. Most of the baggage had been salvaged, and Sherman recovered his trunk. His carpetbag, however, had been lost in the shipwreck.

In the following weeks, Sherman diligently studied business conditions in San Francisco to determine whether to exchange his army commission for "this new and untried scheme of banking." At the same time he worked with Turner and Nisbet to develop and administer the business of the new firm. It seemed to promise well. He found the city at the peak of a wave of speculation and prosperity. Everybody was apparently making money. San Francisco itself was expanding rapidly in extent and construction. Businessmen gladly and promptly paid 3% a month interest for whatever money they could borrow. In addition to receiving deposits and making loans, Lucas, Turner & Co. competed for a share of the continuous stream of gold dust and bullion arriving from the mines. Here, of course, the only chance of profit was to buy the gold for an amount sufficiently less than it would bring on its arrival "back East" to cover costs of shipment and insurance, loss of interest, and a margin of profit to the bankers. With all the financial houses vying for this business, competition inevitably fixed the price paid for the gold. However, the bankers generally believed this was riskless and profitable business. In addition to these activities, Lucas, Turner & Co., like its competitors, sold bills of exchange on their Eastern correspondents. These were most essential to the operations of merchants and importers, as well as to miners making remittances to their families. There was also a flow of Eastern bills of exchange presented by their customers for discount.*

The three partners in San Francisco eventually decided that with a capital of $200,000 and a credit in New York for $50,000,

* See Appendix, "Sherman's Banking Terminology."

they could establish an operation that would surely net a profit. Since Major Turner would not remain indefinitely on the Coast, Sherman agreed to go back to St. Louis to confer with the partners in that city, then return to San Francisco.[33] A letter to his brother John made it plain that he would accept the permanent management of the San Francisco bank only if the St. Louis partners would supply adequate capital. He wrote "My business here is the best going, provided we have plenty of money. Without it, I stick to Uncle Sam emphatically." [34]

Major Turner wrote to James H. Lucas that the bank then owed deposits of $126,000 and was growing with the departure of every steamer. The total balance on its books was $261,000.[35]

Turner was essentially conservative, but even a man of his temperament could quickly become infected with the boundless optimism then pervading San Francisco.

> Business matters have taken a wonderful start [he wrote Lucas] and the probability now is that the three months to come will be the most favorable period for business operations . . . that has ever occurred. . . . It seems inevitable that monied men are to reap a rich harvest before the beginning of winter. . . . The opportunities for speculation in realty [*sic*] estate and in everything else, have no precedent in what has occurred in any other part of the world. All this must be ascribed to the rapid growth of the city and to its final destiny as one of the great commercial cities of the world.

That Turner was already influenced by the "hard money" sentiments prevailing in California is evidenced by his next statement:

> You must remember that there is no currency in circulation here; all business operations are conducted on a specie basis in cash and that the credit system does not now and probably will not exist here to any extent. This . . . will in my opinion serve to protect San Francisco from reverses which have overtaken other newly established towns in the United States.

Events of the next few years must have made Henry Turner recall this prophecy with mixed feelings.

Sherman sailed from San Francisco for New York on July 16, 1853, by way of Nicaragua. After landing, he went immediately to St. Louis by way of Lancaster. Mr. Lucas promptly agreed to the recommendations of Turner and Sherman as to capital. He further consented to erect a building to house Lucas, Turner & Co. at a cost of $50,000. Sherman, for his part, agreed to remain in San Francisco to carry on the business until 1860. When Sherman returned to Lancaster to explain his plans to his wife and her father, they also approved. He thereupon sent to the adjutant general of the army a letter of resignation, to take effect at the end of his leave, September 6, 1853.

Sherman engaged passage for himself and family to leave New York on September 20. The party sailing for Nicaragua consisted of Mr. and Mrs. Sherman; their baby daughter, Lizzie, less than a year old; and her nurse, Mary Lynch. The parents left their elder daughter, Marie—usually called Minnie—in the charge of her Ewing grandparents in Ohio.

The sea voyage was uneventful, but in boarding the S.S. *Sierra Nevada* on the Pacific side, the nursemaid became terrified by the pounding surf through which she was being carried. Her hysterical screaming so alarmed Lizzie that the infant fainted from fright. For sometime afterward the parents feared that this shock had caused permanent injury. Fortunately, they were wrong, and the trip northward was without incident. The Sherman family arrived in San Francisco on October 16 and took quarters at the Clarendon Hotel on Stockton Street near Broadway. Mrs. Sherman's education in the high cost of living in the Golden West began at once. Her husband had to pay $8 carriage hire for the short trip from the steamer landing. Their two rooms with board cost $100 a week, with an extra charge for lights and heat.

A few weeks later, they rented a small furnished frame house on Stockton Street near Green, from a son of the famous English author, Capt. Frederick Marryat.

Everything was different from quiet, peaceful Lancaster. Fleas and flies were thick. The streets were deep in sand that became a quagmire when it rained. Nisbet told the newcomers that, while making his New Year's calls, he had been forced to leave one boot stuck deep in the mud. His other foot was so wet that the remaining boot had to be cut off.

The cost of living was still a nightmare. Eggs were 25 cents apiece; ice cream, $12 a gallon; and strawberries, $5 a pint. However, there were a few delightful compensations for Mrs. Sherman, like the gift of a piano with which her husband surprised her not long after she arrived. It helped her forget her trials and privations, especially when General Hitchcock made his evening calls with his flute and a roll of music. She proved an able accompanist for the General, while Sherman listened contentedly with his small daughter on his knee.[36]

4

Sherman resumed his duties at the bank immediately after his return to San Francisco from St. Louis in October, 1853. One of the first tasks of the partners was the selection of a site for their new building; no decision had been reached by the time Turner left for St. Louis, late in the fall of 1853. Shortly before his departure, he raised Sherman's salary to $5,000 a year; and soon after he rejoined his family in Missouri, Turner himself was made a partner of Lucas & Simonds.

By February, 1854, Sherman had bought a lot from James Lick for $31,000. It was at the northeast corner of Montgomery and Jackson Streets. The parcel was sixty feet square and was bounded on the north by Gold Street, an alley running east to Sansome Street and only seventeen and a half feet wide. Sherman arranged that Lick execute two deeds: one to James H. Lucas for the corner of Jackson and fronting thirty-three feet on Montgomery; the other to Lucas, Turner & Co. for the remaining twenty-seven feet extending to the alley. The purchase was at the rate of $500 a front foot, and Sherman wrote to Turner that very few parcels of business property were available at that price, in fact none that were so well located. Other frontages on Montgomery Street were quoted as high as $1,000 a foot, and actually there was very little for sale.

Sherman would have preferred a location a block farther south but could not obtain one. He considered the Plaza "the official center of the city." His purchase was only one block diagonally from the Plaza, and one block north of Halleck's

HENRY SMITH TURNER
Courtesy of Miss Julia H. Minnigerode

BENJAMIN R. NISBET

Courtesy of Miss Gertrude C. Creswell and California Historical Society

building, the largest in the city.[37] Also, it was diagonally opposite the recently completed Metropolitan Theatre, the "center of polite exhibitions."

In the light of today's concentration of super-skyscrapers along the southern end of Montgomery Street, it is curious to read that Sherman was less attracted by locations south of California Street because of their greater distance from the wharves. Even a man of Sherman's judgment and powers of observation could not possess the prophetic vision of the changes a century would bring to his neighborhood.

San Francisco was showing other signs that it had become a city. On the evening of February 11, 1854, the first coal-gas lights were turned on. In the beginning, only a few of the principal streets and such larger buildings as the Metropolitan Theatre could boast of such illumination; but it was a sign of growth exploited to the fullest by boosters and boomers. Sherman included gas pipes in the plans for the Lucas, Turner & Co. building.[38]

The banker pointed out that "Jackson Street is now a great thoroughfare to the Clipper wharves all lying north of Pacific. All the miners land at Pacific or Jackson Street wharves so that although we are at the present end of Montgomery, we are at the end nearest the heavy business of the country." [39]

Sherman further argued that since all their competitors were farther from the wharves, where the clipper ships docked, Lucas, Turner & Co. might hope to attract some of the patrons of these firms because their new location would be of greater convenience. This emphasizes the importance early San Franciscans attached to shipping, whether steamships or sailing vessels. These were their only mail and freight contacts with the rest of the world. "Steamer day" was far more than a picturesque custom in pioneer San Francisco.[40]

Mr. Lucas had proposed a limit of $50,000 on the investment in the new building. Half the frontage of the Lick property would have been ample for the firm's requirements, but Lick would sell the parcel only as a whole. Therefore, Sherman had divided the lot and the purchase price as above explained. He had instructed an architect to design the bank building with a hallway that could later serve the north portion of the property if the partners decided to improve it. The second and third stories were to be fitted with attractive offices, which should rent easily to lawyers and insurance firms. He believed that even with the bank paying only a reasonable rental for its space, the building would return enough income to pay Mr. Lucas 3% a month on his investment.[41]

Almost before the purchase was closed, the soldier-turned-banker was treated to an experience typical of the feverish tempo of San Francisco business. Henry Meiggs, prominent in political and commercial circles, proposed a deal on the property. If the new owners would turn over the lot to Meiggs for $31,000 and lend him an additional $69,000, he would erect a suitable building, pay 3% a month interest on the total loan of $100,000, and provide Lucas, Turner & Co. with their banking room rent-free. Sherman declined the offer, not, apparently, on account of its several unorthodox features but "because I want to control the tenants." Meiggs's name was soon to become very well known to Banker Sherman.[42]

In the letter that reported the purchase, Sherman also commented on street paving, as related to the Lick property. Jackson Street was now "well graded and planked" and the work paid for. Montgomery was being graded and re-planked in front of the new site at a cost of $6.50 a running foot. He said the building job was up for bids. If the architect's estimate indicated that the cost might exceed Sherman's own limit of $30,000, he was disposed to make separate contracts and to oversee progress himself. He had observed that water was now standing on the lot and proposed to take soundings to determine whether piling must be sunk for the foundations. He was inclined to believe that rock was close to the surface, and if he found this was the case, he was going to "lay the foundations according to the scriptures." He closed the letter by saying, "it is now raining like blazes and the day is dark, gloomy and suicidal." He promised a postscript on the morrow "lest the weather tinge my opinions."

On March 1, the *John L. Stevens* and the *Sierra Nevada* were departing at noon. Sherman believed the former would make the faster trip, so mailed the letter by that steamer. However, he commented that the *Sierra Nevada* would carry duplicates—a common precautionary practice of those days. The promised postscript contained Sherman's own penciled sketch of the new building.

He also informed his friend that he had bought a brick house on Green Street. It was half of a double dwelling of two stories, on a small leased lot which provided only a tiny yard. Both the front rooms had fireplaces, with stoves in the rear portion—very necessary in the cold, wet weather then prevailing. "Fires here are a luxury with coal at $2.50 a bag (about $2. a bushel) and wood $22. a cord." Mrs. Sherman was much pleased with the new home, for which they had paid $3,500. In addition, the ground rent was $30 a month; and at the expiration of a five-year lease, the lessee must either negotiate a new arrangement or remove the improvements.

After they moved into their new home, the Shermans did some entertaining. The banker thought dinners too formal, but he liked to have a few friends come in for little supper parties and games of cards. Refreshments of whiskey punch or wine were offered.

The next letter reported to St. Louis that the well-known banking firm of Palmer, Cook & Co. had not paid the interest on the state of California's indebtedness, mostly held in New York.[43] State moneys to cover this interest had been deposited with Palmer-Cook; now many of the firm's drafts had been returned protested for nonpayment. Sherman feared there would be a run on Palmer-Cook, even though they owned much valuable property. At the very least, their credit was ruined. He concluded this news with a blunt and amazing charge against Palmer-Cook: "[They] have been deep in bribing the present legislature for Broderick[44] but members charge high, and their scheme has failed." Sherman thought the Palmer-Cook trouble might ultimately benefit Lucas, Turner & Co., but "now we are poor and restricted." The number of depositors was growing steadily, but the totals on deposit were not increasing materially. Business generally was dull, and merchants could not collect their accounts receivable. Naturally, their bank balances could not grow under such conditions.

The new building absorbed Sherman's attention. He contracted for a vault "unnecessarily strong, I think" for 16 cents a pound. That would amount to about $2,000. Nisbet had insisted on the great strength; Sherman wrote: "I would like to see a building erected by Nisbet. Pearls and diamonds could not be fine enough. Were I to assent to all he wants the building would cost $200,000. I am determined to reject all redundant ornaments and build for substantial use."

By March 16, Sherman had received fifteen bids on the proposed building and eventually accepted the bid of Brown & Keyser, St. Louis contractors. They had bid $53,000 for a structure to cover the entire lot. Sherman explained that he could have pared the price somewhat had he been willing to omit the granite front on the first story. He had decided that this omission would greatly impair "the solidity and beauty" of the building.

Today, this same distinctive granite front, easily identifiable with Sherman's drawing, is our best proof that the first story of the existing two-story structure is actually the original building that he designed more than a century ago.[45]

The banker waxed enthusiastic as he justified his decision to his partners. The project "will add a hundred per cent to our business. I feel sanguine that the whole building will be a first rate investment. Business is going to that quarter of the city and our removal thither will have a sensible effect." He had drawn a strong contract that would do justice to a present-day escrow officer. It showed all the safeguards against mechanics' and material liens.

Piling had in the end been found necessary. Ninety-six piles had been sunk, at a cost of $28 each. Excavation for a full basement was now under way. The contractors had been given until July 1, 1854, to have the banking room ready for occupancy, and Sherman planned to move the bank by July 11. The remainder of the building was to be finished by July 20.

One of these letters in the spring of 1854 speaks of "my deposit trust fund," and it is frequently mentioned in later correspondence. The reference is to moneys left with Sherman to invest or to lend at his discretion. Some of these deposits were made by customers of Lucas & Simonds in St. Louis, some by friends—usually old army comrades of Sherman's in California. The profitable rates obtainable in San Francisco were all too attractive, so the fund had reached a total of $90,000 at the time Sherman first mentioned it. He allowed these depositors varying rates of interest, from 2% to 2½% per month, payable quarterly. Theoretically, the moneys were entrusted to him at the risk of their owners, but it was Sherman's nature to feel a keen moral responsibility in such matters. Therefore, he urged Turner not to accept any more such funds, unless strong personal considerations made it necessary.

There was a sufficient balance in this trust fund to lend Lucas, Turner & Co. their share of the cost of the building construction. Mr. Lucas would have to pay very little more than the limit he had proposed.

Periodically in the local papers there were accounts of the exploits of the well-known William Walker—a filibuster in Baja California and Sonora. He had many supporters in California and had recruited numerous volunteers in that state. There were enforced federal statutes against such activities; and General Hitchcock, a long-time friend of both Sherman and Turner, had interpreted these laws quite literally. He seriously interfered with Walker's plans. Some of the civil authorities were far more tolerant, as were certain high officials in Washington. Suddenly, General Hitchcock was relieved of his command and was succeeded by General J. E. Wool, who proved far less disposed to interfere. He was not one of Sherman's favorites among the military in California, as we shall see later on.[46]

News of the Crimean War had just reached San Francisco and caused an advance in the price of flour and wheat. The war might affect the movement of merchandise if clipper owners found it more profitable to devote their tonnage to transporting bread stuffs to Europe. There had been an abundance of rain and the mines were yielding well. However, Sherman wrote that business was dull now but "all suppose a good time is near at hand." Lucas-Turner were experiencing a situation quite familiar to all bankers. "We have plenty of calls for money, more than we can accommodate." While interest was being paid promptly, the bank was forced to extend loans that in easier times could have been collected without any delay.

Apparently, Sherman's health had recently given him concern, for he now reported that he felt considerably better. He hoped that his lungs had somewhat adjusted to the climate, although at times he still suffered from asthma.

"Mrs. Sherman though perfectly contented with her new house, still has a very poor opinion of California generally," her husband told Turner. In another letter written about the same time, Sherman ascribed her unhappiness to the infrequent mails from "back home," and the long time they were en route.

Businessmen also probably had strong feelings about the mails. In the present era of instant communication, it is startling to realize the time handicap under which commerce and banking operated in California in the 1850's. In a letter dated March 29, 1854, Sherman commented that he had just received mail from New York dated February 20 or earlier and St. Louis mail only through February 14. Quite regularly, the bank remitted to New York drafts for sizable amounts, which they could reasonably assume would be credited to their account immediately. Yet they could never be certain for several weeks thereafter, and too often they learned of nonpayment or delayed payment of the item.

Noon sailings were a further source of inconvenience. Mail was made ready the night before steamer day, but customers habitually rushed in for drafts up to the very moment the vessel sailed. The work at the bank had increased; and on the eve of steamer days, everyone worked until midnight. Lucas-Turner had two good subordinates in Reilly and Kritchman, but "Reilly begins to groan under his work." Sherman suggested that Turner find in St. Louis a good bookkeeper who would come to San Francisco at his own expense—then Lucas, Turner & Co. would pay him $250 a month. He could live well for $100.[47]

By now, Sherman had come to doubt the opinion generally held by Nisbet and their competitors that there was a real profit in the exchange business. Competition held the charge made to 3% of the amount of the drafts sold on New York. Out of this charge, the bank must pay shipping charges and insurance on all gold dust and bullion sent East, as well as cover the interest on the totals of the drafts until shipments reached New York and were credited to the bank's account. There must also be a margin of profit. "The exchange business is a bore [?] all sound and no profit." *

Just before the mail closed on March 15, 1854, the bank's totals were deposits, $254,940; cash, $565,426; interest and exchange, $43,460.[48]

Sherman closed his letter of April 1, on a lively personal note. He was curious about several pieces of property he owned in St. Louis and asked Turner to inquire of the agent in charge of them "if my estate blossoms as the rose?" He also owned some nearby farmland. If wheat was going to bring $2 and corn $1 a bushel, perhaps this could be sold at a good price; "Vive la guerre!"

---

* See Appendix, "Sherman's Banking Terminology."

5

By mid-April, Sherman learned that Lucas & Simonds had transferred Lucas, Turner & Co.'s New York account from the American Exchange Bank to the Metropolitan Bank. He assured Turner that the San Francisco house would strive to maintain good credit there; but he would not promise to keep $25,000 on deposit because "no one knows better than you that our capital and resources are not in comparison with our great fame, and we often feel the mortification of a poor family of high pretensions." He favored borrowing from $50,000 to $100,000 in New York, if it could be obtained at a fair rate, to make up for the firm's inadequate capital.

Personnel problems can at times be more acute in a small bank than in larger ones. When there are only a few employees, absence because of an illness can seriously affect operations. Nisbet on such occasions was forced to take on additional work. Sherman commented:

> While very willing and industrious [he] occasionally gets a little lively, but the greatest trouble is that he is so deeply imbued with Page & Bacon that he cannot wipe it out. . . . I know we have lost considerable business by this but it cannot be avoided. . . . Neither Reilly or Nisbet have winning ways at the counter. The former looks dull and Nisbet is as short as pie crust and no amount of hints will correct it.

Even with these handicaps, Sherman felt that the firm was prospering, and he hoped in another year to show figures in excess of $1 million. "Neither Mr. Lucas or yourself desire to be small bankers and I assure you that I am ambitious of making our name famous among the nations of the earth." [49]

Even as early as the spring of 1854, a considerable number of California residents were returning to the East. The *Golden Gate* sailed from San Francisco on April 14 with more than 1,100 passengers, some of whom were army officers with their families whose tours of duty in California had terminated. General Hitchcock left the city on the *Sierra Nevada* on the 15th, and a Captain Mason and his wife were passengers on the *John L. Stephens* the same day. Both these officers had made profitable investments in California, and they left their properties in the hands of Lucas, Turner & Co. General Hitchcock gave Sherman his power of attorney in this connection.

Even as conservative a man as Banker Sherman was optimistic about the prospects of the mining industry. An officer of the American Exchange Bank of New York, David Hoadley, wrote him in a doubtful vein as to California's mineral resources. Sherman in replying spoke of "the universal distribution of dust in the mountains, not only in the gulches but in the side hills and on the very [illegible] tops, beside[s] the inexhaustible quantities of fine dust not yet attempted in the lower streams and even in the Sacramento plains." Further, "A scientific gentleman Mr. Marcon [?] was here last night and says all the gold cannot be got out in a century." Then Sherman's native caution regained the ascendancy, for he continued:

> Of course the mines become less and less rich per month and I would advise no one to leave the fertile fields of our west to come to the gold mines but Providence rules these matters and supplies . . . delvers in the earth. Regardless of hardships and inadequate compensation, as long as gold can be had, there will be workers.

A few weeks later Sherman again discussed mining developments, as well as San Francisco's commerce generally, in a letter to Turner:

> I feel some delicacy in entering on a learned dissertation on California matters. It has singular ups and downs, not always to be explained from normal causes but it seems to me that we may

assume that San Francisco is beyond question the great seaport of Western America, that here must center the commerce of the Northwest coast as well as that of Mexico, the Sandwich Islands, etc. Already the coasting trade is a very considerable item and must grow in the exact ratio of the population of their countries. But as you say the yield of gold is the grand criterion. The miners are this season doing famously, the papers are full of big lumps and lucky strikes and every species of mining is paying well, in the rim beds, in the hills and solid rock. The extent of the mining country is vast and the gold is mingled up with all the earth in greater or less quantities. Men are now profitably employed in galleries and pits a hundred feet beneath the surface, at which rate no one can tell when the whole will be exhausted. . . . This city is not so prosperous as when you were here. The merchants complain of high rents and small sales. Competition has forced holders of goods to sell at any price so that one cannot but wonder at the heavy sacrifices. I think these losses must fall on the New York and Boston shippers. This now is working its own cure for few ships are on the way and already many articles of consumption have advanced to a paying rate. . . . There are too many merchants for the business and many of these merchants have inadequate capital.[50] Real estate is not saleable unless for actual use and then the seller asks old prices. There have been several reasons for this—speculation last year ran up the prices beyond their real value, outside of the settled part. The commissioners have not yet passed on the city title to her four leagues and squatters still contend that the city has no real title, that the land not actually in possession is open to squatters and they squat accordingly, but no one apprehends the loss of the lots actually enclosed and in use.[51] Again there was a desperate push to extend the city front the same as when you were here but it again was defeated in the Legislature.[52] Also, the grades adopted by the former council cut deep in the hills; the cost of which was assessed to the property; in some cases amounting to more than the property was worth. To remedy this, the whole subject was given to a board of three disinterested engineers of which Major Barnard, U.S. Engineers and Major Hardie of the Artillery were two. They have just made a report, setting aside the former heavy grades and recommending a system with as little cutting and filling as is consistent with drainage.[53]

Some of the business entrusted to the firm by former residents proved very troublesome. One of these was the collection of rents on a hotel in Marysville, which belonged to a customer named Dr. John S. Griffin, now in New York. The tenants were chronically delinquent and Sherman repeatedly urged Griffin to return to California and give the matter his personal attention. In May, 1854, while Nisbet was in the Sacramento Valley on other business, Sherman wired him to go to Marysville about this problem. Successive reductions of rent and three changes of tenants had failed to improve matters. Such experiences doubtless influenced Sherman to decline repeated requests to invest moneys and to manage properties for nonresidents.

Half of his time was now occupied in keeping a close eye on the rising walls at Jackson and Montgomery. Not content with this degree of vigilance, Sherman employed a man just to watch the mixing of mortar and the laying of masonry. Several buildings had recently collapsed because of defective foundations, and he was determined that no such fate would befall the Lucas-Turner structure.

Apparently a wave of moral reform swept the city about this time. Sherman reported on April 15, 1854, that

> the Council have by ordinance abolished fandango, dancing and bawdy houses and you can walk Dupont, Jackson and Pacific Streets day and night without seeing any of those scenes which made them a disgrace to the city. The more fashionable places on Washington Street are as silent as the [illegible] and you do not now see troops of girls displaying themselves on horseback and carriages [illegible] Such women cannot be changed or reformed, yet their practices are hidden out of the way.

This long letter reported "Mrs. Sherman is tolerably well and our little girl is as fat as a pig and fond of dirt as is natural to children." [54]

The trust accounts described in the last chapter were frequently mentioned in the letters that passed between the partners. In one of them, Turner remonstrated that his St. Louis associates felt that Sherman was crediting these accounts with an excessive rate of interest. Sherman rejoined that the firm needed more money than it had available in its own funds, if it was going to accept all the desirable business offered it. If Lucas-Turner borrowed in New York, it would probably have to pay 10% a year. If it used these customers' funds on which it charged no fee or commission, Lucas, Turner & Co. could pay them a rate attractive to the customers and still retain a margin of profit.

Sherman further pointed out that the bank was at this time carrying all the deposits of army officers stationed in California. New arrivals were customarily directed to Lucas-Turner by present depositors. The latters' good will was therefore doubly important to the firm. Sherman preferred to finance his bank's need for money in this manner rather than to borrow in the East, since the latter course would not be productive of new deposits. The great bulk of the trust accounts came from army officers.

This forthright, even blunt, expression of differing opinions is characteristic of all the correspondence of Sherman and Turner. Separated as they were by thousands of miles, it seems little less than miraculous that harmony was preserved. Sherman put his finger on the reason for their accord when he wrote: "I am thus frank with you because it is our agreement to have no reserve." [55] He could have added that they were two honorable men with unlimited respect for and confidence in each other.

No name appears more frequently in Sherman's letters to Turner than Page, Bacon & Co., whether directly or indirectly through reference to some of its partners. The awe in which they were held by Nisbet has been noted. Sherman did not share this feeling, but it is evident that they and their doings were uppermost in his mind. This was natural enough; both firms were branches of St. Louis houses. Lucas and Simonds had come to San Francisco both in emulation of Page, Bacon & Co. and as its competitor. Its policies and activities were bound to be important to Sherman, although the record is very clear that he did not mistake imitation for competition. He had to guard against this tendency in his assistant Nisbet.

During his daily visits to the new building, Sherman had frequently encountered D. D. Page of Page-Bacon. The latter showed much interest in the construction, and the two men became quite well acquainted. Page, Bacon & Co. owned the corner of Montgomery and Clay, according to Sherman "beyond dispute the best locality in this city." Page wanted to move his bank nearer to the wharves and apparently thought Sherman had made an excellent choice in selecting the site at Montgomery and Jackson Streets. On the other hand, Page told Sherman that he was opposed to tearing down any good building even to erect a better one. Therefore, Sherman was sure Page was responsible for his firm's leasing a lot at the southwest corner of Clay and Battery Streets on which stood a two-story building. Architects were planning to remodel this structure for Page-Bacon's occupancy. Sherman believed this move would bring more business to his own bank's neighborhood.

D. D. Page, his son Frank, and the latter's family were all passengers on one of the outward-bound Nicaragua steamers at the end of April. The firm's San Francisco business was left in charge of a partner named Henry Haight. Sherman's letters make it clear that the friendly relations he had begun to enjoy with D. D. Page did not include his partner Haight. "He has never visited our bank or shown my family a particle of courtesy and of course I have made no advances."

Haight had recently sold his residence on Bush Street to Volney E. Howard for $24,000 and moved into a fine house at the corner of Powell and Broadway, which he rented for $5,000 a year. Sherman's path was to cross Haight's more than once in the months ahead, but they never became friends.[56]

The banker wrote Turner that Mrs. Sherman "is still pining for home" and was already planning on a trip East the following spring. "I don't know what I shall do yet, but if she is no better pleased next spring I may break up, let her go home to Lancaster, there to remain until the expiration of my enlistment." The family's health was again mentioned. Mrs. Sherman was pregnant and expecting to be confined in June, but otherwise she was quite well. "My own health is better than this time last year, the asthma giving me occasional rubs to remind me of its presence. Should I at any time be short or cross, charge it to account of the asthma." He then mentioned that a sick bookkeeper was convalescing for "a week across the bay, among the trees and flowers now in their beauty. I wish I could give myself the same liberty." The necessity of watching the building's progress made that impossible. Meanwhile another employee, named Chamberlain, had been hired; "about 26 years old, strong and good looking and works like a dray horse and don't talk."

The affairs of Palmer, Cook & Co. continued to alarm the business community. Because of that firm's questionable manipulation of the interest on the state's bonds, the American Exchange Bank of New York was "handling them without gloves." Sherman was sure the state would withdraw its funds from Palmer-Cook. Many of the city and county officials would also close their accounts with that firm, provided the other bankers would serve as their bondsmen. (Evidently Palmer, Cook & Co. had utilized this service as a means of getting deposits.) Sherman was approached by the San Francisco tax collector in this connection, "but [I] declined endorsing for anybody, especially a California politician, unless they would promise to keep on deposit with us the full amount of cash expressed in the bond, which of course they could not do."

The War Department had ordered the army officers handling government funds to deposit them in the subtreasury. Lucas, Turner & Co. was therefore threatened with the loss of about $50,000 in deposits maintained with it by Maj. J. G. Barnard and a certain Major Turner (no relative of Henry Smith Turner). The government had recently begun work on the fortification of San Francisco Bay. The work started at Fort Point and Alcatraz Island, and similar improvements were planned for Point San Jose, Angel Island, and Lime Rock Point. Majors Barnard and Turner and some junior officers were directing these works, which it was estimated would cost not less than $2 million.[57]

Barnard and Turner objected to the War Department's order because the subtreasurer was unable to handle their business. Barnard had two hundred men working under him and Turner more than a hundred. Sherman anticipated that eventually the funds controlled by these officers would be transferred to the subtreasury. Messrs. Barnard and Turner would then make lump-sum transfers back into their own accounts with Lucas, Turner & Co., on which they could draw individual checks to their workmen. Sherman was anxious to retain this business, not merely on account of the large amounts involved but because many of the laborers let their pay remain on deposit for long periods.[58]

6

Trust accounts continued to cause Sherman some uneasiness. A friend of the St. Louis partners named Drayton remitted $10,000 "to be invested safely" at 2% a month, payable quarterly. Major Thomas Swords,[59] a fellow officer of Turner's on the march of the Army of the West in 1846, was the owner of another trust account. Turner had promised him that the firm would be responsible for the safety of his investments. Sherman assented somewhat reluctantly but wrote Swords that he must not mention the arrangement to anyone. Even though he fully accepted the moral responsibility, Sherman thought "it preferable to hold ourselves irresponsible save for good faith as agents."

Meanwhile, the firm's own receivables seemed in satisfactory condition; interest was being paid promptly and most were adequately secured.

But there were serpents in this Eden also. One was a Sam Ward, who gave bad checks for part of an exchange purchase and proved elusive when the bank sought a settlement. At times, Sherman's sardonic humor lightened the business correspondence, even when the joke was on himself. One of the boldest confidence men of the Gold Rush era was Baron Steinberger, who had arrived in San Francisco in 1849. He brought letters from both the Secretary of War and the Secretary of the Navy, certifying to his high standing in the cattle business. Armed with these and unmitigated gall but no funds, he had developed a thriving butcher shop on the Broadway Wharf and had made himself a tidy fortune. The process had been easier and more rapid because the Baron seldom paid the ranchers who supplied him with his livestock—or anyone else luckless enough to have dealings with him. In the course of recounting the applications for credit, Sherman wrote Turner:

> Your highly esteemed fellow statesman and friend, Baron Steinberger, dashed at us like a trout at fish bait, but always to find the hook empty. One steamer day he came in and said he must have $150. Of course I told him I could not lend him money. He appealed and promised solemnly to pay in five days. I told him I would not lend him a cent of the money of the bank which was not mine. He appealed to me personally and ass as I was, I gave it. Of course I have not seen him since. Well it might have been worse. This is my individual loss unless your love of Virginia [apparently the Baron like Turner hailed from the Old Dominion] will induce you to step forward and screen from ignominy a full Baron of the Land.[60]

Other smaller fry on occasion wheedled loans as trifling as $10 from the soft-hearted banker, but he was learning! Among such annoying customers was a woman with an ailing baby whose family wanted her to return to St. Louis. They had supplied Sherman with funds to care for her, but she had delayed her departure until there was only enough money left to cover her steamship passage. Sherman bought her a ticket at the last moment to insure her departure.

Far more important was a call made on Sherman late in May by a banker from Sacramento named Rhodes. He wished to negotiate a loan of $20,000 with which to purchase gold dust. Rhodes made a good impression, so Sherman sent Nisbet to Sacramento to inspect the parcels of real estate offered as security. One was Rhodes's bank building and the other a brick structure on J Street between 1st and 2nd Streets, which was leased to a printing office. Rhodes also offered $15,000 of plank road stock.[61] Sherman felt he could make the loan; the borrower would pay 3% a month interest, the principal to be repayable on twenty days' notice. What was equally important, Lucas, Turner & Co. was to have the first right to purchase all of Rhodes's gold dust.

About this time, "Honest Harry" Meiggs reentered the picture. He now had a vast stock of lumber piled on his long wharf. With the stagnant condition of real estate, the price of lumber had steadily declined from $60 to $32 a thousand board feet. Most of the sawmills on the coast had shut down because of the oversupply of planks and joists. Meiggs maintained that he could sell his lumber at $24 a thousand and still break even. The community rated him highly; "a rapid, popular man," Sherman described him to Turner, quite likely to be the next mayor of San Francisco. Lucas-Turner had had considerable dealings with him and he now owed them about $50,000. Sherman had taken all the security he could get to insure the safety of this line of credit. Meiggs for his part had paid his interest promptly; yet Sherman felt a growing uneasiness about this debtor. There was too heavy a concentration in one borrower, and he resolved to call for payment.

One of Sherman's reasons for sending Nisbet to Sacramento and then on to Marysville about the Griffin hotel was "partly that I might scrutinize all our [Meiggs] notes." It is very evident that Nisbet stood in awe of this particular borrower. Either Sherman wished to spare Nisbet's feelings or was fearful of a clash with his subordinate about this line of credit.

Three days later, the banker reported the surprising outcome of his demand that Meiggs pay up: "he forthwith paid in $30,000." Evidently Meiggs then represented that he was closely connected with "a foreign house controlling large sums of money." This made some impression on Sherman, who added "we must keep in with Meiggs, but will hold large collateral always."

By the end of May, the banker's letters reflected his great pride in the new building: "It has grown out of the mud a beauty. It is the handsomest building in this town, and it is admirably built from the driving of the piles to the minutest parts. . . . I enjoy it as much as an artist does a fine picture." The contractors still promised completion by July 1. Sherman was busily prospecting for desirable tenants for the two upper floors. While rents had dropped from the rates prevailing when Turner had been in San Francisco, his partner was certain that the building would return a satisfactory income.

This particular letter closed with the news that Nisbet had returned from Sacramento. Evidently he had combined business with romantic dalliance, as Sherman said he was "much pleased with his visit and a daughter of James C. Fall." [62] Nisbet had been absent a week; and the staff had carried on so successfully without him "I am satisfied that should any necessity arise for him to go away, we can get along. It is well for us to feel independent of anybody. Nisbet's conduct is unexceptionable, only he has his boyish ways for which Nature is responsible and which time will amend." [63]

In June a long letter from Turner caused Sherman to poke fun at his friend:

> Let me join . . . in applauding your resolution to build you a handsome convenient house in the city, where Mrs. Turner can be near her family and where you can have schools convenient. Your farm affords you a convenient retreat for the heats of summer and a place to watch and have trouble about, for trouble is as necessary to real satisfaction as vinegar and mustard to easy digestion. . . . You will be so well off that I fear you will be restless for something to think about. It's utterly useless for you to get me to be sympathetic with you about your national debt [a term Turner frequently used to describe his obligations, both family and financial] as I know too well the value of your estate in Saint Louis.

Returning to business matters, Sherman was happy to report that the firm's profits were exceeding his estimate of $10,000 a month.

The same letter exultantly announced that on June 8

> came into this world a boy of the reddest kind that will need a great deal of watching and if his after career takes as much money in proportion as his birth with doctors, nurses and church fees I

> might as well forego the dream I often conjure up of living in Saint Louis with a small and certain income, with a farm in Illinois to waste that little on. Mrs. Sherman is quite as well as could be expected and William Ewing Sherman has passed most of his sojourn in sleep.

In another paragraph, Sherman confessed his conviction that his wife would never become reconciled to living in San Francisco. Her parents were elderly; it took a minimum of four weeks' travel to visit them. She was going back to Ohio in the spring of 1855, and Sherman had given up hope that she would willingly return to California.

Bishop Joseph S. Alemany had baptized the infant at the Green Street home in the presence of a small group—the Bowmans, Nisbet and Reilly, Major and Mrs. Hardie, and some Ohio friends. (This was the son whose death from typhoid fever in Memphis on October 3, 1863, was one of the greatest tragedies of Sherman's tempestuous life. "Of all of my children he seemed the most precious." [64])

Apparently, Turner had offered to come to San Francisco to relieve Sherman while he escorted his wife to Ohio. His partner assured him that such a sacrifice was quite unnecessary. Friends of the Shermans were among the passengers on virtually every mail steamer, so she would not need her husband's escort to New York, where her brother could meet her. Sherman was hopeful that both Turner and Mr. Lucas would visit San Francisco the following spring, when there would be much of interest for them to see.[65]

A number of applications had been received for rooms in the building, which was now nearing completion. Except for a law office rented to Bowman, Sherman had delayed closing any deals for the space. He wished to choose the best tenants and to secure the most favorable rentals. He was sure that he could obtain a total of $1300 a month, including $600 to be paid by Lucas, Turner & Co.

Despite the dull times, several other buildings were under construction. Haight had told Sherman that Page, Bacon & Co. were moving to Clay and Battery Streets on November 1, but he

THE BUILDING SHERMAN BUILT

No longer a bank; the Lucas-Turner Building sometime prior to 1906.

Courtesy of Society of California Pioneers

THE BUILDING SHERMAN BUILT

On the eve of disaster; the Lucas-Turner Building on March 31, 1906.

Courtesy of Society of California Pioneers

THE BUILDING SHERMAN BUILT

Bricks and ashes; May 22, 1906. East side of Montgomery Street from Washington to Jackson from site of present Transamerica Building at gore of Columbus Avenue and Montgomery Street; Lucas-Turner Building marked by arrow (note the gap in the third-story wall, which bears out the author's theory of the damage caused by the earthquake of April 18, 1906).

Courtesy of Transamerica Corporation

THE BUILDING SHERMAN BUILT

800 Montgomery Street in the 1960's; note the survival of the original pediment and columns at the entrance.

Photographs by the author

had not heard of any other bankers seeking this same neighborhood. Sherman persisted in thinking "the corners of Clay and Washington on Montgomery will always be the center of this city."

Squatter troubles were again disturbing the peace of San Francisco. The land commission was now passing on the titles to the city's land and the squatters spread the idea that San Francisco was going to lose these cases. Their aggressions brought on violence, with a few deaths and many wounds resulting from these fights. One of these brawls had occurred on Green Street near the Shermans' home. A house had been demolished, and a woman and two men had been shot.

The removal of army headquarters from San Francisco to Benicia also caused excitement. Sherman suspected that Washington had ordered this as a slap at General Wool for his promotion of Broderick's candidacy for the Senate, as well as his opposition to the Central American filibusters.[66]

The next letter announced that the new banking room was virtually finished, save for painting and the erection of counters. All this would be completed within a few days. It was now planned that after the bank closed for business on Saturday, July 8, all its effects would be moved to the new location. Operations there would commence on the following Monday. Advertisements to this effect were printed in the newspapers. Sherman proudly asserted: "Our new banking room is without comparison the finest in the city."

In addition to Page-Bacon's recently announced move, Adams & Co. were negotiating for space with the owners of the Montgomery Block. More startling was the news that James King of William, who for some time had operated his own bank, had turned over his deposits to Adams & Co. It had been announced that he would hereafter manage that firm's banking department. King had started business with very limited capital. Being well known, he had quickly secured considerable deposits, but had "not capacity enough to stand prosperity." He had built a fine home on Stockton Street costing about $43,000, had purchased a carriage and horses, had entertained extensively, and had outfitted his bank in a lavish manner. On the other hand, he had loaned heavily on water stock that soon became almost worthless. The borrower could pay nothing, but a firm that had loaned King $50,000 demanded its money. Dull times had caused his deposits to dwindle, and King's liquid assets were nearly exhausted. He sent his family back East to their old home. No one could afford to rent his fine house nor could it be sold at a price even close to its cost. Undoubtedly, King's transfer of his business and his own services was the only alternative to failure. Sherman believed the arrangement with King had weakened Adams & Co. In a few short months, King was to attain a melancholy fame that completely overshadowed his financial troubles and vitally affected the lives of innumerable San Franciscans, including Banker Sherman.[67]

Another competitor named Carothers approached Sherman confidentially during these days and offered to turn over $1,200,000 in deposits to Lucas, Turner & Co., if he could become a member of that firm. Sherman believed Carothers' move was prompted by conditions similar to those that had forced King's drastic action. The banker doubted that Carothers controlled as much business as he claimed and declined his overtures, saying there were already enough partners in the firm. A more compelling reason, he confessed to Turner, was that he had neither the authority nor the inclination to take in a stranger. "It would have been helpful to bring in a man of greater banking experience and more savoir faire than Nisbet, but the status quo is our policy, no change, no modification, so that in a short time our house will have all the elements of strength and durability."

Wright of the Miners Exchange Bank had just purchased a lot at the northwest corner of Jackson and Montgomery Streets (directly opposite the new Lucas-Turner building) for $27,000 in cash. Plans were in preparation for the erection of a very substantial building. Other improvements contemplated for the neighborhood included a new Merchants Exchange on Battery

Street opposite the Custom House. Spirited bidding ensued; it was estimated that the structure would cost $98,000.

During June, Sherman wrote that he had been reelected treasurer of the Society of California Pioneers. Probably he had been elected to this post in 1853, but this is the first time he mentioned it in writing Turner. He had also been appointed one of the marshal's aides for the Fourth of July parade, and had been instructed to equip himself with a horse, saddle, and so on.

> Now if I had a handsome horse and fixtures, [he wryly commented] would not object to make an ass of myself with a blue ribbon across my shoulders, but as I have no horse, and as the fixtures cost some, I'll quietly decline and cross over to Oakland to join the Fourth in that quiet, rural village to whose trees I have taken quite a fancy. Indeed, should Mrs. Sherman consent, I think I would sell my present house and live over the bay. There are now two ferry boats and the County of Alameda will appropriate $25,000. to clean out the bar, the only obstacle to the passage of the boats at low tide.[68]

Trust funds were again a leading subject in several of Turner's letters that arrived on July 1. It is not clear just what position Turner had taken, but apparently he was more in favor of accommodating their friends than was Sherman. The latter wrote:

> As to trust funds, . . . occupying the ground I do, I reserve to myself the right to invest in the name of the owner of the money, which I now invariably do to officers here in the country, thereby throwing all risk on them, but keeping the excess [interest] as our commissions. Where it is manifestly to our interest to keep this money for our customers, Lucas Turner & Co. are of course responsible, but you can see a difference, for supposing that in time we have enough of our own to satisfy applicants? How easily I can invest in the name of these gentlemen, or even return them their funds. With Swords, Drayton and other special friends we act as exceptions to the general rule which exceptions I trust will be as few as possible.

Immediately following the above, Sherman mentioned what was probably a "special" trust account because of the Lucas family: "I am glad to find you sustain my position in the William Lucas account. That too will work itself all right in due time." [69]

Reilly had received a letter from Turner indicating that he "may pop down on us this summer." Sherman said he would be glad to see him but wished he would wait until spring, then bring Mr. Lucas with him. "By that time we hope the seeds we have sown will have produced a tree of fair dimensions with blossoms and fruit."

On the personal side, he was happy to report: "Mrs. Sherman is as well as possible. . . . The youngster thrives, his wants are few and well supplied. Lizzie is the picture of health and I only regret that our small yard and alley are insufficient for her busy legs. The wind blows a hurricane . . . in the evening, the only time when I can walk with her." [70]

Part Two:
Mishaps and Misgivings

7

The next letter, written on July 14, 1854, proudly announced that Lucas, Turner & Co. were now in their new quarters, "all we could expect, plenty of light, easy of access, large, roomy and beautiful." Sherman included a sketch of the sign over the rear partition in the bank, which he had designed—"Lucas, Turner & Co. Bankers" arched over a clock. He also described in detail the signs on the Montgomery and Jackson Streets walls and doors; in addition to the name, these advertised "Exchange on Atlantic Cities" and "Gold Dust Bought," as well as the office hours. "On the exterior we present a respectable appearance and all who run may read."

Some rooms above the bank were already rented at $270 a month, and applicants for the remaining space were numerous. Pile drivers were busy on the site for the Miners Exchange Bank across the street.

The courts had just cleared the title to the block south of the bank. The state of California had claimed that it was overflowed land and therefore state property, but the courts had denied this claim. The decision cleared the way for further improvement of the neighborhood. Meanwhile, a bad fire had swept three blocks built over the tidelands between Jackson and Washington Streets, close to the mail steamers' wharves. Plans for rebuilding were being pushed. Sacramento also had just suffered a major conflagration in its residential district.

Four closely written pages detail the highly complicated litigation involving the steamer *America*.[1] Wadsworth & Sheldon,

New York correspondents of Lucas, Turner & Co. some months earlier had loaned $36,000 to one W. H. Brown to pay the final costs of construction of this new vessel. They took a mortgage on the steamer to secure their loan. At the same time, Brown gave Wadsworth & Sheldon an option to buy a 26% interest in the *America* for $26,000. The steamer was to proceed immediately to San Francisco, and the option to purchase was to run for ninety days from its arrival. A man named Vandewater was appointed the ship's agent in San Francisco until the mortgage was repaid. The *America* had made three trips to Oregon when Brown demanded that Vandewater surrender the vessel to him. A lawsuit resulted; and in the lower court and on two appeals, the decisions were all adverse to Brown. For ten weeks, the steamer idled at anchor in the hands of the United States marshal.

Meanwhile, Wadsworth & Sheldon decided to buy under their option. Vandewater had also acquired an option on another 25% interest in the *America.* Wadsworth & Sheldon requested Lucas-Turner to take a bill of sale on the steamer for their and Vandewater's interests. To pay the expenses that had accrued while the vessel was idle due to the litigation, Page, Bacon & Co. had loaned $5,300 and Lucas Turner & Co., $1,200. When their loan fell due, Page, Bacon & Co. libeled the vessel. Sherman also filed a claim for his $1,200 and for Wadsworth & Sheldon's mortage. The *America* had cost $100,000 in the East and was valued at $130,000 to $160,000 in California, so there was an ample equity to cover all these claims. Nevertheless, the United States marshal in due course proceeded to hold a judicial sale. At the same time, Brown purchased the steamer for $95,000, but since he failed to make the 10% cash payment required by law, the steamer was again put on the block.

Sherman in the meantime had counseled with Cornelius K. Garrison, the agent of the Nicaragua line in San Francisco.[2] Garrison strongly advised Sherman to buy the vessel for Wadsworth & Sheldon and intimated that he would join in the purchase if the other interests wished him to do so. With this reassurance, Sherman bid $95,000 for the *America,* paying $9,500 on account.

"These are large figures," he wrote Turner, "and a large venture, but they [his customers] called on us to protect them and we have done so." That sentence reveals a priceless quality in Sherman. No great success is attainable by any enterprise unless its head possesses a deep, unswerving sense of responsibility. It is not merely pride in a job well done but the instinctive response to the confidence displayed by the customer. An incalculable degree of good will attaches to the man—and the house—that accepts that challenge.

In a short time, Sherman could look back on this episode with real satisfaction. He had been accumulating more than the usual volume of cash, because prudence dictated such a course at that time. In addition, he needed ample funds for the *America*. Presently, Lucas, Turner & Co. paid into court $85,500 in cash on the purchase of the vessel and the next day were paid back $83,000. The balance was left to cover court fees. Sherman had a choice of courses open to him, one conservative and the other speculative. It was like him to let Brown, the original owner, repurchase the steamer. Wadsworth & Sheldon recovered all their advances plus interest and exchange. Probably more money could have been made for his own firm by holding the steamer for resale at a profit, but that did not seem to fit well with Sherman's conception of banking. Not only did he not wish the responsibility of operating a coastal steamer, but retention of the *America* would have made a mortal enemy of Brown.

Evidently Sherman's plans for a bucolic Independence Day in sylvan Oakland missed fire, for he wrote: "We had a great parade on the Fourth and much to my surprise I was chief aide to Marshal Stevenson.[3] I had to act and indeed had the whole management on my hands. These are occasions which I do not solicit, but they attract notice, make acquaintances and further our business. They entail expense on me personally . . . I had to buy a horse." Banker Sherman was being educated in public relations, although he probably never heard the expression.

"Our weather here certainly does contrast with yours for the cold winds and fogs come down over the hills like large billows, sweeping all before it. . . . The children could not be healthier but poor Lizzie is almost dead at being shut up all day. We have but little yard room and Mrs. Sherman will not let her play in the streets."

The ratification of the Gadsden Treaty in the summer of 1854 and the resultant acquisition of southern Arizona brought a scornful remark from Sherman because it appropriated $10 million "for what you nor I would pay as many hundreds."[4]

In late July, the banker complained that while money was plentiful prices were very low. Business in exchange was declining, and Sherman planned to run notices in the newspapers offering to buy gold dust and sell exchange. A few weeks later, he reported that his firm was the successful bidder on $100,000 transfer drafts on the treasury at New York "payable in American coin" at a cost of 1 ¾ %.

Although several substantial buildings were being erected in Lucas-Turner's neighborhood, "times continue miserably dull. Real estate is unsaleable and rents have declined."

Letters to Turner written during the preceding spring had reported Sherman's promise to his wife to take her and the family on an outing to Monterey. Since he had resided there for some time during the Mexican War and still had many friends there, she was anxious to make the journey. A friend named Bowman and his wife had planned to accompany the Shermans.[5] In March, heavy rains had made the roads impassable. By the time better weather prevailed, Sherman was absorbed in the construction of the new building and in the litigation over the *America*. In August, it seemed feasible to make the long-planned journey. He drove his wife, the children, and their nurse in a two-horse carriage, while the Bowmans followed in a buggy. They came back to San Francisco several days sooner than planned because Bowman's affairs required his early return. The families did not wish to separate, so they completed the trip together, following the road up the "contra costa" on the east side of the bay and crossing from Oakland on the ferry. Mrs. Sherman very much enjoyed this excursion and now had a better opinion of California. In view of Sherman's previous residence in

Monterey, it would be interesting to read his report of scenes revisited and of the warm reunions he must have had with old friends like his former landlady, Doña Augustias, and her children. But since our source is a file of business correspondence, we do not find such details.

Sherman believed that Turner had never visited Oakland, so described it for him as it existed in the summer of 1854:

> . . . a low sandy piece of ground on the San Antonio Creek directly opposite this city with oak trees beautifully distributed. The climate is much milder than this as the winds do not blow so hard and the fog scatters before it crosses the bay. The titles to land are not well settled, yet quite a town has grown up there and two steam ferry boats cross with considerable regularity.

Mrs. Sherman was so favorably impressed that she was very anxious to move to Oakland so that her little girl might have more room to play; also, she believed the climate would be better for her husband's health. The poor lady had reason to feel concern on this account. Sherman wrote Turner: "On my trip to Monterey, after riding all day I had to walk all night outside of the houses where we stopped so that I was quite prostrated when I returned." No wonder that the distracted man wrote: "I have little or no faith in my prolonged existence . . . but this asthma is so fixed on me and is so serious at times that I care but little how soon it terminates fatally." Yet in another sentence he proudly emphasized that he had not lost a day at the bank because of these asthmatic attacks.[6]

Mrs. Sherman and the children were well. She was counting eagerly on her visit to Ohio the following spring, but had now concluded that she would return to San Francisco. Nevertheless, her husband still believed that when she went East, he would have her remain there "until my enlistment is out"—he always so referred to his agreement to manage the bank in San Francisco for seven years—"provided always I survive that period."

If it had not been for the trip planned for his wife this next spring, Sherman might have seriously considered moving his home to Oakland. He even indulged in day dreams: "I can get a lot 125 × 225 with fine oak trees and a house large enough for us for about $3,000. We could afford a buggy and cow in addition to our present establishment." Crossing the bay twice daily was an obstacle, but he liked to think of riding about the countryside on Sundays and holidays and "tinkering about a place supplied with flowers, chickens and other rural objects." His more conservative side asserted itself when he closed this subject: "I shall try and fend off the Oakland project unless I find Mrs. Sherman's heart set on it when I shall take it under advisement."

On his return to the bank, Sherman was disappointed to learn that Nisbet had not rented any more of the upper floor space. Within a few days, he himself secured tenants for three of the rooms and placed advertisements in the newspapers for the remaining offices. Letters during this period frequently discuss the ultimate ownership of the building. Sherman favored letting Lucas buy the entire interest for $100,000. He was confident that the property would net him $2,000 a month, but he wished to defer the final decision until Mr. Lucas came to San Francisco. He hoped that would be in the near future.[7]

In August, 1854, San Francisco's financial circles suffered a foretaste of bitter experiences to come. Soon after the arrival of the *Sierra Nevada* one Sunday morning, rumors circulated that a $5,000 draft drawn by Page, Bacon & Co. on a New York bank had been dishonored. The story caused much talk but Sherman could not see that his competitors had been seriously affected. Their exchange business was still the largest in the city.

A confidential postscript on the August 15 letter reported a personnel problem that must have been only too typical of the San Francisco of the fifties. A young clerk, member of a respected St. Louis family, had been discharged by Nisbet during Sherman's absence in Monterey. Although an able worker, he had fallen into bad company and more than once had reported for duty while intoxicated. Sherman himself had warned the young man that he must mend his ways. Nisbet had terminated his employment when he repeated the offense. The banker wrote Turner a sad account of the man's penitence and of his fears of what the news would do to his parents. Finally, in view of his competency (Nisbet admitted he could do twice the work of any other employee) and on his promise to submit to strict discipline, Sherman relented and rehired him. The offender agreed that his necessary expense bills would be paid directly by the bank, he would board where Sherman directed, and would report in detail where he spent his evenings. In addition, he agreed to get along on virtually no pocket money.

More than once, members of the St. Louis firm sought places for their relatives with the San Francisco bank. Sherman frankly warned such inquirers of the pitfalls in the way of the unwary. Capable young men might find no difficulty in performing the tasks assigned them, but how they spent their leisure time was a far more serious question.

The employment of even sober and competent clerks from the East could involve other complications. Reilly, a very satisfactory employee, hailed from St. Louis. In addition to his bank duties, he had helped Sherman keep a close watch on any of the clerks likely to succumb to temptation. However, a death in his family at St. Louis had created estate problems and necessitated the care of a younger sister. Sherman feared he would have to do without Reilly for a long period while he went East to serve his family.

It would be interesting to read Turner's letters to Sherman of July 29 and 31 and find what brought forth the following mixed metaphor:

> You pitch into me like a thousand bricks. Why the deuce can't you let an old soldier [the writer was then in his thirty-fifth year] growl a little occasionally? It's the safety valve without which we should keep an immense quantity of bad humour cooped up. . . . Let me beg you when my letters evince bad temper, be kind enough not to let others see it, and let my asthma bear its full share of blame. Even your good temper and that under absolute control, even you for nights, weeks and months of nights forced to sit, breathing like a broken-winded horse, thankful for a couple [of] hours of repose, would find your nerves and temper somewhat unsettled. For the last seven months I have been compelled

to sit up more or less each night, breathing the smoke of nitre paper and know that this climate will sooner or later kill me dead as a herring.

Turner's reason for "pitching into" Sherman could not have been very basic, since in replying the banker thanked the senior partners, Lucas and Simonds, for offering to increase his $5,000 salary. He could not accept it because, he said, with his partnership interest, he was receiving what he was worth and what he had originally agreed to. He recalled that Mr. Lucas, at the time when partnership interest and salary were fixed, had mentioned expenses that should be incurred for the firm, such as entertaining new arrivals in San Francisco. "We have done some considerable in that way . . . have invited to dine all strangers bringing letters from the interior, have reciprocated favors extended to me. . . . I may at some future time . . . figure it up and submit a bill." But Sherman thought that any increase of salary was unwarranted.

Nisbet felt it necessary that he visit St. Louis, and Sherman thought he could escort Mrs. Sherman to New York. Her husband disliked having her travel so far with two small children. For her part, she was willing to leave the children with her husband "if I can go over to Oakland . . . because that is a quiet rural place not likely to be swallowed up when Sodom's fate overwhelms this unhallowed place." [8]

8

In September, 1854, Sherman received word that the sons of both Lucas and Patterson had been made members of the firm of Lucas, Turner & Co.

In the same period, news of events in St. Louis prompted one of Sherman's rare comments on the politics of his times. Turner wrote to him about the downfall of the mighty Thomas H. Benton, long a power in the United States Senate. "Benton's defeat," replied Sherman, "was highly gratifying and I sincerely rejoice." He continued with the following cynical comments on San Francisco politics:

> Our election here has been a very exciting one. We heard all around that the Know Nothings were organizing in strength. . . . A few days before the election appeared a ticket headed Citizens Reform Ticket with Lucien Hermann as Mayor and most of the other candidates were selected out of the Whig or Democratic tickets already out. It seems the Know Nothings were not aware that Hermann was a Catholic and this was published to show that their creed was misunderstood for their nomination of a Catholic proved that the organization was not opposed to any class on account of religion, but a few days after, only *one* before election, a new ticket made its appearance with Hermann's name left out and a man's by the name of Webb inserted and sure enough the entire ticket has been elected. . . . Garrison bears his defeat badly. . . . Everything is quiet and the general supposition is that our new Mayor and Council will be economical. A new broom sweeps clean, but in one short year these immaculate gentlemen will be

kicked out of office with as little ceremony and thanks as the present.[9]

Lucas, Turner & Co., according to Sherman, "don't have much occasion for lawyer's services." However, Bowman, their local counsel, represented Lucas & Simonds in one matter that seems to have aroused criticism. A man named Hutchinson bought some cattle from one Fenn. Hutchinson paid Fenn by drafts drawn on Lucas & Simonds. When the livestock was delivered, Hutchinson claimed that some inferior cows had been substituted for those he had agreed to purchase. Hutchinson asserted that if Lucas & Simonds had paid the drafts, he would make good the amount; but if Fenn had not received the money, he would insist on a deduction for the poorer animals. Bowman was employed to collect the drafts, and he journeyed to Sacramento for that purpose. He became convinced that Hutchinson's objections were valid. Before the matter was settled, Bowman billed Lucas-Turner for traveling expenses and legal services. Sherman thought he should defer rendering a bill until the affair was concluded. Bowman objected that he was out of pocket and wanted a prompt settlement. Sherman paid the bill and sent it to St. Louis. "Lawyer's fees are terribly severe in this country," wrote the banker, "and what is common to us may seem exorbitant to a gentleman at home. Bowman's charges are high; make me squirm at times." Lucas & Simonds seemed less concerned about the bill than about Bowman's stand in opposition to Fenn, and they really questioned the attorney's good faith.

Two weeks later, Sherman was better able to go to Bowman's defense. A lawyer named Clark had come down from Sacramento en route to St. Louis. He had been present at the meeting between Hutchinson and Fenn and fully corroborated Bowman's account of the transaction. In Clark's opinion, Bowman had acted as prudently as possible. Hutchinson admitted his debt, and if adjustment for the defective cows had been made, would have settled the obligation; but in the meantime, the drop in price of farm commodities had rendered him incapable of paying anything. Bowman was leaving for Sacramento on September 15, in company with a deputy marshal, to levy on the same cattle sold to Hutchinson. "So far as I can learn, Bowman has done all he could to secure the debt." Sherman's description of Hutchinson's embarrassed condition speaks eloquently of the vagaries of California agriculture in the 1850's:

> The time given to Hutchinson was right as all human probability was that the growing crop of this season only wanted harvesting to realize large sums of money, but California is a perfect paradox, a mystery. The various ups and downs are enough to frighten any prudent person. All the large farmers such as Hutchinson, Beard, Homer, Hill, etc. whose names are synonymous with thousands of acres of wheat at a hundred bushels to the acre, turnips as big as a bushel, cabbages as large as an oak tree and onions too large for human belief are all actually failed or failing. —The fact is [illegible] are costly, labor from $3.00 to $8.00 a day, freight to market enormous, commissions, storage, etc. as high as in 1850 and yet wheat is hardly saleable at 90 cents a bushel in the city in good sacks, potatoes 2 cents a pound, barley 2 cents and all produce in proportion.

Other signs of commercial distress were all too evident, but Sherman was too close to the forest to see the trees. He was not the first banker to find himself well into a full-scale recession before he realized that his world was undergoing basic change, not just a momentary ebb in the tide of business.

> The mail companies have stopped the Golden Gate, John L. Stevens, etc. because they sink money every trip and now the old California, Oregon, and Panama are put on the line. The stock of the Consolidated Navigation Company now sells at 39½ to 40 cents, last year [was] par. The plank road stock at 50 cents though it pays regularly 2 cents a month on its par value, yet the Bhoys [*sic*] are becoming rampant at paying at two toll gates between this and the Mission and the city will either have to buy the road or it will end in riot.[10]

Real estate values continued in the doldrums. Sherman foreclosed a mortgage he had made for General Hitchcock on property he had conservatively valued at $20,000. He could not get a bid of even $10,000. He had to bid in the property in Hitchcock's name.

In spite of the gloomy outlook, Sherman reported that the bank was making progress. He would soon be able to operate without the overdraft of $50,000 arranged for the San Francisco house with the Metropolitan Bank in New York. Both exchange sales and deposits were increasing. Loans were at about a half million dollars; and the trust fund, $100,000. Interest on loans was running about $12,000 a month; exchange, commissions, and the like, another $3,000. Expenses were rent, $600; clerk hire and porter, $825.

Apparently, charitable contributions are an ancient problem for bankers. Wrote Sherman: "They still persecute us with charitable applications, some of which cannot be avoided. In most cases I answer that we have contributed somewhat to Catholic, Episcopalian, Unitarian, Jew and Chinese and that we cannot afford to distinguish further among the infinite subordinate varieties."

As to developments in the neighborhood, he wrote: "They are building an infernally pretty house opposite, have stolen in part our design but improve on it by putting a fourth story and making a granite front on Jackson as well as Montgomery." This was the Miners Exchange Bank building earlier mentioned. (Throughout his letters Sherman frequently confined his use of the word "building" to the imperfect participle; seldom did he use it as a noun. On the other hand "house" was frequently written by him when a commercial structure, rather than a residence, was involved. The sentence just quoted is a good illustration of this peculiarity in his language.)

The federal government had not helped the depressed condition of affairs by cutting the appropriations for the fortification of San Francisco harbor. The engineering officers had recommended the expenditure of roundly $1 million to complete the work now in progress. Washington had cut this to $360,000.

With business in a decline and money overly plentiful, Sherman's "trust funds," which he liked to maintain at around $100,000, had climbed to $130,000. He was refusing to take more and, whenever possible, encouraged certain customers to place their investment funds in the hands of some reliable brokers. He was still receiving applications for desirable loans at 3% a month, but as there was considerable money in the William Lucas account for which the firm paid 10% a year, it was obviously poor business to pay 2% a month to any more trust customers, if they could avoid doing so.

He wrote in mid-September: "At no period has our paper [he obviously referred to his notes receivable] been more safe than now," proudly underscoring most of the sentence, and following it with a statement that should have caused him mixed emotions:

> . . . quite a batch of persons having brought accounts to us yesterday and today, caused by the unexpected failure of Carothers, Anderson and Company. I knew they were weak for Carothers intimated to me that he would wind up or make new combinations and wanted some encouragement as to a branch of our house in the country, but today, they closed their doors. . . . All these mishaps help us of course and at the same time impress the necessity of great care in our loans and discounts. There is the true rub, there lies our profit and there our risks.

Then Sherman applied a scale of his own invention to indicate the comparative values of the kinds of collateral offered him:

> I am convinced that mining stocks are 0, wharf stocks about 3, city about 50, state about 70, real estate about 30, and good notes of small amounts made in bona fide sales and endorsed by two good parties about 95. In good endorsed paper we have lost nothing, and it is this very class of notes that facilitates business and makes acquaintances and gives us knowledge of the solvency or otherwise of men . . . I am satisfied that our new house is better than a hundred thousand dollars in our vault.

There is something pathetic about the sentence with which Sherman closed this reference to the new building: "It has a substantial matter of fact stand by appearance which conveys the idea that Lucas Turner & Co. are here for life, and as I say, forever."

By contrast, Sherman was very critical of the shortsighted

planning of their great competitor, Page, Bacon & Co. They had bought a property in which the ground lease at $200 a month had only ten years to run. The building required extensive alterations to fit it for their size. Only superficial inspection had been given it; and when work was about to start, it was tardily discovered that the walls were cracked and the foundations unsafe. The structure had to be demolished. The new building to be erected in its place would revert to the ground owners in only ten years!

Sherman was still sure the Lucas-Turner location was at the best end of Montgomery Street for permanent business. "They continue to build handsome houses all over town and God only knows why—Half of them are vacant and must continue so until we have a revival of business."

The banker ruefully confessed that he had made very little use of the horse he had bought for the Fourth of July parade. "He is an old Dragoon and a splendid animal under saddle." Sherman had driven him to Monterey but since returning had not ridden him enough "to pull down his spirit." The evening winds, the fog and the drab streets through which he must ride had severely limited the banker's equestrian activities. He was sorely tempted to purchase a buggy so that he could take his small daughter driving.

> Poor little thing, she is so shut up that when I go out in the evening after dinner, I have to take her along. Mrs. Sherman is afraid of a buggy in these dilapidated and narrow streets but occasionally indulges in a ride in the omnibus which runs half-hourly from Rincon Point to North Beach.
>
> There are some strange things in this country. You know barley and oats used to be from ten to twenty cents a pound and of course it cost money to keep a horse. Then with propriety the livery stable charged $50 a month. I asked for my bill and it was $50. I remonstrated . . . a horse did not eat more than $13 or $14 of provender but $50 is the price and none of the stables will take less. . . . No more is charged for a horse and buggy.

This long letter concluded with a paragraph of assorted news about mutual acquaintances. A navy officer named Stevens and his wife and children had moved into the house adjoining the

Shermans; "most excellent people," he wrote. A Captain Taney of the navy had arrived with his family. He was to have charge of the new navy yard to be constructed at Mare Island.[11] "Donaldson of the Quartermaster Department has come from the Tejon broken down completely, looks just like Mason did before he died.[12] Old Ben Beall is here but goes down to Los Angeles tomorrow by sea whence he goes to the Tejon where a post is to be built." [13] Turner's former comrade of the Army of the West, Dr. John S. Griffin, had also written Sherman from Los Angeles telling of a loss he had taken in the sale of a hotel.[14] He had just resigned his army post and settled in Los Angeles where he reported he was doing well. He had sent Sherman a box of splendid grapes. The banker also wrote Turner that peaches were quite abundant at $1 apiece—"Don't you want some?" [15]

On September 29, 1854, Sherman acknowledged a letter of Turner's dated August 12. After having read its first sheet with great care he wrote, "I consigned it to the flames as you suggested."

It is easy to guess that the burned paper reflected Turner's growing concern about his friend's health. Sherman felt he had not exaggerated his condition:

> I would be foolish to count on a long life, yet I may go on as now wheezing and coughing for a long time. . . . Of my personal acquaintances the strong have sunk before the scythe of time whilst the weak have gone on defying its edge. . . . I think it right to keep in view the fact that with me life is insecure: San Francisco has a curious climate . . . its fogs and winds will doubtless continue to afflict me with asthma, its coolness and purity may prevent its deleterious consequences . . . My mind is made up . . . to stay here as long as I can fill my present post to the satisfaction of my associates. . . . Until I cry enough I would not have you feel uneasy; much less to impart it to Mrs. Turner. I know that were the necessity to arise you would come . . . promptly to my relief and that you would make any earthly sacrifice.

Sherman was deeply grateful.

Turner must have suggested the possibility of moving his

family to San Francisco if he had to relieve Sherman. The latter felt this would entail unbearable sacrifices for Mrs. Turner. Her mother lived in St. Louis; her children were attending school there—"It is utterly impossible for her to make herself contented here. I see . . . in my family though, my necessities compel me to remain here and Mrs. Sherman knows my determination is . . . as strong as any human resolve; yet she is always uneasy lest her father or mother are sick or lest Minnie should be unwell." [16]

The often-mentioned visit of Mrs. Sherman to Ohio the following spring recurs in the correspondence: "I have made up my mind to let her go home . . . to stay there as long as her parents live." Lest Turner fear that her husband would want to join her he added:

> That will be impossible. I am not able to follow my own taste, even were I to falter in the determination I made to stay here six years. . . . Each day adds to the system and stability of our bank that may enable me to take more leisure and exercise and this is my greatest objection to San Francisco. So forbidding is [*sic*] the outskirts that I would as leave be on shipboard. I now have a horse and buggy and pretend to ride every day, but am half blind with the sand and dust which are worse and worse as they tear down new sand heaps. . . . Next Spring I shall sell out my household traps and take one of our bank rooms and live on the town as we used to do.

Evidently Turner had also offered to come back to San Francisco as a substitute for Nisbet when the latter returned to St. Louis.

> Though I would like to see you very much, I would not have you make a voyage of 6,000 miles without some real necessity. . . . You had better hold yourself in readiness for some future occasion but do not think ever of bringing your family. San Francisco is not so good as when you were here and there is an uncertainty in the stability of men and property that would distress you exceedingly.

Another mutual acquaintance of the two correspondents appeared on the scene in September, 1854. Schuyler Hamilton,[17] a lieutenant of the 1st Infantry and recently an aide of Gen. Winfield Scott, applied for a position at Lucas, Turner & Co. on quite unusual terms. He planned to retire from the army to enter the business world. He offered to work for three months, without wages of any kind, in order to learn banking and business methods. Sherman accepted the offer but declined to set any definite term; Hamilton was to feel free to leave whenever he chose. When Sherman wrote, Hamilton had been with the bank for a week, diligently and cheerfully performing a variety of tasks. The banker explained that he not only wished to do the officer a favor, but "add what influence he may possess. Every little adds." [18] He apparently did not need to mention to Turner that the young man was a grandson of Alexander Hamilton.

A day later, Sherman wrote again of his junior partner, B. R. Nisbet:

> He continues as you knew him. He offends a good many people by his manners but as I know it proceeds from a degree of caution that is commendable, I cannot rebuke him. Any man whose name was not on P.B & Co.'s books is with him *nobody*. Not knowing sometimes the provocation, I can't notice it but I frequently in general terms say how easy it is to say no politely, or evasively answering all the purpose and yet giving no offense. Being somewhat hasty and choleric myself, I am hardly suited to reprove it in others; yet, Nisbet now is certainly most apt and useful. . . . He will always be useful in executing the details. He has told me several times that he has written to you but that you don't write to him. He observes that you write to Reilly and is jealous. Jealousy even among men is a green-eyed monster, so I would suggest that you occasionally drop him a note to keep him in good conceit.[19]

Sherman was fond of the numerous writings of Lt. George H. Derby, who used the pen name John Phoenix; [20] occasionally he sent Turner a newspaper containing Derby's latest article. In mailing a copy of the *Pioneer* in September, he mentioned that Derby-Phoenix had recently arrived from San Diego and was staying at the Tehama House [21] with his wife. "Derby is shy of me since that draft of his came back on which I might have charged him damages and interest but did not, but he knows his credit is not good." [22]

The same letter relayed gossip about a number of mutual acquaintances from army days: "Tis said Folsom is going to marry one of Gwin's daughters just out of school. Ord is going to marry a Miss Thompson, daughter of one of the Land Commissioners. . . . Keyes, a widower of some six or eight months is very sweet on Miss Greenhow [?] a beautiful girl, daughter of the late law [?] etc. author of the History of Oregon." [23]

Business was only "so so." The bank was increasing the number of its depositors, but business in exchange was not growing nor were loans any easier to collect. Generally, money seemed a little more plentiful; good risks had no difficulty in borrowing all they required at 2% a month. Owners of substantial real estate could not afford to pay more than that on mortgage loans for a long term. Short-term borrowings "on the usual security" had to pay 3% a month. (It would be enlightening if Sherman had defined his term "usual security." Probably it meant average risks, neither highly speculative nor gilt edge.)

The banker expected to charge off a few thousand dollars in losses by the year end. The firm held some past-due notes on which interest was still being paid but whose ultimate collection seemed at best doubtful. Nisbet's appraisal of many of these was more optimistic than the managing partner's. Sherman summed up his philosophy as a banker:

> In making business we must risk some. If we are too suspicious and cautious we drive off many men of small means who are growing. My own opinion is that among the smaller class of dealers we find more safety and a better chance of hitting the rich men of 1860. [A. P. Giannini voiced the same opinion many times in the 1920's and 1930's.] Those whose names are current now as large operators are falling as the leaves fall.

After naming several who had failed, he observed that they "in your day would have been first class names, but now are flat broke." Yet Turner had left San Francisco only a year earlier.

Sherman's pride in the new building was obviously tinged with jealousy of any neighbor who seemed to excel him. The following paragraph is revealing of many things:

> An immense quantity of building is still going on to the amazement of everybody. Dr. Wright has built opposite us a more costly house than ours; four stories high and of elaborate finish. It has cut me down considerably although I know ours is a better building, more front and of better style. Still his is higher than ours and of course excells. Ain't that too bad, to be beaten by a man whose name has not been worth writing! I hope it will break him. No I don't. It is an ornament to our corner which I hope to see one of the best in the city.

All of the south half of the Lucas-Turner building (the part owned by Lucas) was now rented except for one room. On the north side, the storeroom and the cellar were still vacant. Sherman had turned away prospects with types of business he preferred not to have as tenants. He hoped for a book or hat store.

His closing observation was that although 1854 must be regarded as a year of unusual depression, yet twice as much brick and mortar had gone into construction as during the preceding year.

9

By mid-October, 1854, Sherman called his friend's attention to a new set of mail sailing dates. Starting the following Monday, a steamer would leave for Panama, but the following week one of the Nicaragua line would depart and alternately thereafter. This meant there would be four mail steamer days a month instead of two. This schedule had been attempted in 1853, but the mercantile community disliked it.

At this point in his correspondence, Sherman's mood became quite somber. "The last fortnight has been more prolific in great and sad events than any similar period I remember. Most tragic and melodramatic was the wreck of the 'Yankee Blade' off Point Concepcion with the loss of some thirty or forty passengers."

The wreck involved the drowning of some thirty passengers, and there was a loss of treasure shipped on the steamer to a total of $462,770.31. Salvagers ultimately recovered a small portion of this sum. The tragedy was heightened by stories told by the survivors of a gang of murderous robbers who terrorized the passengers immediately after the vessel crashed on a reef. Several deaths resulted from their violence, and many acts of robbery were committed. "Some of the survivors had been returned to San Francisco in a destitute condition."[24]

Another sensation that rocked San Francisco during this gloomy fortnight was as Sherman termed it: "the great Meiggs failure, swindle, forgery and flight forming in all its details a perfect epic of crime." The banker probably did not exaggerate when he declared this to be

> . . . by far the most serious disaster that has befallen a community like ours. When confidence in men at best was small, now we suspect everybody for Meiggs was deemed incorruptible, honest though known to be a heavy and daring operator. Up to the very day of his flight, poor people are known to have importuned him to take their small earnings to invest for them. Poor Reilly lost his all, some $1,500.

Reilly had previously been victimized by one Allen but Sherman had been able to rescue him from loss in that case. Quite naturally, Sherman reminded Turner that he himself had had misgivings about Honest Harry Meiggs.[25]

> As far back as last March, I apprehended Meiggs failure but confess I saw no symptoms of dishonesty and then agreed with Nisbet that Meiggs should not exceed $40,000 of debt and to endeavor to bring it to $25,000, for which purpose I overhauled his list of property and took out enough to secure $25,000. Afterwards took another assignment of mortgage for $10,000, since reduced to $6,000—a fine 50 vara lot,[26] and another note of $9,000 secured by the assignment of a bond and mortgage of $12,500. Thus his debts to us amount to $40,000 for which we have adequate security. In addition we have as collateral for any of his endorsements an audited bill against the city now amounting to over $14,000 so that we consider his debts to us amply secured.

Sherman was soon to learn that in dealing with the Meiggses of this world, no transaction, however apparently safe and simple, can be absolutely certain and secure. A good example is the Powell Street bonds, as explained by the banker:

> A contractor named Wetmore had the contract to grade, sewer and plank Powell Street from Washington to the Bay, to be paid by the property holders after the work was completed. It was necessary for him to borrow money. He got of us $35,000 at 5% a month which has been paid regularly up to September. This note was secured to us by an assignment of the contract together with the acceptance of the street commissioners to pay to us the monies

> as collected. However, before the work was done, the City Council assumed the contracts; paid the contractors in warrants and indemnified themselves by collecting the assessments. Wetmore had gone away, leaving Meiggs his agent who brought us $40,000 of the warrants and was to have brought us more for warrants range from 70¢ to 82¢ on the dollar, but he never did, so that note is only secured, say to $30,000. Wetmore also borrowed from us another $10,000 on Meiggs' endorsement. For this we must depend on the excess of security on Meiggs' own paper before described.

Meiggs, as president of the California Lumber Company, had contracted to deliver cargoes of lumber in advance of their arrival. The purchasers gave notes in payment; and when Meiggs endorsed these, they were freely circulated and discounted. A man named William Neely Thompson had given one such note for $10,000, which the bank held with Meiggs's endorsement. It was rumored that Meiggs had endorsed notes on which Thompson's signature had been forged. Thompson himself called a meeting of the holders of his paper "as we supposed to see and separate the spurious from the genuine," but it soon developed that unless the California Lumber Company could be induced to forfeit the contracts Meiggs had signed, Thompson would be unable to pay his notes. Meiggs's failure had rendered the lumber company insolvent, so Thompson too was broke. Thompson had considerable lumber on hand and much other property but no liquid assets; he had a reputation for industry and made so fair a showing to his creditors that they agreed to a composition of his debts. They were to take "cash notes" for 50% and give him time on the balance. Nisbet felt confident the firm would recover all of this debt, but Sherman was less sanguine.

Added to his other troubles during this stormy October, Sherman had been drawn for jury duty and could not induce the judge to excuse him. Thus his analysis of the Meiggs–Powell Street–Thompson complications had not been as thorough as he wished. He was satisfied, however, that unless the city funded the Powell Street warrants, which had been proposed, Lucas-Turner would lose from $5,000 to $10,000. If funded, Sherman expected the warrants to sell between 90 cents and $1. On the credit side, he noted that the bank had already received between 35% and 40% interest. "Of all the banks we come off best for we hold not a cent of forged paper of which Meiggs used near half a million."

On a Saturday when he was free from jury duty, Sherman reviewed the tangled web and apprised Turner of developments. As security on Meiggs's $25,000 note, the bank held a first mortgage on North Beach lots believed to be worth $12,000 to $15,000 and a second mortgage on a building at Broadway and Montgomery Streets that had cost $18,000 and was one of the best in the city. The first lien against it was for $6,000, payable in 1858 with interest at 2% a month. Sherman felt that he could net $6,000 above the prior encumbrance. In addition, the bank had liens on some other parcels at North Beach. All the papers were in Bowman's hands with instructions to foreclose.

Added to the consternation created by Meiggs's flight was the news received by Sherman as he wrote that Smyth Clarke "a gentlemen of high standing, Mayor Garrison's clerk," had just been arrested. At the moment, the banker believed Clarke was involved in Meiggs's frauds and forgeries. A few days later, he was relieved to inform Turner that while Clarke was apparently guilty of serious misconduct, his irregularities were not connected with the Meiggs scandal. Meiggs's possession of blank warrants and other municipal documents was something of a mystery; all the evidence pointed to connivance by one or more officials, and everyone having access to the public supplies was under suspicion. It was rumored that Meiggs had hoped to have his brother elected city comptroller. With him in that position, many of the fraudulent transactions could have been covered up and the records destroyed. Candidate Meiggs actually received a large majority of the votes cast, but was smart enough to foresee the dangers of his brother's plan. Therefore, when Henry Meiggs fled, the newly elected comptroller went with him on the very day that he was to have assumed office. Sagely, Sherman concluded this part of his narrative: "There are many phases of this case that are truly wonderful."

To add to the excitement around Lucas, Turner & Co.'s bank,

another of its borrowers who owed the firm $100 went crazy and blew out his brains!

At noon on October 15, Sherman attended the wedding of Edward O. C. Ord and Miss Thompson, whose engagement he had recently mentioned. The bridal pair were leaving at four o'clock that afternoon for San Pedro, where Ord would take charge of a coast survey party.

The banker also reported the recent confirmation by the land commissioners of San Francisco's claims to its public lands, "embracing limits beyond the calculations of the most greedy. The line is known as the Vallejo line." [27]

During these uneasy days, Sherman and his staff worked on Sundays to omit no steps that would safeguard Lucas, Turner & Co. Sherman, in a second letter, said that he had written their New York correspondent not to be alarmed because Meiggs's name appeared in some of the firm's remittances of exchanges. He made it very clear that the bank had not been victimized by any of Meiggs's forgeries. The papers were full of stories about the scandal and it was essential that Lucas-Turner's "correspondents in New York should not be seized with a panic affecting us." (In today's commercial world, with its many means of instant communication, it is hard to realize the handicap under which bankers and merchants labored when forced to transact all business by steamer mail that took three to four weeks in reaching its destination, with equal delay for the quickest reply! The wonder is that they could carry on at all.)

Sherman must have held up his chin when he wrote:

> We have not nor do we propose to restrict our operations, only to be as cautious as possible. We send forward with this $100,000 of treasury drafts on the New York office—transfer drafts, the very best possible exchange. Before we had the assurance of these, we had collected some considerable bullion, which we sold on the same terms as bought. We receive from Sacramento a good deal of dust which we have run into bars, or coin as we stand in need. The U.S. mint is too slow in its operations to be of any use. They promise to do better soon.

As one other way to trim ship before the storm, he also wrote:

> We had a meeting of bankers some days ago and raised the price of exchange ½ of 1% because the combination steamers have raised the freight by that amount. We also resolved to stop receiving depreciated coin [i.e., foreign currencies] at the value heretofore allowed—francs, instead of being received as quarters will only be taken at twenty cents.*

After all had worked until three o'clock Sunday afternoon, Sherman took Nisbet, Reilly, and Hamilton to his home for dinner.

Among other worries, the loss of the *Yankee Blade* had greatly increased Mrs. Sherman's dread of the sea. She had known some of the lady passengers who had lost their lives.

> She now talks of leaving the children with me so as only to risk her own life. I think a few months will allay this feeling. On the score of economy, I feel willing to send all home, for you will see my account overdrawn some $8,000—against which I have my house and furniture not worth much over $3,500 or $4,000—and yet we live quite economically. [This overdraft mentioned by Sherman was probably a loan he had made with Lucas & Simonds in St. Louis, which is referred to in some of the later letters.]
>
> My horse and buggy are quite hobbies, both good. The horse is a very fine one but so lively that Mrs. Sherman is afraid of him. It is only the playfulness of a pampered colt. I will try and take that out of him, without breaking his spirit.
>
> Now that the titles are confirmed, I would like to buy a hundred vara lot out near the Mission, with a cottage, stable and cow house. Such an establishment would give me occupation—but I forget this Meiggs property will give me plenty to think about. Its foreclosure and sale will require some management.

Jury duty would occupy the banker's time for another fortnight—from ten o'clock each morning until court adjourned. Sherman was thinking of joining one of the volunteer fire companies that were very popular with the San Francisco men of that day. He had been elected first lieutenant of an artillery company but had declined to serve.

---

* See Appendix, "Sherman's Banking Terminology."

He closed this Sunday evening letter with a budget of miscellaneous news items. Among municipal improvements: "The Plaza is graded and enclosed with a handsome iron fence. Montgomery Street from California towards Clay is being paved with square granite stones, one block is finished." Sherman knew that Turner as a good Catholic would be interested in learning that the Cathedral was being roofed. "Colonel De Russy is ordered here in place of Barnard removed and many other changes among the officers is [*sic*] ordered, but since their removal to Benicia it don't [*sic*] concern us so much. Mrs. Hardie had a son some days ago." [28]

Bowman, the bank's attorney, was quite ill; he attributed the condition to the several trips he had made to Sacramento in connection with the Hutchinson-Fenn litigation. Sherman believed Bowman was financially embarrassed, being land-poor at a time when there was no market for real estate. "The fact is this three per cent a month is breaking everybody and it must come down." [29]

A week later, Sherman fumed: "I have been all the time on that d——d jury and must continue there a week more from appearances." However, he had improved the rare moments available to protect the bank on the Meiggs loans. He had secured the consent of opposing lawyers to enter into possession of the building at Montgomery and Broadway, so that he could apply $200 a month in rents to the interest due the bank. With fine sarcasm he observed: "Meiggs is now a gentleman residing out of the state and the law gives those gentlemen ninety days to answer [a suit]. So it will be some four or five months before the smoke clears away and lets us know where we stand and exactly how much we lose." Sherman was still confident that the security he held would liquidate the Meiggs debts, "unless the courts, sheriffs and lawyers consume more than a due share."

Pessimistically he wrote: "Every species of property has declined in value and horses and cattle command prices too low to justify the expenses and dangers of the overland trip. The stock now arriving is in better order than in any previous season."

Nearly eight months earlier, Sherman had shipped some Chinese miniatures to Mr. Simonds. Apparently, he had not had anything to do with their selection or purchase but merely acted as a forwarding agent. Their receipt had never been acknowledged "although I have asked the question pointedly." Even then he had not received an answer. So he inferred that the merchandise had proved disappointing to Simonds. "Though sorry that such should have been the case, I would like to know the simple fact of their receipt."

On the personal side, Mrs. Sherman sent her love and excused her own failure to write Mrs. Turner because "she can say nothing except how she dislikes the country and fears the vast distance that intervenes between this and her home." Her husband expected that when Nisbet visited St. Louis the coming spring, he would escort Mrs. Sherman and her children. They would stay in the East until they would be more content to return. As to himself, he reiterated his intention "to stay here the rest of my time, if not the rest of my days."

> Burgoyne [another banker] now announces that if he can sell his house at $60,000 he will move to Battery Street, corner of Washington. That is following the move of Page Bacon & Company. He is an ass. It may be that some years hence, Battery Street may become the principal street, but Burgoyne now has the best place in the city on this street just midway between the Custom House and the courts. I place great stress on the Plaza and Custom House as fixed points in the city.[30]

The fall rains had commenced and the streets were sloppy.[31]

10

On another steamer day, Sherman detailed his working hours and so gave us a good picture of a San Francisco banker's life in 1854. "I have adopted a plan to get my dinner at home between 2 and 3, a leisure hour, so that I can remain in the office in the evening until the balance is ascertained. Tonight I cannot expect to get home much before midnight at which time the mail closes." (This must have applied only to steamer days, and on this particular occasion Sherman commented that Nisbet, Hamilton, Reilly, Bainbridge, and Fred were all busy at their various duties.)

> We also must wait until the Sacramento boat which the telegraph tells us brings us Read & Company's remittance and list of drafts. We find the business of that house and of Rhodes & Company lucrative and useful. We have always enough gold dust in the assay office to be more than enough to cover their overchecks [*sic*] and the commissions we charge for attending to this business is based upon a calculation of 3% a month for the time the dust is being coined. We coin it when we can purchase other exchange and order it into bars when we expect to ship bullion. For the past two steamers we have had Treasury drafts. Major Snyder, the Treasurer,[32] tells us he has $300,000 more of transfer drafts which will be sold for next steamer, for which we will of course bid.* We have to pay American coin. A good deal of this comes to us as the Engineer officers deposit with us, (usually in

* See Appendix, "Sherman's Banking Terminology," for explanation of bidding on transfer drafts.

sums of $10,000), checks on the Sub-Treasurer paid us in American coin, whereas we pay the checks in California coin. We have had to buy coin, paying from ¼ to ½ premium. All the bankers agreed to sell exchange at 3½ but Drexel, Sather and Church [33] did not stick to their promise, so all have fallen back to 3%. We can afford [it] as our exchange does not stand us but 1¼. Snyder has $300,000 more for sale. His plan is to send notes to each of the banks when a written bid is returned by a certain day when he awards to the highest bidder. We have to judge from accidents how high to bid. Most of the banks here, having agents in the up country, have to buy dust and are cramped for money, so there is not as much competition as we expected. We first paid 1¾ but the last time got [it] at ¾ and on St. Louis at par. We can well afford to pay these rates.

Sherman's incidental reference to "California coin" in the above paragraph touches lightly on one constant and annoying problem of pioneer bankers in California. At the time of the gold discovery there was virtually no coin of any kind in California. The immediate need for a medium of exchange was met very inadequately by the use of gold dust and nuggets. Even when scales and testing devices were available, this practice gave rise to much abuse and downright fraud. All foreign coins passed rather freely, though at varying discounts. French francs at first were accepted at 25 cents. Later they dropped to 20 cents. Obviously the great distance separating the new land from the rest of the Union made it impossible to supply the needed circulating medium from Eastern mints. Therefore, by a very early date, private assay offices, banks, and commercial houses began minting gold dust into coins, bars, and slugs of many shapes and designs. As early as the winter of 1848–1849, Brigham Young had coins made from the bullion brought back to Utah from the Mormon Island placer mines. By 1851, the Philadelphia mint reported coining by fifteen private California mints, which produced one to four denominations of coin each. The denominations ranged from $2.50 up to $50, the latter usually octagonal in shape. Most of this coinage used silver as an alloy, but the grades of weight and fineness were many. The banker who accepted and paid out such a hodgepodge of coins had to tread warily. Foreign coins of all kinds circulated to some extent as late as 1856–1857—Spanish, Mexican, Peruvian, and Ecuadorian doubloons, French franc and five-franc pieces, Spanish pesetas, Austrian zwanzigers, English crowns, Dutch florins and guilders, Indian rupees, Brazilian milreis, and other pieces whose valuation must have added many gray hairs to the experts at the mint or anyone else unfortunate enough to have to appraise them.

On October 23, 1855, the *Alta California* editorialized:

> There probably never had been a single State in the Union so imposed upon with a mixed and debased currency as California. Even before her adoption into the Union as one of the Federal states, the evil began and the old Spanish or Mexican currency of ounces and dollars and their subdivisions were interfered with by clipped coins from the South Coast, adulterated dollars, etc.

In 1850, Congress established a United States assay office in San Francisco, designed to check inferior coinage and correct irregularities in handling gold dust. Two years later, funds were appropriated for a branch mint, which opened in April, 1854. By the end of 1856, it had coined more than $59 million—of which two thirds was in double eagles. Sherman's casual reference to this subject indicates that late in 1854, coins from the private mints must still have been commonplace. The few to be found today are exceedingly valuable collectors' items.[34]

The Meiggs affair had tied up some $65,000 for four months; but if the property sold favorably enough, there would be sufficient to cover interest during the delay.

Merchandise auctions were commencing to indicate a better feeling. Basically, however, Sherman was bearish about conditions.

> Property was too high. Our city is as big and bigger than the country demands, and the interest of money is too high for persons to own unproductive land. Ray is broke and 'tis said Judge Parsons.[35] It seems that all those speculators in wharves, houses, and land of last year are unable to recover. Judge Baker

ditto. I sometimes tremble to see so much change going on, but at the same time are going up all over the city brick buildings of the finest kind. The streets are being extended in every direction, and you would hardly recognize some quarters of the city.

Lumber had risen in price since the Meiggs debacle. Even more favorable to his creditors was the next item Sherman reported: "By universal acclamation the city is going to fund her warrants and debt and adopt the cash system. This will cause warrants to rise; if ours come up to 80, now 70, it will make us nearly whole on the Wetmore note. So good often grows out of evil."

A furniture store had just occupied the first-floor space on the north side of the Lucas-Turner building at $250 a month, and an engraver and lithographer had moved into a portion of the basement. All the rooms save two on the upper floors were rented. These also had been occupied, but their tenants got behind in their rent and Sherman had given them short shrift. The entire building was now bringing in $1795 a month, of which Mr. Lucas' part was $1180.[36] In his next letter, Sherman revived the idea of having Mr. Lucas take over the whole property as his personal investment. With the cost and present rents now definitely known, this was an opportune time for such a transfer.

The letter of November 8 also reported that Nisbet was in Sacramento on a pleasure jaunt. He had written that he was enjoying himself; Sherman added in an aside, "I think in the company of some ladies." He was telegraphing the managing partner daily to keep in touch, and Sherman was glad to have him take a short vacation as long as business did not demand his presence.

A Colonel Stewart had arrived on November 1, en route for army headquarters at Benicia, but was back in San Francisco in a few days. The Shermans invited him to spend an evening with them. He was in a sad dilemma; his wife absolutely refused to come to California even though her husband had been ordered there. His two alternatives, therefore, were a perpetual separation from her or resignation from the service. Sherman was sorry to learn that Stewart had decided on the latter course. The banker felt that if he delayed his decision for a few months, the wife's attitude might change. Lucas, Turner & Co. had purchased the exchange Stewart had brought with him. Sherman at his urging agreed to find an investment of the proceeds at 2% a month. For a long time, the banker had declined to accept any more trust accounts for investment except at the risk of the owner. "I intend to take no more. If any person writes you, you may say as much." A few weeks later, Sherman told Turner that Colonel Stewart was in "elegant health" and was going back East on December 24. Meanwhile, Sherman had shown him much attention, with drives about the city and a trip across the bay. He had also found for the Colonel a $22,000 mortgage loan due in eighteen months with interest at 2% a month. Thereby the bank was relieved of all responsibility for his funds.[37]

Reverting a few weeks later to the investment of customers' funds, Sherman pointed out that his policy of placing them in the name of the owner of the money had one disadvantage. The bank could no longer profit by charging the borrower one rate and paying the investor a lower one. However, the bank retained the advantage of having larger amounts at its disposal when borrowers applied for loans, though relieved of both moral and legal risk. Perhaps for this reason, Sherman now termed this class of business his agency accounts.

Sherman was happy to congratulate Turner on the birth of a son. "Mrs. Sherman says Mrs. Turner prefers girls so she only regretted your child was not a girl. You probably do not share in that regret." Colonel Stewart had brought the news that Turner was building a handsome winter residence on Olive Street in St. Louis. Sherman craved more details.

Additional villainy connected with the Meiggs scandal kept coming to light. Nisbet especially felt very bad about a city warrant on which the bank was counting as an offset to the

Wetmore loan. It had just developed that the signature upon it was a forgery!

> He [Nisbet] was so positive about the signature that I felt easy but now I am satisfied that it was an admirably executed forgery and that other city officials now out of the country are part forgers in connection with Meiggs. You have reason to flatter yourself that this did not transpire during your administration, for these forged securities have been collaterals for three years past. Drexel, Sather & Church and D. L. Ross & Company, the former experienced bankers and the latter an old merchant, have copies of the same as ours and today for the first time it was discovered that the original and genuine paper was paid at the City Treasury and cancelled a long while ago. . . . I will . . . make up the loss as expeditiously as possible.

Sherman was counting on the growing income from interest on loans and exchange charges to offset this blow, but it was nonetheless a grievous one.

From an entirely different angle, Sherman found himself involved in the Meiggs situation. Because the newly elected city comptroller had fled with his brother Harry Meiggs, it became necessary to elect a replacement. Samuel Haight, a brother of Henry Haight of Page, Bacon & Co., was nominated by the Democrats. A certain William Sherman was nominated by the Know Nothing Party to oppose him. This produced inevitable confusion.

> Several papers . . . noticed the nomination, complimenting Major W.T.S. A good many thought I was the candidate so I published a card putting it right. William Sherman is from Rhode Island, brother of R. M. Sherman who used to be a merchant here and was the best candidate. He was elected by a large majority. He's a depositor of ours and a good friend and I did all I could to elect him because I wanted a Sherman to beat a Haight.[38]

Learning that Mr. Lucas had decided not to come to California, Sherman replied "I feared he would not come out. I wish he would, but were I in his place, I'd see California ________ first." Pending Lucas' decision about buying the entire building, his share of the rents was accumulating. Presently, Sherman learned that Mr. Lucas wanted the money invested for him as it was received. Of course, Sherman considered the senior partner in St. Louis a preferred client for whom he would do all in his power. His first inclination was to buy up small unimproved lots with the money as distress sales of such developed.

How often do we hear it said that history repeats itself! However, the repetition is never an exact one. As one reads these discussions of business routine, one startling phrase—certificates of deposit—strongly suggests banking in the 1960's! Sherman proposed as a decided innovation that Lucas, Turner & Co. advertise in the newspapers that they would pay 10% a year on such certificates, for money left on deposit for more than one month. The historical variation here is the diverse markets aimed at in 1854 as contrasted with 1966. Sherman wrote: "There are hundreds and thousands of laboring men gradually collecting small sums of money who would be rejoiced at a choice of leaving their money in a safe place. Now they are forced to deposit in one of those minor banks like Wright's where they [illegible] great risk, though they get 1½% a month." Sherman had in mind the laboring class in a day when savings accounts in a bank or savings and loan institution were all but unknown. He would have been astonished at today's lively competition that seeks sums above a high minimum that are necessarily the property of large corporations or of wealthy individuals.

> I am satisfied [he continued] in six months this would give us $200,000 or $300,000 at 10% a year here, really better [illegible] than we now have our "capital." Why not do it? You may ask, "because Page Bacon do not." I have conversed with Nisbet about it, who says that P. & B. do not. I answer that they do in St. Louis and every old bank does it in every city of the world. The time is come when it will be done here, only we must wait till Page & Bacon do. We must follow not lead.

Sherman did not wish to proceed with such an innovation on his own authority, so asked for comments from Turner and the other St. Louis partners. If they agreed, he proposed to go ahead regardless of what Page-Bacon did.

This letter closed on a nostalgic note; Doña Augustias, his old Monterey friend, was in San Francisco en route to join her children in Mexico City.[39]

On the same day the banker wrote another letter to Turner marked "Private." It presented the case of a young man close to Sherman. The names seem unimportant. Even after this great lapse of time they are omitted, but the episode tells us much of the humanity of the letter writer. It is the tale of three brothers. The second had spent four years as a cadet at West Point but failed to pass his final examinations and did not receive a commission. This was a severe blow to the young man's father. The disappointed youth hit the trail to California in 1849 and spent two years there to no good purpose. He was glad to get back home where he studied law for a time, but chafing at restraints, he soon moved to St. Louis.

> He is of good parts, but lacks industry and system [wrote Sherman], is likely to get into company to drink and smoke to excess especially if the tide sets him that way. I do not ask you to go to any trouble on his account, but if you should, as it were accidentally make his acquaintance and speak a few encouraging words, when you happen to meet, it may be of material service to him as he is sensitive and if he meets with any success is able to profit by it.

There were two other brothers in this case—it resembles a story out of the Old Testament. "The eldest son whom you saw is very different, being more fixed in his notions and habits, actually older than the old gentleman himself. The third son is regarded as the brightest, but for my part the one now in St. Louis was always my favorite." [40]

On Thanksgiving Day, the Shermans entertained all the bank staff and Mr. and Mrs. Bowman at dinner. "Turkey has come down to $8, so we can venture to eat one a year. But it was a dear turkey to me, as with wine, etc. it brought on a very severe asthma which kept me up all night, entirely unfitting me for labor today." [41] A week later the sufferer confessed that it took him two days to recover from the attack. Fear of its recurrence impelled him to forgo attending a testimonial to retiring Mayor Garrison.

In this later letter, Sherman reported that Henry Haight, partner in Page, Bacon & Co., was planning a long Eastern trip in the spring. A man named Ruxton was to have charge of their competitor during Haight's absence. A description of Mr. Ruxton permitted Sherman to joke at Turner's expense. "This Ruxton is a New Yorker such as you admire, short sighted and spectacled, no doubt most exact and safe . . . of a cast of mind likely to offend the class of people we have to deal with. . . . It is said he comes from Duncan, Sherman & Company,[42] maybe to keep an eye to their interests."

Page, Bacon & Co. were to move in a few weeks to their new quarters at Clay and Battery, "a two story brick, beautifully and elaborately finished." Haight had admitted to Sherman that he did not wholly approve of the move. He said the parent firm in St. Louis owned their former quarters at Montgomery and Clay, but proposed to charge the San Francisco house such a high rent that it could not afford to remain there. Sherman reported that dissatisfaction because of the move had prompted the resignations of some employees. All these incidents should prove beneficial to Lucas, Turner & Co., in Sherman's opinion.

The banker wrote one of his rare praises of the weather in California, "The season has been so very beautiful and favorable. . . . The miners and farmers, however, are losers by this late season. The former have no water for washing [gold-bearing dirt] and the latter cannot plough the hard baked soil." However, he added that five lucky prospectors had just dug up the largest nugget ever known, weighing 160 pounds of gold and quartz and worth $26,000.

The new Miners Exchange Bank Building across the street was to have a variety of tenants besides the bank on the first floor. Dr. Wright and his family were to occupy the fourth floor, while the second had been rented by a woman who was installing a waxworks display.

This particular letter closed with the announcement that the writer's infant son "had a *tooth*. So the world moves." [43]

Other losses were listed by Sherman in his next letter. A borrower named C. H. West owed $4,000 "which he promises to arrange when he gets up again but I don't count on it." Another borrower, Moulton, had failed, owing the bank $9,500—but it held an acceptance for $17,000 payable out of the sale of certain properties. Suit had been started to compel the payment of this debt. Except for the loans involving Meiggs, a small sum would cover all other losses. Therefore, in Sherman's opinion, a dividend of $50,000—to be divided among all the partners—could be paid on January 1.

Sherman's letter of December 8, 1854, contained one striking bit of news. The writer admitted he had underestimated the friction existing in Page, Bacon & Co. C. K. Garrison had called on Sherman at the request of Henry Haight. The latter was disgusted at the selection of Ruxton and was generally at outs with the partners in St. Louis. Garrison stated that Haight was ready to leave his old firm and join Lucas, Turner & Co.

> I was much surprised [Sherman wrote], . . . Haight is the strong man of the house. Garrison says they have positive orders not to discount a loan after February next. If this be so they must lose an immense part of their business, as the merchants here must have help about Steamer Day. . . . I had a long conversation with Garrison and told him that I had no power to negotiate on such an important offer, that we had already six partners, and that I did not suppose Haight would come under me. Garrison said he would for a consideration, that Haight was one-fourth partner here, and would expect a like share. I have agreed to have an interview with Haight and may submit the result to Mr. Lucas confidentially. . . . [I] beg you to breathe not a word . . . to any human being . . . for should it come to Haight's partners we know they would be justly incensed. Haight goes home in the Spring, but I think after his first dissatisfaction is over, he will think better and remain as he now is—the head of the house here. The only possible occasion that may arise is my complete prostra-

tion and inability to work, your disinclination to come to California and possibility of Simonds share of one-fourth being vacant. . . . He [Garrison] goes home tomorrow and you will see him in St. Louis.

Sherman had never liked Haight. Long afterward, in recalling these days, he said of him, "He was too fond of lager beer to be entrusted with so large a business." [44] At the end of 1854, none of those concerned could foresee the sensational conclusion of the Page-Bacon story that the next few months would disclose.

The same letter contained one other notable subject:

> We have now one year's full experience and have no reason to regret the retrospect, but there is one item in our contract which . . . aroused my interest in New Orleans, viz. that we pay interest on our capital. . . . I do not think we should pay any interest on our capital. Our labor here ought to be a fair offset for its use. The profits of that use go three-fourths to you in St. Louis and one-fourth to Nisbet and myself. A concession would give each of us the one-eighth of $16,000—or in other words $2,000 per annum more than we now receive. I have lived plainly yet the dividend of $50,000 will not free me of debt. Still a contract is a contract and if insisted on must stand entire.

Sherman's essential fairness stands out here, because, although tartly critical at times of Nisbet, he now championed his subordinate's rights:

> Nisbet has cheerfully resigned his visit home, fills the place of teller and bookkeeper . . . when sickness calls the regular ones away . . . does *more* than the plain strict requirements of the contract. . . . I do not pretend to much useful labor, yet neither sickness nor discontent of my family . . . has diverted my thoughts from the interests of this house. I want these views made known and if concurred in, well—if not we must hold on. As you must ultimately succeed me, you are as much or more interested than I am. [Sherman's pessimism about his asthma made him believe that Turner would succeed him if he died or became incapable of holding his position.] [45]

II

By mid-December, 1854, Sherman became aware that the depression affecting San Francisco business was not just a local condition. Word reached him that one of the bank's Eastern correspondents had suddenly failed. While Lucas, Turner & Co.'s balance with the closed concern was quite small, the news was very unsettling. In writing to Turner about it, he said: "What interesting times you must have handling notes which are good one day, only tolerable the next, slightly at discount, then bad and finally worthless." The notes to which Sherman referred were "bank notes"—promises to pay by private banks that circulated freely like currency. He continued: "Thank fortune what we count cash is cash. Bills receivable at best are only the full representations of cash when paid, but we have no bank notes."

Lucas-Turner's deposits were lower than they had been for a long time "because people generally are hard up and have use for all they could get and more too. We called yesterday some first rate loans because we wanted the money." [46]

A few days later, he wrote Turner again: "Received your New York letter and can imagine your anxiety whilst each day brings accounts of smashes and breakdowns. In the long run, that condition must inure to the benefit of first class private banks. There must be banks of discount and deposit and people who have money will find out where it is safe." While reiterating that "We out here . . . know what is money and what is not," he must have felt he was contradicting himself in view of the Powell Street warrants because he added: "We call bundles of paper cash and some of it may turn out something else. Nevertheless our notes are paid well and I have strong hopes . . . we can recover from the city the Wetmore debt entire."

Wetmore's attorney had begun suit against the city and alleged the public officials had dealt very loosely with Meiggs; among other things, they had not even bothered to take his receipt for warrants delivered on the street contract. The bank still held the contract and Wetmore's attorney had to have it to prove his case. "We will not surrender the contract until we are made whole," Sherman defiantly wrote Turner.

Sherman sometimes referred disparagingly to Nisbet:

> Meiggs' debt was contracted for time exchange, Nisbet's favorite operation and which I absolutely stopped last March. This Wetmore debt was also incurred about the time you went away, before I was well schooled, and as Meiggs paid interest so promptly, and as the city ordinance *was actually passed* for the payment, I did not insist upon closing it up until the development was upon us but we are mighty lucky as it was and I thank the Lord it was no worse.

The word "development" sounds ambiguous; I believe Sherman referred to Meiggs's sudden flight.

The banker realized the value of favorable publicity in a business like Lucas, Turner & Co. He sent Turner a newspaper clipping of an item he had caused to be published locally, copied from the *St. Louis Republican* about "a magnificent present of Mr. Lucas to the City of St. Louis."

Sherman continued to show his resentment toward Dr. Wright for the extravagance he was displaying in the erection of his building. "He is an ass to spend $147,000 for a house in these days. That is $50,000 more than ours cost, and ours is a larger base and better internal arrangements." He grudgingly admitted that the Wright folly at least improved Lucas-Turner's neighborhood.

Turner had instructed Sherman to pay interest on the firm's capital—$8,000 to Lucas and Simonds, $6,250 to Sherman and

Nisbet. In acknowledging this, Sherman made a confidential confession:

> I cannot confide to Mrs. Sherman the fact that I am not saving money. Even with this dividend I am in debt, for as much as I could sell my furniture and house for. I want Mrs. Sherman to take the children home and stay there that I may lay by some for a rainy day, but I can't say a word about economy and the propriety of things but I am answered that she would rather that I was on a farm barely subsisting my family than here with the separation to which she will not grow accustomed. She now says that she will go home in April, leaving the children, thus imposing on me the double charge of maintaining a family here and paying her expenses to and from Ohio. . . . It does seem that ladies where their children and parents are concerned are as blind to reason as mad bulls. Keep this to yourself, for it is not right I should trouble you with such secrets, but you more than suspect it already.[47]

Sherman learned that a son of one of Henry Turner's brothers was en route to California by way of Cape Horn. The family hoped a place could be found for him in Lucas, Turner & Co. Sherman doubtless had misgivings about the nepotism involved but did not voice it. However, he went into considerable detail as to the duties he would assign to young Turner and frankly stated that the firm could afford to pay only bare living expenses until the new employee proved he could earn even a beginner's wage.

Evidently Sherman had some afterthoughts about this nephew, for in his New Year's Eve letter he asked some questions he felt were in order: "Mr. Duer told me he knew him [young Turner] well and that he had been to West Point. Tell me his age, appearance, handwriting and history, that is, when he went to the Point, why he left. This I have a right in confidence to know. This also may enable me to act with more prudence."

In his earlier letter, the banker went on to discuss expenses generally and the policy of economy he was putting into effect. Fitting up the new quarters and the unusually heavy losses and resultant expense due to the Meiggs affair made it imperative that unnecessary expenditures be avoided. He would be happy to have a visit from Turner himself but not at the bank's expense! If the St. Louis partners wanted Turner to make such a trip to review the firm's condition, then Sherman felt they should pay the cost. On the other hand, the writer concluded with this forthright declaration: "I do not think it will pay you to incur the tedium, and danger of the trip, and would not advise you to come out until some occasion calls for it. Such an occasion may arise at any time. You'll have enough of California before you finish your career." Once more Sherman seems to have been apprehensive of his own early demise.

One bane of all accountants and bank operators from time immemorial here raised its ugly head.

> Our bookkeeper, although a young, handy and exact man has not balanced the books for last month [it was now December 15!] and consequently we cannot this mail as usual send the Trial Balance. I regret this, but cannot help it. I suppose your accountants know how inexplicable is sometimes a small error in a set of books. Nisbet has been making a new set of books, dividing the Day Book and Ledger. I suppose it is allright but I insist upon keeping square up and if it can't be helped I will employ an assistant clerk, though I cannot see that we have too much work for our present force.

Schuyler Hamilton had amicably severed his connection with the firm, but dropped in frequently to visit. He was planning to become a street broker. In early San Francisco, men of this calling rendered services similar to those now performed by realtors, insurance agents, and commission brokers. Henry W. Halleck, the well-known lawyer, who was destined both to command and to be chief of staff of the Union Army during the Civil War, was about to leave for the East to marry a sister of Schuyler Hamilton.

In this same letter, Sherman wrote: "Times here continue dull and dangerous. Real estate is still depressed. . . . Since these weekly steamers we have to write so often that the letters will be . . . too frequent to be welcome." [48]

It is only fair to Sherman to say that it is most evident from reading these letters that nearly all of them were written with one eye on the clock. The need to have them deposited in the post office before the mails closed, no doubt prevented any rereading by the writer. Certainly there was scant opportunity to edit or correct them. This explains the occasional awkward phrasing and involved sentence structure that mar Sherman's style. His *Memoirs* display distinctly better English.

On New Year's Eve, 1854, Sherman answered Turner's letter of December 5 from New York and Mr. Lucas' letter of November 30. His response to the latter is characteristic of the utter frankness he exhibited toward these distant partners. Mr. Lucas certainly had it in his power to alter Sherman's fortunes and the course of his life. Even though Sherman knew this, he could differ with Lucas as bluntly as with a recalcitrant borrower.

> I have just answered Mr. Lucas' letter . . . in which he advises us to hold $100,000 subject to their call at a short notice. Of course this we can't do. We have not a dime too much to cover the great wealth we [illegible] and we cannot do business here in deposits or money likely to be called.
>
> That you know, so whatever your necessities may be, don't lean on us at all, until we are past our infancy of existence.

Evidently Turner had questioned Sherman about the bank's dealings with Wadsworth & Sheldon. The San Francisco partner suspected that Turner in these uneasy times was apprehensive about the firm's condition. Sherman replied that usually the bank owed money to Wadsworth & Sheldon. A few weeks later, Turner frankly cautioned his friend that there was serious question as to the firm's solvency. Sherman in his first reply pointed out that the San Francisco bank "at this time have a very respectable balance in the Metropolitan Bank [New York]." Lucas-Turner were shipping them $85,000 in this same mail. He would have remitted it to the parent house in St. Louis but the latter, some time previously, had instructed San Francisco not to remit cash to them unless called for.

"Tomorrow is New Year's Day. We have had four months of unclouded sky, with the groans and lamentations of farmers and miners. Last night it rained and is now cloudy and dark." Sherman expected to make many calls on friends on the approaching holiday. He gloomily predicted that if he took merely a sip with each of them, he would be in for a fortnight of asthma. "I have not escaped one night for the past year and I feel assured that it has occasioned damage greater than my constitution can overcome though it may drag along some time. . . . I look upon myself as merely preparing the way for you at some future day." [49]

The first days of 1855 had unpleasant surprises for Sherman, which added to the distress caused by his asthma. One of these was the concluding chapter about the erring bookkeeper whom Sherman and Nisbet had rehired on a very strict probationary basis. The banker's face must have reddened when he recalled how *only five days earlier* he had described this character in a letter to Turner as "the smartest accountant in this office." The banker had also claimed credit for getting the young man out of debt. We have to guess as to what happened in the interim for now Sherman wrote:

> As to Fred [the bookkeeper] now that he is discharged, hardly a day passes without some bill is presented against him which I assure the holders they deserve to lose, as they held them back as long as they saw Fred in the bank but the moment he was disgraced they came out. I had given him before a chance to amend so I feel no compunction of conscience on his score. I have not seen him since he left the office. Everything in the office works like a charm. Not a dollar short [in] cash since Fred left.

Why was Fred discharged? The mention of cash "not a dollar short since Fred left" arouses a reader's suspicions and the word "disgraced" suggests that he had been caught in wrongdoing. Yet exactly one month later, Sherman wrote:

> Young Kritchman is now very proper in his behavior. I encourage him to visit my family and . . . other gentlemen. . . . He

made me an honest confession of the good lessons he had learned from the past year and assured me that he would die rather than merit the rebuke he received at the time of his dismissal and pardon. You may say to his father that his son is very smart and is now held by us in high esteem.

The above reads like a puzzle from which one or more pieces are still missing.

Even more depressing news concluded this letter:

My health is very bad, dangerous. . . . As prudent men you should have in mind and present here if possible one capable of succeeding me in case of death or if I . . . be useless. I nominate Stone [50] as the best man I know, competent and willing to enter on the task. He will write you on the subject, which I did not break to him until last week when I was forced to notify him that in case I did not recover he must step in and act till you in St. Louis . . . [In my photostat of this letter, only blank space follows, but it is easy to guess the rest of the sentence.] [51]

It is odd now to recall that the pessimistic writer of the above lines still had thirty-six years of life before him; thirty-six crowded years of arduous labor, including military service of incalculable value to his country.

Turner's cautionary remarks about Wadsworth & Sheldon mentioned a few paragraphs back made Sherman wince:

How unpleasant it is to correspond and deal with persons when there is a want of confidence. A banker's life may be a pleasant one but it develops more the disagreeable features of life than any honest calling I know. That mistrust, suspicion of everybody and everything is to me a most disagreeable feature of this our new calling.

Lucas had at last decided to purchase all the other interests in the Montgomery and Jackson Streets corner. Sherman had completed the necessary conveyancing and recorded the deed. Unfortunately, coincident with his becoming sole owner of the building, there had been an exodus of some tenants. Some of them had gotten behind in their rent. Inquiry developed that this was occurring in many other properties around San Francisco; it was merely one more evidence of the depression the city was experiencing. "The fact is times *are* hard. [There is] more difficulty in realizing interest than ever before. Had the drought continued . . . we would have had the devil to pay, but fortunately the New Year came in with a perfect rainstorm and hurricane." Even this good fortune had its drawbacks; all over the city, roofs had been blown off and the interiors of the houses had been drenched. Sherman extracted some comfort from the fact that the Lucas-Turner building had a composition roof of paper, tar, and gravel that had come through perfectly. Sherman's own home had lost most of its roof and the living quarters were damp for days, as the abnormal demands upon the few repairmen necessitated long delays in reroofing the damaged structures.

The neighborhood around Lucas, Turner & Co. was continuing to improve. In addition to Wright's building, the new International Hotel on Jackson between Montgomery and Kearny was now open, and the Parisian banking house of Pioche, Bayerque & Co. had just moved onto the southeast corner of Montgomery and Jackson. Page, Bacon & Co.'s new quarters on Battery and Clay Streets were attracting much attention.

Mindful of the proposition involving Henry Haight, which C. K. Garrison had brought to him, Sherman was keeping a close watch on his competitor. Page, the senior partner, had returned to San Francisco, and Sherman had paid him a courtesy call. He wrote:

> Haight continues disaffected and I think he will go out. . . . [There is] some talk of his and Fisher [Page-Bacon's ex-teller] setting up on their own account. . . . Without the name of Page Bacon & Company I think that Haight will find it harder to obtain the confidence of the community than he supposes.
>
> [Lucas-Turner] continues to grow and we find ourselves constrained to hire more assistants. . . . Have today employed a young man, stepson to Mr. Hooper one of the Commissioners of

> the Funded Debt.[52] . . . [He] is 18 or 19 a fine looking fellow of good education and ambitious. . . . [We] start him tomorrow . . . for $100 a month. . . . As soon as he gets broken in . . . $150. . . . with aid of this young man I hope we can keep up until your nephew arrives.
>
> Mrs. Sherman is preparing to go home in April but persists in her determination to leave the children. She is utterly deaf to all ideas of economy, not extravagant, but not caring for money where the children are concerned. You can see the difference.[53]

Poor Sherman must have been enveloped in clouds of indigo when he wrote his letter of January 15, 1855. The ravages of his asthma were bound to offset even a bright and cheerful background. However, news from the East was bad, business was wretched, and collections were poor. He listed several failures, some of them debtors of the bank. "You would hardly recognize your rich friends of last year. . . . All those men who swore . . . that California land produces ten times as much as any other land . . . are broke. Nothing in California is substantial but the gold mines." The drought had interrupted their operations but the recent rains and snows had revived the miners' hopes. On the other hand this weather also filled the letter writer with gloom because "the streets are muddy and sloppy and the old planks [sidewalks] look decidedly used up."

The banker's good neighbors, the Stevens family, had lost one of their infant sons, eight months old. Mrs. Sherman had handled the details of the funeral and "we all rode out to the new cemetery called 'Lone Mountain' from the conical hill within the enclosure. I don't know whether you ever rode from the Presidio to the Mission. . . . This mountain cemetery is in that desert region." This gave Sherman an opportunity to criticize San Francisco, which he was likely to do when in a black mood. "San Francisco in her ambition to rival other cities is not satisfied alone in rivalling your hotels and mansions, but must imitate your tombs. The disgust . . . that I took for this spot in 1847, will never leave me and where others see beauty of landscape I see only desolation." Even his riding horse had become so wild after several days of inaction caused by the bad weather "that even I am a little fearful that he will run me off some of these high banks left unfinished." Sherman also resented paying tolls of 25 cents when he indulged this hobby; the plank road to the Mission must have been his favorite route. The Shermans had recently crossed the bay to call on ex-Governor Henry Stuart Foote of Mississippi, who with his family had recently settled in an attractive country place. Sherman admired the location and apparently it revived his dream of moving over to Oakland, "but the ferry boat runs irregularly and it is better that I should always be near."

Bowman, the bank's attorney, had formed a partnership with a Mr. Baldwin, said to be an excellent lawyer and a man of some literary reputation. Sherman had labored diligently to reconcile Bowman and another friend named Crockett who had quarreled over some business transaction. The banker's efforts proved unequal to the task and he abandoned it.

Another item of news was that Page, Bacon & Co. had receded from the rule recently announced of making no new loans or discounts; Sherman was "sorry they did not commit the error contemplated." [54]

More mail received a week later did little to relieve Sherman's gloom.

> Your hard times continue and so do ours. . . . Hard is not the exact phrase but dull, flat and stupid. No coin and no gold and no business. Such a period of stagnation . . . has not been seen since the discovery of gold. The break in the drought had roused false hopes; the sky has been unclouded and . . . the sun shines with May brightness.

With business at such a standstill, Sherman decided to mount his horse and ride down to the Pajaro River area near San Juan Bautista, taking his shotgun with him to hunt geese. He started early one evening and got as far as San Mateo, where he spent the night. The hotel was attractive and he had felt well when he started, but his old enemy asthma routed him out of bed and gave him not a moment's sleep. Instead, he walked the streets all night and by morning concluded it wiser to return to the city—"the first time I ever backed out in my life, so I consider myself on the decline."

Sherman was giving a lot of thought to California's troubles and what could be done to remedy them.

> Emigration to this country by steamers has almost ceased and the overland emigrations yearly diminish so that we need population. . . . Meetings have been organized . . . I have taken part. . . . In each I have asserted . . . that the part of the emigrant road that needs most work lies within or near this State. . . . The State . . . should make a wagon road across the Sierra Nevada and also dig wells . . . up the Humboldt . . . as far as the . . . alkali waters extend. With such improvements . . . the emigrants could come along leisurely without fatiguing their animals and stock with the certainty of finding water when they need it and a mountain road easy to be passed with their broken down animals.

A bill to accomplish this program had been introduced in the legislature but "the politicians think they have no business to legislate beyond . . . their State."

Sherman was certain that without increased emigration business was not going to justify existing rent and interest scales. Apparently, Turner had counseled against any immediate action on the "certificates of deposit" issue. At the moment, Sherman was holding his breath as to the condition of some of the smaller and weaker banks that were paying 1½% a month to their depositors. He felt it a most inopportune time to make new loans that would employ the savings funds. Therefore, he was content to defer his proposal until there was some improvement in general business.

Haight had definitely decided to remain the local head of Page, Bacon & Co. Now it was Fisher, Page-Bacon's ex-teller, whose nose was out of joint. He wanted to join Lucas-Turner, but Sherman saw no place for him.[55]

12

Despite his asthmatic attack in San Mateo, Sherman was so favorably impressed with the "good hotel, fine oak trees and green grass, contrasting so well with the appearance of things here, that I prevailed on Mrs. Sherman to take the children and ride down on the stage." Mrs. Bowman accompanied her. Sherman and Bowman followed shortly and spent one night in San Mateo, but returned because of the ever important steamer day.

The news brought from New York by the *Golden Age* must have quickly erased all recollections of the brief outing. The details of Wadsworth & Sheldon's failure were not only bad in themselves but also calculated to shake the public's confidence in banking generally. Lucas-Turner, at the instance of its Sacramento correspondent, Read & Co., had remitted Wadsworth & Sheldon $18,000 to meet obligations of Read's about to fall due. This remittance had reached Wadsworth & Sheldon just before their doors closed and they had used the money for their own purposes.

The Metropolitan Bank had very generously protected Lucas-Turner on some of its own drafts drawn on the bankrupt firm; but Read & Co. still owed past-due bills, despite the remittance made to pay them. Fortunately, a small balance remaining due on the steamer *America* transaction was still in Lucas, Turner & Co.'s hands and was being held by Sherman as an offset to any amount owing by Wadsworth & Sheldon. Sherman correctly foresaw the more remote damage done by this failure: "So far as absolute losses are concerned amidst the crash of our correspondents, we may esteem ourselves fortunate, but the moral effect is far worse. . . . If they break, persons reason very naturally that we may. They cannot know that we speak the truth when we say our losses thereby are trifling." Sherman was frankly surprised that public reaction had not been more serious. He could not trace any withdrawals to this news, but sales of Eastern exchange were lighter than usual. That could well reflect loss of confidence.

Burgoyne was one private banker who now admitted confidentially to Sherman that he was going to wind up his affairs and withdraw from banking. Some of his customers were leaving him because he could not accommodate them with loans. Lucas, Turner & Co. took over about $130,000 of his receivables falling due in the next thirty days. In payment, Sherman gave him three time bills. The bank's main objective was to secure the future deposit and exchange business of these best customers of Burgoyne. The latter's plight was to Sherman the best possible proof that a bank in San Francisco must have adequate capital to survive. He wrote Turner: "You and I have embarked our fortunes and reputations in a dangerous crisis in monetary matters and if we steer our ship through the present . . . with moderate profit but unimpaired names, we will have accomplished enough to satisfy ambition."

Consistent with his proposal to improve transportation into California, Sherman with Turner's approval had subscribed on behalf of the bank to the newly organized Sacramento Valley Railroad. Its builders expected to have twenty-three miles completed and operating by the end of 1855, "a direct line towards Nevada and the best populated part of the mining region, and will at once pay. I am Vice-President and have been solicited to be President but have most positively declined." [56] Sherman had wisely announced that the bank as such would not subscribe to any railroad stock and proposed to let this stock stand in his own name at least until it paid a dividend. (In his own thinking Sherman was anticipating by a number of years the policy of the legislature in not allowing banking companies to own stock in any corporation.) Mr. Lucas had evidently warned Sherman not to make any loans to railroad contractors. He assured Turner that he agreed this should be the bank's policy.

Sherman had heard indirectly that Mr. Lucas was planning an early trip to San Francisco. Sherman hoped this was correct and urged Turner to come also. He recommended the months from March through June. He had heard that the Panama Railroad was now running. That would be the best line to patronize, especially as their ships on the Pacific side were the best.

Turner had written Sherman to ask

> if I don't feel like a Colonelcy in a new regiment. It never entered my mind but if, when these failures are occurring and rumors of others flying about, I would not like to be tempted. If all men were personally honest, the business of banking would be beautiful, but in my experience of life I would assign it a low place in the catalogue, as it develops the worst qualities of the mind, mistrust and suspicion of everybody. As long as Lucas & Simonds don't break I will try and hold on. I would not be at all astonished to hear that Page & Bacon of St. Louis were gone.

Earlier in the same letter, Sherman reported having heard "that Page & Bacon have lost heavily by Belcher & Bro." [57] This was another firm of private bankers in New York that had just failed.

Turner had spent some time in New York City following the Wadsworth & Sheldon failure. Not having Turner's letters to guide us, the steps he took are not entirely clear but from Sherman's expressions of satisfaction, it is evident that both Read & Co. (the Sacramento firm) and Lucas, Turner & Co. were faring better than had seemed likely when the New York bank closed. Sherman wrote:

> The community feel increased confidence in our standing in consequence of this event. The prompt action of the bank and your own course is well known here so that Lucas, Turner & Company never had higher grounds than we now possess. For the past week we have had a perfect rush of new accounts of the very

best kind. Burgoyne's withdrawal from business is the principal cause and he does not hesitate to advise his best customers to come to us.

Burgoyne had advertised his withdrawal from business in the newspapers and had invited his depositors to come and get their money.

"The notes we took from him [Burgoyne] are paid as fast as they mature and we shall be perfectly able to anticipate the heavy time bills we advised on last mail. Our balance [deposits undoubtedly] last night was $966,000 and before this month closes it will be a million." Evidently, Turner had frowned on Lucas, Turner & Co. issuing its own time bills to pay for the loans purchased from Burgoyne. "Had I received your letter I doubt whether we should have made this transaction although I feel certain it is the best single transaction we ever made. . . . Our number of depositors have in four days increased at least fifty, of our very best men."

More help was going to be required to handle this growing business. They had built an addition to the vault; the original was presently used only for money and storage boxes of merchants, the other for books and records. The building was now lighted by gas, a great improvement in working conditions, where night labor was required.

The totals of Lucas, Turner & Co.'s deposits to which Sherman was referring so proudly look trifling today, when major banks have both deposits and loans running into the billions. All comparisons are a matter of contrast. Therefore, a glance at a few other statistics will help us bring the 1850's into sharper focus. In 1855, the population of the whole United States totaled about 27.5 million people. Today the figure is crowding 200 million. A special census authorized by the California legislature near the end of 1852 showed the state's population 264,435 and San Francisco's 36,151. It was generally believed that these figures erred on the low side. By the end of 1853, California was estimated to have 308,000 with nearly 50,000 of that number in San Francisco. By 1854, emigration from California had begun to slow the rate of increase and it seems fair to assume that San Francisco's population was still around 50,000.

How these figures are dwarfed by comparison with the Census of 1960 which gave California 15,717,204 and San Francisco 740,316! Furthermore, in the unregulated laissez-faire economy of Sherman's time, numerous banks competed for San Francisco's business, nineteen in 1853, and twelve in 1854.[58] The very existence, let alone success, of any of them seems the more miraculous when we recall that none of these banks was more than six years old. Remember also that less than ten years before, the lusty metropolis of 50,000, which they served, had only about 200 residents.

Sherman was still trying, with scant success, to prevail on his wife to take the children and the nurse with her when she went to Ohio in a few weeks. By this arrangement he could save enough money to buy or build a good house and a stable. His wife's objection was that she did not wish to stay away from her husband so long in view of his many asthmatic attacks.

> I have my eye on a lot on Rincon Point . . . with a small cottage which for $2,000 could be enlarged enough for us. This would give the children yard room to play in instead of the street as now. The owner asks $6,000. I want to trade my present house in, for it is on leased ground, $30 a month four years to run. . . . This lot is near the Marine Hospital on Harrison Street near First and commands a good view of the city. . . . Mrs. Sherman . . . is perfectly willing to leave the children there as there is no danger of drays and wagons. This change would cost me some six or seven thousand. The lot will be very valuable in time. . . . I am hardly able to pay the California rates. I might . . . get you to raise it for me at 10% a year. I might . . . take part of the William Lucas fund, but would not do so without consent.[59]

Within a week, Sherman had closed the purchase of the Harrison Street property from a son of Commodore John D. Sloat, and deeded him the Green Street property as part of the purchase price. He had hired a contractor to build an addition to the new house. He hoped to find some couple who would occupy it with him and look after the two children during Mrs. Sherman's absence.

Though no blame could attach to Sherman, his timing of the Harrison Street purchase proved most unfortunate. Before the addition to the house was even completed, San Francisco was to experience a major financial crisis that had far-reaching influence on Sherman's future. It would then be too late to abandon or even to modify plans for the new home. The purchase and the improvement of this property were to cost the hard-pressed banker dearly and saddle him with debt that it would take him years to repay.

A private bank in Stockton, Robinson Bours & Co., had opened an account with Lucas-Turner. Sherman was opposed to establishing branches in the interior but was glad to have good correspondents in Sacramento and Stockton. He wanted to form a similar connection with some reliable concern in Marysville. With that done, he felt the bank would have as many correspondents as were desirable.

Pioneer bankers ran some risks peculiar to their times. Rhodes & Co., Sacramento correspondent of Lucas, Turner & Co., had shipped $15,000 in gold dust on the river steamer *Pearl*, en route from Marysville to San Francisco. Rhodes drew on Lucas-Turner to pay for the dust. The *Pearl*'s boiler burst just as she passed the confluence of the American and Sacramento Rivers. The vessel was a total wreck, and between fifty and sixty persons lost their lives. One of the casualties was the express messenger in charge of the gold dust. This was supposedly lost in the wreck, although later it was recovered from the river. On news of the disaster, Sherman at Rhodes's request stopped payment of the draft. On recovery of the dust, the draft was paid.[60]

Despite the general dullness, the bank's business was continuing the spurt Sherman had earlier reported. "Our depositors have grown beyond parallel . . . and the number of new accounts each day gives promise of great results. . . . Last night our cash balance was over a million and tonight will run up to $1,100,000." (I am sure that by "cash balance" Sherman meant total deposits.) "Notwithstanding the general cry of hard times we have been pressed less for loans and discounts than heretofore." The notes purchased from Burgoyne were liquidating according to schedule and Lucas-Turner had already retired a part of the term bills it had given in payment for them.

In retrospect, one reads of Sherman's exultation over this expanding business and the increased prestige of his firm with sadness. His elation was destined to be so short-lived! Even as he wrote, distant events beyond his knowledge and control were creating crises and problems greater than he had ever faced.[61]

Part Three:
Bank Runs and Rescues

MRS. WILLIAM TECUMSEH SHERMAN

Painting by George P. A. Healy, 1868.

Courtesy of National Collection of Fine Arts, Smithsonian Institution

SHERMAN'S HOUSE ON RINCON HILL,
SAN FRANCISCO, 1856

When the photograph was taken, the Sherman family resided in this "cottage . . . near the Marine Hospital on Harrison Street near First [which] commands a good view of the city."

From the files of California Historical Society

13

Sherman undoubtedly found it hard to restrain himself when he wrote his letter of Sunday, February 25, 1855.

> This steamer will convey . . . accounts of the most terrible financial storm that has ever devastated any community. . . . We have resisted [?] it well and come out safe. . . . I must . . . give you a faint account of it and if my ideas are loose and scattered, remember that for a week I have hardly slept, not from asthma but from a rigid distraction of nerve, mind and body. . . . On Saturday arrived the *Oregon* and quick as lightning flew the intelligence that Page & Bacon of St. Louis was bankrupt. Crowds assembled all along Montgomery Street and a run on P&B & Co. began. Meetings were called, circulars drawn up certifying to the fact that the house here was not liable for the debts of the home house, and that they were abundantly able to pay every cent of their deposits and certificates in California. The excitement was naturally allayed. On Saturday night I went down to P.B. and Co., found Mr. Page, Haight and Ruxton together with many prominent citizens in consultation. I took Haight to one side and asked him frankly how he stood. He said the blow was entirely unexpected to him, that they had for some time been pushing forward money to the relief of Page & Bacon, that P. & B. of St. Louis owed this house $250,000, that they had to their credit with their other depositors [depositories?] $600,000 over and above their drafts, that on Saturday morning they had coin and bullion in vault $1,200,000. Bills receivable $600,000 and that they owed their Depositors and Certificates $1,700,000. The run on Saturday took out $300,000 cash. On Saturday night there was a consulta-

tion which resulted in a publication that they would continue business, as theretofore in their old bank. Last Monday was the day for their new co-partnership and removal to the new bank on Battery Street. On Sunday night Folsom came to see me but I was out and he left me a note to meet him at P.B. & Co. I found there Parrott, Larkin, Downey, Paine, Folsom and many others representing heavy real estate interests here.[1] A card had been drawn up similar to the one signed in St. Louis. The card read, "We the undersigned etc. having made a personal examination etc. do hereby pledge our property, etc. for PB&Co.'s depositors." Folsom wanted my advice. I told him such a card would most certainly allay the growing storm, but that I thought they should make the personal examination of cash on hand, certificates of deposit out and balances of accounts liable to sight check. After a long conversation with Parrott and Folsom outside, back of P.B. & Co.'s office, I left them and next day learned the sequel. As Folsom entered the office where sat all these gentlemen, Paine remarked, "Well, I suppose we have nothing to do further than sign the paper." Folsom rejoined, "What about the personal examination we propose to certify?" "That would take too much time." "No" said Folsom, "We have the night before us. We can add up the balances and see the amount due Certificates and count the cash by weighing and counting as fast as possible." I had pointed out these to Folsom and gave as my opinion that ten gentlemen could in four hours arrive at a very fair result. During this conversation Haight . . . overheard and not wanting this personal examination turned the conversation and said with a card expression of general confidence, he thought he could carry the house through. So the . . . pledge was avoided and lucky it was so to the proposed signers. On Monday the house opened as usual. Deposits were made and checks drawn but of course the balance was falling off for no one would buy exchange. No new certificates were issued, but old ones came pouring in. Tuesday and Wednesday the same. The [illegible] seemed to have ceased. No run on anybody else, and our deposits growing all the time. I thought the crisis passed, but still refused all loans and discounts and insisted on all payments due. . . . On Thursday morning our cash balance was $1,145,391. That was the 22nd of February during which there was a firemen's procession and the streets were filled with crowds of spectators and actors of the scene. Page Bacon & Co. did not open their bank. Many thought it was on account of the parade and holiday, but soon it was whispered round that they had stopped. I knew it early in the morning from Mr. Casserly, the lawyer who told me L. [?] B. Wells was appointed the receiver. . . . In the course of the day came out the enclosed circular, the most egotistical and incendiary production that was ever thrown upon an excited people.[2] It was the spark that exploded the mine. Whilst the public was absorbed in the celebration, quiet people were drawing their money [out] of the banks. Thursday night our balance ran down to $1,065,250, a falling of $80,000. During the evening arrived the Nicaragua steamer with New York [mail] dates to January 20 from which it seemed the excitement there about Page & Bacon had subsided and that all the California drafts had been and would continue to be paid. . . . All thought that this news would restore public confidence and such would have been the case had it not been for the false assertions in the Page & Bacon circular.

However, returning to ourselves . . . not a clerk left the office until we had the balance of each man's account and that due certificates that amounted to $530,000. We had a little over $400,000 [almost illegible] in actual cash and $700,000 in notes with additional securities—State, City & County & scrip, with some $100,000 in mortgages. Certificates of Deposit are held mostly in sums of $4, $5, and $600 and must be paid instanter. . . . I [subtracted] enough to meet demand notes due next [day] and such as owed interest and counted certain of my personal friends who would . . . take my word, thereby counting some [illegible], leaving a balance of cash $65,000 to be paid in case of a run.[3] . . . We all went home entirely comfortable but when I reached the office . . . Friday I was thunderstruck to see the crowd and tumult. Adams & Co. closed, Wells, Fargo & Co. afraid to open, Robinson & Wright's Savings Banks closed before a dollar could be called for and the assertion in every man's mouth that all must break, because Page Bacon & Co.'s circular said so. "There is no coin in the country" a base deliberate falsehood, conceived in folly, knavery or downright malice. . . . We knew where we stood and were determined not to break. Our bank is a large roomy one on a corner with four large doors easy of access. A crowd inside and outside but our tellers were as cool as possible. Reilly a shade more erect, stiff and exact. . . . Nisbet lent a hand

and Henry kept filling the trays out of the bags in the vault. Soon a crowd of friends, officious and otherwise, poured in to inquire "For God's sake, what are things coming to!" I explained "What others are doing, we know not," but . . . Lucas, Turner & Co. would not break and that any person feeling even nervous to go and get his money. My own personal friends simply took my word. Some took security for their balances and to some we paid bullion. . . . By noon we had paid $337,000 of cash. After seeing the machinery working easily, I went out, saw all I could promptly, assured them of our ability and determination to stand this run, and to such as I could confide [in], that we might be pushed unless we would lay our hands on $65,000. . . . We succeeded in getting the crowd away by 12 or 1 o'clock. Still, one by one or in groups came [with] checks and certificates and by 3: P.M. our trays looked slim enough, about $40,000 in small gold and silver, 50's and 20's all gone. Things looked bad, yet so far as we were concerned the excitement was done. . . . I knew of one or two certificates liable . . . to be presented, the holders of which were nervous but restrained by . . . pride. . . . A man named Pearson drew from us . . . $25,000 which he . . . still has in his room. Mr. Parrott . . . offered him a mortgage on all his Montgomery Street property valued at $250,000 but his answer was he would not take a mortgage on all San Francisco. . . . I saw our clerks begin to look alarmed. Nisbet decidedly so as he feared I trusted more than was prudent on my army friends, but I knew they were true as steel. During the day there was a desperate run on Davidson and Company, Drexel, Sather and Church, Sanders and Brenham, and Tallant and Wilde, but strange to say none at all on Palmer and Cook and Co.[4] This is accounted for thus; they receive all the City, County and State taxes which are now in their hands and not liable to sudden call. They have very few Certificates of Deposit and their depositors, few in number, are such a class as can be reasoned with. . . . I have always kept a kind of visiting acquaintance with them and on Friday determined to see if I could not make a raise from them. It was successful; I got $10,000 on my simple promise not to use it unless it could carry us through the day. I got this about 3:15 P.M. . . . Nisbet's friend, Kellogg[5] brought in some $4 or $5,000 from his assay office and other of our friends little sums. . . . So the word went out that the run had ceased and deposits were coming in.

Our clock seemed provokingly slow, but at last it pointed to 4.

. . . We had $45,000 left without having pledged one dollar of our securities. . . . We did not rest. All hands worked till near morning, but . . . our cash was balanced and stood [Friday night] $781,370. [I am sure here again Sherman meant his deposits] . . . I rode out to Folsom and told him by midnight he *must* raise us $17,000. He was very sick, looked very bad . . . promised to send his man Van Winkle to see me by 10 P.M. I then went to Dick Hammond [6]—he has the . . . fund for building the Custom House here. . . . Smiley is contractor and some weeks since had Hammond's acceptance for $25,000 at 30 days on which we advanced $10,000. My object . . . was to get Hammond to anticipate and pay this. . . . he said if I would give him my word to have it for him the 1st of March, I should have $30,000. You can imagine my satisfaction. He promised to come down by . . . midnight and close the matter. . . . I came to the office where every soul was engaged. Van Winkle came and said he had the promise of $25,000. . . . Maynard thought he could get $2,000 by 9:30 but in due course came Hammond and Smiley, also Jones of Palmer-Cook. By . . . midnight we knew the actual balance of each account. There remained due Certificates $50,000 and depositors $80,000—total $130,000—Cash on hand $45,000. Balance to be raised . . . $85,000. But we went over our Balance Book . . . for such accounts as were in Oregon, the South or the interior, impossible to come by the next day . . . and asserted . . . that with $40,000 we could pass the morrow. Jones of Palmer Cook & Co . . . agreed with Hammond if he, Hammond, would let us have $40,000 he Jones, would pledge the house of P.C.&Co. to see us through. Hammond assented and made me his check on the Ass't. Treasurer. For it he holds no voucher or receipt only my word that he shall have it . . . by the 1st proximo. It was a noble act on his part which I shall never forget. . . . More than any one thing [it] has carried us through with triumph when the veterans failed for want of nerve and courage. . . . I [saw] the Treasurer Major Snyder. . . . He said the check [Hammond's] was good. . . . We [met] at his office at 8:00 A.M. and . . . I then received the $40,000 in American gold. . . . When we opened we had a very fair show. Instead of an exciting day, it was one of absolute calm. $34,000 was deposited and $32,000 drawn out. . . . Last night our balance was $792,307 of which $117,000 is in actual coin. So the battle is over, and we are not dead by a d——d sight!

We have had a perfect rush to congratulate us. I don't think that Haight wanted to ruin us, but . . . he thought when PB&CO. could not stand, no one else could. Page, Bacon & Co. are dead as hemp in California. Salt won't save them. Adams & Co. are dishonest, craven, cowardly, all through the land they caved in.[7] Nothing but air and impudence to stand on. Wells Fargo agents—better but were unable to pay. . . . Colonel Pardee, the head of the house says he is working night and day to convert his bullion into coin, says he will open tomorrow or Tuesday. I have no faith in them. Banking and expressing are different trades and hereafter will be kept apart. Davidson is the recipient of the aid of the Jews and foreigners. He stood the run well and from foreigners raised outside assistance. Drexel, Sather and Church like ourselves have much capital and means that has enabled them to get through safe. I have explained Palmer Cook and Co.'s secret. Sanders and Brenham and Tallant and Wilde are very small concerns.

In the country our little friend Rhodes has weathered the storm. Read and Co. caved in at 12 Noon Friday. Robinson Bours and Co. was the only house in Stockton that survived and same of Mark Brumagim and Co. of Marysville. . . . A magnificent future opens before us. . . . I shall not lose sight of the lesson taught by this awful calamity. Among the merchants . . . as their notes fall due, they know not where to look for money. Very little . . . from the mines in consequence of the drought. . . . In town here all is in the hands of individuals scared to death, buried in the sand or hidden away.

In the past eight days $3,000,000 of coin has been paid out.

By Page Bacon and Co. from Saturday to Wednesday	800,000
Adams and Co. on Thursday	200,000
Davidson to date	800,000
Lucas Turner and Co.	400,000
Drexel Sather and Church	400,000
Palmer Cook and Co.	200,000
Sanders and Brenham, Tallant and Wilde	200,000
Total:	3,000,000

This is no exaggeration. Page Bacon and Co.'s contention is . . . false. . . . . Had Haight gone on . . . until the Nicaragua boat arrived with confirmation of his drafts being protected and had he abstained from that suicidal and incendiary circular, this city would have been spared this calamity. Were it not for the pernicious effects upon business generally, I would not regret these events for it has shown the strength and ability of the true, and separated them from the false and unsound. California is hereby thrown back three years—but the mines are still here. . . . We have a city with its wharves, warehouses and stores and dwellings . . . although individuals must be ruined, the general welfare is not annihilated . . . my judgment is as good as many who know more about . . . commercial technicalities. I find mathematics as applicable to banking as to artillery, but better still I find how true are old army friends.—Hammond has acted nobly and I shall reciprocate it. Schuyler Hamilton,[8] Colonel De Russey,[9] Major Towne, Trowbridge and other officers sustained me and inspired public confidence in our assertions and Stevens of the Navy has afforded active and effectual aid. On the merchants and business men generally, I am down; instead of coming to the rescue, they sat in their offices scared and paralyzed. . . . Several of them came last evening to renew notes but I gave them my mind and told some of them they had shown us no confidence . . . and that from us they should reap the fruits. . . . There are honorable exceptions which I shall remember always. . . . The newspapers which . . . will be sent you, will give other views. . . . Some . . . have taken a reasonable view of events, but . . . the *Alta California* . . . increased the trouble by announcing that all the banks would inevitably *go*.

On Sunday evening, Sherman added a page. Creditors of Page, Bacon & Co. had met that afternoon. "Some arrangement was made . . . to pay certain of their creditors in cash and the rest in drafts on New York." Haight had told Sherman on Friday that his bank had $840,000 in New York. "If they extricate themselves they have lost the prestige of their past success."

Sherman was worried about the last payment the firm owed for the loans it had purchased from Burgoyne. This involved $47,000 and the bill had changed hands and evidently he feared they might be called upon to pay it twice in New York. (The practices of issuing "first and second of exchange" apparently entered into this.)

Sherman closed this long chronicle of woes with a bitter

reflection: "What terrible casualties we incur. . . . I thought in leaving the Army that wars and rumors of war could be forgotten but it is one continuous strife. . . . Indeed all are lucky that can report themselves in existence." [10]

In this grim recital of the passions aroused by runs on banks, a few human touches stand out in warm relief: gallant young Captain Folsom, one of San Francisco's best known and wealthiest citizens, now ill with the malady that was soon to kill him, bestirred himself to aid his embattled friend, and other army comrades of Captain Sherman's like Major Hammond risked government funds in his custody, solely on the banker's solemn word. No wonder that Sherman termed them "true as steel" and declared that he would never forget their noble acts.

Sherman added an ironic postscript to his chronicle of disasters:

> Mrs. Sherman is the only person *not* rejoiced at our success for she says if we had broken I would have gone home, but I'd blow this house into atoms and squeeze dollars out of brickbats rather than let our affairs pass into the hands of a rascally receiver, or a more rascally sheriff. I believe I express the joint feeling of . . . every member of the House of Lucas, Turner and Co. in saying that I would sacrifice a hundred thousand dollars rather than to stop one day. In the midst of our manifold troubles, I have forgotten to communicate my satisfaction at seeing that the run on your house was so easily met. Ours here was not aided as yours by the long history of the partners, or long standing wealth.
>
> You know what little faith people have in wealth afar off. But now everybody is satisfied that we know where to get money when it is needed.

This reference makes it plain that Lucas & Simonds had also withstood a run in St. Louis, brought on no doubt by the crash of their competitor, Page & Bacon.

On February 26, 1855, Turner wrote to Sherman, giving details of events in St. Louis that were related to San Francisco's Black Friday:

> Page & Bacon . . . reopened the doors. News received with much eclat. . . . Desperate efforts are being made to bolster up

> the credit of this house and to establish . . . the impression that their recent suspension was wholly in consequence of bad faith and treachery . . . of their New York correspondent, Duncan, Sherman & Company. . . . I can assure you that the credit of Page & Bacon is . . . far from being re-established. . . . It is announced that before resuming, William Bacon . . . obtained an extension for payment of $300,000 due Duncan, Sherman & Company. Isn't it rather singular . . . they should seek . . . accommodation from such a source? . . . It has leaked out that they have . . . obtained similar indulgence in small amounts from $3,000 to $5,000 from other parties. These rumors . . . show this house is not yet out of its troubles. . . . I give you all the information we can gather . . . for the security of your own interests.[11]

On February 28, Sherman referred again to

> the Battle of the 23rd of February. [I] can only add that since the great day quiet has prevailed, money returning to our vaults steadily. Our own notes have been paid better than might have been expected, so that we feel beyond all chance of danger. Today [there was] a fair demand for exchange so that we must ship some $50,000 of coin and $20,000 of bullion. . . . I will write them [the New York correspondent] that they must be content with a small balance until we feel it perfectly safe to increase our shipments. . . . No doubt that Page, Bacon & Co. have destroyed themselves by endeavoring to send forward so large a portion of their depositors' money to the relief of the Home House. As those funds appear to be held in New York . . . [for] this house, it is possible that the firm may recover in part their lost ground but [if] . . . any portion of the funds . . . have been diverted from the control of the partners here, then this House is irrecoverably gone.

Sherman added important details about the Sunday meeting of Page-Bacon's creditors. Depositors with balances due them of $400,000 had agreed to accept the firm's certificates of deposit with interest at 1% a month, payable in three installments—two, four, and six months from date. This enabled the House to reopen, but Sherman wrote:

> So completely is confidence in them destroyed that this very course gives them six months to die in, for when the last install-

ment is paid, they will be abused and by a public that is convinced of Haight's inability to meet a crisis.

Adams & Co. are hopelessly insolvent and have acknowledged it. Wells, Fargo & Co. resumed quietly, but I shall not forget their selfishness in leaving us to bear the brunt of a panic in part created by them. No house in this city has recovered so promptly as we. Although not a word has appeared in the papers at our instance, I did at one time think of exposing the falsehood, egotism and malice of Henry D. Bacon's letter to Sam Brannan & Co. in New York, but . . . am glad I did not . . . for so many *cards* have been published by the insolvent and disgraced banks that it would be bad company to be found in. . . . Haight's statements were so contradictory and inconsistent . . . and I. C. Woods [manager of the now defunct Adams & Co.] flummoxed and floundered beyond his depth and comprehension that the public has no faith in bankers. These men brought on us the run which has established us on a firmer basis than ever. Monday, deposits $12,000 more than checked out. Tuesday $44,000. Today was deposited $161,000 and $141,000 drawn out. . . . We have cash on hand $180,000. . . . This run was a tornado required to purify the elements . . . it has not been so disastrous as at first sight appeared. The aggregate amount of money lost to individuals is not great and is widely distributed. It has destroyed two small savings banks and two great despotic concerns that assumed to themselves all the glory and merit of their office. Poor Nisbet's model hero, Haight is in the dust and he has no apology for him. That one stumbling block is out of our way and a proposition can be entertained on its merits, without being knocked into pi—by Henry Haight not approving. If greatness should now be thrust on us by this misfortune . . . I will try and keep cool and profit by the lessons. . . . So long as you . . . maintain the high character you now enjoy, I will strive to keep the child worthy of the parent. . . . For the past week we have all, clerks and principals worked nearly all night. I sat up [with] Stevens' dead baby. Today attended the funeral, and yet tonight must make up the mail. . . . You may dismiss all fears of any danger to us for we are out of the woods.[12]

Sherman's reference to the large remittance made by Page, Bacon & Co. in San Francisco to the St. Louis house concerns the climax in the failure of the two banking firms. While Lucas,

Turner & Co. may not seem to have been involved, this disaster to its principal competitor precipitated the gravest crisis in the affairs of Sherman's bank. Therefore, the major details of the catastrophe seem a very pertinent part of the Lucas-Turner story. When the St. Louis bank found itself seriously embarrassed because of heavy loans to railroad contractors, it called upon the San Francisco firm to remit to it the major portion of its surplus coin. One account says that approximately $1 million was shipped East on two steamers. Storms and accidents delayed the vessels' arrival.[13] Another version of the same occurrence gives the amount shipped as $2 million.[14]

Apparently, a double tragedy resulted. The money, whether $1 million or $2 million, left San Francisco just *before* its presence in Page, Bacon & Co.'s tills would have saved the coast firm. It arrived in New York for credit to the St. Louis bank *after* the parent establishment had closed its doors! This is a classic example of the vital role played by primitive communications in the economy of the 1850's.

In both St. Louis and San Francisco, some at least of the Page-Bacon partners struggled to regain their lost position. The elder Page was a large owner of realty, and he drew heavily on his resources to reopen the bank. The St. Louis firm resumed business for a time but finally closed on April 4, 1855. In San Francisco, Page, Bacon & Co. reopened on March 29. On May 1, the S. S. *Sonora* arrived with word of the failure of the parent house. This immediately resulted in attachments being levied against the San Francisco firm for more than $98,000. After paying out all ready cash of some $117,000 the firm confessed judgment for $400,000 in favor of the certificate holders whose previous forbearance had permitted the reopening of the bank in March. Its doors were now finally closed.* A maze of tedious and expensive litigation followed. Nine years later there was still a half million dollars owing to its luckless creditors.[15] One bank historian wrote of it long afterward, "The actual extent of losses

---

* For additional details, see Appendix, "The Page-Bacon Failures as Viewed by F. W. Page."

suffered by the public through the failure of this firm will never be known."[16]

February 23, 1855, was long remembered in San Francisco as Black Friday. Seven of its nineteen banks had closed, six of them permanently.[17] Some of the largest and most prominent financial houses were among the casualties. Throughout the interior, banks fared even worse. Sherman's pride in the showing made by Lucas, Turner & Co. was certainly justified.

The student of economics would be hard put to find a better example of unrestrained laissez-faire than the financial structure of California in the 1850's. In the absence of regulatory statutes or supervisory authority, the managements of the banks had been left to their own devices, had fixed their own policies and standards. Black Friday would remain for years a potent argument for banking legislation and state supervision. The mood of the public toward such conditions can be surprisingly patient and long suffering. Black Friday was only the first of lamentable and avoidable bank crashes. Eventually, there would be mild approaches to regulation and supervision of banks but they met the usual fate of halfway measures. Not until early in the twentieth century did the California legislature pay real heed to long continuing abuses and dangers. The California Bank Act of 1909 was a half century overdue.

14

Sherman's mood on March 1, 1855, was distinctly cheerful. California had enjoyed "magnificent rains giving a new tone to public feeling . . . the sky has cleared . . . and the day is beautiful." Not having heard how much gold was being shipped on the departing *Golden Age*, the banker asked himself what would result should California cease making the heavy shipments of the precious metal that had come to be taken for granted? Maybe there would be "weeping and wailing in Wall Street" but it seemed to Sherman that if more money stayed on the Coast a better market for real estate would probably develop. Thrifty folk might buy and improve small acreages instead of entrusting their savings to banks. More farming should then follow and that would be good for society. "We are going to have a good time and who are better placed than we to take advantage of the new epoch!" [18]

In gloomy contrast was the letter of the following week. "I am confined to my house from a severe attack of asthma which came near ending my earthly operations." Dr. Bowie [19] had been called in; his remedies eased the attack but left the patient weak and debilitated. He was convinced that one of these seizures would sooner or later prove fatal.

> Don't think I feel any fear, [he assured Turner, but] I am exceedingly sorry that I bought that lot and began building a house. . . . It is now pretty well determined that Bowman, Mrs. Bowman and Nisbet will occupy the house for a year from April 1st and I will board myself and children with them. . . . This is

not entirely to my liking but Mrs. Sherman is so determined not to leave her children without some responsible female person in charge. [Sherman had assented] rather than be at the expense of hiring some *lady* who would have to be fed on sugar plums and treated with all the consideration of a lady though a hireling. That class of housekeeper is peculiarly disagreeable to me.

Nisbet had received a letter from Turner which mentioned a long one he had written to Sherman. It had not arrived. "I feel anxious to learn the details of your St. Louis financial troubles," he wrote Turner, even though he had read much about them in the newspapers,

> let me beg of you, let your necessities become ever so urgent, don't diminish our capital by a single cent . . . it would be fatal. See what havoc that policy has produced to . . . Page, Bacon & Company. . . . Since we opened this house the . . . times are all changed. We have got along quite well and if we are true to ourselves, I don't see why you and Mr. Lucas cannot look with certainty to a high name and all of us to fair profits. . . . In California a bank must have a large cash capital . . . moreover . . . the reputation of wealth won't pay checks here. If Page fails, Lucas may, is a natural inference. Page has failed but Lucas has not, and we must take advantage . . . of the fact. We are getting the very best kind of depositors and are discounting little or nothing and that of the very best. . . . Old notes . . . are being paid with astonishing promptitude.

Sherman then displayed a rather surprising boldness of vision: "when mortgages have declined in value [he must have meant the mortgaged property] I am going to increase security and diminish interest, say 2½ or even 2 [percent]."

Again he exulted in the "splendid rains." Everybody was looking forward to a good year. Evidently the St. Louis partners had proposed to raise Sherman's salary.

> I feel duly complimented at the offer of $10,000 salary. It would be most acceptable but I would much rather see the item of interest on our capital left out [of] the contract which would be a concession of $2,000 to me and $2,000 to Nisbet. . . . If you

> choose you may give me the $1,000 additional making me $500 a month. With this modification it would be prudent to declare a dividend of say $50,000 per annum; leaving the accumulated earnings as a safety fund and increase of capital.

Sherman had several times argued that the bank should not pay the partners interest on the capital. He did not like to think of that capital as borrowed money on which interest was paid regardless of conditions but as a fund to be maintained intact for the protection of depositors. If the bank prospered, dividends could be declared as earned, but no interest paid on a debt. In his thinking on this point, it is curious to see how Sherman anticipated by many years the later legislative enactments that the capital and surplus of a bank must remain unimpaired.

Having taken this forthright position, Sherman assured Turner he would abide by whatever the St. Louis owners decided to do, adding "now is the time to lay a safe foundation for a safe future."

The banker also explained two expense items. He had been urged by St. Louis to recoup himself for entertaining on behalf of the bank. Such expense had now amounted to $1,400 from November, 1853. The second was a $45 charge for a dinner he had given the staff in appreciation for their extra nights on duty during the run. He hoped Turner would not think it extravagant!

Sherman's sense of humor impelled him to record what he described as a "semi-comic" incident of the recent runs on the banks. I. C. Woods, the head man of Adams & Co.

> lived in a large brick house . . . on Stockton Street. His mother, sister, wife and family and her beaux . . . were present. Door bell rang, servant opened the door to two women, one large with child and the other carrying a valise and bags. "Does Mr. Wood of Adams & Co. live here?" "Yes." "Come in Mary," said number one, "this is the place. Lay down the things. I am going to stay here." And into the parlor she bolted. "Ahem! A beautiful place. Mr. Woods' home? Mr. Woods' home is my home. Mr. Woods has all my money. As long as he has a home. I have one. When he goes into the street I go to the street. That will do, Mary. You can

> go, tell them I am all right. Mr. Woods' home is my home," and there she stayed. The beaux tried to coax and force her but 'twas of no use. They sent for a lawyer, but she deliberately announced the fact that she expected to be confined in a few days and had saved her money for that event, and therefore she had a better claim on Woods as long as he had a roof over him than on anybody else. She would not budge until removed by force by a police officer.

Equally ironic humor was attached to an incident involving Henry Haight. Some months previously friends and admirers of this gentleman had circulated a subscription list "a la California," wrote Sherman, "(a custom I hope is as dead as Adams & Co.) to present [Haight] a testimonial on account of his eminent financial qualifications and generous qualities etc. prior to his departure East." Sherman on casting his eye over the paper when it was brought to him to sign, observed that the subscriptions totaled about $17,000 from many of San Francisco's most prominent citizens.

> I would not sign Lucas, Turner & Company for obvious reasons but put my own and Nisbet's down for a comparatively small sum. [Sherman must have made a wry face when he did this.] James King of William was treasurer of this fund and deposited it with Adams & Co. When they broke, the Committee who had given Tucker the order for a magnificent set of plate . . . went to King to claim this fund as a special deposit not to be put in the general assets but King has just that much sense of conscience that he said they were like any other depositor. . . . So Haight will lose his plate. The entire committee will most likely be sued by Tucker for damages, etc." [20]

Another week seemed to confirm Sherman's announcement of improved business. On this steamer day, Lucas, Turner & Co. sold the largest amount of exchange up to this time—nearly $135,000. It also shipped $175,000 in bullion plus about $10,000 in Eastern exchange deposited with it. Once more, however, the banker declared this exchange business was not profitable. He had tried to get the other houses to raise the rates to where the sellers could make ½% or 1% on exchange sold, "but the bankers . . . will not cooperate cordially."

As explained in the preceding chapter, Page, Bacon & Co. were open again for a few weeks after March 29. Sherman doubtless chuckled grimly when he wrote: "Yesterday and today [Page, Bacon & Co.] advertised to sell $200,000 of exchange on New York at *par*. Think of that. Oh, what a fall was there, my countrymen! When but a few weeks since, their exchange was sold by the million and now they have to beg the public to take a small sum at a sacrifice of 3%."

Sherman was hopeful that with Page, Bacon & Co. and Adams & Co. out of the picture, gold dust and bullion could be bought at a cheaper price. At the moment, the demand for bullion for shipment was strong and the bars were selling for ¼% off.* "We cannot tell till this bullion is sold, refined and placed to our credit, what profit we make."

Major Turner's long-expected nephew arrived on the morning of March 14, 118 days around the Horn on the *Morning Light;* Sherman called it a quick passage. He was given a few days to see the town before starting to work. "He looks easy and good natured but not very energetic. Still he may wear well." Sherman planned to set him filing letters, balancing passbooks, and performing messenger duties. "He comes in at the foot of the ladder. . . . If he works up he will have a fair chance." Sherman said he could safely associate with the other young men in the office and hoped he had character enough not to get into scrapes. "If he shows any proclivity that way, he will get hauled over the coals."

Evidently the excitement and melodrama of Black Friday had worn off by the time that Sherman wrote:

> This life of ours is a terrible drudge. All day questions of thousands of dollars must be despatched without hesitation, and

* For explanation of this term, see Appendix, "Sherman's Banking Terminology."

here is night with piles of money to be arranged, counted, etc., boxes of bullion to be packed, notes and drafts to be arranged, and classified, letters and lists written. Our clerks have hard work. . . . Midnight will not let us off this time, and instead of getting lighter, it is getting harder each steamer.

Sherman's house on Harrison Street was nearly ready. In again mentioning his plan to board himself and the two children with Mrs. Bowman, he added: "It is touch and go with Bowman. He can't pay his interest to General Hitchcock. . . . I'll have to take a deed for the property in lieu of the mortgage. General Hitchcock has bad luck, but the property which falls to him is very good unless San Francisco be the baseless fabric of a dream." [21]

The handicap of uncertain communication under which the banking business operated in the 1850's is again demonstrated in Sherman's letter of March 23, 1855. On one steamer he received four letters of Turner's, written January 20, 21, and 30, and February 6. All these should have arrived on earlier boats, but had been delayed by severe storms in Illinois. Apparently, Turner had considered coming to San Francisco because of the panic.

I wish you had come [Sherman wrote to him], but I think you will be satisfied I did as much as was necessary on the occasion, not only meeting the run but availing ourselves of the reaction which is being slowly felt. Money here is infernally scarce, property is unsaleable. . . . The worst feature . . . is the effort . . . of the large property holders to throw off the city debt. The City Council had passed the ordinance authorising a Board of Commissioners to fund the present city warrants by issuing in their stead Bonds with interest at 8 per cent payable semi-annually in New York.

Some of the larger property owners brought to light an old clause in the city's charter limiting its debt to $50,000. That amount had been greatly exceeded, and the legislature had to authorize any change in the charter. The opponents of the measure petitioned the state senate to defeat the modification (the lower branch of the legislature had already approved it).

> My own opinion [declared Sherman] is that if this step should be successful it will produce more trouble than the forgeries of Meiggs and the breaking of all the banks. These warrants have been considered the very best kinds of collateral at 60 cents on the dollar. We hold a good many of them as collateral and $40,000 of our own by the Meiggs flight, so that our interest in this move . . . is great. . . . I am in correspondence with several members of the legislature. . . . I take it the petition was accompanied by material aid, without which nothing can be done here.

Sherman sent with this letter a copy of an advertisement he had placed in some of the papers. It set forth new rules for the conduct of the bank's business. In brief:

> Checks on other banks received before 3: P.M. will be presented the same day. Those deposited later will be held till the next morning at the depositor's risk. Parties desiring to renew notes must obtain bank's consent the day previous to the note's maturity.
>
> Overdrafts will not be permitted, unless parties interested obtain the necessary credit or deposit collateral beforehand. Certificates of Deposit will be issued as heretofore, payable on demand without interest.
>
> Two other classes of certificates will be issued: 1st, Certificates at ten days sight bearing interest at the rate of seven per cent per annum.
>
> 2nd, Certificates for six months and over at the rate of ten per cent per annum. After April 1, 1855, bank hours will be from 10: A.M. to 4: P.M.

Sherman explained that a number of checks deposited late in the day that Adams & Co. closed could not be presented to them for payment. One depositor had refused to make good on an Adams check he had deposited. The interest-bearing certificates were the innovation that Sherman had proposed as an experiment shortly before the February panic. Now there was more justification for such a savings medium. Even Mr. Henry Haight was said to approve the new rules. Sherman reported that "Haight told a friend . . . we had hit it exactly if we only stuck to it. Page, Bacon & Company's overdrafts on the day of failure were $200,000."

Sherman expected to occupy the house on Harrison Street by April 10. Mrs. Sherman would start East on April 16. So far her husband had not secured an escort for her but was sure one would be found. He himself had had two very severe asthmatic attacks. His doctor believed damp walls at his present dwelling were partly responsible and predicted Sherman would enjoy much better health in his new quarters. "That," sighed the patient, "will be some amends for my folly in building at this critical time."

Turner must have written that rumors had reached him that Nisbet was going to leave Lucas, Turner & Co. Sherman was sure the report was groundless. "With his little follies I prefer him to any stranger," the banker replied.

A fragment of a page concludes this letter and starts in the middle of a sentence about a sketch of San Francisco that Sherman was sending. The banker had marked on it the location of the Lucas, Turner & Co. building. The view was looking east on Sacramento Street toward the Bay.[22]

A man named Fisher left San Francisco for St. Louis at the end of March. He wanted to open a branch of Lucas, Turner & Co. in Marysville and planned to confer with the partners in St. Louis about it. Sherman saw some advantages in having a branch in Marysville—sale of exchange, purchase of gold dust, and the like—but would not take the responsibility of such a step. To succeed at a point so distant from San Francisco, a manager must have unlimited signing powers and authority. He felt such latitude should only be shown a partner; on the other hand, he opposed adding any more partners to the firm.[23]

Apparently Sherman's argument in favor of "no interest" capital had not persuaded the St. Louis partners to modify the contract in this particular. On March 31, he told Turner:

> I'm sorry you are so positive on the . . . interest on our capital. . . . I have presented the subject more strongly and before making any change in our entries I will await a reply thereto. . . . I feel bound to write strong whatever occurs to me. All I ask is a fair hearing; if you disagree of course I submit with due grace, for I am well assured of your hearty and honest support. In the matter of our coming to the assistance of Lucas & Simonds or their coming to ours in case of pressure, we are too far apart for that. The history of Page & Bacon's late failure illustrates more fully than any argument I can use of the extreme danger of a house here diminishing its actual cash for in case of alarm it is useless to attempt to raise money outside.

Then follows a passage that could have been written by any banker, trust officer, or family counselor who advises women about their investments:

> I wrote to Lee telling him I would use his money as requested. It is not for him but for a lady and you have no idea how nervous they become or what long letters I have to write to allay their fears. For John Lee [24] I am willing to do any amount of labor but I want him to appreciate that high rates of interest are not alone for the use of money, but for the extraordinary risks of this country.[25]

On April 8, "a most beautiful Sunday" following fine rains, Sherman reported that the move to the new Harrison Street house had commenced the previous day, and that he expected the Shermans and the Bowmans to be fully settled in the new quarters very shortly. Mrs. Sherman was excited by the prospect of her early departure on the 16th and was relieved to have her family so comfortably housed. The banker hoped to be able to hold his expenses to $400 a month. With business at a low ebb, and real estate almost unsalable, he found it hard to understand why the cost of living remained about as high as ever.

In San Francisco, he wrote, "everything wears a most gloomy face . . . the city credit is dead. Warrants are of no value and repudiation . . . may be attempted. This will materially hurt us as we hold some $40,000 on our own account and as much more as collateral for notes." Sherman reported that the bank was restricting its lending to a very low minimum of short-time paper of the highest credit.

> We are strong and intend so to remain until we hear what effect the news of the general smash here will create at home. I apprehend when in St. Louis it is known that the house here has failed [i.e., Page, Bacon & Co.] that there will be a run again on Page & Bacon and should it force them to close again, I feel certain this house will no longer struggle . . . but go into liquidation. This cannot but benefit us in the long run, but in the meantime it will shake the public faith in all banks, especially of the St. Louis houses. . . . We are sufficiently warned.
>
> Messrs. Aspinwall and Chauncey [26] are here. They paid a visit to the quicksilver mines [27] and . . . saw the valley of San Jose with which they are perfectly charmed. They see things in their prime and may carry such news that may counteract any unfavorable impression these mercantile houses may produce by their gloomy apprehensions. They go next week to the gold mines where also they will see things in their brightest garb, for there is plenty of water and miners are doing well. All our troubles here result from having spent too much in houses and streets, incurring debts at 3 per cent a month which must ruin anybody who is at all in debt. I hope as times mend, interest will decline but it will not unless securities are better.

Sherman was glad to be able to report one improvement in the bank's business; they were now making money on the sale of exchange. It was costing the bank from 1% to 1½%, while the firm could buy gold bars at from ¾% to ½% off and net a premium of ⅛% on them in New York.* After deducting costs and shipping charges this resulted in a clear profit to the bank.

The elder Mr. Page of Page, Bacon & Co. had called on Sherman frequently. The latter's sympathy was aroused by his changed appearance. Page solicited Sherman's support of a proposal that had been made by Mr. Aspinwall—that the San Francisco banks discontinue the sale of sight drafts on New York for more than $1,000. Aspinwall, in lieu of same, would have the

* For explanation of these terms, see Appendix, "Sherman's Banking Terminology."

banks issue all these larger drafts at three days' sight. Sherman could see advantages in this and although unwilling to bind himself, did attend a conference at Page, Bacon & Co.'s new banking room to discuss the proposal. For the first time since the run of February 23, he encountered Henry Haight; he looked "cut down terribly." Aspinwall's proposal was fully debated, but in the end Sherman's idea of a higher charge for exchange was generally favored; namely, 3½% on bills payable at sight and 3% on three days' sight bills. This was later modified to 3¼%.* An agreement was drawn and was circulated for signature by all the bankers. Everyone agreed except Drexel, Sather & Church. Drexel, described by Sherman as "a cautious old fox," wanted a day's delay to think over the idea and to consult his partners. Drexel, said Sherman, "did not clearly define his objections." Sherman had inserted a condition in the plan: "provided it met the concurrence of the principal dealers of exchange in California." He cynically weighed the chances of success: "The bankers here are guilty of the same sin that afflicts the whole community, viz a willingness to sign any obligation and bolt it when their interest requires it. All have plenty of excuses to justify themselves."

Sherman had dined with Mr. Aspinwall, and the latter had offered his services in seeing that Mrs. Sherman was offered every courtesy and care during her approaching voyage. A lad of sixteen who would be a fellow traveler was going to assist her with her baggage in crossing the Isthmus. Her father would meet her in New York. The children were well and very happy in their new large yard.

For some time Sherman had felt it advisable from every standpoint that Turner pay another visit to San Francisco. If Turner approved of this suggestion, Sherman hoped that his friend might arrange to come at the time of his wife's return so that Mrs. Sherman might have the benefit of his escort.[28]

* See Appendix, "Sherman's Banking Terminology."

15

Some days later Sherman reported that the *Golden Gate* had brought the first newspaper stories of New York's reaction to San Francisco's Black Friday. The city was astounded to find how casually the East had accepted the news. "It will take us down considerably" wrote Sherman. He then went on to detail further failures in San Francisco—a warehouseman who had issued receipts for nonexistent flour, as well as a large milling concern. The warehouseman was overdrawn on Lucas, Turner & Co.'s ledgers about $1,100. Sherman blamed himself for this loss, as he had taken the man's word that the overdraft would be covered in two days. His alibi was that the failure of the millers had carried him down with them. The same defaulting millers owed the bank $5,000, which was the only remaining note purchased from Burgoyne when he went out of business; Burgoyne had endorsed the $5,000 note, and Sherman was delighted to point out that he held sufficient margin in other collateral taken from Burgoyne to make good the $5,000.

Another failure also was causing Sherman concern. Brown & Keyser, who had built the Lucas-Turner building, had put all their contracting profits into a new brick structure on a leased lot at the corner of Broadway and Dupont Street. A short time before, the old wooden buildings on the site had rented for $1,000 a month. Now the larger and newer improvements had only a few tenants; their rentals totaled only $714 a month, while the ground rent was $750! Sherman had loaned these contractors $5,000 on the security of their lease. He was now trying to negotiate an adjustment with the agents of the absentee owner of the lot. A certain Naglee was one of these agents; Sherman ruefully remembered that Naglee "hates me like pisen [*sic*] and I reciprocate it most cordially." He told Turner that he was reciting all these items because they showed how depressed San Francisco real estate now was.

Despite the discouraging state of both real estate and mercantile business, Lucas, Turner & Co.'s deposits and exchange business had increased but "so far as collecting interest and notes, it is like pulling teeth. We are doing everything to make losses as few and small as possible, but it is evident . . . they will be considerable."

Duncan, Sherman & Co., Page, Bacon & Co.'s former correspondent in New York, had not written to Lucas, Turner & Co. but apparently had made overtures to do business with the firm through the St. Louis partners. Sherman wished "to decline any close alliance. If they make any specific request, we can answer it, but as to opening accounts and using them . . . as agents I think it would be bad policy. . . . Their name smells bad here."

His response to another subject mentioned in Turner's latest letter was even more forthright:

> You . . . ask me in confidence about Garrison.[29] I have seen a good deal of him and unquestionably state that he is a very, very *unsafe* man. He is vigorous, violent but unscrupulous. No criterion but Number One! If I were associated with him in business, I could not sleep. Success has heretofore marked his progress but I think he is catching it now, big licks too. He had to take Horner's property and he was the active agent in selling the city slip property which the courts have decided to be illegal and suits for large amounts are brought against him individually.

Again Sherman was enthusiastic about his new house, especially its large yard, with

> bushes that make it refreshing. The distance is great, but I walk it twice a day sometimes for there are planked streets within one square. It is pretty far for Nisbet, but it is necessary for him to live out with us. He thinks he can get along without a horse and I

think so too. Your nephew is a funny little fellow, very naive and pleasant. As good natured as possible, and has made himself useful and ornamental. I have no doubt he will be of service to us and vice versa.[30]

The next letter dwelt again on Sherman's surprise at

the coolness with which the monied world treats our difficulties and the continued plenty of money and high price of stocks. The knowledge of our true difficulties . . . will manifest themselves by degrees. The run was nothing but . . . property holders and merchants are in debt and are paying 3% a month, which is gradually eating them [illegible] is a slower and more consuming process from which there is no relief. . . . We have had abundant rains. . . . Farmers and miners must do well this year but farm produce is so low that there is no encouragement. In the mines is our true wealth and I shall early in May make a large tour taking the Southern mines and the Northern mines [31] as far up as Shasta, provided always I can snatch an interval between two attacks of asthma to make a fair start. . . . On my way here I called to see Garrison, but he was not in. I left word that I wanted to see him but suppose I must go to his office. You will perceive that he is in trouble with his company. I know that during his agency, he loaned large quantities of money to Horner, Beard, Peter Smith and others, all of whom are dead broke.[32] . . . Garrison has to rely on mortgages, some of which are second. Now this property is utterly unsaleable, taxes are heavy and street assessments worse. If this money be his, he may in time recover it, but if it be the money of others, or of his company—if they press him, he will be in a devil of a way as no money can now be borrowed here on real estate or any kind of city security. Again, he whilst mayor, was instrumental in causing the sale of the slip property, and was one of the commissioners into whose hands the first cash payments went. It seems now there was some flaw in the whole concern. The present city government repudiates the whole transaction and as property has declined so much, the buyers have begun suit against Garrison in his individual capacity for damages and the lawyers think he will be held, in which event he is a gone coon. I shall maintain friendly relations with him and his brother, but devil the cent has either now, or shall they have out of this concern.

The above is what a banker would term a confidential and unfavorable credit report. It is one of the few instances in these letters where the shrewd manager of Lucas, Turner & Co. was apparently proved wrong by future developments. Bancroft, writing about Garrison more than thirty years later, said, "He acquired a princely fortune, with which he transferred himself in 1859 to his native state, there to continue figuring as a magnate." [33]

Sherman reiterated his philosophy as to credit in these disturbing times: "We are operating very closely on the principle of safety rather than profits. . . . It is probable that by this course we may drive away some good and enterprising customers but *n'importe*. The world has not stopped yet."

That same evening Sherman was going to Martinez to attend a sheriff's sale of a ranch against which the bank had levied execution on a judgment for $2,200.[34]

The next letter told of a new development. It was another example of how the free enterprise system, when thwarted on one sector, casts about for new avenues in which to apply its energy and ingenuity. Sherman wrote Turner that "flour and grain have of late been shipped to Europe and even to New York. Flour of native wheat is now quoted at 6 to 7. Imported U.S. 13 to 14." (It is curious to find Sherman referring here to California-grown wheat as "native" and wheat shipped from the Eastern seaboard as "Imported U.S.") "I doubt somewhat whether our native flour will bear the voyage to Europe or New York yet the merchants will test this question and may give an outlet for the surplus. At all events this fact will deter shipments of grain from home and from Chile."

Sherman, in writing his letter of April 30, 1855, little realized that the above incidental paragraph of his letter actually heralded a tremendous change in the economy of California. Often before he had proved himself a shrewd observer. Now as to wheat, it is true he was a cautious and doubting prophet. Within a few years, he could marvel how greatly he had understated his hope that grain shipments from the East and Chile would be deterred; from home or anywhere else he could have added! Five years after he wrote the above, California produced 6 million bushels of wheat. Before the time of his death, this was to grow to 40 million, and California would then be second among all the states in the production of wheat.[35] Even as San Francisco merchants and financiers worried and faltered in the 1850's, a vast new business was awaiting them just a few years ahead—hundreds of windjammers laden with burlap bags of hard durum wheat plowing the seas to Liverpool, Marseilles, and Genoa, to Shanghai and Sydney; grain elevators and long railroad sidings at Port Costa; and flour mills at Stockton and South Vallejo. Behind all these future hives of energy, the great hinterland was about to be quickened and expanded to supply processors and shippers. That quickening and expansion would know changes in emphasis and direction but it would never cease.

Again Sherman was cheerful about the good weather.

> The roads to . . . the mines unobstructed, so that there is a . . . demand for goods of all kinds. The up-river boats go up loaded and the trade to Oregon and coastwise is rapidly increasing. . . . The fact that emigration to us has in a measure ceased . . . dispels the illusion under which we labored when you were here that San Francisco would grow till it became like cities at home. . . . There is less population now here than two years ago.This is no disadvantage for mechanics and loafers are driven to the mines and interior. . . . Every day we become better . . . known. The New Yorkers and Boston people begin to point us out as the safe house through which to send their drafts. . . . Today we have sold about $160,000 of exchange . . . have on hand about $75,000 . . . drafts, $43,000—Government Treasury drafts . . . which cost us from 1½ to 2% premium. Selling at 3 gives us a fair profit. Our bullion stands us ½ off, will likely sell at ⅜ premium, giving us ⅞ profit. Admitting freight, insurance and commissions to amount to 3% an offset to exchange, but not having enough bullion and exchange, we must ship American gold coin on which we barely clear ⅛. Still our rule is to sell all the exchange we can. . . . We think we are right in confining our remittances to bullion and not dust. Therefore have not bought any dust since you left. . . . We

have it run into bars and buy the bars at market say ½ off. Both Rhodes and Robinson Bours & Co. find it more to their profit to sell the dust out and out to some of the freight houses.*

Relations with these interior bankers sometimes produced problems, for example:

> Robinson Bours & Co. did a thing which I checked peremptorily at which they are not well pleased. Without our consent, direct or implied, they had blank drafts struck off, headed "Agency of Lucas, Turner & Co." intending them as drafts on you, on New York and New Orleans. When the blanks were ready, they wrote down that in the way of exchange they considered themselves as acting as our agents and would sign drafts "Lucas Turner & Co. by T. Robinson Bours." The most unadulterated piece of impudence, which I gave them to understand most particularly. Agencies in the interior would be useful, but the risk far overbalances the advantages. I know that Mr. Lucas will not entrust his name to an irresponsible agent.

Sherman had thought of a possible new avenue of safe and profitable business. Let buyers of gold dust in the mining regions ship their gold to Lucas, Turner & Co., the latter to pay them in coin at $16 an ounce. The bank would have the dust converted into coin or bullion for the shipper's account, charging a moderate commission for the service. He planned to explore this idea on his coming visit to the mines. He was going first to the southern mines, then to Sacramento and the northern mines as far as Yreka. If letters to Turner arrived irregularly for awhile, it would be due to this tour.[36]

The vagaries of banking in San Francisco in 1855 are well illustrated by two letters of Sherman's to Turner, both dated May 8. Obviously, they cannot have been written many hours apart, yet their contents and tone present strange contrasts. A reader is struck by the ordeal undergone by their writer because of rumors, garbled intelligence, and sheer inability to ascertain

* See Appendix, "Sherman's Banking Terminology."

the facts. Sherman's experience on that one day was an incontrovertible argument for an overland telegraph system. The handicap of delayed communication seriously crippled any business operation even in normal times. When bank and mercantile failures had already undermined public confidence, this forced reliance on postal intelligence, always several weeks old, was too great to be borne. A man's reason and nervous system could not be expected to withstand such tension.

The first letter reported the *Sonora's* arrival on May 1 with news of the final failure of Page & Bacon.[37]

> A new tumult arose and amidst it the rumor got abroad that Lucas & Simonds had failed—how, why or wherefore was a mystery, and yet through the night of the first it was universal. It was said some of our drafts had come back protested. Our letters from New York and St. Louis were most flattering and one from the Bank contained the telegraphic despatch from you of April 4, announcing to them the failure of P & B and that it occasioned no excitement, that on the contrary P. & B. had turned over to you their collections. To our numerous friends who called during the night we showed these letters, and they carried them around to all the papers. Still the report was so general, and so perfectly is all confidence destroyed that we knew that we would have a renewal of the scenes of last February. So we sat up all night, posted up and saw exactly where we stood. During the last month we have made very large payments, $75,000 to the city, of borrowed monies, and $137,000 remitted to cover our bills for the Burgoyne purchase. So we were not so strong as a few weeks ago. Nevertheless we feared not.

Sherman was apprehensive that the report which he was sure was false, would be swiftly carried into the interior. "This will of the wisp was harder to combat than a real substantial danger. Late at night a person from the *Alta California* . . . said a friend . . . had actually seen one of our drafts for $45,000 protested." Sherman recalled that Lucas, Turner & Co. had issued drafts for that amount to Burgoyne, payable at various dates in the future. Since none was due at the time the mails left the East, it could not have been protested for nonpayment.

> I had a friend trace the rumor from mouth to mouth till it finally settled down on a Mr. Cohen,[38] one of the assignees of Adams & Company who then exhibited a notary's certificate of protest of Page, Bacon & Company's order on Duncan, Sherman & Co. for our draft in favor of Burgoyne & Co. for $45,000 due May 19. . . . Cohen swore he heard the rumor before he opened . . . the above protest. It was so outrageous a perversion that Tom Stevens of the Navy [39] volunteered to whip Cohen. . . . I could hardly restrain him, but went myself and saw Cohen at Palmer, Cook & Co. and told him what a villainous thing I thought it was, but Cohen obstinately denied participating in the rumor, but he lied for that was the draft the editor of the California saw. Nothing like a protested draft was seen here. In the evening paper I offered a thousand dollars reward for any draft of ours protested for non-payment and on the morning of the 3rd, published this explanation. Nevertheless strange to say so perfectly is all confidence in banking and Bankers' cards destroyed that a slow gradual decrease of our deposits occurred. . . . Deposits have been drawn out in the past week by depositors who were not disturbed during the great run. . . . I have felt more sore about this than the former trouble for it has been like a slow pestilence in camp, with none of the exciting influences of an ordinary panic. . . . This ruinous failure of Page & Bacon impairs our credit and prospects. If *they* fail people contend *we* may. All with whom we converse hold out the brilliant prospect to which we succeed but this slow reduction of our deposits shows their words and actions do not tally.

Several small business failures had resulted from this latest panic. Some of these unfortunates were customers of the bank which was thus indirectly involved. However, confidence in Lucas, Turner & Co. was slowly being restored and by May 8, they were again selling some exchange—always a barometer of the public's trust.

The Nicaragua steamer arrived on May 7, with New York mails to the 12th of April (Sherman in error wrote "May 12"). "Everything still prospers there," he noted. "No news of the failure of Lucas & Simonds, so that is dead."

Sherman had gone to Sacramento on May 4 to lend what influence he could to the passage of the funding bill for San

Francisco's debt. The bill was passed, providing for a refinancing at a rate of 6%. The banker felt his presence was unnecessary, there was such "an universal concurrence of opinion . . . this will at once make saleable securities which have laid dead in our hands for months." Sherman planned to exchange the bank's warrants for bonds and ship the latter to New York either as collateral or for sale as need should determine.

Sherman expressed himself as agreeably surprised at the prosperous state of affairs in Sacramento;

> . . . the levees increased and strengthened. I, J. and K. Streets raised as high as the levees and planked. . . . A very handome house (state or court) is erected on the site of the old one burnt down. Business too looked brisk, every steamer arriving . . . loaded down and even sailing vessels were carrying freight. I am told . . . interior towns are in like manner prosperous . . . all the doom falls upon this city. Now that P. & B. are broke sure, I suppose we can count on no more *after* claps.[40]

Unfortunately we do not know how many hours intervened before the second letter of May 8 was written; probably it was the product of the midnight hours. "The day is over . . . and the tide has turned," it cheerfully begins. Deposits had been declining at rate of nearly $50,000 a day. On May 7, the bank held only $180,000 in coin and bullion.

> Today deposits have increased to $1,250,000 [this figure is scarcely legible] and several new accounts, among them Wm. T. Coleman & Co.[41] son-in-law of Mr. Page. This is owing to the news by steamer last night that Lucas & Simonds had not only not failed but that P & B had turned over to you their collection paper. Now that Page & Bacon are dead, this heavy cloud that has lowered over us so long will clear away and everything will assume a better tone. I'm glad it is passed and if you . . . keep your business in hand, I'll pledge my best efforts, body and mind to keep this house safe and sound. No amount of profits will induce me to risk beyond the monies absolutely in our control. We cannot operate on our deposits here, further than to use a small part for call loans of the quickest kind and for gradually accumulating bars for shipment. I know this will meet your

> sanction. People tell me we don't make enough noise, don't publish enough, don't operate for [illegible] but I know such reputation is illusory. I would rather have the reputation of the safest, most prudent and best conducted bank of the country than all the newspaper fame that preceded the down fall of Adams & Co. I have heard from various quarters that orders are being received by merchants here to remit our drafts. This must follow as a matter of course from the name of the home house.

Sherman ventured the guess that on the approaching 16th, Lucas-Turner's shipment would be close to $250,000; moreover, the bank was now netting very close to 1% on exchange sales.

In addition to the good news about the restoration of San Francisco's credit as a municipality, Sherman informed Turner that the city had a new charter that would prevent it from incurring further indebtedness and should diminish the cost of local government. Many land titles had been confirmed by the land commission. The miners were insuring greater permanence for their industry by constructing many ditch systems. Altogether, Sherman thought he saw signs of better times to come; "if I am right, we are in the exact position to be advantaged by them. . . . We are as easy as an old shoe." [42]

The banker's third letter written to Turner on May 8, was headed "Confidential" and had scrawled across its face: "Confidential for Major Turner or Mr. Lucas." It referred to a communication received from Turner about Nisbet and continued:

> His character is identically the same as when you knew him. He is vain, young and of bad manners. Has no reverence for years, no respect for superior education or any qualities but money. This is the fault of his training and education. He is good hearted and is certainly an adept at figures and the transaction of ordinary business but has no general comprehensive sense. . . . He has the keenest instinct at detecting a failure and I confess he has saved us from several missteps into which I would have been betrayed. . . . He has qualities that I have not and vice versa. Therefore, he is helpful to us. My whole study has been to let him improve as his years come on, and it was partly for this purpose that I wanted

him last Spring to go home and stay there a few months that he might see we could get along without him. Events have however given an opportunity for he sees that had he been alone here, this house would have been swept [away] in a single day. He has *no friends*. . . . He is only friendly with the prosperous, and an open enemy to a failing house. His manner has offended many gentlemen whose good will is very important to us. I have spoken to him about it and he has always exhibited such signs of contrition that he's made me hope for improvement. The simple idea of his position is enough to inflate a young man. If he were old, modest and industrious, he would be invaluable, but as he is, his merits and demerits are so nearly balanced that it is a question which way the balance turns. G.[43] was mistaken in saying that he frequents bawdy houses. He has lived in Bowman's family for more than a year and always slept at home. He did drink a good deal once and when in liquor is a perfect dunce, but for many months he has almost entirely abstained. A visit of six months home would benefit him much, but things are now so placed that he cannot be spared. . . . for the present I do not think it politic or prudent to do anything hasty or rash. Permanency is a desirable feature in a bank. I have no trouble in maintaining my position as Head and if the safety . . . or . . . material interests demand it, I believe I . . . could be harsh. . . . I defy anybody to point out a more faithful set than our office exhibits. . . . When the rumor got out . . . they sat up all night til 7: A.M. and were at their desks at 9: for which I . . . complimented them. . . . All of P. B. & Co. employees have been here offering their services but I don't want them. Their school was a bad one, the one that gave Nisbet his bad features. . . . Even Haight offered his in any capacity. Think of that. Your proud man (not to me but to Nisbet). Haight knows . . . I think he was privy to a desire to break us to soften his fall. . . . He was not at all concerned in the story last raised, that I know, but it would be wrong for us to aid . . . any member of that House.

Sherman hoped Turner would come to San Francisco in the fall and remain three or four months as a guest in his home. If possible he urged Turner to make the trip at the time of Mrs. Sherman's return from the East, so that he might serve as her escort.[44]

A strange circumstance lurked in the background of the concluding paragraph of this letter. When he bought the Harrison Street residence, Sherman borrowed $7,000 from Lucas & Simonds. He now wrote: "I'll arrange that $7,000 note next mail and diminish Bragg's account by that sum." This suggests that Major Braxton Bragg was another of Sherman's army friends whose funds, left with his bank for investment, were called by him his "trust accounts." The two men had known each other at West Point. That acquaintance had ripened into friendship during the Seminole campaign in Florida. A few years later they were to become even closer during Sherman's brief career as superintendent of the Louisiana State Seminary of Learning and Military Academy. Bragg was to be influential in securing that post for his friend. Yet within a decade, these two were to command opposing armies on the field of battle, where one was to suffer defeat and final surrender as a prisoner of war to his good friend, the San Francisco banker of 1855.

16

It was May 14; the banker wrote: "We have dragged through another hard week's business—dull and suspicious—all accounts drawn to the lowest notch, and some of our best exchange customers buying coin and shipping on their own account." Sherman did not wonder at this when he considered how the public's confidence had been betrayed.

> We have got to be patient and live down such mistrust. . . . The country . . . never was in a more prosperous condition . . . and so late and plentiful have been the rains that the farm products must be large enough to supply all possible wants and afford considerable for export. . . . Factories of different kinds are being established such as breweries, starch factories, etc. A law has passed to stop all gambling houses and a vote is to be taken on the Maine Liquor Law.

Page, Bacon & Co.'s failure was still a very live topic in San Francisco.

> Feeling against Mr. Page for having withdrawn so much money from this house is deep and bitter, and . . . against the other partners for having permitted it, but more especially for making such representations after the first failure as induced their friends here to endorse for them to the extent of four hundred thousand dollars, besides renewing their business whereby hundreds of thousands were sent forward in . . . exchange which must return protested. . . . This return of drafts which were paid for . . . holds the community in suspense . . . a dread of failure in quarters where it is difficult to guard against. . . . Real estate remains

depressed on account of the quantity . . . in . . . foreclosure and sale. Page-Bacon's new bank, their splendid property corner of Clay and Montgomery and other valuable property must be sold. . . . Also our *vis a vis* Wright's Bank. . . . An immense quantity of most valuable real estate must be sold this summer . . . will keep property down and rents also.

The next paragraph sounds incredible.

A new bank with capital of 3 millions of francs is contemplated under the management of Argenti[45] with Haight as Cashier; the locality . . . a new house on Kearny Street corner of Sacramento. Argenti has bad personal standing, was forced to stop business two years ago by reason of bad moral character, keeping a woman openly and on one occasion taking her to a ball, where both were ignominiously expelled. I know him well enough to believe no project of his can command confidence, nor can Haight now exercise any good influence. He intimated to Nisbet his desire to come into our employment but I refused peremptorily any thought of it. One day I met Mr. Page on the street. . . . He spoke of his high respect for Mr. Lucas, but called Simonds an old Presbyterian, etc. and then remarked . . . "I hear you offered that fellow Haight $1,000 a month to come into your employment!" I told him it was utterly false . . . and he expressed himself pleased to hear it. I infer there is a complete breach between all the partners. . . . Page & Bacon blown to atoms . . . venom and hatred . . . sown among them.*

It was time to close the mails so Sherman ended this brief letter: "We have had a right busy day, but . . . balances smaller at night than morning . . . sold only $85,000 exchange."[46]

Perhaps the shortest letter in the whole collection—less than a page long—tells that the *John L. Stevens* had just brought the startling news of the wreck of the *Golden Age*[47] on which Mrs. Sherman was a passenger. Her husband was immensely relieved to learn that there had been no loss of life.[48]

At the end of the month, the banker was still conscious that the fall of Page-Bacon had hurt Lucas, Turner & Co.,

* See Appendix, "The Page-Bacon Failures as Viewed by F. W. Page."

. . . because it brings discredit to our locality. . . . Had it not been for that idle rumor we should have led off in the new era, but Drexel, Sather & Church have the advantage. Their stand, corner of Clay & Montgomery, is better than ours [the first time Sherman ever admitted a location two blocks farther south was better than the Lucas-Turner site] and they evidently control large capital. Our neighborhood has been sadly afflicted by recent events, hardly a solvent house within a block of us save Pioche, Bayerque and ourselves. . . . We are at an end of the street, an end pointing to deep water but its rapid development of last year is checked. . . . Selling goods has revived because the miners are doing well. . . . Our city is too large for its business. . . . There is more money in town now than ever before, but it is not in the banks, nor do borrowers know where to find it.

Sherman expected that this money would ultimately be invested in real estate, but the high taxes were a deterrent, "how the cat will jump, I can't say." In the meantime, the bank's deposits had increased slightly and on the day he wrote, more than $200,000 in exchange had been sold.

"You speak rather mysteriously of something you are going to tell me soon, but as I am not personally interested I can afford to wait." Then as if to belie his own words, he added:

Look out, we all have a share of curiosity and I rather think you are down on Mr. Simonds. I confess I have a grudge against him for I took the trouble to send to China for miniatures for his family, which commission I thought was handsomely executed though he never had the politeness even to acknowledge their receipt. You also hint that the home house ought to have a man like me at its head. Fortunately you cannot see two thousand miles the blush of a modest man. I do believe you have not meant to flatter, but really are deceived into the belief that I am *some*, but don't let that belief carry you beyond a fair amount of confidence. . . . You must know by this time that I don't love money but that ambition is mixed with my plans. I am going to accept . . . to have my salary $6,000 in lieu of $10,000 on the condition ratified by the House that interest on capital should be let up. . . . You give us a capital of $200,000 and we do the work for our respective shares. Our expenses . . . are high . . . [and] added to

> $16,000 a year of interest would be a greater load than the capital should bear. As it now stands, it is simple, fair and right, and . . . gives me the nerve . . . for tight occasions. I am fully aware that in foregoing the $4,000 increase, I benefit Nisbet to an extent of ⅛ of $16,000 or $2,000, but the success of this house is my first interest; if it prosper and rise . . . I . . . have an occupation, a living salary better than any immediate savings. If . . . misfortune [should] occur . . . my reputation and occupation would be gone.

Sherman then told Turner that a few days before he had been offered the nomination of the Regular Democratic Party for city treasurer at a salary of $4,000 per annum. His duties would have required not more than two hours a day of his time, with a clerk paid by the city. He had told the committee that waited on him that he was not a politician and not a Democrat.

> I never voted for a President in my life. My family, friends, and relatives are nearly all Whigs. They said if I would run, no questions would be asked . . . except if I were a Know Nothing. I admitted I was not a Know Nothing, but . . . I preferred to stand back to be sure the Whig Party has ceased to exist. . . . I . . . therefore declined the nomination.

Shortly after reaching Lancaster, Mrs. Sherman read with mixed feelings her husband's letter saying that he had declined the nomination for city treasurer. Added to the family's annual income, $4,000 would have been most welcome to her; also, if "Cump" had accepted the Democratic nomination, she would have rejoiced to see him triumph over the Know Nothings. As a devoted Catholic, she feared and disliked that political party because it was strongly anti-Catholic. Yet she was also a loyal wife, so wrote her husband: "Such is my confidence in your good judgment, I knew at once that you had made the proper choice."

Reverting to the wreck of the *Golden Age*, Sherman wrote:

> Mrs. Sherman has always dreaded such an event, but . . . she suffered so little . . . I am in hopes she will feel that shipwrecks

> are not such dreadful things. . . . All travellers should experience a wreck once . . . that delightful sensation of timbers grinding and crashing underneath. The huge mass of iron and timber and copper cracking and splitting under ocean's powerful grasp like dry leaves in the hands of a strong man. I despair of Mrs. S. ever getting a reasonable, a practical view of such things for she will not be convinced that the Creator made *all* the world for use of civilized man or that the sea was made for any purpose but to drown people who are fools enough not to stay at home. Nevertheless when there was danger, she was cool and brave.

He turned to affairs of the bank and continued:

> I have been to Sacramento, also to Benicia and along the Contra Costa [49] and Monte Diablo. In a few days I go to Stockton, Sonora and Southern Mines. . . . My principal object is to make acquaintances. . . . I do not intend to establish an agency in this country but if we can get parties to remit us gold dust for coinage or to be run into bars, we can afford to advance after receipt of dust, at a reasonable rate and with commissions.

Surprisingly enough, he reported "all is smooth again; money is easy . . . old debts being settled as fast as could be expected." One good bit of news; he had collected a $7,000 draft on the S. S. *America* transaction, with 10% a year interest and a 3% that must have been a commission. Lucas, Turner & Co. had originally handled this deal for Wadsworth & Sheldon of New York, which had since failed, owing Lucas-Turner on other accounts. Sherman was now insistent that this latest recovery not be paid to Wadsworth & Sheldon or to their successors but be applied to their indebtedness to Lucas, Turner & Co., which would reduce that loss to about $2,000.[50]

Turner had been urging Sherman to put into effect his proposal of three- or five-day sight drafts mentioned in earlier letters. He regretfully reported that he had been unable to secure agreement among the other bankers to follow the proposed practice. Drexel, Sather & Church were leaders in the opposition to the plan. "Without a joint action . . . it would be suicidal for us to attempt it."

Again he ruefully admitted that Drexel, Sather & Church were giving Lucas-Turner stiff competition since Page, Bacon & Co.'s enforced retirement from the field. Sherman was not sure he knew the reasons for this:

> It may be that many say . . . if Page can fail so shamefully, any St. Louis house may do the same or . . . that cursed rumor turned people's suspicions against us; it may be I have been over cautious, or . . . maybe our bank is inconveniently located to the bulk of business. . . . There is no use concealing it that business has returned to Clay, Sacramento and California Streets. Along Jackson Street some of the heaviest failures have occurred . . . houses under execution or . . . foreclosure. . . . Yet I am not discouraged.

One interesting sign of progress was that the mint was now turning out coin at the rate of $100,000 a day. All of the gold was now going there rather than to the assay offices, and coming out in $20 pieces instead of in bars. There was less profit to the bank in shipping coin than bullion, but this was only a reiteration of Sherman's old contention that the exchange business had never been profitable.

The land commissioners were continuing to confirm many of the Spanish and Mexican land grants. One of these especially interested Sherman—the so-called Bolton and Barron Claim, covering three square leagues of land that included the Mission Dolores (San Francisco de Asís) and much valuable property around it. This title had been confirmed on June 5, 1855. The United States Supreme Court on March 10, in approving John C. Frémont's title to Las Mariposas Rancho, established a principle that the commissioners applied in the Bolton and Barron case.[51] This land was owned by a Philadelphia association that had been incorporated. Sherman had taken thirty of its shares as collateral on one Horner's indebtedness to the bank.[52] At the time, the value of these shares was quite problematical; now they should bring anywhere from $30,000 to $60,000. Sherman had sent the stock to Turner some time before, and feared it had passed out of the firm's control. But if Lucas-Turner still owned it—the prospect thrilled the banker! He wrote that the land commissioners' decision "has produced a perfect howl among the squatters, who hang everybody even Chief Justice Taney, in effigy. So the race of fools is not dead yet, even in California." Palmer, Cook & Co. were heavily interested in the Bolton and Barron Claim and two of the firm were sailing for New York, even as Sherman wrote, presumably because of this favorable development.[53]

A grim line in the next letter reminds us that the steamer trip to San Francisco in the 1850's was not exactly a pleasure cruise to the tropics: "Nicaragua steamer yesterday. Cholera killed twenty-two on the *Cortes*, but the Panama route is healthy."

Turner evidently had written that the New York firm of Duncan, Sherman & Co. were thinking of opening a bank in San Francisco.

> They would start brash [commented Sherman], but soon would haul in, for they would be beset by borrowers to cover up old [illegible]. The only thing that can save the old fogies is to obtain money at lower interest for with rents and property steadily falling, it bears hard on them to be paying 2 to 3 per cent [a month]. It has killed Folsom[54] prematurely. . . . As near as I can ascertain, his debts amount to about $325,000. His estate used to be valued at $2,000,000 . . . enough was improved to yield . . . $20,000 a month . . . recently fallen off to . . . about $10,000 to $14,000. . . . Unless his executors can [secure] a large loan elsewhere, the interest will eat up the estate. . . . Folsom would never sell but leased and . . . it worried his life in compromising and suing lessees and collecting rents. . . . One who inherits San Francisco property is good for a martyr's fate. Poor Folsom, I knew him as a cadet and in his better years before wealth sealed up the fountains of feeling once bright and fair. Of late he has been morose and cross, but always energetic, fair and honorable.

Sherman ascribed to Folsom "more than any twenty men" the credit for having the alcalde titles confirmed by the city. Halleck, Peachy, and Van Winkle[55] were the executors named in Folsom's three-year-old will. Sherman was sure Folsom would have remade the testament had he been warned that death was imminent. He was convinced that Folsom planned to found a charitable or educational institution, rather than leave his fortune to his family, because "his mother is married against Folsom's wish and he has seen little or nothing of his family since he went to West Point."

Sherman reported that another of San Francisco's wealthy leaders, William D. M. Howard, was very ill at a farm near San Mateo. Coming to California a little before the Gold Rush, he had, like Folsom, prospered amazingly in a few years but like him had burned himself out in the process and was to die, still in his thirties, in 1856.

"A great many here," Sherman wrote Turner, "are going through . . . bankruptcy. . . . There must be an immense quantity of dishonesty for the bankrupts are really living more comfortably than those who pay their way."

As a postscript to the subject of "California coins," dealt with in an earlier chapter, it is interesting to read Sherman's comment on the change now rapidly taking place:

> New bullion is becoming more and more scarce . . . and we will, each steamer, be forced to send more and more coin, or what is the same thing, mint bars. So many counterfeit slugs are in circulation that all the banks have refused them, and we now buy them as bullion according to fineness. The old slug is now obsolete. Soon will follow other California coins, and it will not be long before we have nothing in circulation but the U.S. coin. Now it becomes us to prepare for this—a merchant can ship his own coin as cheap as we can. He can insure of Aspinwall at 1⅛, and can therefore afford to ship his coin at about the price we charge for exchange. Therefore the large merchants now send the actual gold instead of bills. How can this be remedied? . . . We influence the agents of the steamship companies and we do get Garrison to return ¼% if the bills of lading are signed, receipted and paid for, so that he may assert, as he does . . . that he charges and we do pay 1½ freight. This is a subterfuge that is disagreeable to me and does not elevate Garrison in my esteem. . . . Now comes insurance . . . in which we have reason to expect a reduction—1½ is too high; it is more than Aspinwall charges and places

us at a ⅜ disadvantage . . .* We must know exactly what we have to pay, and if others get [it] at less, we ought to get the same else we compete at a disadvantage. I intend to write a pretty strong letter to the bank. [Sherman probably meant the Metropolitan Bank in New York, or Schuchardt & Gebhard, of the same city, with whom Lucas, Turner & Co. had been doing business since the failure of Wadsworth & Sheldon.] I have already alluded to the subject to them but have not given it the weight it merits. So long as I feel that on all exchange . . . we are losing money, I can't . . . exert myself to enlarge the business. Glory is poor enough in the army but infinitely more so in business.

Sherman said that his wife was "getting impatient about us out here. I write her the most encouraging accounts of the children." He had feared that Turner might wish to visit San Francisco before Mrs. Sherman was ready to return. Now the situation was reversed. Turner felt he could not leave his wife just yet, so Sherman was going to write Mrs. Sherman to defer her homecoming until Turner would be available as an escort. On the east-bound trip the selection of an escort at the last moment had worked quite well, but Sherman was unwilling to risk finding as happy a solution of that problem for her return to San Francisco, "the scramble among passengers this way is worse than going Eastward."

Then follows the first intimation that Sherman had changed his mind about the prospects of the firm in the years to come.

I take it the great fame of D. D. Page was the impulse in James H. Lucas' mind that resulted in the establishment of this bank. D. D. Page is fallen and infamy has succeeded his past good name. The California bubble has burst, and we have escaped. Now how does Mr. L. feel? Does he still wish to have $300,000 of his fortune here 6000 miles away [56] among an adventurous gambling community? I don't want to represent things worse than they are but if Mr. Lucas has changed his mind and doubts the policy of saving [?] his estate, of establishing some of his family here, it is time for

* See Appendix, "Sherman's Banking Terminology."

him to think of it, and to impart to you and to me such change of mind.

Were the case a new one, I am satisfied you would not establish a house here, for you have a reliable basis of wealth, population and of credit in St. Louis to use profitably all your money and time. Whereas here, it is no use in saying that Mr. Lucas' wealth is unknown. Our general reputation in New York is gradually being felt, and here we are pretty well known as careful, prudent people. Yet we cannot claim any more excellent position than our neighbors. I throw out these ideas that Mr. Lucas may freely impart to you any change of opinion growing out of the change of circumstances. . . . As he is the wealth of the house . . . should he desire it . . . I think I could gradually withdraw so as to suffer no material losses, or impair his good reputation. We have . . . a good start, a fair prospect and as I gain experience, we ought to make more money, but of course you must keep in view some successor, for if we have many such years as this, one man could not stand it long, without relief.

Reilly was expected to go East on the August 15 steamer, and be in St. Louis before October. The time of his return to California was uncertain. "Reilly is honest, true and faithful and has enough brains for a plain, un-educated man, of not enlarged views. He is *not* a Know Nothing." [57]

As an afterthought the banker added that he had recently made a short trip to Benicia "and another to the quicksilver mines in company with Steptoe.[58] Steptoe remains at Benicia to await some action of the President regarding his qualified declension of the governorship of Utah." [59]

The correspondence of two intimate friends is usually excellent source material for one who chronicles their activities. However, he can find himself seriously handicapped when one man's letters are unavailable. In the instant case, we find Sherman in July was about to advise his wife to postpone her return to California because Henry Turner could not leave his own wife and escort Mrs. Sherman on the trip. Yet in reading between the lines of the very next letter from Sherman to Turner (in St. Louis), we must conclude that Turner in the intervening three months had visited San Francisco and returned to St. Louis! Why did he so swiftly change his plans, just when did he arrive, how active was he in the affairs of Lucas, Turner & Co. while in San Francisco, and when did he leave there for his home? The records available afford no answers to these questions, and since those answers were known to both parties, they naturally are nowhere spelled out in Sherman's subsequent letters to Turner.

Turner's stay at the new home on Harrison Street with Sherman's family, and his other activities while in California would make an interesting story. Was he in the bank, for instance, on September 13, when a Chinaman was arrested for trying to pass adulterated gold coin? Maybe he detected the attempted fraud [60] or summoned the police. No doubt the dignified Major Turner's account of such an incident would be well worth reading, but this is not a work of fiction, so it must go unread.

17

Late one Sunday evening in November, 1855, Sherman commenced a letter—"not knowing how I will conclude," said he. San Francisco bankers still had to worry about the weaker brethren among them. Two days before, Sherman had been informed that one of the smaller banking firms, Sanders & Brenham,[61] could not survive next steamer day unless someone supplied them with $30,000. If they received that help, they would immediately give notice of their withdrawal from business and pay off their certificate holders and depositors. Without the $30,000—they must fail. Another bank disaster, even though a small one, could spell trouble for all the other houses, so Drexel, Sather & Church; Wells Fargo & Co.; Palmer, Cook & Co.;[62] and Lucas, Turner & Co. agreed to let them have the required money. On Sunday, Garrison, together with Jones of Palmer, Cook & Co.,[63] called to inform Sherman that Sanders & Brenham would not open the following morning and that the $30,000 advance was in jeopardy. A conference developed the fact that depositors were drawing out their money rapidly. If the assistance rendered by the four good Samaritans did not prevent a failure, then they "would have a bad set of effects to divide amongst us." Sanders & Brenham also now asked for another $30,000, but Sherman refused to advance a quarter of this amount. If the endangered bank could not find four other friends who would supply this additional fund, then, insisted Sherman, they must refund the original advance. Otherwise, he felt very sure the first $30,000 would disappear in a futile attempt to stave off failure.

Sherman informed Turner that, should he become convinced that Sanders & Brenham would not weather the storm, then he proposed to withhold two or three boxes from his contemplated shipment of bullion on the next steamer. This could come in very handy if the failure of this one house started another run on all the banks. "San Francisco is an awful place for a panic. We have no place to look for assistance and of course we could not in an hour collect in our monies. Our notes are about as you left us." (This last sentence is the first positive reference to Turner's recent presence in San Francisco.)

The country was suffering from "drought in the mountains. No gold coming down at all." The bank was being very conservative in extending credit, but as evidence that the small amount loaned was of the best quality, Sherman proudly pointed out that of $75,000 of notes falling due on the previous Saturday, not one missed payment.

At five o'clock on Monday morning the banker added a postscript to report on Sunday night's final conference of the four banks. Sanders & Brenham had cut their second plea to $18,000; if supplied that sum, they felt they could carry out the program first proposed. Garrison offered to raise this amount, but required a first call on the assets to protect it. This would have left the $30,000 advance unsecured. Sherman refused, and Mr. Sather backed him in this position. After long discussion, Sanders & Brenham, as Sherman put it,

> caved in, paid us our $7,500 each and agreed to close. I don't think their failure will produce any feeling, I believe it has been anticipated. But if it should, it is at a very unfortunate moment when all the banks are short. We have not exchanged checks yet with other banks and cannot tell how accounts stand. We hold $300,000 of checks, but know not how many are against us.

(This was before there was a clearing house in San Francisco. Each bank had to send its representative to every other bank to present checks for payment.) "We have only $130,000 [?] in coin which is low, but would suffice always the day after steamer [day] when nothing is done but to try and recuperate from the strain of the day before." Lucas-Turner's Marysville correspondent had also drawn some $20,000 of checks against a gold shipment which had not yet arrived. If Sherman refused payment, it would break the Marysville bank. "So it seems," he concluded this dreary recital, "there is a concurrence of tight circumstances this morning." Small wonder that he said he had only slept some two or three hours and was now finishing with the mail and "looking around" before the bank opened.

He admitted to feeling "anxious that no stampede . . . occur. . . . Of course want of sleep may make my nerves less strong than usual, but I must scan the accounts . . . and throw out every check that overdraws or raise some money before bank hours." Sherman also planned to warn some of his heavier depositors about wild rumors that might start from the news of Sanders & Brenham's failure. Should the mail steamer delay its departure, he promised to write Turner a later report.[64]

The next day Sherman was happy to be able to advise his friend that their neighbors' failure "has seemingly produced no effect. Everybody knew they . . . had no capital." When one large firm withdrew its balance, Sanders & Brenham were left without resources. "They also are good livers," Sherman commented, "and their expenses have gone beyond their earnings." It had proved to be an unimportant incident, but his concluding line eloquently reflects the state of the writer's nerves: "The simple feeling that our depositors . . . are all here on the spot and may demand in an instant all their money, whilst we must wait till our notes mature is the most acute and harassing that I can conceive of."[65]

Sherman's next letter starts in a relaxed, domestic vein: ". . . Sunday evening. I have just finished dinner, seen the children in bed . . . kindled a fire and am now seated in the room you occupied." That forenoon the banker had taken a long horseback ride with a friend named McKee—out to the Mission and the high hills behind it, then to the ocean beach, returning by the Presidio.

Then he went into detail about the Sanders & Brenham collapse, adding: "All the papers commented on it in every style of ridicule and satire, flinging . . . at all banks the fact that the public has no means to know what constitutes our capital or what use it is put to. No names were used by any save James King of William, who excepted Drexel, Sather & Church, Tallant & Wilde [66] and ourselves. King all the time is pitching into Palmer, Cook & Company." [67]

King published a steamer edition of his new paper, *The Evening Bulletin*, and Sherman sent Turner the latest copy, and continued about this editor:

> He says all banks use their deposits . . . although any sensible man knows that we could not afford to hire an expensive room, employ clerks . . . and do all the labor . . . keeping accounts without some return, yet there is a class of people who think their idle dollars are kept ready for them at all times. . . . Our deposits have fallen off about $100,000. . . . Merchants all have laid in large stocks of goods. . . . As yet the rains . . . have been so slight as not to have the . . . effect of getting out the gold. . . . The upcountry merchants are all behind . . . in their payments. . . . Consequently those here are short . . . peculiarly the case with the jobbers, who must pay . . . importers and are yet not in receipt of their own money. . . . Tomorrow . . . I will be beset by applications . . . we cannot grant. . . . Jobbers have active accounts, draw large checks . . . make large deposits but . . . their balances are small . . . often on the wrong side. . . . However . . . [they are] the best credit and the best papers for discount. . . . Their presumption is great and I have given several offense by refusing them discounts and . . . actually returning their checks [unpaid].

Then follows our first intimation that Nisbet is now in St. Louis: "Nisbet will be astonished to learn that I actually so refused Castle Bros., Schloss Bros. and McKee.[68] All came to me in anger but soon found they reckoned without their host." (Here a defaced letter sheet prevents verbatim quotation. Enough is legible to tell us that Sherman warned these customers that checks refused payment must be blamed on the parties signing them, knowing there were insufficient balances in their accounts, and *not* on the banker who declined to make an involuntary and unauthorized loan.) The next passage reveals not only Sherman's philosophy as a banker but also the state of his nerves in these uneasy times:

> I am determined not to put myself in the power of these men, even if I break down our business, for the danger is great of letting them let up [on] their customers and lean on us without limit, and the anxiety to myself individually is too great for endurance. . . .
>
> I have got my discounts down to $550,000 and have only promised some $10,000 for tomorrow whilst we have $50,000 due, so that I feel easy. . . . I propose to bring our discounts down to $500,000 and keep them there . . . for the feeling against all banks is now chronic. The palmy days are past and time alone can decide the future for the banking interests of California. We are making a steady dead loss on our exchanges, and can't help ourselves unless we promise the contract for Treasury drafts or unless you succeeded in getting reduced rates of freight and insurance. [It is evident that Turner had undertaken on his return to the East to seek relief on freight and insurance rates charged the bank. The reference to "the contract for Treasury drafts" is not clear.] And in discounts we are almost restricted to the moneys actually belonging to us, as such are beyond the call of parties here.

Schuchardt & Gebhard, the bank's New York correspondent, had just arranged to let Lucas, Turner & Co. draw on a number of European banks. Sherman planned to advertise these new connections in the hope of developing additional business.

Then follows the news that Sherman expected his wife to return soon on the *Golden Gate*, accompanied by Nisbet and perhaps Reilly. The latter was on Sherman's black books:

> I feel more than ordinarily provoked at Reilly's treatment to [*sic*] Mrs. Sherman. . . . He did not go to Lancaster, he did not write to Mrs. Sherman till he had been three weeks in the U.S. and then only in answer to her inquiries for her letters. He was taken sick . . . and yet had time to spend a week in Baltimore. [It

is curious to find residents of California as late as 1855 still referring to the Eastern seaboard as the "U.S." as if California were a foreign land.] It was unpardonable after the favors both Mrs. Sherman and I had shown him. Reilly has too high an opinion of himself—his honesty is his chief merit. . . . He don't [*sic*] like to work too hard and thinks himself indispensable. . . . Mr. Bainbridge is worth two of him. Holland, Little and Morgan [69] are better bred and better tempered and [if] . . . Reilly has concluded to remain in St. Louis, understand that I say amen. If he is on his way out, I will put him to work as Receiving Teller but he has lost all claims to an extraordinary confidence on my part. If it should be as his brother says, that he does not propose coming out to California till January, please say to him . . . that I don't care a d____ whether he comes or not . . . for were he in his death struggles, he should have borne the message to Mrs. Sherman he solemnly promised to do on parting with me. I depended on Reilly's seeing Mrs. Sherman to assure her of the health of the children. These disappointments to Mrs. S. render my post more difficult as she is hostile beyond measure to California and my remaining here and I trusted to more propitious events to reconcile her on her return, but everything has proved adverse. . . . Do not for a moment understand me as wavering in my original undertaking, but Mrs. Sherman's discontent added to the cares and necessary labor of my post makes it about as much as my precarious health can stand. Last week the labor and care forced me to keep my room Saturday and Sunday, but now I feel about as well as usual. Bainbridge . . . looks over the notes, sees to the bullion and keeps the General Ledger. All the others are employed as you left them. Your nephew is so slow, and so often indisposed that I have been compelled to hire a young man in his place—Babcock, nephew of the Pacific Mail Steamship agent [70] and formerly one of Page, Bacon & Company's employees. [He] . . . has excellent reputation and . . . has done an immense deal of work. . . . I employed . . . for two months from 5th inst. At the expiration of that time, I expect Nisbet and Reilly . . . back. Should Reilly not return I may make Bainbridge useful. . . . I am not . . . satisfied with ______, he is noisy and extravagant. I fear his honesty. Your nephew is . . . too slow and prefers all kinds of business to his specific work. I cannot keep scolding him. . . .

Don't be astonished to learn that he has returned home. I hope you won't break with Nisbet; he had many good qualities and I do hope after a year at home he will have become proof to drink and . . . be more deferential to others. He has capacity for what I need here very much—a rapid execution and intuitive knowledge of figures and bookkeeping.

Sherman reassured Turner that the accounting was quite in order, "but all the letter writing devolves on me . . . besides the thousand calls outside and in the bank make more physical labor than one of my constitution can endure, but the arrival of Nisbet's brother [71] soon will make that all right."

(Across the page dealing with Turner's nephew and Nisbet the word "rewrite" is written in large letters, as if Sherman changed his mind about transmitting the contents. No substitute sheet appears in this correspondence.)

The next news reported by Sherman heralded a period long to be remembered in the history of San Francisco:

. . . two murders worse than usual—Wall and Williamson of Monterey were murdered on the Salinas plains, and last night General Richardson [72] was shot dead on Clay Street just below Montgomery by a gambler. The bells rang and the city was in commotion and the Vigilance Committee was again talked of. I have been through the city today but no signs of riot. The murderer is in jail. Should the lawyers get him off, I have no doubt we will again have lynch law here.

Once more another bank's troubles were a source of worry.

Palmer of Palmer, Cook & Company is back. King is into him. I have no doubt they are short of cash. Jones [of Palmer-Cook] applied to me . . . yesterday for $25,000 to take their bills on New York. [In other words, to pay cash in San Francisco for Palmer, Cook & Co.'s check on a New York bank.] He assured me Palmer-Cook had $100,000 but with . . . present feeling . . . could not . . . sell exchange. After satisfying myself that Palmer had made some sales in the East and on Jones' solemn assurance . . . I let him have $15,000 . . . all I will do for them and should I see them toppling, I will make Jones secure these bills in transit,

While Sherman did not mention it in his letter, he undoubtedly remembered that Jones of Palmer, Cook and Co. had been one of the few bankers who had lent Lucas, Turner & Co. a helping hand in the bad times of the preceding February.

The same letter stated that Mrs. Sherman was expected to return home about the 30th of November.[73]

18

The jobbers of San Francisco and the special problems they created for the bankers formed the main theme of Sherman's next letter. He pointed out that these jobbers were regularly heavy purchasers of merchandise which they sold on credit. While considerable capital was employed in their business, they always leaned very heavily on their bankers.

> I have watched their operations closely [he wrote Turner] and confess they scare me. Checking heavily without regard to their accounts . . . on steamer day actually exhausting [them] during the day and replenishing at night. Of late . . . instead of depositing at 4 o'clock enough to make their accounts good, come in with notes for discount. . . . Sometimes having already paid their checks, I could do nothing better than take these notes without security or endorsement. [I assume Sherman means third-party endorsers; surely the jobbers must have guaranteed these notes they were substituting for cash deposits in their own accounts!] The heaviest of these were Castle Brothers, Harold Randall & Company and J. H. Bosworth & Company.[74] I had expressed to each . . . that instead of presuming upon such accommodations and discounts, they . . . come beforehand to ascertain whether it was agreeable to us. . . . Money has been tighter and tighter every steamer [day] for the past two months because the rains are late and the gold does not come from the mountains. . . . The failure of Sanders and Brenham and threatened danger of Palmer, Cook & Company has [*sic*] kept deposits low. I was determined to contract . . . discounts . . . to put a stop to the practice . . . a growing evil and . . . most dangerous. . . . As I could not stop it

by mild measures, I was determined to do so by severe ones. So last steamer day finding checks of large amount passing in from the . . . parties named, I instructed Morgan . . . when parties had no money to their credit to answer "No funds. Call at 4 P.M." By 2 o'clock it was known all over town that we had refused the checks of persons of very high standing and many called to enquire the reason. I . . . explained . . . the checks would doubtless be provided for but that we would not pay checks in advance of deposits. It was half past four before Castle made his deposit. I expected him to say something so . . . stood close. He went out . . . immediately returned with a friend and asked for his balance. I told him if he would call in the morning we would give him his balance if he had any. He walked away . . . made . . . a remark about our not paying his checks. . . . I told him he drew them taking his chance and [it] . . . proved a bad one. About half past five I went . . . to dinner . . . got back . . . about 7 o'clock. . . . Morgan told me Castle had come back and made so much fuss that he struck his balance and gave it to him, $25,000. . . . This balance embraced his checks not yet collected, some notes Fred had discounted . . . and some checks on Stockton and Sacramento which are considered collections until . . . paid. I . . . gave Morgan and Fred to understand they are not clothed with such discretion and the like must never occur again. The next morning Castle published a notice which I send you. . . . On succeeding days appeared the second notice. . . . Castle Brothers are . . . a good jobbing house . . . English, and have a good opinion of themselves. The other jobbers make common cause with them because they will be incommoded if the other banks do as we have. All of them have except Drexel, Sather and Church. . . . They have their hands full as I know. . . . I published but one notice but as Castle Brothers had given their figures to the *Chronicle*, I made the editor come to the bank and see for himself the true state of Castle's deposits.[75]

Any experienced banker is bound to read the above paragraph with amazement and incredulity. It is commonplace to find a customer resenting his banker's refusal of a loan. It verges on the ludicrous, however, when a businessman inserts an advertisement in the newspapers to protest the refusal of a bank to pay his checks when his account is overdrawn! In this respect at least, times have changed for the better.

Sherman continued:

"I would not have done this had not they seen fit to make public their view of the case. I did not care so much about the details as about stopping a practice that has been too much in vogue . . . and which . . . might run any bank dry in the midst of any steamer day when we have so much of our cash invested in bars and exchange for shipment. Take [our] present case. We had about $160,000 in bars and exchange. We had to expect all accounts to be . . . low and if Castle Brothers could check out $60,000 or $100,000 and other jobbers the same, they might have actually exhausted our coin. . . . Another consideration was that we could not discount for smaller and better customers because we could not tell how much the jobbers wanted . . . these jobbers never kept a balance. They were heavy borrowers and considered themselves so good . . . they thought I ought not to ask [for] endorsers or collateral. . . . Beside[s] they never buy a cent of exchange. I am glad I am rid of them. The checks of Annan, Talmadge & Coghill [76] are refused in the same way, but esteeming them careful men, I addressed each a note explaining why I had so acted. Coghill came up immediately and acknowledged I was right. Annan, Talmadge & Company replied by a letter which I also enclose. [Regrettably no copy is with these photostats.] Both these houses are stronger than ever in their confidence in us and . . . that is the feeling among merchants who borrow little or none. The person who keeps a balance . . . has reason to complain that his balance should be used by a jobber to keep up prices. . . . The day after last steamer day, McCreery [77] . . . asked me about the Castle matter. I answered that Castle insisted on his right to draw as much as he pleased without asking. He replied "Do you want us to deposit every hour of the day?" "No, the day *before* if you choose." ". . . you won't pay our checks if we make them good same day?" "No. How can I tell you will make them good?" "Would you pay my check [McCreery's] for $10,000 if I had no money in bank?" "No, emphatically." "Then make up our account." "Good." I then inquired, "McCreery, of what use is your account to us? Have you ever a balance idle?" "No." "Did you ever have a check refused here?" "No." "Did you ever apply for a reasonable discount without success?" "No." "Then have you personally any reason to complain?" "No—but the jobbers contend that they have a right to check all day, provided they make the account good that evening or next day." . . .

It places a bank in the power of a few merchants who can gradually tie up all the moneys of a bank however large. . . . These big jobbers had been allowed the habit at all other banks. . . . They seemed determined not to give it up. My remedy may have been a little harsh but it was effectual. I know . . . every dollar that our good customers want and . . . can sleep soundly without the dread of Castle Brothers and their fellows drawing our every cent in pursuance of a custom that ought to have died last February.

While this question was being debated on the street, Sherman encountered Haight and asked him what he thought of it. Haight admitted that he was in part to blame. While Page, Bacon & Co.'s deposits were between $1.2 million and $1.5 million, they actively sought the jobbers' business, but he sadly observed that they were the last to come to the firm's rescue when troubles overwhelmed them. In fact, Page-Bacon had nearly $200,000 in overdrawn accounts when they failed and seemed likely to realize next to nothing on them! Haight also believed the jobbers had brought about Burgoyne's downfall.

Sherman added some more comments in his letter:

Brewster [78] is one of the heaviest [jobbers], he came to see me yesterday . . . said Drexel, Sather & Church could not accommodate him as much as he wanted and desired to know if I felt disposed to lend some assistance. I told him . . . the sooner the jobbers contracted their operations the better. I . . . did not encourage him. . . . Indeed Arrington,[79] Brewster, Coleman, Castle, Harold Randall & Company and a few such houses would absorb the capital of a large bank and if mercantile reverses should come, such as prevailed here in '53 and '54, they would break any bank. I know that Arrington has lost $30,000 on coffee. Generally . . . the jobbers have done well this year but they have immense amounts out on credit and if . . . the winter should be a dry one . . . will see a mercantile row . . . just as we have seen in real estate . . . capping the climax of the financial history of 1855. Maybe I am not sufficiently courageous for success. . . . it is one thing to overturn one's own neck and head, and another to overturn the wealth and name of others who have trusted to me and . . . expect rather excessive caution than excessive boldness. I fear you will suppose . . . I ought to have temporized more . . . but. . . it made me nervous and I could not stand it any longer. . . . It has not lost us more than half a dozen accounts which kept no balances . . . bought no exchange but were borrowers without limit. It has given confidence to the large class who do keep balances and whose loans are comparatively small and . . . [who are] willing to get endorsers or security. . . . The jobbers think us rather mean and no great bankers. I have reduced our discounts to about $500,000, discount[ed] at 2½%, and am gradually getting in the old . . . debts. I don't think we ought to declare a dividend until I pay back all my trust funds, until the city funds her debt or . . . we recover a judgment and generally . . . recover the ground lost in the disasters of this year.

In reading the last paragraph, we for the first time find Sherman on the defensive. He seems to have feared that his Eastern partners might criticize the course he had pursued. More and more since the Black Friday of February, 1855, one senses that Sherman was tiring physically and nervously. His fighting spirit remained undaunted, but, perhaps unconsciously, he sensed a deterioration in the moral fiber of the men about him. San Francisco's future in the years immediately ahead shone less brightly, less surely. Could his bank thrive in this trying climate?

In addition to the worries caused by the jobbers, Sherman was being plagued by routine administrative problems. The continued absence of Nisbet and Reilly deprived the manager of their greater experience. Nisbet's brother had not arrived and Sherman wrote: "I have too much to do. . . . All in the bank are a little crowded. . . . Cash don't [*sic*] balance at night as close as it should . . . too often short . . . only possible chance of short cash is in wrong payments . . . or actual peculation. . . . As soon as Reilly comes I will divide the cash and hold the paying and receiving tellers responsible each for their files." He then detailed how he planned to rearrange the staff so as to minimize the risk of employee dishonesty. Evidently his resentment toward Reilly had cooled in the face of his present need for more competent assistants. He at least felt sure of Reilly's honesty.

> This is a large force [he admitted], worst of all, this receiving and paying out money involves labor expense and risk . . . yet the deposits are so fleeting as to afford no adequate compensation. I've got one fellow on his way to the penitentiary for forging a letter of credit whereby he got $500 . . . and another, for attempting a forged check in which he was not so successful. So you see all the rogues are not caught yet.

Then follows additional evidence that the generally disturbed state of affairs was wearing down banker Sherman:

> I have seen many of our friends since you left and all agree that you ought to reside here. If I must devote my concentrated thoughts to the dangerous part of loaning money, I cannot hope to be very courteous or friendly. . . . That is the greatest danger one runs. A banker, especially in California, can have no personal friends for they will want to borrow money.

Another threatening cloud on the horizon was the likelihood of more bank failures. Sherman had learned only too well that nothing else was so calculated to destroy confidence and undermine the morale of the community.

> The court [he wrote Turner] today made an order that Palmer, Cook & Company should deliver to Naglee [the receiver of the bankrupt firm of Adams & Co.] some $120,000 of Adams & Company's money. If they have to do it, although they have had ample time to gather it in, they may be very short. I hear they intend to appeal, but don't see how they can appeal without giving security and no one will go security now. I fear their doom is sealed. . . . Now every fellow is for himself. No bank will now aid another and it is well for since Sanders & Brenham deceived their fellow bankers, there is an end to that sort of faith. I wish Palmer, Cook & Company would disgorge this money. . . . They have no depositors except such as are heavily indebted, so that the losses would be on the part of public treasurers whose bondsmen they are. You will see that King [of William] gives them no peace.

Despite the high mortality among the city's banking firms, new ventures continued to find the field attractive:

> Garrison told me all about the new bank. They begin in Wells, Fargo & Company's office, corner of California and Montgomery, about the first of January [Wells, Fargo & Co. having removed to the Parrott's building, formerly occupied by Page, Bacon & Co. and Adams & Co.], with a cash capital of $600,000.?? [the double interrogatory is in Sherman's hand] and a confirmed credit through Morgans of New York for $500,000 for which they pay 8% per annum.[80] Now if this is true, they will have a great advantage. I told Garrison I would turn over to him the jobbers and some borrowing customers like McKee that we can well spare, but Garrison says he will put up a big sign—"No overdrafts allowed." I can tell him signs won't do.
>
> Louis McLain is now at the head of Wells, Fargo & Company. He and Parrott and Inge but they are cautious, timid, prudent men.[81] Drexel, Sather and Church are too deep for me. They either have more capital than I think or are playing a bold game. They *lose on every ounce of gold shipped as we do*. Bars are still at par here, whilst freight and insurance are the same, 1½ each. I trust that we have got the contract for Treasury drafts, or that you made better terms for shipment. At present we are losing on exchange. Parrott tells me from Page, Bacon & Company's books, their losses on dust and exchange will not fall short of half a million."

Mrs. Sherman had reached San Francisco on the *Golden Gate* the Thursday preceding this letter,

> . . . with the exception of a cold, in tolerable health. She is again established as the head of the family and things already assume a family-like appearance. Both children are robust and happy. Bowman is well but Mrs. B. has the blues—dispepsia or neuralgia or something that makes her unhappy. I rather suspect she will not be satisfied at being a boarder instead of the head of the family, but both Mrs. Sherman and I will try and pay her for having consented to look after the children during Mrs. S.'s visit. Bowman has purchased the lot next me, will . . . at his leisure build a cottage . . . which will afford Mrs. B. more occupation and authority.[82]

19

By the end of steamer day on December 19, 1855, Sherman had recovered his usual buoyancy: "Though money is awful tight, I feel . . . much more comfortable in consequence of taking down the jobbers in time. Having discounts down to $500,000 I was easy as an old shoe. . . . You may bet high nobody tries to overdraw without first obtaining a credit. All who left us [except] Castle and Harold Randall have returned."

Aspinwall's Panama mail line had just exceeded the bid Henry Turner had made for the firm on treasury drafts. Sherman felt that the mail and steamship company was unfairly invading the banking field. He told them he would endeavor to get better freight rates from the Nicaragua line on Lucas-Turner's shipments of coin and bullion. Garrison, Aspinwall's competitor, quoted Sherman a lower rate, so he advised Turner that he would henceforth patronize the Nicaragua line. The risk from filibusters no longer seemed great and was protected by insurance.

Sherman then had the painful task of informing Turner that he was sending the latter's nephew back to St. Louis as soon as he was able to travel. The young man was at present confined to a sickbed. Sherman thought he might make a good engraver, lithographer, or draughtsman. "He is not calculated to succeed here. . . . The sooner he gets to some calling suited to his capacity and talents the better. . . . He cannot fix his attention . . . to books."

Another employee was proving both intemperate and insubordinate. While Sherman was away from the bank, a friend of this clerk brought him a bottle of champagne, which, in spite of express orders, he proceeded to open and drink before he balanced his cash. For some strange reason, the cash remained out of balance. The thirsty teller was discharged. Increasing cash shortages were giving Sherman much concern. He was forced to pay more personal attention to the custody of the bank's cash. Reilly had apparently written that he was not returning to San Francisco. "I don't regret his [decision]," Sherman wrote. "His honesty is beyond reproach but he is whimsical and slow and does not supply our wants. . . . I would prefer Nisbet with all his faults. . . . [He] writes me that he will be out in January." It was not too hard to secure competent clerical help. Sherman's chief problem was to find time for all the correspondence that he felt only a partner could handle. He explained that, because of this demand upon his time, he must greatly curtail personal correspondence.

Major Thomas Swords [83] was one friend whose letter Sherman had not yet found time to answer. This case was probably typical of many that had confronted him. Evidently, some time after Black Friday, the banker had managed to collect Swords's investments and remitted him in settlement. Swords must have questioned Turner as to Sherman's reasons, for the latter now wrote: "[I] will satisfy him that in sending him his money, I was governed solely by a desire to save him anxiety, for I know he felt anxious about his money, and moreover it is not right we should guarantee the safety of any private fund at an interest above 10%."

Sherman concluded this letter by saying all were well at home. "I have traded Weston [his horse] for a big, strong, tame grey, so that Mrs. Sherman can now ride without fear and trembling. I had to give boot as Weston is not accounted a safe draft horse." [84]

His next letter tells of a new routine he had adopted for steamer days. He now dined at home but instead of returning immediately to the bank, he slept until 11:00 P.M. Then he arose and went to the office. By this time all advices of remittances had been prepared and all accounts balanced. He was now ready for the final actions that must be taken before the steamer sailed. On the preceding night he had worked with the clerk who had replaced Turner's nephew and also his friend Schuyler Hamilton.[85] He kept them busy copying the outgoing mail. About 4:30 A.M., Sherman and Hamilton lay down on sofas and slept until 7:00,

> when I have begun again. I will write no letter but this as I am not well enough and have much to say to you. About Nisbet, I coincide with you that it was best to allow him to return, but . . . regret he was not . . . allowed time . . . to reform . . . in habit. . . . I can see how Robert Nisbet[86] could not be spared. . . . Now I know that Nisbet will be here in a month and have arranged accordingly. Capt. Hamilton is . . . with his sister . . . so I have invited him to assist me . . . before Nisbet's arrival. But when Nisbet arrives, are you all willing that he should be at the head of the house? I was very sick last week. . . . I may die at any moment. . . . My asthma has so fixed itself that the least cold settles on my lungs and last week I had congestion of the lungs. . . . I am not well now. My head throbs and I have a bad cough. I can see that all are alarmed, Mrs. Sherman very much so. . . . I am weak and pale. . . . I am in no fit condition to be entrusted solely with too much. You probably think I am too apt to be alarmed at my health. I do not fear death . . . but think what I must do in anticipation. If Nisbet is here . . . he must manage things until you find a successor, but Nisbet and I are not enough unless both of us are . . . well. You should be here . . . to realize anything like the grand plans first conceived. . . . Were I in your stead I would not come here with your entire family for a one half interest. In case of my death . . . Stone[87] is still the best man. He has every inclination I know. I never breathed a syllable to him until last week when . . . Dr. Bowie began to hint . . . I might have to leave. I sent for Stone and [told him] that in case of my death, I would leave a power of attorney for him to act in my stead until . . . you at home could replace me. . . . All I asked of him was if it met the concurrence of the interests at stake that he should succeed me. I wanted him to buy my house and furniture and pay me something for my putting him in the way. I . . . think . . . it would be well to manage . . . an ⅛ interest and having three resident partners . . . as long as I live. . . . When I die let Stone have my ⅛ without salary. I leave these things to you. . . .

> if you think best to trust to Nisbet in case of my departure, so be it . . . but if I were looking at another person as pale as I am, with such a cough and . . . liable to congestion of the lungs, I'd mark his tombstone at once.
>
> My own opinion is . . . I will live this year but . . . I will . . . be a little timid of . . . next winter. . . . I must cease from this night work. I must let up my mind from the gnawing care. I must shake off the importunities of many borrowers and must keep off these committees on which they . . . place me in spite of myself, and most of all I must wear overshoes [and] be careful of myself, a thing that is impossible. If I get to thinking, I don't care whether I've got shoes on or not. . . . Mrs. Sherman is doing her best, and is so much better contented since her return that I feel provoked at my illness.

One feels sympathy for this sick man, forced unwillingly into committee assignments. However, how startling to recall that a little over four months later, this same asthmatic, overworked banker was to find himself the major general in command of the San Francisco division of the California militia! Though that body lacked some of the essentials of a military organization, the fact remains that Sherman was persuaded to assume the role in the midst of one of the most turbulent crises in the history of American cities. Even a very able-bodied man, free of all other responsibilities, would have been justified in refusing such a post.

> I have lost but two days at the office since you left [he wrote Turner] and then people would come out to the house to bother me so that I had . . . to refuse to see anybody. . . . That is one thing necessary in a banker; he should ever be present to transact his business. . . . I have made it a point to stick to the office like wax. . . . I must take more outdoor exercise and . . . try to shake off the care that eats up one's soul. With my experience . . . I would rather be anything . . . than a California banker, and why Stone wants to come in seems a mystery to me. . . . He would be a good acquisition and infinitely better qualified to step into my shoes than Nisbet.

Sherman emphasized that all of the above details were intended solely for Turner, but he could tell the other partners that Sherman's condition was precarious.

Garrison, Fretz, Ralston and Morgan have begun with a flourish, $700,000 capital, $500,000 reserve fund in case of loss of a shipment, and as they are the stuff that mostly prevails in this community, let them rip.[88] [So Sherman heralded the start of a new competitor.] Some of our customers will go there of course but I am not afraid of any emigration of the good ones. We can spare them a dozen that will be an advantage to get rid of. Old McKee still gives me trouble. He tries to overcheck [*sic*] till the [next] morning but it's no go.

This letter contained a message for General Hitchcock,[89] whose inquiries about his real estate had gone unanswered due to Sherman's illness. "Tell him . . . that to sell now would be ruinous for there is no demand . . . for real estate. We expect some change . . . in the spring." He then concluded on a somber note: "Give heed to what I say of myself. . . . Do not think me scared or trifling. It is a serious truth." [90]

Thirteen days later Sherman wrote in an altered mood. He began the letter: "My dear Major"; in most of this correspondence he had used the salutation: "My dear Turner." It acknowledged receipt of a letter dated December 15, which antedated Sherman's despairing recital of the critical state of his health by three weeks. The latest letter of Sherman's that Turner could have had when he wrote was the one dated November 18, reviewed in an earlier chapter. Illness had been mentioned by Sherman but rather incidentally. While we do not have the text of Turner's December 15 letter, Sherman's reply suggests that Turner was either telepathic or very prescient, for his letter had a tonic effect on his ailing friend.

The *Golden Age* is in [began Sherman's acknowledgment], with your very kind letter of December 15, clothing me with a discretion and power with regard to Nisbet, and offering me . . . in addition to my present reasonable compensation, to give me a house rent free. . . . I cannot do less than thank you and Mr. Lucas for such signal marks of your favor. I want to do right and the measure of . . . compensation is beyond my merits. . . . If I were . . . strong [and] able to count on a future, I would shrink from nothing and would ask little more than a good fair maintenance of my family till such time as the end would demonstrate that my services have been well or ill paid. I . . . have been undergoing a dangerous probation, one that I tremble at . . . in which I have committed errors. . . . That is past. The losses incurred were great, but compared with others of older minds than mine, not unfavorable, but each day convinces me that to bank on our capital we have at times ventured too far, and I fear in myself a growing suspicion and timidity . . . for risks must be incurred and the question is, just how much. During Nisbet's absence I have worked too hard for my strength yet nothing that a strong man would feel. . . . When he returns I will feel that he is under a ban, that I will not be relieved of responsibility by taking his advice . . . that if I should think proper to visit Marysville, Sacramento or interior towns on business, I will leave behind in charge one in whom you feel a want of confidence, yet mechanically, he can relieve me . . . of the necessity of writing so many letters. . . . Schuyler Hamilton now does and I have experienced sensible relief therefrom. In the bank . . . daily routine . . . goes on as smoothly as possible. Although the accounts are low, [they] were never better, because I have . . . extinguished that ruinous practice of overchecking [*sic*]. Our up/country accounts have given me some trouble. Rhodes responds promptly, so does Bours, but Wilkinson & Company of Marysville, and Langton of Downieville and Strange of Murphys are constantly overchecked and writing down to protect their checks as the dust will follow in a day or so. . . . Gold dust is very scarce; the weather has been intensely cold and the miners can't and won't work. . . . The merchants try and send checks down here to keep their credit up, and these interior agents draw as much as they dare. I have conversed with Sather and the other bankers and all represent the same.

Sherman then admitted what every large city banker knows full well:

We want these interior correspondents and it is hard to say "thus far shalt thou go and no farther." . . . I will be watchful and guard this interest as well as I can. . . . Money is very tight. . . . As deposits are low, I restrict loans and discounts . . . I have now only $480,000 out. Some of our best customers who used to have large balances now are borrowers. . . . It requires great discretion to discriminate . . . that too with delicacy, to refuse a reasonable accommodation to an old customer gives offense.

Sherman cited an instance:

When I was very sick, could hardly breathe, much less speak . . . one of our steadiest customers applied for a loan of $3,000 to pay freights. I had told Bainbridge to decline everything and say I would be at the bank in a day or two. [The customer] showed some impatience and came out to my house where Dr. Bowie had given positive orders that I should not talk or be disturbed. The girl told [him] I was sick and could not be seen. He returned to the bank, showed . . . impatience and finally ordered his account to be made up . . . and moved [it]. . . . As soon as I got down, I went to see him and the moment he saw how sick I had been, he apologized. . . . I told him under the circumstances he had no cause of offense. . . . He admitted he had been hasty . . . he had never borrowed money outside of our bank and . . . felt nettled that I had not left orders for his particular case. . . . I explained . . . we had four hundred cases somewhat similar, etc. etc. . . . He admitted he would rather trust us than anybody else. He bought his last exchange of us and . . . his account is again on our books. . . . This case illustrates my situation. . . . San Francisco seems peculiarly inimical to my health, and . . . the care and anxiety [of] attending half a million of outstanding [loans] don't help me much. It was this . . . that influenced me in my last letter to dwell on the necessity of . . . another partner who enjoyed the confidence of the firm. I am . . . willing to take Nisbet with his proclivity to drink, to bad company, and to trifling with subjects too delicate or serious for his comprehension . . . but I should suppose Mr. Lucas and yourself . . . would prefer . . . somebody here who in case of my death . . . would relieve you of the apprehension I know you all would feel. . . . I don't intend to die . . . but I would be false to my trust were I to conceal . . . that I am liable to our common enemy. I named Stone because . . . I believe him honest, honorable, capable, and probably better qualified . . . than myself. I don't propose to burden the house . . . with more partners. . . . All I will agree to is that [Stone] should acquire or buy Patterson's or Nisbet's shares. Your letter gives me

> discretion to coerce Nisbet, but I have not the heart to drive him out if he behaves . . . tolerably well. If you . . . with an absolute knowledge of the past felt a delicate regard for him, how can you expect me, in a manner dependent on his experience, to act with more sternness?

Sherman reiterated the precautionary measures he had taken to prevent confusion should he die. He had executed a will and also a declaration that except for property specifically mentioned, anything in his name belonged to Lucas, Turner & Co. Stone's authority during any interim after Sherman's death had been minutely described. Stone was to buy Sherman's house and furniture at a fair valuation and assume the payment of Sherman's $7,000 note to the St. Louis house of Lucas & Simonds. He also enclosed a catalogue of the sale of Captain Folsom's estate. Sherman felt the properties had sold well. He closed with the remark that he wanted to think longer about Turner's offer to have Lucas, Turner & Co. buy Sherman's Harrison Street house.[91]

A letter written the next day reported that Mrs. Bowman would be a passenger on the Monday mail steamer. Her husband was sending her East for a visit. He hoped to have a house built on the lot next to Sherman's by the time his wife returned to San Francisco. "Mrs. Bowman must have a house to tinker at," commented Sherman. During his wife's absence, Bowman would continue to live with the banker.

The latter also planned to have Nisbet board with him on his return.

> Our house is too large for our small family, and servant hire still keeps up amazingly high. Nisbet will in my opinion get married to Miss Thornton before spring. Her friends make inquiries after his movements from which I infer he does not correspond with her. . . . As he is naturally fickle, he may fly the hurdle yet. . . . It may be best for him to marry.

But there were weightier problems than romances in Sherman's staff.

> This is a devil of a country [he told Turner]. I have just been interrupted by Mr. Pickett [92] of Pickett and Mount [?] who . . . informed me . . . he could not get through steamer day one of the tightest of the season. They owe us $4,500 . . . due yesterday. . . . [We] attached, being the first attaching creditor and therefore amply secured. He had a good stock of goods. . . . Several failures have occurred here and at Sacramento and Marysville but . . . by none are we losers.

A few lawsuits in which the bank was interested were proceeding slowly. Sherman mentioned specially the suit against the city on the Powell Street paving bonds. In this matter Lucas, Turner & Co.'s attorney was sanguine of success and this would mean much to the bank.

Referring again to the "tight steamer day," Sherman wrote:

> All the bankers have been here and admit it is the dullest day of the season. I have so restricted borrowers that I have not been at all pushed and I have taken less paper than was paid in. Our notes maturing to-day were $65,000, every cent of which was paid. . . . William T. Coleman and Hussy, Bond & Hall [93] bought . . . exchange of us today.

Sherman was pleased at the arrangements Turner had made about insurance of the firm's shipments of coin and bullion. He also planned to give Lucas, Turner & Co. a deed from himself and wife to the Harrison Street property to cover his indebtedness in the event of his death. On the health score, he wrote: "I feel about as well as usual . . . and will try to escape colds."

This brief letter [94] closed with news of the death of one of San Francisco's best-known citizens, William D. M. Howard.[95]

20

On one steamer day in mid-January, 1856, Lucas, Turner & Co. was shipping $130,000 of coin and bullion. Under the new arrangement, Sherman could save $400 in charges by routing it by way of Nicaragua. However, William Walker's filibustering activities in that country were at their height, and Sherman feared that treasure might be seized from the steamship. Even though the insurance carried would probably protect the bank, he decided to pay the higher Panama rates, $2,000 in this case, and avoid any risk; he so advised Turner in his next letter.

It told too of the welcome arrival of the rains, a warm downpour which he hoped extended to the mining region because

> money is awful hard to get. . . . It is the hardest . . . task to resist the demands of old and good customers for money which in ordinary times they never need, but the low state of deposits . . . and small amount . . . in certificates and timebills makes it . . . necessary to cut close. If we had had more money these hard times, we could have had an amount of new business and customers but it is best to cut the coat . . . to the cloth.

Then the banker was once more the parent.

> Lizzie is developing very fast and talks all the time . . . hardly time to sleep, so many things are passing [through] her brain. Willy is dogmatic and short "No—Yes—" and monosyllables generally. He is very strong and fat, and has not been sick a day since you were with us. Mrs. Sherman is quite well . . . much more contented. . . . So . . . everything is working . . .

smoothly. . . . Nisbet ought to be here before next steamer day so I may conclude my night work is . . . over.[96]

Two weeks later Sherman, in a contrite mood, acknowledged Turner's

> long letter of December 21. . . . I feel . . . that in those long nights, when alone I carried on the correspondence . . . I must have written so carelessly as to convey an utterly wrong impression of my feelings. I admit all you say. . . . Any depression . . . I may have experienced was the consequence of ill health and . . . the bad state of things here, but in no wise connected with the relations between yourselves and me. I certainly have, and ought to . . . expressed my entire satisfaction at the confidence reposed in me and the advantages conferred on me . . . which I know are beyond my deserts. I have written too much and must learn to curtail. Any depression of feeling . . . was . . . the effects of a disease which I cannot control and . . . the downward tendency in the solvency of men and . . . every species of security. It was impossible . . . to have a confidant and . . . I piled my troubles and sorrows on you a little too thick. At times here things have looked black enough, city defaulting, state dishonest, county . . . in no credit, merchants overstretched . . . real estate of no saleable value. You must excuse me if I felt keenly these concurrent dangers. . . . To the world I think I have never shown a sign of apprehension . . . but I have . . . feared losses which have not occurred, and felt uneasiness about people which may have been unnecessary. . . . Fluctuations in business are natural but . . . harder to endure here than anywhere else, for when money gets scarce here . . . pressure comes from every quarter . . . deposits run down . . . borrowers increase . . . and the bank cannot get money except by foreclosure or suing without getting any good of it. . . . Rains have fallen in abundance, gold is beginning to come down. Borrowers are a little easier. . . . Maybe times are mending but I have got rid of many old debts, have shaken off our worst accounts and been as liberal as . . . justified to our best accounts. . . . Discounts down to $450,000, and [this] steamer day feel no fear of overdrafts which I have stopped effectually. Our business and prospects are as good as ever but I . . . would not go through last year's cares for all the money in our trays. I am not disposed to growl . . . would rather be associated with

> you and Mr. Lucas than any two men on earth. . . . Since my severe attack in December I have been about as well as usual. I have asthma . . . every night but can generally keep it down by nitre paper. . . . Only when [a] cold is . . . added . . . I have to sit up. Now that Nisbet is here to keep one of the keys [this must have referred to the bank vault] and to do the bulk of correspondence, I can avoid exposure and . . . diminish the risk . . . [and] give more . . . time to those out door operations so necessary. . . . Nisbet will stay at our house. . . . He is disposed to do his very best. . . . I have no doubt he will avoid those irregularities that gave us so much concern.

Some latter-day literary psychiatrists have sought to diagnose Sherman's alternate moods of depression and exhilaration during the early months of the Civil War as symptoms of a manic-depressive psychosis.[97] The high and low emotional levels exhibited in some of the letters just reviewed might be considered additional evidence to prove their claim. Sleeplessness, a driving energy, a mind obsessed by many worries, the urge to write—since there was no one with whom he could talk—these might support such theories. Many persons even believed Sherman was crazy in 1861, but fortunately for the Union, General Grant and General Halleck did not. Long afterward, Sherman wryly remembered those days: "Grant stood by me when I was crazy, and I stood by him when he was drunk."

Few writers are competent to apply medical terms to Sherman's condition in the winter of 1855–1856. Moved by compassion, it seems more fitting to give weight to the oft-repeated assaults of asthma. He was compelled to sit up at night gasping for breath. He was choked by the dust of ill-paved streets of the mushrooming city, where the wind vied with labor gangs in removing the sandhills. The manic-depressive is often bowed down with imaginary woes. If Sherman's apprehension about further asthmatic attacks seems exaggerated, it should be remembered that even though death delayed its arrival until long years afterward, its weapon then was again asthma. Impressive also was the mounting concern bound to be felt by any conscientious guardian of his friends' and customers' fortunes in the stormy climate of pioneer San Francisco. Add to these burdens the tedium of business correspondence and the minutiae of banking routine, then we do not need the jargon of modern psychiatry to acquire a sympathetic understanding of Banker Sherman's condition. I am satisfied that Henry Turner reached the same conclusion.

Sherman's next letter summarized more general news about San Francisco:

> The Limantour [98] [Claim] has been confirmed by the Commissioners, but as they made a prior confirmation to the city, I don't see that inside the city limits this fraudulent claim will have any effect save to prevent sales. Judge Norton [99] has also decided that the sheriff is not the proper officer to collect the State & County taxes, although he has done so ever since the organization of the state. These decisions all . . . encourage that mistrust that prevents real estate from recovering . . . a saleable price. The city government also remains tied up, can make no appropriations of money, so the streets remain in a most dangerous state. King continues to pitch into Palmer, Cook & Company who have not failed, but manage . . . to get along although it is manifest cash is very scarce with them. They could not pay the Adams & Company money and for some reason, Naglee has taken as part payment a certificate of deposit with certain real estate collaterals.[100] . . . Our suit against the City was argued in Sacramento last week but it will be some time before a formal decision is rendered. . . . probably in case of an unfavorable decision, we will get the judges to withhold it and unite with other scrip holders in a desperate effort to get another funding bill passed.[101]

Sherman enclosed newspaper clippings with details of these matters.[102]

The slow mail service finally brought to Sherman on February 19, 1856, two letters of Turner's dated January 3 and 18. Again they had a good effect upon the lonely banker:

> [I] feel well rewarded in your expressions of commendation . . . in the Castle case. . . . It was an outrage for any set of

merchants to claim such rights. . . . Now I know I was right and the best people have acceded. All the banks now profess to allow no overdrafts. . . . It is a matter of some feeling when a check of a good customer comes in, to refuse it. Discretion must be exercised. My orders are to the teller, if the check of a good customer overlaps a little, to exercise his discretion; if a check is all over [overdrawn] to say he has orders not to pay. If I am by, they are referred to me, if I am not by, Nisbet or Bainbridge must decide. . . . I find they venture but little.

Sherman by this time had convinced himself that one of the employees he had discharged was indeed dishonest. For several months he had been plagued by constant cash shortages—never an overage. Since he had dismissed the man he suspected, weeks had passed with never more than a dollar shortage and occasionally an overage.

After twenty dry days in February, the city was again gladdened by rain at eleven o'clock in the evening. Sherman went home but would write another letter on the morrow should there be news to report as the steamer would not depart until noon. The next letter bears the same date as the preceding one so was probably written early the following morning. The writer hoped to pay a dividend provided the bank was successful in its suit against the city on the Powell Street paving warrants. He also called Turner's attention to newspapers he was forwarding:

You will see that the feeling towards bankers has not yet improved. . . . The legislature has in view . . . a bill to regulate our business. Many think the legislature has no right to expose our affairs but as we must take out a license, I . . . think they can impose . . . conditions before granting such license. . . . Were the bankers to refuse a publication of their capital and resources, it would be . . . not favorable to our business. . . . If we are forced to pay taxes not only on . . . real estate and capital but upon all moneys used . . . in business, it would be a serious item.

Reading the above points up how far we have come in a little more than a century! One might say that this interest shown by the legislature in 1856 marks the first attempt to regulate banking in California. It is noteworthy that Sherman did not oppose regulation in itself but felt a natural concern as to its operation. Even more interesting is his shrewd sense of the dangerous effects of declining to disclose capital and resources. In the laissez-faire atmosphere of the mid-nineteenth century, he was in advance of his times. His reactions to both these questions should further allay the doubts of the psychiatrists.

Sherman also sent Turner another newspaper clipping showing that

> some prying fellow has got hold of the tax returns . . . and made an exhibit therefrom of the resources of all of us [i.e., all the banks] which is not flattering. . . . In returning for taxes I . . . scheduled all property which we have been forced to take and our capital as $100,000. I at first returned our . . . capital as $150,000, but when the city repudiated her warrants [the basis of the suit then pending in the California supreme court] I knocked off $50,000 and would only pay on $100,000.

One of the letters written by Turner during this period is available to us and refers to several of the questions discussed by Sherman. Writing from St. Louis on the 31st of March, he acknowledged Sherman's letter of March 5:

> The Nicaragua line has suspended . . . because of Walker's recent seizure of the Transit Company boats . . . therefore only two mails a month between New York and San Francisco. Your course in "overchecking" seems to work well, and being in accordance with the only safe mode of doing business whether in San Francisco or elsewhere, I must . . . congratulate you on the boldness you displayed in being the first to lead off in this measure of reform. . . . I see . . . a bill introduced in your legislature for regulating the business of bankers, also the invidious article published in the *Times* newspaper [reference is to the San Francisco journal of that name, mentioned in Chapter 21 hereof] touching the returns made by you and other San Francisco bankers upon which . . . taxes [are] predicated. . . . This article was quoted in the New York Evening Post . . . whereupon your friend Meigs of the Metropolitan Bank replied to it. . . . The proposed action of the legislature may be a more serious affair, and unless counteracted may cause considerable injury to . . . banking in California.

I shall feel anxious about the matter until I . . . hear of the adjournment of your rowdy legislature. Mr. Lucas returned from New Orleans . . . seems quite elated at discovering the high standing held by our respective houses in that community. It is now well understood that both you and us [*sic*] keep within legitimate banking limits and . . . no two houses . . . enjoy a larger share of public confidence. . . . No better evidence of this than what we see exhibited in Meigs' note [enclosed]. Our friends of the Metropolitan Bank are proverbial for their prudence and caution and were they not well satisfied of your position, they would be very chary [?] of committing themselves in your behalf.

Your brother [John Sherman] [103] has been appointed Chairman of a committee of the lower house of Congress . . . for the purpose of taking testimony in a contested election case [in Kansas] . . . The appointment of your brother gives great satisfaction to the abolition prints. . . . I fear that he has prejudices on the subject of slavery which it will be difficult to eradicate. Still my faith in the name inspires me with the hope that even justice may be expected from him. The committee will be here . . . on their way to Kansas. . . . I shall endeavor to see much of your brother during his sojourn.

Turner had recently seen a West Point classmate of Sherman —Captain R. S. Ewell of the First Dragoons.[104] Ewell had questions for Sherman; could he operate successfully in San Francisco on a capital of $10,000? Also, what did Sherman think of Ewell investing in sheep in New Mexico and driving them overland to California? [105]

To return to the February 19 letter to Turner, Sherman continued:

I will go up to Sacramento day after tomorrow and . . . see some members. . . . If they think some bill must be passed, I will endeavor to have it modified. . . . If real estate is allowed as a basis for banking, it would be advisable to schedule some . . . improved property, such as my house, the Meiggs house . . . and with Mr. Lucas' consent, this banking house, leaving out such as . . . should be sold as soon as a market offers. Business . . . is exceeding dull

> and real estate cannot be sold. . . . The weather has been beautiful, not a drop of rain. . . . I hope the rains have not ceased. . . . Not enough has fallen to satisfy the . . . miners . . . enough to ensure a long mining season. [Otherwise] I would not count on much change during the present year. . . . Very few ships have arrived and . . . business has been absolutely dead.

Before closing this letter, Sherman visited the wharf where the steamer from the Nicaragua line had just landed. (The semaphore atop Telegraph Hill had signaled its approach shortly before.) He was anxious for news about developments in Nicaragua and found these disquieting. Because the administration had refused to receive the minister sent to Washington by Walker, the latter had broken off diplomatic relations with the United States. "I suppose Uncle Sam feels bad," was Sherman's sardonic comment. Other disturbing news from Central America induced Sherman to continue shipments by way of Panama. This time the remittance was only $130,000.

> We are all as usual out home [he said in closing]. Willie is a picture of health and rowdyism. Lizzie is delicate but very bright. Doyle [106] goes home this steamer. . . . He will visit St. Louis where he will see you. King [James King of William] has damaged Doyle a good deal but he can't complain as all who were concerned with Adams & Company ought to expect that. Palmer, Cook & Company hold out in spite of appearances . . . it seems will weather the storm. You need not fear my committing us in that quarter.[107]

Extremely cold weather in the East delayed the mails to California, so that when Sherman wrote prior to the next steamer day, he had no St. Louis mail to answer—an unusual occurrence. It did, however, emphasize what the banker called

> this wide separation [which he termed] unfortunate as if I write unfavorable accounts of anything, the whole case is changed before a reply is had. If in accordance with my suggestion, any proposition comes whereby Stone could be admitted to our house, I will not act . . . but lay it away for future action. . . . Measures . . . in case of sudden accident to myself . . . do not concern me so much now as before Nisbet came. He is perfectly steady . . .

cheerful and I have no fault to find with him. . . . I control . . . all the business, make all loans and discounts and he corresponds and sees to the books. . . . In all our recent loans and discounts . . . for the past year, we have made few or no bad debts. The interest account . . . grosses $20,000 a month; taking off expenses, freights, interest, etc. . . . we may count on $12,000 clear a month.

Two hurdles stood in the way of the dividend that these profits seemed to justify. One was the suit against the city on its repudiated warrants, already mentioned. The other Sherman referred to as "this ridiculous suit of Smiley against me." [108]

Again California was plagued by a dry season. Save for one night, in six weeks not a drop of rain had fallen.

The streets are dusty, the mines dried up and the . . . season is now far advanced. If we have no more rain, we shall have another hard year. . . . The gold was beginning to come down quite briskly but [with] this continued drought . . . receipts are falling off fast. Bars are no longer to be had and our shipment will be almost entirely in American coin and exchange.

I went up to the Railroad celebration. . . . Much to my surprise, had to make a speech which was chronicled as decidedly energetic and applauded. . . . Building of . . . only 22½ miles of railroad in California is a fact that would inspire the dullest mind. The road will be a magnificent . . . property. . . . I doubt whether its stock can recover from . . . increased cost and interest on loans made necessary by the fact that the heaviest subscribers failed. . . . The contractor and . . . directors have put the road in . . . hands of Mr. Moss, trustee to secure his advances. It is in receipt of $600 a day which will pay running expenses, interest and something besides but . . . must go up to a $1,000 a day before . . . overplus will justify dividends.[109] . . .

I also made a visit to Benicia last week taking Mrs. Sherman and the children who enjoyed it much. . . . Willie . . . is very large and strong and almost beyond control. If he goes on at the same rate he will be able to make his way in the world.[110]

Two weeks later, Sherman received the consent of the St. Louis partners to the purchase by Captain Stone of Sherman's interest in the firm in the event the latter's condition made that necessary.

> I have placed it away for future action. I am now as well as ever. . . . Asthma makes it necessary to keep a supply of nitre paper on hand. . . . I hope I am over this winter. . . . I have seen Stone who has received your letter and feels much pleased at the possibility of his succeeding me. . . . He felt disposed gradually to draw out of his present business with Wilkinson but I advised him to hold on for it is not prudent for us to increase the number of partners. . . . Nisbet and I can do all the business that . . . falls to our share. I do not propose on any contingency to leave California during the period I agreed upon, no matter what the consequences, though satisfied the low position of San Francisco and its salt atmosphere is not favorable to my malady.

One senses that Sherman may have begun to regret his approaches to Stone. The latter's "pleasure" at the prospect of succeeding him must have stirred mixed emotions. Stone's reaction seems natural enough, but the tentative arrangements agreed upon could well have created a delicate situation for each of them.

> The drought continues [wrote Sherman], hardly any rain since December. . . . The fogs and winds from the sea . . . indicate the summer . . . has set in. . . . January, February and March have been cloudless and warm. Today was quite hot. . . . The miners are all disappointed and it is said the farmers will lose their crops. At the south all is dried up . . . cattle are suffering. . . . In writing . . . to the house yesterday, recapitulating losses charged . . . I used some words about Wadsworth and Meisegaes [111] that I hope will not be misconstrued. I spoke of them being pious men. I meant hypocrites in the worst sense, who are active members of one of the Protestant churches who use the standing thereby acquired to cheat. You no doubt feel the same disgust I do at that hypocritical assumption of religion. Real piety is too holy a feeling to be treated by worldly hands, but hypocrisy is all the baser for its attempt to steal so pure a garb. Wadsworth is one of those smooth tongued men who are active in soliciting church contributions and charities . . . active member of Mercantile Library Association. . . . [He] told me he held produce to secure

> that note. I pinned the lie on him out of which he attempted to worm, but if I can catch him he shall have no mercy. I am now pretty well posted on the standing of men . . . and the risk I take in every loan. We have made very few bad debts in last eight months. . . . The old items . . . caught us . . . so sudden was the reaction in property and consequent failure of so many men. . . . I do not think we suffered anything like the losses every [other] banker did. . . . If the mines are tied up for want of water, it will require great prudence on the part of every solvent business man. Provisions are quite high, potatoes are 6 cts a pound, meat 25 to 37 and flour is about $15 a barrel. Dry goods and groceries are low. I think interest will go up to 3 per cent [a month] again, instead of declining as we all expected. 2½% is still current.

Illustrative of judicial ethics in the 1850's, Sherman remarked that while no decision had yet been handed down by the California supreme court in Lucas, Turner & Co.'s suit against the city, one of the justices of the court had advised a friend of Sherman to buy some of the city's warrants involved in the case! They were quoted at a very low price at the moment.[112]

21

Although in his letter of March 4, 1856, Sherman referred rather contemptuously to "this ridiculous suit of Smiley's against me," actually that suit developed into a serious threat.

The banker felt reassured when the case was "referred to Edward Stanly,[113] the best reference possible for he is above corruption." Major R. P. Hammond, collector of the port, had wanted to help his friend Sherman during the Black Friday run on Lucas, Turner & Co.; therefore, he had deposited $40,000 with the bank,[114] which already held his acceptances for that amount in favor of Smiley, payable on *completion* of construction of the customhouse. Sherman had previously taken these acceptances as collateral to a loan made to Smiley. The building had *not* been completed on February 23; and, strictly speaking, Hammond should have retained possession of the $40,000. Sherman agreed to return this sum to Collector Hammond, after Lucas-Turner had survived the run. Hammond's action was admittedly irregular. He was taking a heavy risk, but there was no dishonesty involved, especially as Smiley had full knowledge of what was being done and interposed no objection at the time.

When the building was finished and the acceptances became payable, Smiley and Hammond disagreed about matters unrelated to the $40,000 transaction. In the subsequent lawsuit between them, Smiley for the *first* time claimed that Sherman had received the $40,000 for the sole account of Smiley, free of any conditions, and demanded that the money be paid him.

On the first day of the hearings, Smiley's attorney called only two witnesses in support of his claim. Palmer and Jones, partners in Palmer, Cook & Co.,[115] testified that they had overheard the conversation between Hammond and Sherman at the time the latter received Hammond's check for the $40,000. Sherman said this was true; but as most of his negotiation with the collector had been at the latter's home, the conversation in the bank had been very brief. However, Palmer and Jones added fictitious details, according to Sherman, that supported Smiley's claim. On the other hand, neither recalled anything about the very important agreement to return the money to the collector after the run.

Bowman, as attorney for the bank, submitted testimony showing that since February 23, Smiley had borrowed various smaller sums and repaid them together with sizable interest, "a thing hardly probable if he had on deposit, as he claimed, $40,000 all the time."

Sherman in disgust added a postscript to one letter: "Jones . . . admitted on cross examination that Palmer, Cook & Company are interested with Smiley in the profits of this contract and of course in the result of this suit. A pretty witness!" No wonder that he also wrote: "The whole case is so absurd that I would give it no thought only the Law is such an uncertain thing and I will not neglect the case from over confidence."

Two weeks after writing the above, Sherman may have thought the statement last quoted was prophetic. He now wrote to Turner:

> The most serious thing that has occurred to us is the strong and villainous effort made by Smiley's lawyers for that $40,000. Hammond testified for us exactly as it occurred . . . and Williams, the attorney on the other side saw the case was inevitably lost unless he could defeat the plain . . . assent given by Smiley to the return of the money to Hammond, and by an absolute sale by Smiley to a man named Dall of his interest in his claim, and patching up mutual guaranties, they made out that Smiley was no longer interested in the suit and was therefore competent as a witness. Referee Stanly admitted him but with the qualification that he

could judge of the credibility to which it would be entitled. . . . Smiley swore the case right square up. Said the $40,000 was an absolute payment to him on the contract, that he loaned us the money, that two days after he called on me for a settlement, that I commented . . . that Hammond required its return—that he forbade it, that ten days after, he called again and was informed the money had been returned, when he said he would hold me responsible. All this is pure falsehood, and yet being defendant, my hands are tied. . . . The reason he assigned for his long silence and delay was that he was afraid of Hammond, afraid he would stop his supplies, and waited till he had settled with Hammond and his partners. Hammond was removed [as collector of the port] in September, yet his suit was not begun until December. I think Stanly understands the case, although [admitting] Smiley's testimony and getting him to swear he did not consent to the return of the money to Hammond gives the case a serious turn. . . . Hammond swore that Smiley was the first person to advise him that I had returned the money to the Cashier of the Custom House, and added it was all right. Smiley swears he never said such a thing. . . . I think there is no doubt that Smiley used those very words . . . for Nisbet says that Smiley came in . . . the day I went down with the money. . . . Nisbet told him I had just gone down with that money. He said that was all right and . . . followed after. It makes me sick to find how men will perjure themselves for a little money. . . . Smiley has sworn false for he never by sign, word or gesture intimated but that he was perfectly satisfied that the money was returned to the Custom House, but lay silent for nine months. . . . Smiley never thought of this claim until his lawyers told him there was a chance of his recovering, and lawyers here are no better than robbers. Baldwin and Bowman [Baldwin must have been a lawyer associated in the case with Bowman] feel no uneasiness. . . . A few pertinent inquiries of Stanly . . . at the close of the argument gave me the assurance that he felt Smiley was more deeply interested in the result than his affidavit showed. [Reference is doubtless to the document wherein Smiley advised the court he had transferred his interest to Dall.]

On April 17, Sherman was happy to inform Turner: "In the Smiley case . . . Stanly has decided . . . wholly in our favor."

He enclosed a copy of the opinion. After summarizing the highlights of the controversy, he concluded:

> . . . you will see Stanly paid no attention to that [Smiley's testimony on the witness stand] . . . thereby treating Smiley's whole testimony as perjury. . . . I was up at Sacramento last week and Nisbet telegraphed me that the decision was in our favor. . . . As I walked out in front of the Orleans,[116] I saw Smiley, a large, strong man leaning against one of the posts, talking to Mayor Van Ness [117] of this city. . . . I could not resist the temptation and . . . said "Well, Smiley, I suppose you have heard the news?" "No, what?" "Why Stanly has decided that suit against you, but of course you expected that." No, he didn't. . . . I then with some feeling said "Did you presume to think that you could impose on such a man as Edward Stanly by such a cock and bull story? . . . You know that from the 23rd of February till you began this suit, you knew that Hammond had the money and you never intimated to me . . . but that you were wholly satisfied therewith." I expected him to strike me, but he showed so much confusion that Mayor Van Ness turned and left him. Those lawyers made Smiley perjure himself, poor devil. I pity him but I shall lose no chance to tell all who ask me what I think of them. Palmer, Cook & Company reckoned without their host this time and I know they feel confounded.[118]

In pursuing the Smiley suit to its conclusion, we passed over many paragraphs in the letters of this period that discussed other matters.

In March, 1856, a representative of the Washington Territory called on Sherman to apply for a loan to finance warfare against the Indians. In the banker's opinion the government would have to spend millions and take at least a year to accomplish results. General Wool had most of the troops of his department in Oregon and Washington. Sherman refused on behalf of Lucas, Turner & Co. to assist in financing this operation.

He repeated his firm resolution to go no further at this time with Stone. He encouraged the latter to continue in his brokerage business, "the very school," wrote Sherman, "that will prepare him for my succession if necessity should force me to abdicate, but you may bet high nothing short of absolute certainty of death will induce me to surrender my present post." Sherman regretted that he himself had not had the advantage of such an apprenticeship.

The drought continued to plague both miners and farmers. All through the mining region, huge piles of dirt had been stacked to wait for a sufficient supply of water to extract the gold dust.

> Merchants complain . . . of the short remittances from the interior. . . . When interest is at 2½% a month, a merchant can hardly afford to lay out . . . his money [for] a whole year. The miners don't care for they won't pay interest as long as they can buy on credit . . . As the law is utterly inoperative on them, their creditors have to wait their pleasure.
>
> Nisbet continues perfectly exemplary. . . . We ship per steamer . . . $165,000 in American coin . . . $40,000 in bills which covers our sight exchange. A good many people are sending money . . . for stock investment in the States. They . . . want time paper. . . . It is the best for us as we can make more than exchange by use of the money before remitting. . . . On time exchange we make money, on sight it continues touch and go. Freight is 1¼, other charges as heretofore.

Turner had written to Sherman that leaders in St. Louis business were energetically promoting construction of a good overland wagon route to California. Sherman was happy to hear this, "That . . . will be more certain to bring . . . a railroad than . . . hasty legislation by Congress. I have written my brother John in Congress to advocate any appropriation for this purpose. Until emigration flows this way again we are doomed to dull times. . . . Land can now be bought cheap and titles are . . . becoming more secure." [119]

In his next letter, Sherman criticized C. K. Garrison's publication of a statement of his bank's condition.[120] Sherman admitted that $700,000 capital was impressive to depositors, but careful observers were bound to note that cash on hand exceeded the amounts due depositors. How could Garrison bear all the expense of running a bank yet realize nothing on his deposits?

The bill regulating banks had passed one branch of the legislature. Its fate in the other house was uncertain, but Sherman thought it likely that Gov. J. Neely Johnson would veto it as unconstitutional if it reached his desk.

Once more the proposed wagon road was mentioned. A public meeting had been held in San Francisco and a committee of fifty-three men named to prepare and circulate a petition to Congress. Sherman was elected its chairman. The measure received universal approval, and Sherman hoped by April 20 to mail a petition bearing 150,000 signatures.

Sherman was a very busy man in late March and early April. The Smiley case was plaguing him, he was serving on a federal grand jury, and now he bore the responsibility of chairmanship of the wagon road movement. One wonders when he found time for his banking duties. It is easy to understand why he abandoned plans for "a short excursion into the country."

The following paragraph from a letter of April 4, 1856, arouses in the reader a sense of foreboding. Sherman could not have been aware when he wrote it, but it was actually the prelude to a dramatic tragedy:

> "I . . . send you a leaf from the *Sunday Times* in which you will observe he pitches into us, but his attacks have been so indiscriminate, having repeated the same abuse of all bankers . . . that this paper has not been noticed by a single individual or press. . . . So far as we are concerned the paper might be published in Ireland. The fellow wanted blackmail and so far as I know, has not made a cent. His printing office *was* in our building, but before he put us on the list he had the good sense to move out. . . . I would have visited on him some act of displeasure such as tossing him and his press out of the window.

Curiously, Sherman only refers to the *Sunday Times* editor as "he," but in the next few weeks his name was to acquire a sombre and deathless notoriety—James P. Casey.[121]

Another tenant had also vacated the second floor of the Lucas-Turner building (although under more conventional circumstances); Colonel De Russey, of the army engineers, had moved his office to one of the nearby army reservations.[122] That made three vacancies and reduced Mr. Lucas' income for the present. The practical Mr. Sherman improved the opportunity to do some painting and repairs made necessary by recent earthquakes.

The bank's deposits were now $574,918; it was shipping $210,000 in coin and bars, and had sold $35,000 in exchange. Maturing notes in a total of about $120,000 had been paid, and new loans had been made for approximately the same amount. Loans now totalled $530,000.[123]

Regarding the promotion of the overland wagon road, Chairman Sherman reported that editor Nugent [124] of the *Herald* had published an article about the subject that seemed to threaten the Union if the federal government did not recognize California's vital interest in the project. In the banker's opinion, Nugent's views were not shared by many San Franciscans. Sherman, in common with most of the community, believed that "California ought and will build a good road to the frontier near the sink of Mary's river,[125] and that the general government ought to build the road east as far as Kansas." A company based in St. Louis was willing to construct and equip the road provided it received a mail contract and a strip of land three miles wide along the route. Sherman decidedly preferred having the federal government build the road and then have the St. Louis concern, with which Turner was now connected, operate a stage and freight line over the route. Sherman, however, feared that high cost of feed, interruptions by snow, theft of animals, and the like, would prevent the operation being profitable. Yet, as he seemed glad to hear that Turner was interested in the project, he must have included some governmental subsidy in his calculations, although the letter does not so state.

Some rain had fallen since his last letter, "but it is again bright and clear and again faces are long." Mrs. Sherman and the children were all well and "my ground looks very pretty and is a source of much pleasure. Willy is already trying to climb the fences and bushes and it is impossible for the buggy to leave the yard without his . . . demanding a ride." [126]

By mid-April, the Nicaragua steamers discontinued operations. "Affairs connected with that line are in . . . confusion. Of the merits of the controversy, I know nothing more than you. Garrison is . . . its agent and I would not be astonished if he is at the bottom of the claim set up by Walker's government." The military reverses that Walker was then sustaining foretold his final defeat, in Sherman's opinion.

The letter writer then switched quickly to the domestic front and a lighter vein:

> Willy would make a sensation in a fair in the Fiji Isles, and would excite the palate of some epicure there, but he is a hard specimen for civilized people. He walks over us all rough shod, and rules his poor sister Lizzie without a particle of charity for her inferior strength of body and purpose. . . .
>
> I continue ordinarily well . . . and Mrs. Sherman thinks asthma is not my only chance [of death] but a foolhardy exposure of life and limb. . . . A few days ago I went on board the bark Emily Banning . . . to witness the operations of a diving bell. . . . I saw a party go down and return . . . looking . . . fine and fresh . . . and being invited to go down, I did so. . . . [I] went down to the bottom of the bay and returned none the worse but wiser by the trip.

Despite the favorable termination of the Smiley case, Major Hammond was far from free of troubles. Word of these had reached St. Louis, and Sherman summarized the situation in answer to Turner's inquiry. He was not sure he had all the facts; the story was quite complicated. In paying for the new customhouse, Hammond had exceeded the appropriation but claimed he had the approval of his superiors and proper receipts for all disbursements. In addition to this charge, there was a $48,000 fund Hammond had received from his predecessor, Sanders.[127] This had been reserved for certain suits pending against Sanders as collector. He had been ordered to pay the fund to the assistant United States treasurer, but instead he lodged it with Hammond. At this point, as Sherman explains it, both Sanders and Hammond seem to have been infected by the loose practices prevailing in pioneer California:

It was understood between him [Hammond] and Sanders that this money should be invested in a part of the ranch over the bay where we took that ride. Hays being Surveyor General [128] and largely interested in the same claim and assuring them that a patent would soon be issued and they would make a good thing of it—whereas property has gone down, down till now there is no value to anything. Lands held at $300 an acre when you were here are now sold at $3 and I expect soon that people will be afraid to acknowledge they own any property at all. . . . Both Hammond and Sanders have been indicted for this transaction. . . . They can't . . . raise the money. Hammond owes us $4,000 on the same note you saw here and has made a deed to us of a good many town lots in Stockton, partly to secure the note and partly to have his property beyond risk of attachment . . . the only accommodation he has ever had of us. . . . I think his leaving us that $40,000 the night of the Grand Smash up entitles him to this.

Sherman again referred to his brief absence from San Francisco:

Last week I went to Sacramento and Marysville taking . . . Mrs. Sherman and Lizzie. It rained all the time hard, but so welcome was the water that we found no fault. We rode out and saw General Sutter [129] who was much gratified. He is rid of all his claims but the Hock Farm . . . is now settled . . . cultivating the grape and fig and fruit. . . . Last year the grasshoppers took everything but this year he has the promise of much fruit. He irrigates by a steam pump. Sacramento is much improved since you were there and the railroad runs twice a day to Folsom. But the taxes are 5% so that they are bad off there as we are here, but they don't seem to be aware of it. Marysville is comparatively out of debt, looks well and has three or four squares well built of brick houses, but the railroad will cut off much of their trade for goods can be delivered at Folsom for some $3 to $5 a ton less than Marysville, where the Yuba [River] is already nearly filled up and the Feather [River] daily shoaling. The hardest rains of the season have been since the last steamer and their effect is magical. The country is now beautiful, all green and flowers. The wheat and grain crop is certain and a great deal of snow must have fallen in the mountains. . . . [It] rained hard for three days . . . value of it more than ten millions of dollars. A most universal sentiment prevails of better times, but I see no evidence of it yet. . . . Many failures continue."

After detailing the trouble he had encountered in collecting three drafts on a supposedly good letter of credit, he exclaimed in disgust: "I think interest should be 5% a month to incur such risks."

Sherman was happy to report that he hoped to have all his trust accounts paid back by the end of 1856.

As he wrote in his letter of April 17, the memorial to Congress about the overland wagon road was starting East on the outgoing steamer. It was in two bound volumes. The very next mail received in San Francisco [130] further emphasized the urgency of the problem. The *John L. Stephens* arrived on May 2 with accounts of serious rioting at Panama. With the Nicaragua route already closed, "and the other threatened by a wild and irresponsible mob," San Francisco faced the prospect of complete isolation from the rest of the world. No wonder that Sherman wrote:

The wagon road must be built, so pitch in or see California madder than now if such a thing were possible.

I have written to Mr. Meigs thanking him for the prompt denial of that silly *Sunday Times* [article] which was clever on his part as the character of the paper was unknown in New York. Lest the other article which I sent to you might also attract attention, I sent him a copy of Mr. Stanly's report. [This referred, of course, to the Smiley case which had apparently been unfairly dealt with in some newspaper article.] Dall is asking a rehearing but Baldwin says there is no chance. No decision in the City case [about the Powell Street paving warrants]. Why I can't conjecture. . . . Every day's delay increases the chances against us. A great many suits have recently been started against the city on warrants for the legislature rejected the bill for funding. With the example of bad faith on the part of the city, it is small wonder there is so much dishonesty here.

We get more customers quietly—some good, some bad . . . all more or less borrowers. . . . On open accounts, balances are all small. . . . I restrict our discounts . . . trying to regulate them according to our interest, but it is very hard to control them. I . . . believe that Garrison has more money than I gave him credit for. He makes a statement every now and then showing a steady increase of loans and discounts with a diminishing balance in New York. Amount due depositors . . . is small. Such is the case all over town. I believe our deposits are about as good as any. We had another failure among the bankers yesterday. Argenti, Cavalier & Company did not open . . . in consequence of the return of some French drafts protested. They have never had any deposits and their failure hardly gave them a newspaper slap.[131]

Derby puts forth this morning a hit at the fulsome descriptions of the recent school examinations . . . good enough to . . . enclose in this.[132]

There is a movement . . . to enlarge the present Mint[133] or build a new one. . . . Ground contiguous to the present Mint will cost as much as to build . . . on Sansome Street in rear of the Custom House on . . . Custom House block already owned by U.S. . . . Alsops Company are trying to sell their building on California Street, as bad as the present cramped building. It is much to our interest to have the new Mint on the Custom House lot. I have written to the Secretary of the Treasury [in care of] John F. Lee[134] under expectation that John Sherman has not returned from Kansas. It is worth your while to . . . watch this movement . . . and if you could bring any influence to bear, do so.

Evidently Sherman shared the apprehension recently expressed by Turner, concerning his brother John's politics, for he wrote:

[John Sherman] is, I fear, committed to the new black Republican party, but I hope . . . he will not be led into any extreme party. . . . All Ohio politicians are opposed to slavery and its extension but I cannot think he would advocate any measure . . . to bring the influence of other states on the general government on that vexed question. . . . I am afraid of it and have written him to remember what other good and great men have done in like cases . . . Clay, Jefferson, Ewing[135] and others whom he must respect. He is young and ambitious and may at the outset of his career commit some fatal errors. The slave states have claims to sympathy for the institution is fixed on them by bygone ages. Instead of being badgered . . . they ought to receive the assistance of all national men in regulating their affairs according to their own judgments.[136]

Part Four:
The Eye of the Hurricane

22

During May, 1856, a series of startling events demoralized Lucas, Turner & Co.'s operations, just as they disrupted the lives of everyone in San Francisco. Slow loans, exchange problems, pending lawsuits, and all banking routines were perforce relegated to the background.

Mention has been made of the vigorous editorials of James King of William in the *Daily Evening Bulletin*. Municipal corruption and fraudulent elections were frequent targets of its editor's attacks. In one of these, he bluntly charged that James P. Casey had been an inmate of Sing Sing Prison in New York.

Casey was a versatile rascal. He was an expert operator as well as a beneficiary of that peculiar San Francisco institution of the 1850's—ballot-box stuffing. A box some two feet in length and half as wide and as deep was equipped with a false bottom and inner slides. A skilled manipulator could insert in the box ballots which he had previously marked. In numerous elections of the period, many fraudulent ballots were mixed with the legitimate, outnumbering the latter and tilting the count for the benefit of the candidates favored by the stuffers. These gentry became so bold that in some instances, the total votes recorded in a precinct exceeded the number entitled to vote there. Such was the artistry of the double-back-action ballot box, that at a municipal election late in the fall of 1855, Casey had been declared elected a supervisor by the voters of a precinct of which he was not even a resident and in which he had not previously been announced as a candidate!

The issue of the *Bulletin* exposing Casey was on the streets at about 3:00 P.M. of May 14. Between 4:00 and 5:00 P.M., Casey strode into the newspaper's office on Merchant Street between Montgomery and Kearny, to demand an apology. King contemptuously ordered him off the premises. As he left, Casey vowed he would kill the editor. A little later that afternoon, as King was crossing the northwest corner of Montgomery and Washington Streets, Casey approached him, calling out: "Defend yourself." He then drew a revolver and shot King in the breast. "Oh, God, I am shot," King cried and staggered into the Pacific Express office, where he collapsed. Dr. Beverly Cole soon arrived and administered first aid. A little later the stricken man was removed to a room in the Montgomery Block.

Word of the shooting spread like wildfire. King was quite popular, and his fearless exposure of the city's corrupt politicians and criminal element was much admired. Everywhere the cry was raised that the assassin should be lynched. Casey's friends quickly became alarmed and spirited him to the county jail on the north side of Broadway between Kearny and Dupont streets, where his crony, Sheriff David Scannell, could be counted on to shield him from the angry crowds that were gathering rapidly.

Soon Mayor James Van Ness appeared and begged the multitude to disperse and let the law take its course. He was howled down with shouts of "Where is the law? Where is Cora?" (This scornful reference was to the many delays in retrying the assassin of United States Marshal William H. Richardson.)

Almost spontaneously public sentiment evoked memories of the Vigilance Committee that had cleansed the city in 1851. Frightened citizens concluded that it was again needed. On the evening of May 14, the great bell atop the Monumental Fire Engine Company's headquarters on the Plaza sounded its tocsin. Scores of aroused members rushed from their homes and within a few hours, several of the committee's former leaders were addressing the ever-growing crowd. There were loud demands for the reorganization of the committee. William T. Coleman, who had been its president, agreed to head it once more. In the next few hours, other meetings were held and the enrollment of members started. Fifteen hundred joined the first day; soon the total swelled to five thousand.

In a few days, permanent headquarters was established in a two-story brick building on Sacramento Street between Front and Davis. Each member was given a number and was known only by that. (Coleman was Number One; Isaac Bluxome, secretary of the committee, was Number Thirty-three.) The membership was divided into several military companies of infantry, two of cavalry, and four of artillery. Ships in the Bay supplied four pieces of ordnance, which were mounted on the roof of the headquarters. This building quickly became known as Fort Gunnybags because of the bags filled with sand that formed a breastwork for the cannon. The lower floor of Fort Gunnybags contained the armory and drill room. Here were stored the firearms that were rapidly assembled from all over the city. The second story was occupied by the offices, committee rooms, and eight cells for prisoners.

Few episodes in the history of the West have excited as much interest and controversy as the activities of this 1856 Vigilance Committee. The literature on the subject is voluminous. Bancroft alone devoted more than seven hundred pages to detail the events of that stormy spring. He did not content himself with the role of a mere chronicler; but with aggressive partisanship, he filled numerous pages with a defense of the Vigilantes and the denunciation of their opponents and critics. His bias and sympathies are so mingled with the facts that his account must be read with caution.[1]

Since this narrative deals with William Tecumseh Sherman, the banker, I do not propose to undertake a study of the committee's proceedings or of the phenomenon of Vigilantism itself. However, to the degree that it monopolized much of Sherman's time, and stands out as the greatest external influence in his San Francisco career, it must loom large in our story.

Sherman's own account of the events succeeding May 14 must be our primary source of information. Despite the distraction of the explosive happenings around him, he found time to write his steamer letters. Unlike the heavy correspondence previously reviewed, his principal letter dealing with the Vigilance Committee has been published in part. In its December, 1891, issue, *Century Magazine* printed long extracts of Sherman's letter of May 18, 1856. Before finding it in that magazine, I had obtained a photostat of the original letter, which is in the possession of the Missouri Historical Society of St. Louis.

It is probably the longest of Sherman's letters that I have seen. *Century* published the first sixteen pages with some omissions. A few of these are inconsequential but the failure to reprint others results in the avoidance if not suppression of Sherman's account of some of his own participation in the fateful events of the third week of May. These omissions cannot be deemed minor. Still harder is it to understand why the editor of *Century* left out the next four pages, which Sherman added as a postscript on May 20. These include expressions of his views about the committee and its doings. Certainly those views were neither trivial nor irrelevant. Why were they omitted in the 1890's?

In republishing this letter in these pages, nothing legible has been deleted, so that I believe that what follows is the nearest to a complete publication of Sherman's account of events up to May 20, 1856, that has appeared.[2]

It is most unfortunate that the latter pages of the original letter in the possession of the Missouri Historical Society were damaged by water. Even its exact length cannot be ascertained. The twentieth page is in part illegible, and I have been informed that the balance, including the writer's signature, was virtually destroyed.

This is Sunday [began Sherman]. Mrs. Sherman is at church. The children have the whooping cough and all else at home is as usual, but abroad is danger and this steamer will bring you news of most distressing character growing out of the shooting of James King of William by Casey, editor of the Sunday Times, the same man who so recklessly attacked all the bankers and decent people of this city.[3] I will send you so many newspaper extracts that I may confine my letter to my own personal history, and I beg you to preserve this letter in view of any untoward events in which spite of all caution I may become involved.

Shortly after the sailing of the last steamer several gentlemen connected with the Volunteer Companies of the city mentioned that Governor Johnson[4] would offer me the appointment of Major General 2nd Division California Militia. I expressed a strong disinclination to do anything at all and hoped the Governor would do no such thing. The Governor soon after called in person and offered me the appointment. I expressed a dislike to do anything that might distract my attention from business. He assured me that the Legislature has passed a law reorganizing the Militia, making it imperative on him to make some high military appointments, among whom he proposed Ned Beall, Woodworth,[5] myself and others—that it was simply for the purpose of organization and that no expense would be incurred and little time needed to perform its duties. I gave a reluctant consent which at the time I felt was imprudent.

Last Saturday, feeling the want of exercise, I crossed the Bay to Oakland, got a horse and took a ride over the mountain toward Monte Diablo and making a circuit back to the city. On my arrival on Monday I found a commission awaiting me, which I accepted and wrote for a copy of the laws governing the Militia, meaning to take my time to appoint a staff and do what seemed requisite.

On Wednesday after bank hours I came home and about 8:30 o'clock, Mr. Bainbridge and Holland came out and told me that King had been shot by Casey and that excitement ran high. King's articles have all been provoking and I have long expected him to be attacked, and therefore was not astonished, and had the populace got Casey that night and hung him I would have rejoiced, but Casey was smart enough to have himself confined to the jail before feeling had become concentrated. The Mayor called out the Volunteer Companies, three of infantry, amounting to some sixty men turned out, a few straggling mounted men and about a dozen men stood by two guns, six pounders. That night passed off without violence and next morning, Thursday, I went to the bank as usual, found everybody intensely excited, threats to take Casey and Cora and hang them, and a revival of the old Vigilance Committee. A public call was made for the old members of that committee at a certain room around which all day was gathered a large crowd.

I went to the Mayor Van Ness, a large, good man, but as usual so mussed up and involved in old business that he could do nothing. I then saw the officers of the Volunteer Companies, and found them wavering. I went to the Jail and found the Sheriff, a strong gross bluff, athletic man, surrounded by his deputies in a kind of ante room, excited and apprehending an attack on the Jail each moment. I examined the Jail and found it utterly indefensible, its rear wall flush with the ground and overlooked in all its parts by houses all around—a perfect trap in which a small body of men could do nothing. I suggested to the Sheriff the immediate procurement of plank and materials to parapet the walls and make it tenable against a mob attack, every moment apprehended. I then became satisfied the volunteers could not be depended on and so informed the Mayor and that I would not identify myself with them and that though I held the Governor's commission, I should not attempt any exercise of military authority. To have done so would have been to make myself odious and ridiculous. I informed the Mayor that the Jail could not be defended, that a mob could occupy a few of the buildings and completely drive out any posse the Sheriff might command. What complicated matters was that the Sheriff and his friends are shoulder strikers, the very class against which is raised this storm of indignation. Colonel West, Major Johnson[6] and a few of the Volunteer officers, thought maybe in the course of the day they could prevail on some of the Volunteers to act. When I pointed out to them that the only possible way to hold the jail against a mob was for the Sheriff to occupy the jail with his deputies, the police and such citizens as would serve as a posse, and the military companies to occupy such buildings roundabout as would prevent their occupation by the mob.

I then went about my business, but went down town that night with Nisbet, walked about town, and found as I expected that the volunteer companies had not turned out, that there then had been no mob but that the Vigilance Committee was in session enrolling men, and keeping up a secret dread of some violence.

Friday was the same, continued excitement but no direct attack on the jail, or direct interference with the civil authorities. On Friday afternoon the Mayor called on me, saying he had telegraphed to Governor Johnson to come down, and had received an answer he would be down that evening, and he requested me to meet the Governor at the boat at 9:30. About the same time, a formal writ was served on me, commanding me to meet the Sheriff at the 4th District Court room at 3:30 p.m. I went and found about a hundred people who had been summoned. The Sheriff called out the names of all on whom the writ was served, and it seemed about one third had come. These were mostly lawyers or persons in some way friendly to those in jail. There were some exceptions, Judge Norton, Thornton, Peachy, Billings, McAlister, Baldwin and others.[7] The Sheriff commanded all to accompany him to the Jail, to obey the law and prevent rescue. I did not go, but told the Sheriff that I had to be at the Sacramento boat on its arrival.

I came home to dinner and before leaving the table, Hall McAlister and another gentleman came out and said that the posse comitatus at the jail composed of some sixty gentlemen had organized at the jail by electing me as Captain, that it was understood to be indefensible and all wanted to see me. I explained to him that I could not act as Captain of a Sheriff's posse, that the Sheriff was of law and necessity to command their services, that I was Major General or nothing, that there were no forces and I could not exercise military command at all, that I had an appointment to meet the Governor with whom I should probably be engaged all night, but that I had no objection to give my advice and counsel.

I went with them to the jail, found there the Sheriff, his deputies and policemen amounting to about thirty men, and the citizen posse. They clustered around me, anxious and concerned. The duty was a most disagreeable one, to defend a jail against an infuriated mob, to defend two such scoundrels as Casey and Cora. I told them frankly that the only influence their presence could exert was a moral one, the consciousness of sacrificing their comfort, and endangering their lives in the maintenance of organized law as against the violence of a mob. I pointed out the weak points and concluded that to defend the jail successfully, certain buildings outside must be occupied. Upon examination this move was too late, for the Vigilance Committee had them all filled. There was no alternative but to desert or stay in that open corral. The night was bright moonlight and beautifully serene, contrasting with the tremulous fears of the doubtful and the growing passion of the determined.

I became satisfied that unless King (from whom bulletins of health came forth almost every hour) died, there would be no direct attack upon the jail, until the Vigilance Committee had strengthened themselves by enrolling their entire force.

At 9:30 Friday night, I went to the Sacramento boat to meet the Governor, found his brother and Captain Garrison [8] waiting for him too. The *Senator* came along the wharf. We stood at the after gangway but the Governor did not come ashore. Soon we heard he had passed up the wharf having landed from the lower deck at the forward gangplank. So we followed him to the International Hotel and there found him. Johnson is a young man, very pleasing in his manners, a lawyer of intelligence and I am satisfied if he had the power would sustain the law. We told him all that had occurred, described to him the then position of things, the small civil force the Sheriff had, the danger of the posse of good citizens who at his call were now gathered together at the jail. So we went thither, where he saw for himself how utterly indefensible the jail-yard was, open to the rear, overlooked on all sides by brick houses with parapet walls, no part of the interior of the jail safe from shots, but the cells which are full of prisoners—the wall at one corner almost undermined; a large wooden gate on a side alley which could be cut through in a minute. Indeed if I were forced to meet an armed mob, I would rather be in an open prairie than in that jail.

The Governor, seeing the entire mass of people arrayed against the civil authorities, the only military force in existence sharing the feelings of the people, the cause of the civil authorities being a bare naked principle with two such vile wretches as Casey and Cora as its exponents, whom we would all delight to have executed speedily and on a gibbet.

All of this time the Vigilance Committee was strengthening its numbers, then 2500—now 5000, having at its head such men as William T. Coleman, the brothers Arrington, Flint of Flint, Peabody & Company, Miers F. Truett,[9] and indeed all the large merchants, active controlling members, whilst Parrott, Ralston, Drexel, Sather and Church [10] and most rich men are contributing means and countenance sub rosa.

I suggested to Johnson for us to go right to their headquarters, at the Turn Verein Hall on Bush Street, and we all concluded to go, Garrison, the Governor, his brother and myself. We reached the Hall about eleven o'clock at night—found it lighted up and a stream of people coming and going. At the door we found H. Channing Beals [11] to whom we announced ourselves. After a little delay, we entered a vestibule and were shown into a bar room to the right, where we sat down and Mr. Coleman, President of the Vigilance Committee sat down and had a very general conversation in which Coleman said the purpose of the association was not designed to subvert the law but to assist it in purging the community of the clique of shoulder strikers, ballot box stuffers and political tricksters generally, that the courts and juries had become of no use, and that they must be purged or spurred on, that they did not meditate violence and were willing to await King's fate; if he dies, Casey to be tried speedily and executed. All this was fair and we almost coincided with him in opinion. At first he intimated a desire that Casey should be given up to them, but Governor Johnson told him distinctly that he would enforce the law as speedily as its forms would allow, but he would never consent to Casey being taken from the Sheriff's custody, but that if the Committee felt any uncertainty about Casey's being safe in custody, there was no objection to a few men of their number being admitted, who were to be considered an assistant guard, but under the control of the Sheriff. It was then agreed that if such an arrangement were made, that the Committee should pledge themselves that those of the Committee so admitted should not attempt any violence or league with those outside, but if a change of purpose became necessary, the Committee men should be withdrawn and reasonable notice given.

Coleman then went into the large hall and after some time returned with six other gentlemen, with whom further conversation was held, all to the same effect and the treaty was made verbally, Governor Johnson telling them that he treated with them as individuals and not in their capacity as a body of men leagued together for a purpose unknown to the law. We were there till half past one at night, and parted with a clear distinct understanding that no mob violence was contemplated at all, and no demonstration on the jail should be made until their guard was withdrawn and reasonable time thereafter to enable the Sheriff to resume the status quo.

We agreed to meet at the jail at two o'clock to admit their ten men, the Sheriff being at liberty to keep as many as he pleased. We went to the jail, found the Sheriff disinclined to admit the enemy, but as he could not depend on the citizens to defend the jail, he became satisfied his only chance of life was to save time, and therefore consented. At two o'clock Friday night, ten men of the Vigilance Committee were introduced and the room in the jail placed at their service, and one or two of them were allowed to stand or sit near the cell door in which Casey is confined. Coleman and Truett came with their posse, assured themselves that Casey was there, and we all left thinking under the circumstances that it was the best thing then at our choice. We all parted Friday night at three a.m. satisfied to await King's fate, and believing that the community at large would be satisfied.

Sunday, twelve o'clock.

Governor Johnson has just sent for me. He is on Jackson Street, International Hotel. My belief is that the leaders are not able to control their men, and that they will be forced to extremity. I believe Casey and Cora to be doomed if the Sheriff resists and blood is shed. No man can forsee the result, all the elements of the Paris Committee of Safety are here and once put in motion, they cannot be stopped. I regret having been placed in this position but I am bound in honor to serve the Governor of the state to the best of my means and ability.

2:15 p.m. I have just returned to my house. I went to the International and on my way saw crowds hurrying in the same direction. When I reached the hotel, I found the Governor and Mayor on the roof along with many others. He simply pointed towards the jail which you remember is on Broadway near Kearny. All the houses commanding a view were covered with people. Telegraph Hill was black with them, and the street was a complete jam. He told me that the Committee had sent him word at 10:30 that they would withdraw their men and the treaty was at an end. Johnson went immediately to the jail and found the Sheriff with his deputies and a few citizens. The Sheriff has been firm and constant and he very properly asked the Governor to give him some orders how to act in case the Committee demanded his prisoners. The Governor told him then if they appeared with sufficient force to make resistance idle, he might surrender his prisoners under protest. This is humiliating but I think he did right. If the Sheriff should fire on that mob, the immediate result would be terrific, whatever the future effect and consequences yet in the lap of futurity may be.

Well, shortly after the masses of people began to move towards the jail, crowning all the houses and hills, soon followed by the Committee in full organization—2500 men armed with muskets, rifles, a field piece, beside at least as many more arm in arm, silent, orderly and quiet whilst at least five thousand men flocked as to a show. When I reached the roof of the International, there must have been at least ten thousand people within a rifle-shot of the jail. Soon a man rode by on a white horse, followed by a carriage which stopped at the jail door. Soon a shout announced success and soon the procession began to move from the jail down Kearny to Pacific, Pacific to Montgomery, Montgomery towards Sacramento when I lost sight of them—it was headed by two platoons of about sixty or eighty men with bright muskets, then the carriage with Casey with two files of armed men on each side, then followed by a promiscuous crowd. A great many armed men appeared to remain at the jail. This Vigilance Committee seem to take the old one of 1852 as their model and as that one hung their prisoners at 3: p.m. on Sunday, I take it for granted that before the ink dries on my sheet, Casey will be hanging from some beam out of some Committee room of that Power that now governs San Francisco. Soon after the passage of the crowd, Sheriff Scannell and his deputy, Harrison, came on the roof of the hotel to see the Governor, but he had disappeared. We descended from the roof to his room but he was not there. We searched through the hotel without success. Whilst this was transpiring, Scannell told me that Coleman and Truett [12] were the spokesmen, that they demanded Casey, whom he surrendered under protest. They took Casey from the jail and dispatched him in the manner I have stated, and then demanded possession of the jail. This not being contemplated, his instructions did not cover the case so he and his deputy ran down to see the Governor, and thus far has not seen him. But I did not stay long. I came home. San Francisco is now governed by an irresponsible organization claiming to be armed with absolute power by the people. The government is powerless and at an end.

I don't care if they take the jail, the courts, and what they please. Coleman told me he thought they could control the movement. I doubt it for reasons I will now proceed to explain, in continuation of the events yesterday.

On Friday night we made an agreement with the controlling members of the Vigilance Committee that to be assured of no complicity of the Sheriff with his prisoner, that they should have a force of ten men nominally under the orders of the Sheriff. Yesterday—Saturday—the Sheriff suggested to Johnson to try and get the number diminished to five, when he would reduce his force in proportion, this under the supposition that no attempt to take the prisoner should be made until King's fate were determined. So yesterday at 1: p.m. the Governor asked me to walk with him to the Committee to make the proposition. We found new men, a new tone and a positive refusal to reduce the number. In reannouncing the conditions agreed on the night before, we claimed that *reasonable* notice should be given, *that* too, they denied. New elements were at work and outside pressure was brought against them which they could not resist. An absolute issue of fact presented itself, and Governor Johnson found himself in a most delicate position; to have conferred with an illegal body, to have admitted spies and enemies in the jail. We asserted so positively this change of promise, this want of truth, that we agreed to bring Garrison. We found him about 4: p.m. and his memory was positive, and with him, we again went to the Committee rooms. Again a change of men, more rabid than ever, asserting openly that they never contemplated a trial of Casey save by themselves. This was so utterly at variance with their stipulations of the night before, that we sent for Coleman and Arrington and one other who was present the night before, and these had to confirm our version of the agreement. Quite an angry debate followed among themselves, showing a division of purpose, the very object we had in view but as always the more violent prevailed and the honorable stipulations of Friday night were thrown on Mr. Coleman individually. Coleman reiterated them, and as no conclusion could be come to, they asked to advise with the Society and agreed to come to the International Hotel at 8:30 last evening.

They did not get there until 9:15 and made short work of it. The Society had overruled Coleman and would make no promises or pledges, but simply agreed to give the Governor notice before they withdrew their men, which we all knew was to be the signal of attack. This morning's notice—the taking [of] Casey are told, but what has been done with him, you will hear along with this letter.

The hanging of Casey and Cora are small trifles compared with what may follow. The Vigilance Committee are now in full possession of San Francisco and in a free American country where we pay taxes of four per cent on full valuation, we now are at the mercy of irresponsible masses. To be sure, the heads and guiders of this business are deemed some of our worthiest and best men, who profess to improve on the law and its administration. They may succeed. They say they did so succeed in 1852, and a few days or weeks will demonstrate. There are vast numbers of men here desperate, too lazy to work in the mines, unable to go away, strong for mischief and powerless for good. This class did not exist in '52. At all events, I am not implicated with it and though it may be impossible, I will endeavor not to provoke the special enmity of our new rulers.

(Here is where *Century*'s printing of Sherman's letter ends. What follows is a copy of the legible portions of the balance.)

Tuesday night, May 20. The steamer *John L. Stevens* was to have sailed today but she broke some part of her machinery and cannot get off till to-morrow evening. The *Golden Age* is now out 29 days; some accident must have happened to her or the steamer on the other side, and her non-arrival complicates the condition of affairs. I will now resume the thread of my story. Contrary to my expectations, the Vigilance Committee did not hang Casey or Cora either. I went down town on Sunday night and found the streets filled with people but it was understood nothing would be done that night. Yesterday passed off in like manner, it being understood the executive committee would *review* Cora's case, and try Casey who was expected to make many revelations showing up our politicians and implicating others. 'Tis said some five or six whom King had attacked, threw dice as to which should kill him, and the lot fell on Casey. Yesterday King was supposed to be better but last night he grew worse and rapidly failed till 1:30 today when he died. The news flew all over town. Stores were all closed and people were seen hurrying towards Sacramento and Front Streets where the Committee have their rooms, believing of course the culprits would be hung at once. Ever since, the streets and houses in that neighborhood have been filled with crowds eager to behold two men hung, but up to this moment, 10:00 o'clock at night, no execution has taken place. The Committee works with absolute secrecy and nobody knows what is done or what is to be done. I wish they would hang them and let the people go back to their work, for as long as something remains to be done, the excitement cannot subside, and people cannot return to their work. Business of all kinds has been in a measure suspended, yet strange to say, every note due yesterday was paid, and there are less borrowers this steamer [day] than on any former occasion. Of course during the uncertainty of sailing on the part of the steamer, less exchange has been sold, but I have no doubt that tomorrow the balance will be made up. I have just come up from the bank. All buildings on Montgomery Street and some principal cross streets are draped in mourning, and an immense line of people are forced to enter Montgomery Block where King's body is laid out. I did not go in to see him, but I directed Nisbet this evening to put up some black over the main entrance to our building, not over the bank for the reason that I did not care about our building being the only one unmarked with crape. I look upon King as a small part of this affair; his death by violence was to be expected, and that Casey should be his murderer is not astonishing. What I oppose is the usurpation of all civil and criminal power by a committee of citizens with absolute mastery over our lives and property. To this I will give no sign of submission or assent. A great deal of money, it is said, has been raised to defray the expenses of this Committee, stated as high as $75,000 which I much doubt. A subscription was handed me by Castle [13] the same with whom I had the difficulty about overdrafts, headed with Drexel, Sather & Church with $100. I declined to sign it, saying I had paid full and too much taxes for the support of government, and I would now contribute nothing to destroy that government. Of course this was reported to the Committee, some of whom waited on me, professing the highest respect, and urging me to resign my commission of Major General. I answered my commission was worse than useless as I had not a single man to command, but that I should not resign till I thought proper, which shall not be as long as this excitement lasts. When this subsides, I probably will, but not from any reasons which the Vigilance Committee can offer. Today, another committee, headed by Abel Guy,[14] a French banker, waited on me with another subscription list, stating they knew I was not favorable to their cause but hoping that I was convinced of the wisdom and firmness of our new rulers and would in consequence change my resolve, but I told them to make themselves perfectly easy as nothing could change my resolve to contribute not one cent out of my private purse or the bank to support the movement. I believe [damaged manuscript] . . . was on the lookout today for some demonstration looking like a threat, and kept the money arranged so as rapidly to put it in the vault, lock it and change the combination of the keys, but nothing of the kind has occurred and probably will not. I cannot believe that Coleman, Truett, Flint or such men will carry measures to extremes, but now law is at an end. The courts have all adjourned sine die, the police are not on duty but the streets are full of armed men, marching to and fro with loaded muskets and mounted sentries ride through the streets looking mysterious. This Committee has such an organization that they can do what they please and if they stop short when they have executed Cora and Casey, which they must, and have warned off the shoulder strikers which they are doing, it will be the most wonderful movement of this kind in history. It is said they have notified some 70 to quit and if they cannot pay their own passage to New York, they are provided with tickets at the Committee's expense. So at last we are turning the tables on New York. Between you and me, 'tis well King is out of the way; if he had recovered, he would have been the veriest tyrant on earth and his paper would have been law. Casey's execution will end the Sunday Times, thus two birds are killed by one stone. Is this the operation of Providence?

(Our knowledge of this long but incomplete letter must end on this cynical note.)

William T. Sherman was not the only Law and Order partisan in his household. If anything, his wife was even more outspoken in her denunciation of the Vigilance Committee than her husband himself. While his sentiments originated from his deep-rooted devotion to the law and the constitutional safeguards for enforcing it, hers sprang from more emotional and personal causes. She disliked James King of William intensely because, she wrote her parents, "he has been writing outrageously against men of education and standing . . . venting personal spite in a blackguard manner and calling it zeal for the public good." Moreover, King had "dealt in false personal abuse of Father Gallagher rector of the Cathedral." This of itself was enough to make Ellen Ewing Sherman fiercely indignant.

> King deserved to be cow-hided [she wrote], but he carried arms always and repeatedly announced that if any approached to attack him, he would fire. . . . He goaded Casey to madness and Casey shot him. . . . I am delighted that Cump by his recent appointment as Major General of the militia will act prominently against the Committee and my only regret is that he has no force sufficient to quell them. . . . Mr. Bowman urges me to suppress my views since they are unpopular. I have such a contempt for the popular side of this question . . ."

Sherman seriously proposed that his wife and Lizzie immediately return to Ohio and remain there until his "term" in California expired, but she wrote her parents, "Much as I would like to be with you, I could not deprive him of the comfort of a home and family for so long a time." Instead of preparing for flight, the courageous lady copied the sixteen-page report about the Vigilantes, which her husband had written to his St. Louis partners, and proudly mailed it to her mother and father.[15]

23

There is an unexplained gap in the Eleanor Sherman Fitch Collection of letters between May 4 and July 2, 1856. This is in part compensated by the long letter of May 18th and 20th reprinted in the last chapter. We do not have any letters written by Sherman to Turner during the six weeks between May 20 and July 2. I am convinced that Sherman wrote to his friend during the period. Not only was it his custom to send a letter by each mail steamer, but also we have a record of other letters written by him during these weeks. Two to his father-in-law, the Hon. Thomas Ewing,[16] were reprinted in the same issue of *Century* as were the extracts from the May 18/20 letter in the preceding chapter.

These letters to Ewing were dated May 21 and June 16. While recounting the story of the Vigilance Committee, the first adds nothing to the facts already reviewed. The second narrates events up to June 16. Sherman's *Memoirs*[17] also recount this whole series of happenings.

King died on Tuesday, May 20. By coincidence, the Vigilance Committee's trials of both Cora and Casey had been set for the same day. The committee appointed counsel to defend the two prisoners; and their trials generally observed legal formalities, although they were expedited more than in the regular courts. Both defendants were convicted and were sentenced to be hanged.

King's funeral was conducted by the Masonic order at the Unitarian Church on Stockton Street on Thursday, May 22.

The church was filled to capacity and a large assemblage, unable to enter it, thronged the nearby streets, then followed the cortege to Lone Mountain Cemetery.[18] While the obsequies were in progress, Cora and Casey were hanged from the second-story windows of Fort Gunnybags. An equally large crowd witnessed the executions.

Sherman hoped that with these criminals disposed of, the Vigilance Committee would adjourn, and San Francisco could resume its normal way of life. However, the committee gave every indication of continuing its announced mission of reform. Ballot-box stuffers and other undesirable characters were driven into exile. Armed representatives of the committee patrolled the streets.

Therefore, Governor Johnson wired General Sherman on May 30 to meet him at Benicia. At their conference, the governor stated he might be compelled to call on the militia to enforce the laws. Having neither arms nor munitions, he proposed that application be made to General Wool, in command of the Pacific Department of the Army. The government arsenal at Benicia was supposedly well stocked with both guns and ammunition. The two men called on General Wool and inspected the stores in the arsenal.

After some hesitation, Wool stated that if Governor Johnson issued a proclamation commanding the usurpers of power in San Francisco to disband and to permit the civil authorities to resume their functions, he, General Wool, would on application, furnish General Sherman the muskets and munitions needed to equip the militia under his command. With this assurance, Johnson returned to Sacramento and Sherman to San Francisco.

The governor directed Judge David S. Terry [19] of the supreme court to issue a writ of habeas corpus commanding the sheriff of San Francisco to bring before him one of the prisoners confined in Fort Gunnybags by the Vigilance Committee. As expected, the writ was disregarded, and the governor then issued the proclamation discussed at Benicia. It was stronger than Sherman had anticipated and declared the county of San Francisco to be in a state of insurrection.

In the meantime, Sherman had begun the organization of his militia. Numerous citizens enlisted in response to the proclamation that he issued as major general. The governor then applied to General Wool for guns and ammunition to equip Sherman's companies. General Sherman was thunderstruck to learn on June 5 that Wool had notified the governor that he had no authority to supply the munitions requested and so declined the governor's application. Sherman wrote General Wool and pointedly reminded him that he had promised the munitions to Governor Johnson in Sherman's presence at Benicia.

General Sherman felt compelled to publish a card in the newspapers. In it he deplored the illegal status of the Vigilance Committee and its actions. He recounted his efforts to raise militia to carry out the governor's proclamation and stated that he had planned to arm his troops from the government arsenal as agreed to by General Wool. Now that Wool's change of mind or heart had defeated his plans, Sherman was resigning his commission so that Governor Johnson might take whatever steps he wished.

Sherman was attacked in the pro-Vigilance press and at the same time was criticized by the governor for resigning when he did. Johnson appointed Volney E. Howard [20] as major general to succeed Sherman as commander of the militia.

Sherman's letter to Turner of July 2, 1856, which is in the Fitch Collection, was also published in part by the *Century Magazine* in December 1891. The omissions in this abridgment command our special attention. They are certainly more than incidental! A reading of the full text of Sherman's letter gives us a better knowledge of both his reasoning and his actions at that critical time. *Century*'s incomplete version left out Shermans' report of an important precaution he took to safeguard the small supply of arms in the possession of the militia. In this connection, he showed the same grasp of tactics that distinguished his Civil

War career. Other omissions create a false view of Sherman's own opinions, including his uninhibited estimate of the supreme court of California. Therefore, this letter is reproduced in full below.

Another steamer day is approaching [Sherman began]. As the 4th of July intervenes, it will make it awkward to us, so that I will beforehand write my private letter. The last advices explained the condition of public affairs up to the 20th ult. at which time the Vigilance Committee were in full blast. There was an apparent submission to them, which looked like a perfect calm, but every thinking man knew that at any moment the whole might explode. Sure enough, on Saturday the 21st occurred one of the most disgraceful scenes that can be imagined. It seems that General Howard, who succeeded me in the management of the military affairs here, was gathering arms and munitions, picking them up wherever they could be found. A small schooner, the *Julia*, had about 130 [?] muskets on board, and whilst on her way to the city, was intercepted by another small vessel with Vigilance Committee men on board, headed by one Durkee,[21] who took the arms and the three men in charge in custody, and on reaching the city the arms were taken to the Fort of the Committee and the three men turned loose; these were named Phillips, Maloney, and McNab.[22] These men went before the U.S. District Court and filed a complaint against Durkee for a piracy on the waters of the Bay, and the Committee finding themselves about to be embroiled with the U.S. government, discovered that Maloney was a bad character, a ballot box stuffer, and accordingly issued their orders for his arrest. This order was placed in the hands of their Chief of Police, Hopkins,[23] who proceeded to the room of R. P. Ashe,[24] Navy Agent, brother-in-law of Dr. Moses in your city. He has been a most violent opposer of the Vigilance Committee, and he was captain of one of the companies enrolled under my orders. His room is over Palmer, Cook & Company's bank and Judge Terry of the Supreme Court, was staying with him. Terry, too, is a most violent opposer of the Committee, is the judge whose writ was disobeyed, and who has honestly opposed the progress of this Committee by all the influence he possesses. When Hopkins reached the room and asked Maloney to go with him, Ashe, Terry and others present, put Hopkins out. He immediately sent word to the Committee rooms for more force to arrest Maloney. Ashe, Terry, and the others in the room with Maloney, took such weapons as they could get, and started for one of the armories used by one of the state volunteer companies on Jackson Street between Kearny and Dupont.

On leaving Palmer, Cook & Company's building, they were followed by Hopkins and others, who endeavored to seize Maloney, but Ashe and Terry interposed, and they had nearly reached the armory when Hopkins seized the gun in Terry's hands, a scuffle ensued, a pistol went off and Terry, a strong, fine looking man, excited, announced himself a judge of the Supreme Court, commanded the peace, and endeavored to escape from Hopkins, who held his gun with his left hand and with his right grasped Terry by the hair or neck cloth. Then Terry drew his knife, showed it to Hopkins and stabbed him in his left shoulder. Hopkins by this time had Terry's gun, with which he ran down the street, crying he was stabbed or killed. Maloney, Terry, Ashe and party thus reached the armory which is in the third story of a fire engine house.

Then arose such a tumult as I never witnessed. The Vigilance bell pealed forth its wildest clamor and men ran calling "Hang him, hang him!" All kinds of stories flew about that Terry had shot Hopkins dead, and indeed it was hours before the truth was known. All stores were closed; so wild was the tumult that I had the money put in the vault and locked, and commanded all the clerks to stand by. Crowds of people with muskets and swords and pistols poured by up Jackson Street, and a dense mass of men filled the street from Montgomery to Stockton. Knowing Terry and Ashe to be desperate men and hearing that some fifteen or twenty of their friends were with them, I took it for granted that blood would be shed, but after some talking they concluded to surrender, and were conducted under strong guard to the Vigilance Committee rooms.

At the same time, all the armories of the State Volunteers were surrounded, cannon placed in front, and all surrendered, giving up their arms and accoutrements, a regular *coup d'état, à la Louis Napoléon.* Thus from that day, the state of California ceased to have any power to protect men here, in defense of her sovereignty. General Howard managed badly—he allowed the different companies to have their arms at different rooms, all of which were of course known, and were picked up by the Committee. When the Volunteer companies were organizing, Lt. Colonel West came and asked me about their drills. They had arms. I ordered him to drill at nights in their rooms, and then let each man take his musket to his home, scattering them as much as possible, but Howard, I suppose, allowed West to keep his muskets at the different armories, so he lost them all at one blow.

Since that day nothing has been done in the military way except by the Vigilance Committee who have their rooms fortified and whose companies are marched through the streets at all hours. Some are being uniformed, and some bands of music are now being formed, so it may be they intend to keep up their military power a long time.

In the meantime Terry is in the cells of the Committee. At first they were disposed to treat him well, allowed his wife to see him, but of late they have changed and now they permit no one to visit him. I enclose you a slip containing a letter from Mrs. Terry, and I know you will agree with me that this is a case of such cruelty, that without knowing we could not believe such a thing could be enacted in an American city.

For ten days Hopkins has been lying on his bed, with reports coming every hour that he was getting worse and even dying. The newspapers, a perfect curse, have been inflaming the public mind, and that *Bulletin*, the cause of all this civil strife, announces its dictates, which are promptly obeyed. To it Judge Terry is indebted for the cruelty shown him. When it was generally understood that during his confinement, he was to have a room and be allowed the company of his wife, the *Bulletin* announced that such would not be the case, and that the editor was *happy* to announce that Judge Terry would not be treated a bit better than Casey and Cora, that he was confined in the same kind of cell, that he would be tried by the same law, and if found guilty, suffer the same penalty. It has now been almost certain that if Hopkins died, Judge Terry would be hung. If Hopkins recovers, then he will be banished. At all events he must be made to resign, but he will not resign, he says. He would rather die than be dishonored. If forced to leave the state, he still remains Judge of the Supreme Court, and as Judge Heydenfelt[25] is away, it virtually breaks up the Supreme Court, that court on which we all depend, we for our city case,[26] on which we believe the judges have passed favorably.

Yet this decision is not yet rendered, and therefore as an effect of this outrageous decision, we have to incur the risk and expense of going over the whole case again. Of the judges of the Supreme Court, Murray [27] is an able lawyer, but has all the vices in the calendar. Heydenfelt is an honest, honorable good man, but the extremist "states rights" Calhoun man,[28] he is now abroad. Terry is young, resembles you in appearance, probably taller and heavier, highly honorable and bade fair to make an excellent judge, but he was imprudent in this matter for as judge he ought to have kept aloof on the score that the questions involved might come before him as judge. So satisfied was I of this that, when in command here, I requested Johnson to call him to Sacramento, which he did; but when I resigned, he came again to this city and the result is he is in the power of the Committee. Still he is a highly respectable man, and Hopkins is a loafer. Now when Casey killed King, the cry was that King was a good citizen and Casey a scoundrel—now the case is reversed but it makes all the difference in the world, whether your bull gores my ox or my bull yours.

I hope Hopkins may recover, in which case the Committee can do nothing to Terry, but if he dies, we may have further commotion. I am sick of this whole matter, and I believe the community is fast becoming so, and therefore I will drop the subject, leaving the newspapers to keep you advised of the progress of this singular revolution. I am out of it, and believe I have lost nothing in public estimation in what I did. At all events it is a lesson I will never forget—to mind my own business in all time to come.[29]

In order to finish the story of the Vigilance Committee, so far as Sherman was concerned, two of his letters to his brother John [30] and an extract from a third one follow. These were reprinted by *Century Magazine* (also in December, 1891) and are taken from their pages. By inserting them here, we are breaking the sequence of the letters to Turner, but the unity gained in the account of the Vigilance Committee makes that desirable.

My dear Brother [the letter of July 7, 1856, reads], The steamer sails to-day and will bring you news of the same character as the two past. The Vigilance Committee is in full blast, still exercising full control; has Judge Terry in their power, and, had the man Hopkins died, they would have hung him. Now the probabilities are they will send him away. Where the matter is to end I cannot imagine; but I think the community is getting sick and disgusted with their secrecy, their street forts and parades, and mock trials—worse, far worse, than the prompt, rapid executions of a mob or lynch court. Since my resolution I have kept purposely aloof from all parties, either one way or the other. Being in a business where large interests are at stake, I cannot act with that decision that would otherwise suit me. I do not think that there is any necessity for the interference of the Federal authorities, but that before we can hear from Washington the matter will be over and forgotten.

Another letter to John Sherman is dated August 3. It reads:

Here in this country the democratic, common element prevails to such a degree that, as you will have observed, the influence of the Governor, Mayor, and all the executive authority has been utterly disregarded. For three months we have been governed by a self-constituted committee, who have hung four men, banished some twenty others, arrested, imprisoned, and ironed many men, and who now hold a judge of the Supreme Court in their power, the authorities being utterly unable to do anything. . . . There is no doubt we have had a bad administration of law here, and more than a fair share of rowdies; but I think the committee itself no better, and if we are to be governed by the mere opinion of the committee, and not by officers of our own choice, I would prefer at once to have a dictator. The committee is now in a bad fix. The man whom Terry stabbed is well. The Executive Committee of Vigilance are willing to acquit him; but before they can act in such a matter, by their by-laws they must submit the case to a Board of Delegates, composed of three (3) from each of their military companies. This Board of Delegates, of course, want action, and they insist that Terry shall resign his office and go away or be hung. There is a sloop of war here, the *John Adams*, whose commander says that he will intercept any ship that attempts to carry Terry off. So that it will be difficult for them to banish Terry, and it is not impossible that they may yet hang Terry to save themselves the consequences of his return to the bench. If there is not an entire revolution and withdrawal from the Union, then all these acts of violence must come up before our courts on action for civil damage; and it is likely if Terry returns to the bench he will have some feeling against the men who have kept him imprisoned for some two months with daily expectation of death or banishment. We are waiting to hear what President Pierce [31] will do in this matter. I doubt if he will interfere as long as the trouble is local, and as long as those men do not try to bring about an absolute revolution, which I do not think they have yet contemplated. My own opinion is the committee is tired of its position, but finds it difficult to withdraw from the complications in which they are involved.

A brief extract from another letter to his brother, dated August 19, 1856, reads:

It is pretty generally acceded to that Terry's friends in the committee had to log-roll and stuff the box in order to save him. I know that some of the most conservative of that committee hurried Terry aboard the *John Adams* at two o'clock at night to save him from the vengeance of the more rabid faction. The committee yesterday had a grand jubilee, and for the time being are retired from the public gaze, but nobody can doubt that in any case of danger to themselves they will again come on the tapis.

24

Marking it "confidential," Sherman commenced his next letter to Turner with what was certainly an understatement: "The action of our Vigilance Committee has somewhat engrossed our attention and to some extent withdrawn my thoughts from our more immediate interests." One banking problem, however, had become so annoying that Sherman could no longer delay commenting on it. This concerned the commissions charged in New York by the Metropolitan Bank and by Schuchardt & Gebhard. These commissions were absorbing all of the firm's profits and more from the considerable volume of business involving drafts on New York. Sherman had tried unsuccessfully to obtain more reasonable rates. As a last resort, he boldly proposed to the St. Louis partners that Lucas, Turner & Co. and Lucas & Simonds jointly establish an agency in New York to handle their own transactions there.

Sherman reviewed the charges he had been paying:

On bills of exchange bought by Lucas, Turner & Co. and sent to the Metropolitan Bank, Lucas-Turner was making a profit of from 1% to 2½%.* Gold bars shipped to the San Francisco bank by its upcountry customers were bought from ¼% to ½% off their gross content. American coin had to be received at par and it was impossible to break even when the bank reshipped it to New York. Since money retained in San Francisco could be

* For explanation of terms used in these paragraphs, see Appendix, "Sherman's Banking Terminology."

readily, yet safely, loaned at 2% a month, it was obviously to the bank's interest to keep down the volume of these remittances and to obtain instead the greater return from local loans and discounts. To assist this process, Lucas & Simonds had some time before guaranteed the New York bank on Lucas-Turner transactions to a total of $50,000. In addition, Lucas, Turner & Co. received no interest on its balances with the New York bank except on amounts in excess of $25,000. Even so, the Metropolitan Bank had just increased its charges from ⅛% to ¼% on *all* items, including American coin, deposited with it by Lucas, Turner & Co. "All accounts agree in classing Mr. Williams [the Metropolitan's vice-president who had informed Lucas-Turner of the increased charges] as a fine gentleman but his idea of our submitting tamely to a charge of ¼% for handling . . . over $300,000 of American coin per month is beyond my endurance."

The doubling of the handling charge on such sizable amounts, when added to freight, insurance, boxing, and the like, would necessarily entail a loss of at least $3.35 per $1,000 on all such shipments. These cost calculations allowed nothing for clerk hire, rent, or other overhead, of which the exchange business should bear a part.

Assuming that Lucas & Simonds was doing business in New York at least equal to that done by Lucas-Turner, Sherman figured the New York bankers were making a clear profit of $30,000 a year or more from the two firms. He had been further aggrieved to learn that Wells, Fargo & Co. were paying only 1% insurance on their shipments, three other banks of about his size 1⅛%, while Lucas, Turner & Co. could not get under 1¼%. Small wonder that he declared: "Wall Street is a monster swallowing up all things."

Schuchardt & Gebhard, in Sherman's opinion, earned their commissions more easily than the Metropolitan Bank, and with a minimum of risk. This firm handled all foreign bills received by Lucas-Turner. They merely forwarded the bills for collection to the various points in Europe and charged 1% for the service.

They also accepted Lucas, Turner & Co.'s thirty-day and sixty-day sight bills for ½%. Lucas-Turner always remitted equivalent funds well in advance of the maturity of these bills.

Sherman's proposal was that the two related Lucas firms open an agency in New York. Its first step would be merely to perform the services now rendered by Metropolitan and by Schuchardt & Gebhard. Next, the agency would undertake collections and commissions for other Western and Californian banking houses, "taking *no risks whatever*. If you or Patterson could go [to New York], that would be the best plan. If you cannot, I would be willing. . . . I believe we are now well established here. . . . Stone [32] can take my place perfectly well." He repeated his previous favorable opinion of Stone's character and personality. Sherman was willing to sell Stone his interest in the partnership "on terms that would not draw a cent from the business." He would move his family to Ohio, to remain there as long as Mr. and Mrs. Ewing lived. He felt certain he could dispose of his home on Harrison Street on fair terms, perhaps to Stone. With the proceeds, he would repay his $7,000 note to Lucas & Simonds. For his own compensation, he proposed that the St. Louis and San Francisco houses each pay him $3,000 a year, with some adjustment in his favor if the New York enterprise ultimately grew into something more than an agency for the two banks.

The next paragraph reveals that personal as well as exchange problems entered into Sherman's proposal:

> For myself, I would as leave remain here all my life even with asthma, which is worse here than in any other spot I have thus far found, but I find Mrs. Sherman, though personally as comfortable as she could be anywhere . . . repeating that no earthly consideration will make her consent to live here longer than the term for which I agreed, so that I have staring in my face . . . this fact that in a couple of years I must cast about for a new occupation. . . . With bank failures and a country falling lower . . . all the time, I cannot . . . expect to make an independent fortune. All I expect is to make this house respected . . . [to] form a foundation on which to build when the good time does come.

Sherman proposed paying Stone $5,000 a year plus the one-eighth interest he would sell him. Lucas, Turner & Co. would save more than half of its present charges for New York exchange. He felt the change, if agreed to, should be made at the end of the year. If the partners had other ideas as to who would best fill the New York place, Sherman would abide by their choice. Lucas was now in Europe and Sherman realized any decision must await his return. In the interim, he planned to preserve absolute silence about his proposal, even to Mrs. Sherman.[33]

Again an unexplained gap in the Fitch collection of letters leaves us somewhat in the dark as to what transpired in the following six weeks. We know that Sherman continued his steamer letters for the next copy available (that of August 18, 1856) begins "as I wrote you last mail."

As it was more profitable to ship bars or gold dust than coin, Sherman had taken steps to secure shipments of bars and dust by some of his upcountry correspondents. To do this, he made secured loans at 2½% a month to three bankers to enable them to buy the miners' output. Strange, a banker at Murphy's, received $5,000, John M. Rhodes at Sacramento $25,000, and S. W. Langton at Marysville $25,000 under this arrangement.

> I soon discovered that Strange was getting beyond his depth and I closed down on him, and I fear we will lose something. . . . I found Rhodes also loaning too heavy, thus checking for money believing the dust would be down in a day or so. . . . I found the evil originated with Rhodes and Whitney upcountry and prevailed on Rhodes to break with them, and took enough of his bills receivable, endorsed by him, to cover his balance. . . . Now he keeps money to his credit. Similar consequences occurred with Langton & Company at Marysville. Stone is in partnership with Langton who has an express from Marysville to Downieville, Nevada [City], Forest City, etc., at all which places he has agencies to buy dust. The dust is sent to Stone who has it coined or run into bars. . . . They have an office at Marysville and . . . six points in the mountains at . . . which . . . they keep coin

wherewith to buy dust. This requires a good deal of money in advance of purchases. . . . In competing for the purchase, they occasionally advance money to secure the purchase of the dust on Sundays, the day when the miners clean out their dust and sell it. . . . I went up to Marysville with Stone and . . . made an examination of their accounts which are well kept. . . . [They] show a fair profit on their . . . purchases, but I observed some . . . advances stood over longer than seemed prudent so we went up to Bidwell's Bar to see the operations of one of the grand companies to which Langton & Company are in advance some $12,000. Bidwell's Bar is about forty miles from Marysville on the south fork of the Feather river. . . . [We] reached there at noon, so hot we could hardly breathe . . . walked down to claim called the Junction just below where the two forks of the Feather unite. A man named Hart is the contractor for the work, which consists of a dam and flume about forty feet wide 1400 feet long . . . to carry all waters of the river out of its natural bed whereby the bottom is to be exposed and worked. They believe from the formation of the shores and surrounding hills that there is an almighty amount of gold there, which they propose to make before the winter rains come and sweep away the whole. It is a joint stock company, the works cost $130,000. Hart owns three saw mills and is part stockholder and contractor. Now if they are right they will get a large return for the labor and expense, but it is possible all their labor may be in vain. It is a grand gamble and . . . unsafe . . . to lend money on. So I have notified Stone if he wants to make ventures of that kind, he must not use our money. . . . He concluded to wind up with Langton . . . leaving Langton, who is an express man, accustomed to large risks, to venture as much as he pleases. I could not but admire the skill and boldness of those mountain men to risk so much on a chance. All the business of the mining country is gambling. They put all they have and all they can borrow on a chance, which if successful, they make their pile, and if they lose, they try it again. I think, independent of the claim in question, Hart is good for his debt to Langton & Company, yet the more I see, the more satisfied I am of the risk attending advance of money to interior houses. Being on the spot, they become infected with the mania. Each little office tries to do a banking business. They draw checks on Marysville and San Francisco with looseness, thinking it all right if they send

> down in a week or so a corresponding amount of dust. By checking it saves . . . sending coin up to them, which makes their profits so much the more.
>
> Langton has a good deal of property, a dwelling in Marysville, an office and dwelling in Downieville, a brick office in Forest City and horses, wagons, etc., strung along his express line. But I don't like their risks and shall draw in and keep all our means here, buying bars when we can and when we cannot . . . ship coin. . . . On exchange . . . we are steadily losing. . . . This is very disagreeable and grates on my conscience all the time.

After this firsthand view of the high risks inherent in "up-country" business, Sherman could derive small comfort from present conditions in the city. "As failures continue we must occasionally meet with a loss, so that in my judgment, the business of California is about at as low an ebb as possible. Other bankers here know this . . . but all hope for an improvement. I hope so too." One senses the lack of conviction in these words.

Despite Sherman's expressed intention to eschew the Vigilance Committee and all its works, it again became a topic for his steamer letter. He began a paragraph with fine irony:

> The Vigilance Committee have at last finished their task. We are now a highly reformed people. Today all their firms are parading the streets on a grand jubilee, celebrating their victories, and rejoicing at the regeneration of society. I have not been down the street to see who have closed their stores in obedience to the *Bulletin*'s orders, but we have not, and I do not think any of the bankers have. . . . I hear a good deal of under expression that it is all folly, this presentation of swords and banners to companies of armed men who at most have conquered their own fellow citizens and made the authorities of their own selection a by-word and laughing stock.

While Sherman was in Marysville, he wrote Turner that Judge Terry's case had been decided by the committee. The Judge had been awakened in the middle of the night and informed that he had been found guilty. However, with that information went the decided qualification that, since the committee's two forms of punishment—death and banishment—were not suited to his case, he was at liberty to depart. Judge Terry immediately went to a friend's house where Mrs. Terry was staying. Soon afterward, some of the committee warned him that because of hostile feelings in the community it would be well for him to take refuge on board the naval vessel *John Adams*, then lying in the harbor. Terry followed their advice.

When this news became known the next morning,

> the Red Republicans [34] fumed and the *Bulletin* thundered forth its threats against the Committee, advised its deposition and the appointment of a smaller one, which could act more promptly and positively. Meetings were called and for some time there was danger that the worst elements would prevail, but the Committee held its [illegible] and Terry was out of their power.

The next afternoon the Sacramento boat carried Terry and a party of his friends to the capital where they were received with honor.

> I have no doubt [Sherman added] that Terry owes his safety to Captain Boutwell, U.S. Navy,[35] of the *John Adams*, who publicly stated that no ship should take Terry out of the harbor if he could prevent it. As Hopkins had recovered, they could not hang Terry . . . they could not banish him without coming into contact with Uncle Sam, and they had to set him free. . . . Having accomplished their great aim of purification, they are about to retire . . . have broken up their fort and reduced their expenses . . . will keep up their organization . . . in case they are threatened or if society relapses into its former dangerous state. . . . Robberies and murders are going on all over the state, as though they had not hung two or three scoundrels and expelled some twenty. . . . The amount of deep seated vengeance smothered up in the minds of those who have been ironed, imprisoned and insulted will . . . cause ten fold more crime than has been punished. I do not think even this Vigilance Committee would recommend it as a permanent institution, yet it is . . . fixed on this country as surely as any other part of our government. When ever any part of the people have real or fancied grievance, they will not appeal to the law, but organize a Vigilance Committee and pitch in. . . . If people will admit there is a reform and behave accordingly, I will no longer

quarrel with the breach of principle and dangers through which we have passed."

Sherman was quickly mindful that Terry's release would permit the state supreme court to function again. He hoped it would soon hand down a decision on the bank's case against the city over the Powell Street warrants. "I hope his [Terry's] prejudices," he wrote with tongue in cheek, "won't lean him in favor of San Francisco after his seven weeks city hospitality."

The banker believed there were signs of returning activity in real estate. The new city charter had gone into effect in July, 1856. Under it, taxes were expected to be lowered, and a more economical municipal regime seemed likely. All these factors should make real estate more salable.

If Congress passed the wagon road bill,[36] which now seemed most likely, and if also the railroad bill should carry and the Nicaragua line be reopened, then San Francisco's handicap of isolation would be lifted. Each of these possibilities would be most welcome to the city's businessmen.

Then Sherman first mentioned a radical change that was going to occupy much of his thoughts in the coming weeks.

> If we were down on Battery Street, we would do a much larger banking business. Many persons deposit with Drexel and Garrison[37] who would prefer us, but our building here is so secure and complete, and I was instrumental in having it built that I can hardly think of moving. If I could rent this to some good purpose, I would make the change. Battery Street is the longest and best arranged for business, and Montgomery Street is fast losing its character as the money street. We have a mortgage on a building on Battery . . . opposite Garrison's and diagonally opposite the Custom House and Post Office which I can get, and it could easily be adapted to our purpose.

Sherman's attraction to Battery Street and his change of heart as to Montgomery strike us curiously today. It must be reiterated that the use by the mail steamers of the Jackson and Pacific Streets wharves acted as a powerful magnet to business. This was augmented by the proximity of the customhouse and the post office. The removal of aggressive competitors like Drexel, Sather & Church and the house headed by Garrison to sites two blocks nearer these focal points strongly influenced Sherman's thinking. In terming Battery Street the "longest," a review of the map can be misleading. Montgomery is just as "long," if we disregard the terrain. Telegraph Hill ascends very abruptly north of Broadway. The same is true to some extent of Sansome, but Battery continues a fairly level course along the east foot of the hill. When Sherman wrote, more wharves had been constructed only one block east of Battery almost as far north as Lombard Street in an area lacking direct east and west access from Montgomery Street. Lucas Turner & Co. were two long blocks farther west than these competitors, and the connecting streets were narrow, poorly paved, and heavily traveled.

The concluding paragraphs of this letter combine grief and tragedy with domestic gossip and Sherman's own cynical humor. He sent Turner such condolences as he could on the loss of an infant, together with genuine concern about young Wilson Turner, who had accidentally lost an eye. He then predicted Mrs. Sherman's confinement about October 1. "Lizzie and Willie are perfect specimens of health. . . . The boy is the admiration of the town and I think he can hold his own with a two year old anywhere."

The final paragraph told of a Mrs. L. who had recently arrived in San Francisco, apparently from St. Louis. She "has talked me to death," he grumbled, "I got her off to Marysville this afternoon and had to advance her $70, which I hope I'll get back. . . . San Francisco is a horrid place. Everybody going away or arriving is dead broke and charity is no small item in one's expenses." Reverting to his new acquaintance he asked: "*Can't she talk?* and she thinks Mr. Lucas and Mr. Patterson and Mr. Turner are her warmest admirers and friends. With such an array of friends how could I refuse her? . . . Please drop the General . . . I was a Captain, but I doubt if I ever was a General." [38] This doubtless refers to Sherman's brief term as major general in the California militia.

25

"The summer has been unusually boisterous," the next letter began, "cold and foggy. On some days we have been able to dispense with overcoats." (Sherman was writing on the 4th of *September* in 1856!) ". . . I hope it is a sign of a hard winter. The two past winters have been dry ones. . . . All hope the coming one may . . . wet the ground good. Dry is not the term for the earth now. It is burned to quality of brick." Sherman believed that hard times back East might increase immigration to California—something very much needed by the state. He reported that settlers were now arriving with families and household effects—"they are a good class." He was still eager that Congress should pass the wagon road bill. Regarding the "agitation of the railroad, you know I think the railroad is a present impossibility."

The San Francisco mint had shut down for repairs, so the bank was getting more bars rather than coin for shipments, but that was affording only temporary relief from the excessive ¼% charges on the shipment of coin.

He was chagrined to have to report a sizable loss from an unexpected quarter. A customer, P. Kuhtman & Co.,[39] had for some months deposited a number of thirty-day and sixty-day drafts on a New York firm, Gupoke (?) & Company, under a letter written in German by the latter firm, which Sherman understood to be a guarantee to pay such drafts at specific rates.

A checking of the New York firm had shown them in good standing. Lucas, Turner & Co. bought a number of such bills from this customer, all of which had been duly paid, until Kuhtman cashed one for $6,000, then failed before it could be collected in New York. Gupoke refused to pay this draft; and, according to Meigs of the Metropolitan Bank, the so-called letter of credit was calculated to mislead Sherman into believing the German wording bound Gupoke when it did not. "I will try to get something out of Kuhtman," wrote the disillusioned Sherman, "though a trifle. Seems utterly impossible to steer clear of these chances . . . impossible to ascertain the standing of commercial houses here. They may be today a store full of goods and . . . the appearance of wealth. Tomorrow a sign will show them . . . agents for so and so of New York."

Yet, surprisingly enough, the banker noted that money was easier. As he wrote, the balance sheet showed discounts less than usual and deposits quite respectable. But like thunder ever threatening in the mountains, an oft-recurring theme troubled him. "If this Vigilance Committee excitement would die down . . . business would assume a lively turn." The latest flare-up resulted from the refusal by the federal court to admit John Durkee to bail on the charge of piracy growing out of his seizure of the *Julia!* The Vigilance Committee angrily notified its members to be on the alert.

> We are liable at any moment to be aroused by its tocsin notes [Sherman told Turner]. I wish this matter could be got over but . . . fear . . . as the parties more and more equal each other in strength, some sudden . . . provocation may cause it all to break out again. I would not have the judge . . . swerve one iota from the course he would pursue in times of . . . quiet, but it would be well not to arouse the pride of . . . men who think they have saved the country. . . . At the same time I don't see how we are to escape the necessity of putting down . . . resistance to the Law, for it will be repeated . . . until subdued . . . or until some outrage causes the more peaceable inhabitants to rebel against . . . this Executive Committee.

Under the terms of the so-called Consolidation Act, much street improvement work was being done, with the cost assessed proportionately to each lot owner. Fortunately, none of the bank's properties had been so taxed, but lots Sherman had acquired to satisfy some of General Hitchcock's [40] mortgage investments had been so taxed. Sherman had received several offers for the General's properties but was holding them for a higher price. One prosperous year should greatly improve the real estate market. Most of the sales now being made were distress situations.

Real estate mortgages were obtainable at 1½% a month. Lucas, Turner & Co. was receiving 2½% a month on loans and discounts with collateral. Sherman wrote:

> One of our notes for $7,000 laid over today [that seems to have been the idiom of his times for saying an obligation had become past due]. We take it the house—Lowe, Ebbetts & Company—has failed. We hold 200 barrels of butter as collateral, which I think will cover principal and interest. By recent failures we have succeeded to a good many funny things—a lot of drugs, dye stuff, butter, pick handles, etc. Generally speaking, I do pretty well.

The next few sentences throw light on the personnel problems of the 1850's. Sherman had just lost one of his best clerks, Holland, "a model of industry, good sense and fidelity." He was shipping out to accept a position in Hong Kong. During the dull times, hundreds had gone to Oregon, Chile, Australia, and Asia. Sherman expected all of them would return. He had innumerable applicants for Holland's place and was trying out a young Swede,

> well educated, sober and industrious . . . but not quick enough at figures. . . . [I] will give him a fair trial. . . . If he doesn't suit, . . . no difficulty in filling his post. . . . We are better off by the emigration of the non-producers. . . . The western emigrants are best for farming and foreigners for the mines. The Chinese are coming in pretty thick and the rascals pick up a great deal of gold. . . . Deposits today $690,000.

Sherman once again thought about the Vigilance Committee, this time in a postscript: "Judge McAllister[41] will not release Durkee on bail on grounds . . . he is to have a speedy trial. The Vigilance folk, I guess, will hardly attempt to take him out of the hands of the U.S. authorities. The cursed newspapers which thrive on excitement will do all in their power to keep it up."

The banker was assured of a busy period just ahead. He had been drawn on the grand jury by the Court of Sessions.[42]

Sherman omitted his usual letter on the next steamer day because someone in Lucas & Simond's office had informed him that Turner had probably gone to Europe. Actually, he was visiting relatives in Virginia and wrote Sherman from Middleburg on August 31. Sherman hastened to send a letter by the succeeding steamer, when he believed both Turner and Mr. Lucas would have returned to St. Louis. Lucas had written Sherman from Berlin on August 4, 1856, and had been much reassured by the latter's account of affairs in San Francisco. After all he had passed through during the perilous Vigilante days, Sherman was heartened to know that "my course is approved by those whom I feel bound to serve."

Since his last letter he had, despite his urgent protests, been made foreman of the grand jury. Once more, regardless of good intentions and of wary avoidance of trouble, he found himself embroiled in a community quarrel in which passions ran high. San Francisco's free-wheeling journalism had gotten out of hand. The grand jury brought in indictments against the editor of the *Sun*[43] for libel, and against the editor and printer of the *Sunday Times*[44] for numerous offenses. The Sisters of Charity[45] had charge of the County Hospital.[46] The *Bulletin*[47] had published a series of articles attacking the sisters' administration of that institution. The grand jury in reporting on the hospital, in Sherman's words, "had to do them justice and denounce the accusers as influenced by base or sectarian motives."

Another target of Sherman's grand jury was the extravagant administration of the school system. There were about twelve schoolhouses, one a high school, and the cost of maintaining them added materially to the tax rolls and compounded the real estate problem about which Sherman so frequently commented.

> Most of the families here [observed the banker] are of Eastern people who rent their houses, own no property and insist on maintaining this . . . school system at the expense of others. Yet the . . . Common School is one of our political crys and whoever dares to question it is sat upon by editors and nameless correspondents. . . . The Grand Jury has been pitched into by the *Bulletin* and other papers. . . . I will send you [a copy of] our Report . . . that you may see how completely . . . we are under the government of the *Evening Bulletin*, edited by my old clerk, Thomas King,[48] whom I hope some Casey will dispatch. . . . As long as we . . . crave for excitement and scandal, . . . there will be a *Bulletin* and a King. . . . [We] hope that one paper soon will improve and stop this . . . private and public calumny.

Sherman wryly closed his report of this episode: "By the *Bulletin* the foreman of the Grand Jury was denounced as a Roman Catholic and that was the reason for the defense of the Sisters of Charity. So you see I have credit in high quarters for piety, and this letter is my Sunday sermon." [49]

The proposed move to Battery Street was still uppermost in the banker's thoughts.

> I know our business will be much increased by it. . . . All the heavy importing business has been . . . moving to Battery Street ever since the failure of the banks [Black Friday, 1855]. "The best . . . have kept no bank accounts. . . . Several have opened . . . with us on condition that we would bring our office more convenient to them.
>
> The office we are to occupy is owned by Stevens & Abell.[50] The interest of the former is in my name as security and it is possible . . . we may have to own one half of a large 3 story building at $25,000. This interest has cost Stevens ½ of $84,000. . . . Location is now fixed by the new Custom House and Post Office. . . . Stevens & Abell have sold . . . some land . . . in the Peralta Tract and . . . expect to make many more. . . . Though I feared Stevens would lose his [illegible] in the present depression, it looks . . . as though he would come out with something left.

A review of the income statement of the Montgomery and Jackson building reflects the depressed condition of San Francisco business at this time. Where the rents had formerly totaled about $1,500 a month, they were now only about $800. The bank was paying $300 for its own quarters and was entitled to one half of any excess of the over-all rentals over $600. Sherman had closed a deal to rent the bank space for $200 and proposed to pay this and $300 more to Mr. Lucas. Sherman still blamed himself for the erection of their building,

> but the same mistake was committed by Parrott, Brannan,[51] and the so-called most prudent men of the country, but will do all I can to rectify it. I still think people . . . will at some future time think it worth while to walk two squares to deposit their money in such a strong, safe building as ours. . . . I hope before one year expires, Stevens will have redeemed his property and . . . we can return to our present office, and carry with us as much business as we want.

Sherman frankly stated that he would not advise anyone to invest in California, "even if [a] dollar would buy all Montgomery Street." If Mr. Lucas thought differently, Sherman was certain he could acquire many desirable properties for him "but I don't advise it for I have no confidence in men and things here, and believe we have not seen the worst yet."

One of Sherman's bêtes noires, as mentioned in an earlier chapter, was H. M. Naglee.[52] It will be recalled that he owned or was managing agent for a lot at Broadway and Dupont, which he had leased to the contracting firm of Brown & Keyser.[53] The ground rent due Naglee and associates was $750 a month. They erected a substantial brick building costing $28,000. From time to time, Brown & Keyser borrowed from Lucas, Turner & Co., giving this ground lease and building as security. When the general crash occurred in 1855, they deeded the property to Sherman. At the outset, their rents were running about $1,500 a month. This soon dropped to $1,000—then $800. At this stage, Sherman withheld payment of the ground rent and endeavored to prevail on Naglee to reduce the amount of same on account of the depressed state of business. He proposed that they consider lot and building of equal value and agree to divide the total rents received on this proportionate basis. Under the ten-year ground lease, Naglee was obligated at its expiration to purchase the building from Brown & Keyser at its appraised value. Sherman proposed that Naglee be credited on this purchase price with the difference between the stipulated ground rent of $750 and the amount he actually received on the 50–50 division of rentals. Naglee proved obdurate and would not consider any change in the amount paid him as ground rent. Sherman then proceeded to apply the total rents he was collecting to the liquidation of the debt due the bank, before Naglee could get possession because of the defaulted lease.

Sherman discovered a clause in the Brown & Keyser contract with Naglee, whereby if any default continued for thirty days, the total rents for the entire period of the lease could be declared due. As holder of the title, Sherman realized that if this clause were strictly construed he could be held liable for $85,000! "I saw Naglee's game," he wrote Turner, "a blacker hearted scoundrel never lived." Sherman quickly assigned the lease to a janitor who swept Bowman's office. The bank had now collected $3,200 in rents and applied them on the $5,000 debt due it. Sherman emphasized that no breach of the lease had occurred while he personally was in possession, because Naglee had never demanded payment of *him*. Instead, Naglee proceeded to sue Sherman individually for $85,000 on a constructive breach:

> He [Naglee] and his lawyers thought they had me dead on that breach. Ever since August, 1855, this case has been [pending]. . . . Yesterday the judge decided that *I was not liable on the breach*. So . . . they have utterly failed. . . . I am liable for about four months ground rent at $750 and would have willingly compromised on that basis but Naglee was after his pound of flesh. . . . [He] has calculated without his host . . . By trying for too much he has lost some $5,000 of rents. . . . I am free of this incubus. . . . As long as I can keep my wits about me, such a villain as that Naglee shan't get to windward of me."

Sherman reported that mercantile failures were occurring daily. Since his last letter, three involving Lucas, Turner & Co. had been reported.

The details of one of these bankruptcies illustrate the poor business ethics prevailing and the difficulties encountered by a banker when he sought to collect. A certain William Bailey had given his note for $941 to a customer of Lucas, Turner & Co., who had pledged it to the bank as collateral. When Bailey failed to pay, Sherman hurried to his store and found his business sign had been removed and that of another firm put up. The stock of merchandise was the same as it had been before the signs were switched. Sherman was informed that Bailey had sold out and gone to the country.

> After an absence of a few months [Sherman wrote scornfully], [Bailey] will return from the country and take the benefit of the bankrupt law and resume . . . business. . . . He has failed twice before and is quite well off *thereby*. . . . Of course it is a plain swindle, but in these Vigilance Committee times when the merchants make the law, these things are encouraged. . . . They [the merchants] begin to see if they tolerate such practices, all credit and business must cease. . . . The law and practice of San Francisco is to look mildly on these failures. . . . This I regard the most serious feature in this country. . . . Any banker who can sleep quietly in San Francisco must have the nerves of a man marching over mines—not of gold but powder. I am too suspicious and have too little faith in this country to succeed.

A postscript to the latest letter made it plain that the Vigilance Committee was still uppermost in men's minds. "The . . . Committee still keep the arms of the State and the Governor won't recall his proclamation." [54]

On October 19, Sherman acknowledged a letter that Turner had written him from New York. It had informed Sherman of Mr. Lucas' arrival from Europe and that both men were about to return to St. Louis. Turner's trip to Europe had been abandoned for the moment. Equally interesting to the hard-pressed banker in San Francisco was word that Turner had successfully renegotiated their commission arrangement with the Metropolitan Bank. Henceforth, New York would charge Lucas-Turner only ⅛% on its shipments.

In the meanwhile, Sherman had done pretty well by melting his gold receipts into bars for shipment. The local mint had at last resumed operations and coin would once more have to be shipped.

The preceding steamer day had been one of the lightest in point of shipments that Sherman had ever experienced. It was the last day for the payment of taxes, which pulled down deposits. Collection of accounts receivable by the merchants was also suffering for the same reason. A little rain had fallen, not enough to benefit agriculture but sufficient to drive the miners from the riverbeds. Two more mercantile failures had just occurred, but neither was a customer of Lucas-Turner. Even so, the banker glumly closed this paragraph: "It is a question if ever again private bankers can recover the ground lost by the failures of the past year."

Lucas, Turner & Co. was now located at Battery and Washington Streets.

> We moved to the new office last Monday [Sherman wrote] and have as yet experienced no marked change. Our yesterday's operations must have equalled our neighbors and we beat them in the interchange of checks. . . . In the very heart of the merchants, it will require great caution in loans. . . . I was forced yesterday to refuse a great deal of money [i.e., loans]. . . . Failures occur among the regular borrowers . . . but these failures leave us in possession of liquor, butter, dried apples or property, which is hard of sale and . . . won't pay checks.

It was characteristic of Sherman not only to take the blame for actions that resulted badly, but to offer to assume all the adverse material consequences. He felt it might well prove that the move to Battery Street had been an error; so he wrote: "If in this I have yielded to appearances and been mistaken, I am perfectly willing that all my interest in the house should stand forfeit."

Then he asked whether the St. Louis partners had enough confidence in California to take property instead of cash for their coming dividend? The bank had ready use for all the money it could retain. During times like the past two years, the volume of business transacted had increased faster than the profits. The withdrawal of sizable amounts of cash would harm the firm, while it could readily spare its real estate.

Sherman apparently knew that Turner was in need of cash at the moment. He therefore proposed that Lucas-Turner divide $72,000 as a dividend in the following manner: Turner to receive his share of $9,000 in cash; Sherman's and Nisbet's portions to be applied on amounts they owed, thereby not lowering the firm's cash: The shares of Lucas, Simonds, and Patterson to be taken by them in fractional ownerships of the following parcels of San Francisco real estate:

1. The Meiggs house and lot at the corner of Broadway and Montgomery Streets—it had cost $28,000 in 1852 and was on the firm's books for $12,000, now rented for $100 a month; [55]
2. A lot with sixty-foot frontage on Market Street near the Oriental Hotel [56] and facing Battery Street, running through to Stevenson, on the bank's books for $20,000, described by Sherman as "a very valuable lot . . . on the supposition that San Francisco is not a humbug";
3. A small lot on Montgomery Street near Pacific, valued at $3,000;
4. A fifty-*vara* lot at corner of Powell and Greenwich Streets, valued at $5,000;
5. A fifty-*vara* lot and dwelling on Chestnut Street, valued at $4,000;
6. Two fifty-*vara* lots in the water near the new Pacific Mail Steamship Company's site on First Street, valued in 1853 at $12,000, but standing the bank $3,000;
7. A few additional small parcels.

Sherman suggested that Turner, with these data before him,

consult the other partners and advise him of their decision. If Mr. Lucas preferred cash, the bank would have to reduce the volume of loans and discounts. "For myself and Nisbet," he concluded, "we are as economical as possible. I grudge every dollar I check for. I restrict Mrs. Sherman to [illegible] to maintain the household. . . . As soon as I saw we could not keep a horse and cart, I dispensed with both."

Then he showed one of his rare signs of resentment toward the partners other than his friend Turner and Mr. Lucas:

> If Mr. Simonds and Patterson think they can avoid these bad debts, [?] say to them if they will come out I will surrender the helm with cheerfulness. . . . I have not taken real estate as security for [illegible] years because . . . it is no security. We deal altogether in endorsed notes, and items of personal property and goods which are sure of conversion. . . . We have to do as other bankers or drive away custom. I had to stand the brunt of the overcheck game [57] and take all criticism among the merchants, but they now admit the correctness of it. Now on steamer days we know beforehand how much can be asked for . . . but I assure you it is the hardest thing to refuse money to a man who tells you the secrets of his business . . . that his salvation depends on a . . . small loan for a few days. When our loans . . . are at $500,000 we are comparatively easy . . . when . . . up to $600,000, too much for safety.

Sherman wished that Mr. Lucas would pay the San Francisco house a visit and thus determine "whether this is a temporary or permanent institution, whether we should secure present business with usual risks or be cautious and slow in progress." He went on to review the imposing list of San Francisco banks that had failed to date, "an idea that has caused me much solicitude. . . . The real causes were that expenses and losses were greater than were compensated for by 3% a month."

Another care was gnawing at Sherman's composure:

> Our taxes and licenses . . . are enormous. I had to pay over $5,000 taxes yesterday, at rate of $2.30 on every $100. Bank capital assessed at $150,000. I . . . think [the] same money we have

invested here [if] used in St. Louis . . . the net profit would be greater. Whilst every sort of expenses and profits . . . have declined, we have to pay our clerks and bookkeepers from $200 to $300 a month. . . . I would reduce them only other banks pay the same. Don't suppose me in the blues. I study the losses rather than profits for they are rocks on which others, wiser and better than I, were wrecked.

"Old timers" were predicting a hard winter. Heavy rains might bring "flush times" but Sherman doubted it; there were now more poor people in San Francisco than in any other city of its size.

Judge Shattuck[58] had just handed down opinions in three cases quite similar to that of Lucas, Turner & Co. versus the City of San Francisco. The bank's case had been before the supreme court for more than six months. Sherman was sure Judge Heydenfelt was opposed to the city repudiating its debt. He also believed the other two judges, Murray and Terry,[59] though probably sharing Heydenfelt's opinion, feared that a decision in favor of the bank would bring down upon them the wrath of the newspapers. It would be so easy for the press to charge the court with favoritism because Sherman was a Law and Order man and strongly disapproved of the Vigilance Committee's treatment of Judge Terry. Now, with Judge Shattuck's favorable decision in three similar cases as a precedent, the supreme court would be on stronger grounds if it ruled against the city. Such an outcome would materially improve the fortunes of Lucas, Turner & Co.

Bowman,[60] the firm's attorney, had been nominated for the state senate by the Democratic Party. Sherman had advised him not to seek the office because "the Vigilance Committee and Black Republicans have united and will probably carry the city and county. They are very anxious to get an amnesty act passed by the next legislature to exempt them from prosecution. To this the Black Republican candidates are pledged, but I doubt if the regular Democratic nominees will give such a pledge and this will defeat them."

During the 1960's, marked by violent riots and insurrections throughout the cities of the United States, many Negroes seemed to forget, if they ever knew, that the Republican Party was organized by men dedicated to the abolition of slavery where it then existed and to the prevention of its establishment elsewhere. Passage of the Kansas Nebraska Act in 1854, with its repeal of the Missouri Compromise, brought about the demise of the Whig Party, deepened the split between Northern and Southern Democrats, and made inevitable the founding of the new Republican Party. As one of its leaders declared after a meeting in Ripon, Wisconsin, on March 20, 1854, "We went in [as] Whigs, Free Soilers and Democrats and came out Republicans." Sherman himself within a few weeks referred to the Republicans first as "Red Republicans," then as "Black Republicans."

Old-line Democrats showed their contempt for the young party by calling its members "black Republicans" or referring to it as the "nigger-loving party."

"I have no idea how this state will go for president," Sherman's letter continued, "I shall vote for Buchanan, but if Frémont should be elected I think he should be installed and tried." His next sentence is quite revealing as to his opinion of Frémont:

> "I . . . try to believe that our government ought to be strong enough to endure the Devil himself for President for four years. My idea is that if Frémont should be elected he will in six months break with the abolitionists, at all events with the dangerous faction of the Republican Party.

From the vantage point of today's knowledge of the calamity into which America was soon to be plunged, Sherman's next sentence startles us. Reading it in a paragraph which closed a routine business letter—dashed off because of the imminence of the hour for sailing—we wonder if the writer possessed powers of precognition. In a few hasty lines, he displayed a greater grasp of the realities than most of the statesmen of his day, who could choose and weigh their words with deliberation. It was characteristic of Sherman to favor the moderate course that might still halt extremists of either stripe at the brink of the abyss.

His judgment of men and events as a prudent banker also seemed to qualify him to assess national issues with clear-eyed calm. Already, in 1856, was visible the greatness that manifested itself in his handling of Gen. Joseph Johnston's surrender, a foretaste too of his confrontations with Secretary Edwin M. Stanton in the last weeks of the Civil War. In 1856, this man was ready for the cruel responsibilities of the 1860's.

> I would submit to almost anything [the clairvoyant sentence began] rather than see the United States in danger of civil war, but the sample . . . here shows we have engrafted on our people all the dangerous elements of anarchy and civil war. . . . A dissolution of the Union cannot be peaceful. I remember well Mr. Clay's [61] speech in 1850 . . . and the picture he drew of an attempt to make two republics of one present one. Should desperate men bring about civil war, an awful calamity, you in St. Louis would be the first to feel the blow. Slave property is too weak there to stand a day against the fanatical sweep of the Germans [62] and Northern people in your very midst. The election of Blair [63] shows St. Louis county to be opposed to slavery, but I won't believe that such an issue will ever come. Even if Frémont should be elected, I hope the South will cheerfully submit, for the future may show him better than his hope of success makes him appear.

In the midst of this discussion of business and politics, Sherman digressed in a very human manner:

> I came near forgetting to tell you that Mrs. Sherman presented No. 4 just a week ago—a boy, large 10½ lbs., fine and healthy. All well. We are to have him baptised by Mr. Gallagher this evening. . . . We name the child after Mr. Ewing—Thomas Ewing Sherman.[64] My other children are in perfect health . . . that is one great merit in this country. My house and lot are in very fine order and afford plenty of room and playground.[65]

A few days later, in writing his good friend, Lt. James Hardie,[66] then stationed at Benicia, about the birth of this son, Sherman brought up the very distasteful encounter he and Governor Johnson had had with General Wool the previous summer. Probably Hardie's position as regimental adjutant prompted Sherman to reopen the subject; his high regard for Hardie doubtless made him wish to have his friend hear Sherman's side of the dispute.

> I was sorry [he wrote] to see Johnson recall the old question of General Wool's refusal to give arms to the State. He makes use of a letter I wrote him . . . in June last. . . . I suppose this will make the General wroth.[67] It is impossible to avoid the issue. He did promise, emphatically. Of this I feel not the shadow of a doubt. He might have afterwards reconsidered . . . under a new aspect of the case . . . refused what at first he was inclined to grant, but in denying his promise, his memory . . . or his intentions are bad. . . . It placed me in an awful category out of which I could with difficulty escape. . . . Even now, I would prefer to have the whole matter sink into oblivion, but if the issue of veracity must come, I cannot help it. I don't intend to say or write a word more . . . but if the matter comes in such a shape that self-protection demands it, I will recall other facts, small in themselves, but going to show that between the 1st and 6th of June, his mind underwent a change, adverse to his first friendly offers to the Governor. I am in no wise an advocate of Governor Johnson. I have not seen him since June, nor has anything passed between us since, but as to facts . . . within my hearing and observation, I must bear testimony when called on.[68]

26

Late in October, 1856, Sherman again visited the Sacramento Valley.

> I went to Marysville to stop Langton & Co.[69] checking on us and to make an arrangement with the best house there, Macy, Low & Co.[70] who hereafter will do their business with us. I took from Langton . . . some of their bills receivable and security for the balance of their account. . . . Their risks are . . . not according to my notions. Stone is their agent here and has not kept them well enough in hand. These upcountry fellows are the devil's own; because they hang up the sign of Banker, they think they can check ad libitum. I am glad we never established agencies in the interior, for I know Drexel, Sather & Church are sick of theirs. Rhodes [71] has sold most of his real estate and told me he found his business so unprofitable that he is going . . . to draw out. . . . The poorer classes do not deposit in banks . . . and merchants do so to secure occasional assistance, so that all the banks are kept down almost to their own capital.
>
> Whilst in Sacramento I saw Governor Johnson for the first time since my resignation. I thought he might have some feeling . . . but he does not . . . said under the circumstances, he expected it. We conferred freely . . . and especially as to the question of veracity . . . between him and General Wool. . . . I . . . advised Johnson not to write any more letters but wait till the Legislature met and call for a . . . committee to take testimony. . . . I think he will do so.[72]. . .
>
> His insurrection proclamation still existed and, very properly, he would not revoke it until the Vigilance Committee surrendered

> the arms belonging to the state. When I got back to the city Flint and Dempster[73] came to see me on some business. When I asked them why they did not surrender the arms they said they were afraid . . . that they might be used against them in this election. I scouted such an idea, when they offered to place them in my hands provided the Governor would withdraw the Proclamation. I began a correspondence which resulted yesterday in the Vigilance Committee making an actual surrender of the arms to the Quartermaster General of the State and Johnson put his Proclamation in my hands for publication. I procured from Judge Freelon[74] a statement . . . that as the arms were surrendered, there remained . . . no longer any obstacle to enforcing . . . civil and criminal process of his court . . . and having learned that the arms were . . . shipped to Sacramento . . . I caused the proclamation to be . . . published.[75] So the election is held today in profound peace.
>
> I voted for Buchanan but in the State, City and County . . . I picked . . . the nominees I preferred.

Sherman thought the new location was having a favorable influence on the bank's business. But money was tight and collections poor. Not enough rain had yet fallen to increase the production of gold.

The latest mail to reach San Francisco from New York brought news most disquieting to Sherman. The Russian consul in San Francisco, as the agent of his government, had made purchases for its far eastern provinces bordering the Pacific. To realize the necessary funds, this official had been drawing on a New York banking house—Lucas, Turner & Co. had handled many of these drafts. It now developed that one for $30,000 and another for $34,000, each at ten days' sight, had been refused acceptance in New York. The Russian official there was certain they would eventually be paid, but no authorization had yet been received from St. Petersburg. Sherman feared the drafts would be returned protested and that Lucas, Turner & Co. would have to remit New York for them. The transactions provided that in such an event the bank would be entitled to 15% damages plus interest at 10% until reimbursed, "making a good investment," observed Sherman; but in the meanwhile this unexpected debit of $64,000 was quite inconvenient. His initial investigation of the transactions had disclosed that the bills covered the purchase of the cargo of the ship *American King* of Boston by the governor of the Russian colony at the mouth of the Amur River, approved by the governor of Kamchatka. The New York bank admitted it had sufficient funds to cover the drafts, *but* they were earmarked solely for *marine* purchases, whereas the San Francisco consul had drawn on New York for what were considered purchases for the land establishment. A slight technicality perhaps, but it was little comfort to learn that other San Francisco banks had similarly become enmeshed in the mazes of Russian bureaucratic accounting.

The Nicaragua steamers had resumed operation, and they offered lower freight rates on the bank's shipments of coin than did the Panama steamers. A steamship of this line would sail from San Francisco on the 20th of each month; and as Walker's regime seemed firmly ensconced in Nicaragua, Sherman proposed to patronize this route unless the Panama mail line moderated its charges.

Although Turner's letter is unavailable, we can easily infer from reading between the lines of Sherman's correspondence that the St. Louis partners were giving very serious thought to the suggestion that they open a New York agency. If they decided on such a step and were inclined to send Sherman east to run the new office, then it was evident they were also weighing Stone's [76] eligibility as the manager of the San Francisco house. Turner was plying Sherman with questions about Stone. "You know him pretty well," Sherman answered. "I think him honorable, honest, but like most officers, too prone to believe the word of men. *I* feel that weakness. . . . It takes hard knocks to shake one's confidence in . . . men of honorable bearing." He repeated his earlier criticism of Langton and of Stone's failure to control the Marysville man's credit operations. Sherman had left with Macy, Low & Co. the securities pledged by Langton to protect the balance due Lucas-Turner. This balance was to be reduced in the near future to $15,000, for which Stone would remain as guarantor. Stone, wrote Sherman,

> has control of about $50,000 of which the larger portion belongs to Captain Clary.[77]. . . They [Langton & Co.] buy a great deal of gold dust from which we . . . get bars. Stone tells me one Eastern firm is ready to buy him out if he wants to turn his attention to something better. . . . I . . . hardly know what to say about Stone. He would give his right arm to succeed me . . . would work hard to please you . . . might do better than I have done but my idea of a banker is a Jew . . . without feeling, who is not to be moved by the appeals of a man in imminent peril of ruin. I cannot but be moved in such cases and am afraid of such men as McKee [78] who makes more noise and fuss, and I would give a thousand dollars out of my earnings if he would go away—but he won't go away. . . . Some borrowers are necessary . . . it requires the nicest calculation . . . to select these. . . . Whether Stone or anybody has the exact qualifications for such a post, I don't know. I mistrust myself but an older man than either of us would better keep clear of these errors which all have committed. [Sherman was thirty-six, Stone a few years younger.] . . . [I] think it may be unwise to branch [out], you can make better use of your money in St. Louis. . . . If I were Mr. Lucas, I would have but one bank . . . right under his eyes, unless . . . to found an establishment for one of his own family.
>
> Everybody says we'll have good times after the election, some say after the rain falls, but I think it will be some years before property, government and men are well enough established here to make business satisfactory.

After once more assuming the blame for the erection of the Montgomery and Jackson Streets building in the face of such an uncertain future, Sherman reverted to one underlying cause of his unrest: "I would never have breathed a syllable of going East had not Mrs. Sherman constantly talked about Minnie, her father, my health, etc. All these are as well as I can make them. . . . We are more comfortable here than there, so I don't want you to make a branch in New York for me."

He reiterated his wish that Mr. Lucas come to San Francisco, see for himself and then give most careful thought to future planning.

Wanting to be fair to Stone, he continued his answer to Turner's question: "I think well of Stone. . . . In ordinary times he would do better than I. Whether in a run, he would have the nerve, nothing but the thing itself will determine. . . . I hope he will have the sense to avoid the folly I committed of holding, even for a day, a public station." [79]

"Nothing but the thing itself will determine!" How often would Sherman be forced to apply that crucial and ultimate test to the mettle of many men!

On November 5, a postscript was added to the above letter:

> The election . . . passed very quietly. . . . [It is] generally admitted that Buchanan carries this state, but the Peoples ticket has carried this city . . . a compound of Republicanism and Vigilance Committee . . . I admit is made up of better material than the Democratic or Know Nothing tickets. . . . [I] hope we are now through the agony, and people will no longer give this . . . excuse for neglecting their business and not paying their debts.

Once more his domestic situation was commented on:

> Mrs. Sherman is now able to ride out . . . the boy . . . looks hearty and strong. Mrs. Sherman has just sent down her letters . . . I see one addressed to you. What business she has with you I don't know. She always sends messages which I . . . forget to transmit. . . . She got hold of one of your letters . . . and said . . . something was in the wind about a change. . . . I told her the Bank [Metropolitan] had receded from an exorbitant charge which rendered a change unnecessary . . . it would be abandoned. If . . . she writes about any such thing, don't mind it as I won't go to New York unless the interests of the house make it necessary, which I now doubt especially if the Bank doesn't make any difficulty about the [Russian] drafts which from . . . Mr. Meigs' letter, I think will be the case.
>
> We ship $200,000 bullion and coin . . . $12,000 of bills . . .

would ship more but . . . money [is] very tight. . . . I will in the next fortnight curtail . . . should those cursed drafts come back.

Sherman proposed to make his next shipment by way of the Nicaragua line, if conditions remained quiet in that region.

"Johnson has published a letter for which I was sorry, quotes an old letter I wrote him in June. . . . Wool did promise and it is idle for him to deny it."[80]

Two weeks later the embarrassment caused by the dishonored Russian drafts was still uppermost among Sherman's worries. The dry season had virtually shut off gold shipments from the placer mines. A large number of ship arrivals had produced an abnormal demand for loans to pay freight and unloading charges at the same time when everyone wanted cash to pay taxes. To cap it all, the auction of the large Folsom estate had further depleted every one's supply of money.

Sherman more than hinted that an Eastern trip by Turner might ease the pressure if a clearance did not soon arrive from St. Petersburg. He sent him a full file of the papers involved so that he could adequately present the firm's case to the New York bank. As a last resort, Sherman urged that the federal government be requested to have its embassy make representations to the Imperial Russian government. Unless the latter remedied matters very soon, Sherman pointed out that the Russian consul in San Francisco would find "this will so damage his credit that he will be unable to raise a dollar for the necessities of his office."

Sherman reported the results of the auction of the Folsom estate, which had attracted much interest.

The small lots down towards my house sold very well, it is a desirable quarter for dwellings. On North Beach it brought very little and strange to say in the heart of the city far below estimate. . . . The Union Theatre on Commercial just above Kearny, 80 × 60 feet and a good sized building, only . . . $8,600 and his magnificent homestead, 140 × 275, highly improved with a good dwelling, stable lots, house, etc. only $10,000 for a lager beer garden. Folsom spent on that lot in improvements near $90,000.

> Won't he be wroth in his grave at the Dutch music and dancing on a Sunday? . . . It was a sale subject to probate . . . a bid of 10% will cause it to be sold anew. I think that will be done. . . . Sather will buy it . . . would cut up in small pieces and sell for double.

This must have been Captain Folsom's home at the southwest corner of California and Montgomery Streets, on which the Clunie Building has stood for half a century. In this year of 1968 it is soon to be razed to make way for a low, single-purpose banking house of the Bank of America. It immediately adjoins the space occupied by the same institution's huge headquarters building, now nearing completion on the southwest corner of the block. This will be the tallest structure in all California, fifty-two stories rearing 760 feet above the street level. Oddly enough, the western portion of Folsom's holding which was long ago his fine gardens will again be landscaped and form part of the courtyard of the skyscraper.

The writer reverted to the proposed New York move: "I take it for granted that we cannot dispense with the aid of the Metropolitan Bank and . . . [the] New York agency must be abandoned. . . . I am convinced that the advantages . . . from such agency are not of sufficient certainty to warrant an experiment."[81]

By November 20, so much exchange on New York had been sold, that Lucas, Turner & Co. had to ship $240,000 to cover. The bank's insurance policy protected shipments on any one steamer only up to $200,000. Therefore, on this occasion, Sherman sent $100,000 by the Panama line and $140,000 by way of Nicaragua. Much more exchange had been applied for, but because of its unprofitable nature, Lucas-Turner had taken the business only of its best customers. Loans and discounts were about at their average, but the general shortage of money had depressed total deposits. Actual cash on hand after steamer day transactions stood between $180,000 and $190,000.

This letter was written on Thanksgiving Day, but because it also happened to be steamer day, the bank stayed open until noon. The staff was still working at 2:00 P.M. Sherman reported all were well at home and closed "my health better than for several years." [82]

About December 1, the *Golden Age* brought Turner's very important letter of October 30, 1856. We cannot report his exact language but Sherman's reply gives us quite a definite idea of that letter's content.

"I have read [it] with great care. . . . Together with what had occurred here since, [it] is conclusive as to the proposed change which I have dismissed from my mind. . . . [Stone] is too easy and good natured for this place." He repeated the facts of Stone's connection with Langton & Co., whereby Lucas-Turner had

> procured a great deal of gold bullion and used to advance against the gold dust receipts. . . . Langton for a long time kept his business well in hand, but by degrees he began to check for more dust than he sent down and repeated it so often that . . . when I examined his affairs and became satisfied they had not capital enough to carry on . . . on their scale . . . I advised them to reduce number of their offices and keep . . . business within limits, but . . . they lent money to various parties in Downieville because of . . . their gold dust . . . on which they were making 5 per cent a month. I then fixed a limit for which I took collateral security. Sure enough the very next steamer, they exceeded the limit some $10,000. I drew a draft on Langton for $20,000 and . . . necessary papers to attach in case the draft was not paid . . . sent a young lawyer with it to Downieville. He returned with the money but Langton came along, offended at the harsh and summary proceeding, and took . . . his account to Davidson, the very thing I wanted. This was about a month ago. . . . Today Davidson refused his checks. Stone is not a partner of Langton, but . . . had such confidence in him that he is largely in advance of him, consisting mostly of money given him by officers and others for investment. Stone immediately . . . got out the necessary papers . . . to secure all he could.

Sherman went on to detail Langton's scattered real and personal property, as mentioned in an earlier chapter: "A diminutive

Adams & Company concern," Sherman called it, "and in the country believed to be wealthy, but it will take Stone some time to convert these into money. In the meantime, the persons who have left their money with him will become alarmed and may compel him to make . . . larger sacrifices than he can stand."

Sherman then expressed the thoughts that had now crystallized in his mind about Stone, as his successor. "This . . . makes him out of the question and when he returns from the country, I will advise him, if possible, to regain his commission in the Army. At the time I broke with Langton, to enable Stone to carry on his business, I discounted for him some $20,000 of notes, all of which I believe to be good, secured by real estate and other collateral."

Evidently Major Turner's letter mentioned a loan Lucas & Simonds had made Captain Clary for $20,000, apparently borrowed for the benefit of Stone. Sherman knew that Clary owned some good San Francisco real estate, whose sale Stone had discussed with Sherman. Without having Turner's letter, the relations of Stone with the funds of both Captain Clary and his wife seem complicated. Turner may have solicited Sherman's aid in collecting the moneys due the St. Louis house. After discussing that affair, Sherman reiterated his faith in Stone's honesty which he said was "the universal opinion here among officers and citizens."

(According to a letter Sherman wrote to Lieutenant Hardie at this time when Captain Stone's financial world was crumbling around him, "Mrs. Stone had a child born last night . . . it seems everybody is doing their full share in increasing the population." [83])

> It seems [Sherman continued his letter to Turner] that nobody is proof against this country. The temptation of large profits is the soul of gambling and business here has partaken of that character. . . . I know that our business has been conducted as strictly as I know how and our losses have been less than those of any bank here . . . yet were we to close short, we have some notes that would not realize their face. . . .
>
> I take it that banking consists of using the moneys of others, but

here the community are firmly of the opinion that they have a right to use the banks. I hope in time confidence will return when moneys will be more freely deposited and allowed to remain and I prefer to stay it out. . . . I have dismissed the . . . New York agency from my mind. . . . I find that Mr. Ewing [84] heard something of it in St. Louis. I never said anything to him and Mrs. Sherman found it in a letter from you she got out of my pocket. I don't think Nisbet has heard of it yet. He is strongly in favor of some agency there that would save us commissions, etc. . . . but I admit the necessity of using a strong institution there to guard against the consequences of a loss of a steamer or the delay in collecting such exchange as the [Russian] drafts, so . . . best to let things remain as at present.

From his report of a torchlight celebration in honor of Buchanan's election, Sherman brought himself back to the very mundane topic of difficulties with personnel, reporting a brush he had had

with Babcock, our general ledger clerk . . . a smart fellow but cross and snapping. Henry, the porter, used to sleep at the bank, but he got married and wants to sleep at home. We have five young men in the office. . . . I told them to arrange it . . . turn about . . . that one would sleep here. Babcock replied . . . he would not. I of course discharged him on the spot. I hate changes but will not permit insubordination. I deem it necessary some one should sleep here. . . . As to hiring a private watchman, when we pay high wages to five young men, it is out of the question. Babcock will be here tomorrow to beg off, but the spirit he evinced is not proper . . . he should exhibit it elsewhere.

On the domestic front,

Master Willie made his appearance today in breeches . . . the most ridiculous picture you can conceive. He is a buster. Lizzie has had a bad cold and is slightly deaf. I hope it will be nothing permanent. The baby is developing rapidly.

We have had some fine rains and the effect was instantaneous. I think we are going to have a good winter . . . and may look for a prosperous year. I hope . . . for it as you must be tired of my complaints.[85]

27

In view of Page, Bacon & Co.'s [86] sensational failure a year before, Sherman was greatly surprised in early December by a call from Frank Page.[87] He presented a letter of credit signed by the old St. Louis firm of Page & Bacon and wanted to cash a draft on them for $20,000, payable on four months' sight. Sherman knew that the firm had failed for more than a million in liabilities, so he looked askance at the paper. Because Page insisted that the draft would be paid at its maturity, Sherman inferred that the St. Louis house expected to be refinanced within four months. Nevertheless, he refused to have anything to do with Mr. Page's application.

He wrote to Turner, "I know from Parrott [88] who has had possession of their books [i.e., Page, Bacon & Co.'s] for more than a year that they have . . . about $300,000 of . . . worthless bills receivable besides considerable overdrawn accounts. I am going to have a peep at them if I can." One of the partners of the bankrupt firm had always maintained that if the St. Louis firm of Page & Bacon paid even a reasonable amount of its debt to the San Francisco house, the latter could right its affairs. Sherman commented: "I . . . guess he counted bills receivable as all cash, but as Parrott says, there is the considerable item of $300,000 bad debts. . . . Nearly all the rich men of 1853 are bankrupt." [89]

The next letter was written just after Sherman's return from a brief stay in Sacramento. He felt that many recent events warranted comment. First, he reverted to the election: "The vote of

California shows in what estimation Frémont is held here. We all prefer the safe administration of such a man as Buchanan to the uncertain course of the Frémont faction." (The vote certainly did not bear out Frémont's vaunted popularity in his adopted state. Buchanan received 53,000 votes, Fillmore 36,000, and Frémont only 20,000.) "We want a wagon road to California," the letter continued, "long before any . . . legislation . . . on the Great Railroad project, concerning which I feel much misgiving. Politicians cannot build that Road. Any bill in Congress will clog its ultimate completion unless Uncle Sam will build it . . . with money and land united."

Sherman, like most men, enjoyed seeing his actions justified by later events. "Our Grand Jury report is being vindicated by experience, for the schools have exhausted their money and must all be closed, instead of being lopped off as we recommended."

Among Sherman's usual comments on business conditions, he once more said: "The servants and laboring classes, who alone are saving and prosperous here, will not trust banks." He stressed again the unfavorable climate for the safe and profitable lending of money:

> Merchants . . . [are] encouraged by law to fail and prefer their . . . friends as creditors. With these facts staring me in the face, I cannot hold out . . . those prospects of great profit . . . we had reason to expect. I hope you will get the government contract for transfer drafts at any price under 3 per cent. . . . That would be something certain, however small . . . and take so much business out of the hands of those New Yorkers who absorb all profits.

Evidently the St. Louis house was still having difficulty with Captain Clary. "I have every reason to believe," Sherman wrote, "he has money and land in St. Louis, beside . . . considerable here. I don't like his paying . . . in driblets. I have his endorsement for $5,000 . . . if he has not discharged that draft when you receive this, I want it enforced."

Sherman then added a new chapter to the tale of Captain Stone's misfortunes:

I wrote you . . . by last mail . . . he had gone up country to attach all of Langton's property . . . leaving his brother-in-law and his clerk named Liverich [?]. . . . A few hours before the departure of the steamer on the 5th instant, that clerk, who had had complete control of the books, disappeared . . . no doubt he went off on the *Golden Gate.* This fact was telegraphed to Stone who forthwith returned, leaving his business with Langton to be pushed . . . by a lawyer in Marysville named Mesick. When Stone got back, he . . . suspected his clerk . . . guilty of peculation. . . . By a close . . . examination of the books, it appears he has been abstracting a large quantity of money and covering it up in Langton's account. Therefore Langton is not indebted to Stone as much as Stone thought and . . . represented to me, by between $20,000 and $40,000, the latter . . . no doubt the nearer. . . . Stone is so completely disheartened and dejected . . . he will not . . . tell me the full truth. He has . . . for months allowed that clerk to rob him of large sums . . . all the time supposing . . . it was Langton's acts. . . . Not having access to his books, I could not detect this, but so satisfied was I that Langton was carrying on . . . recklessly that I broke with him and long since refused him any credit, or even the privilege of checking on us against gold dust shipments. What Liverich has stolen is a dead loss to Stone. . . . Though of respectable family he has nothing of his own. . . . Now it is known . . . he has been gambling . . . large sums . . . also that although he had a family in New Orleans, he has kept a mistress in handsomely furnished rooms. . . . How Stone could have been ignorant of all this passes my comprehension. . . . Mesick attached all of Langton's property, money and notes throughout the county and put sheriff in possession, but as Langton had learned by telegraph that his checks on Davidson were going back protested, he . . . put away enough money and bills receivable to cover him and his deposits which are small. . . . Stone's attachment only took . . . offices, furniture, mules and wagons . . . to him of little value. . . . Then Mesick came back to San Francisco with one of Langton's favorite expressmen, representing that . . . costs of suit and sheriff's fees would eat up everything. Stone was forced to . . . raise the attachment and trust to Langton to settle as he best could. I suppose Stone will lose by Liverich $40,000 and has tied up with Langton as much more. . . . Where did all this money come from? . . . Captain

Clary must have given Stone [illegible] in money here and that acceptance of $5,000. . . . Stone had his Benicia farm . . . valued at $31,000 . . . on which he probably raised $20,000. . . . Balance of money consisted in funds placed with him for investment by soldiers and officers, mostly small sums. . . . Generally . . . he made loans for other parties by taking notes . . . in their names, but a great deal is in his own business and will be lost. Stone feels very bad. . . . He has hopes . . . he may catch Liverich and recover some of the money. . . . That is a sad chance. His chance of getting something from Langton is better. I have assured myself that the notes and securities we hold are good . . . part has been paid. I . . . feel very bad about Stone but business is business and he must shift for himself. All that Clary let him have is gone. I hope Stone will regain his post in the Army. . . . He would prefer to do something that would enable him to repay those who entrusted him with money, but California is no place to recuperate in.

The next paragraph of Sherman's letter called for ink of deepest indigo:

The Supreme Court has decided that all the bonds of the State of California . . . above $300,000 are unconstitutional and not binding on the State. . . . About $3,000,000 of state funds . . . forces the legislature to pass a law acknowledging these bonds and submitting the law to a vote of the people at next general election . . . September, 1857. In meantime, money has gone on [i.e., has been shipped East] to pay the January coupons but next July coupons will not be paid. . . . I doubt if when the vote is taken . . . the people will assume this vast debt.

Well might the *Sacramento Union* exclaim: "The world of civilization will pronounce the verdict of judicial repudiation against the State of California. Let but a single failure to pay our interest promptly occur . . . and the name of California will become the scorn . . . of all men who prize public faith and individual honor."

Even though it breaks the continuity of our narrative, the importance of California's reputation as a good credit risk seems to justify a digression on this subject. Bancroft shared the sentiments expressed above by the Sacramento editor:

After leaving the constitutional question untouched for five years, to bring it up now and decide against the validity of a debt of more than $3,000,000 would look like a deliberately planned and executed act of dishonesty. . . . In that light, the decision was regarded as a public calamity.

But the masses were not dishonest and when it was pointed out by the judge that the question could still be submitted to the people of adopting the indebtedness of the state, with the addition of appropriations for necessary future expenses, they consented and a bill of submission being passed by the legislature of 1857, voted to pay $4,000,000 rather than endure the ignominy of repudiation.

A diligent search has failed to disclose the details of the popular vote. Bancroft is silent on the point. In response to a direct inquiry I made in 1967, the California state treasurer replied: "Upon checking we are unable to find any period of time when State of California bonds were in default." This official statement seems to justify the assumption that the bonds were eventually paid.[90]

Repudiation of the State debt was not the only thing that worried Sherman as he wrote in mid-December:

Another decision says the City cannot be forced to pay the City Comptroller's warrants, and this hurts us badly. . . . Another decision absolves the county from paying her warrants. . . . The Supreme Court has virtually absolved the State, County and City from paying their debts on technical grounds. . . . We hold no State or County bonds or . . . indebtedness . . . but in the City Comptroller's warrants, we hold the Powell Street contract for $35,000 with about $48,000 of warrants as collateral. . . . We hold a few other warrants [?] . . . representing debts of $5,000. So here we have $40,000 . . . lost, I term it, but the lawyers say yet the city must pay.[91] . . . Our Supreme Court . . . is not above suspicion. At the time our case was argued, Heydenfelt was abroad, yet he rendered the decision, the others concurring. Baldwin insists he never read the papers for in the decision to which I refer you, the court did not pass on . . . our claim on the warrants. We claimed on the contract and on the warrants too.

> The contract was made by the Street Commissioner by virtue of a resolution of the City Council . . . contract was subsequently approved by a committee of the . . . council. The Supreme Court says . . . council had no right to delegate their power. I send you all the decisions . . . beg you to read them carefully and see how all State, County and City debts to . . . $5,000,000 have been virtually repudiated. Every banker and moneyed man in California is injured by these decisions, and the probability [illegible] that the people will ratify and confirm all these debts and economize in future.

(The one short illegible word is very important to the sense; if Sherman wrote "is," then he contradicted his own opinion stated a few paragraphs earlier.)

> If such be the result, these decisions . . . will be the best thing that ever happened to the State, for all these corporations were recklessly incurring debt which in the end would have made them all bankrupt. . . . By practicing economy, the evil may in time be remedied. The city is practicing economy—at night there is but one lamp to a block. The public schools will be closed. The police is reduced to barely enough men to attend the courts. The Fire Department goes begging . . . and the City pays none of her bills. . . . Business is awful dull. . . . All . . . [are] convinced of what I have always known . . . this is essentially a poor country. . . . Gold does not leave any profits behind. . . . Profits of business are being eaten up by expenses. . . . People who have some thousands of dollars live in a garret, lend their money at 3% a month on tip top securities, are growing rich, whilst the big merchants, big property holders and big bankers too are doing comparatively nothing. A great many people are going away. . . . Notwithstanding all this, I am better satisfied than if things were driving . . . headlong like they were when we began here. If we could only have foreseen this state of things . . . how we might have saved! By not building, we could now have the best property in the city for two-thirds the cost of the building. This property [i.e., the new Battery Street location] is going to be the center. . . . Tallant & Wilde [92] are moving down on January 1st. . . . Pretty well admitted that . . . Battery Street is to be to Montgomery . . . what your Main Street is to Fourth [this refers to St. Louis].

Sherman then reverted to the famous Limantour Claim,[93] discussed in an earlier chapter:

> The almost certain proof that [it] is a fraud and forgery . . . now before the U.S. District Court. I was on the Grand Jury . . . the other day when Limantour was indicted for using a forged deed. The evidence is conclusive. . . . I cannot tell what occurred in the Jury room but a good deal has leaked out which you will find in the newspapers. . . . [Limantour] has since tried to escape but was arrested. . . . I was always convinced his claim was spurious as none of the old inhabitants ever heard of Limantour until after 1852. . . . This exposé removes a cloud on all the titles in the southern part of the city. . . . If now the same exposé can be made in regard to the Bolton-Barron Claim[94] out by the Mission, of which I do not doubt the character, our city titles will be pretty well established.

Reverting to the very sore question of Lucas, Turner & Co.'s large claim against the city, Sherman wrote:

> I have seen Sullivan, one of our State Senators, who believes the entire San Francisco delegation is in favor of some compromise whereby these city warrants will be funded or paid, but he agrees with me . . . that the mountain boys will never vote to pay the State Bonds. . . . I will . . . leave no stone unturned to convert these warrants into money. . . . Misfortune loves company. . . . All our neighbors are heavier losers than we. . . . All . . . have . . . State, County and City indebtedness. I have always mistrusted our public securities, but was drawn into this Powell Street contract at the outset of my administration.

Despite this gloomy picture, Sherman had not finished his pessimistic portrayal:

> I always mistrusted everything in this country and am now more suspicious than ever. . . . Suppose [that] in St. Louis every public security will . . . in three years . . . become valueless, real estate and buildings . . . decrease in value . . . from 20 to 100% per annum, and half your business community were to fail each year, what would be the result? This is no overdrawn picture of this city. . . . We are in for it and must brave it out. . . . I will be

> as watchful as I can . . . to keep safe the capital and reputation of the house and trust to the future for profits.

Again we find Sherman did not hold an equal regard for all the St. Louis partners:

> For myself, I expect no profits, but would be most happy if I could add to your and Mr. Lucas' fortunes, but I don't feel the same consideration for Patterson or Simonds.
>
> I . . . think you ought to come out . . . to consult with me before November when I must make up my mind about this building, whether to take it for the mortgage or to return to our old stand. . . . Mrs. Sherman knows now that any hopes she may have entertained of going East are futile . . . that we must . . . stick it out.

The independent-minded bookkeeper, Babcock, was again the subject of comment: "His brother is agent for the mail steamers, with whom it is in our interest to keep on good terms. He came . . . and made such excuses . . . that I agreed to let Babcock return if he would . . . understand that my orders are not to be questioned. . . . He is now at his desk."

Then Sherman's mind reverted to the perennial problem of safeguarding the bank's assets, and he continued:

> Our discounts are well distributed now. . . . We have a good class of customers, probably the best in the city. . . . Everything works smooth and if we don't prosper it is because nobody does. Sather is going home tomorrow . . . his second trip this year. I think his business has fallen off but . . . there is nothing like the business of former years. . . . The sooner we all get to the bedrock as the miners say, the better. We have had some rains and a good deal of snow in the mountains. . . . Miners are at the moment doing little, but have big piles of dirt ready for the rains.[95]

A letter to Hardie written a few days later shows that the loss of confidence caused by Captain Stone's defaulting clerk was widespread.

I can well understand that the misfortunes that have swamped Stone should shake confidence in everybody, but you may rest assured that I am not going to be caught by such people as involved Stone! It is utterly impossible from the checks in our Bank that any clerk or teller could abstract money and cover it up on the books, like Liverich, Stone's clerk, did.[96]

At the end of the month he again wrote Hardie, who was stationed a few miles away at Benicia:

We had quite a snow storm yesterday and from the appearance of the Coast Range, I think you must now have snow on your parade [ground], looking quite like Christmas times at home. I hope they are merry times. We are all well out home save myself. . . . I hardly expect ever to be perfectly well here. The Creator never made my animal part for this locality. . . . A happy New Year to you and Maggie and little ones.[97]

Part Five:
Withdrawal with Honor

28

January 1, 1857, ushered in a truly wintry month. Writing on the 3rd, Sherman told Turner: "All the mountain country is frozen up, the roads are almost impassable . . . We had a beautiful and pleasant New Years Day."

The mail steamer would sail at noon on the 5th, so Saturday the 3rd was steamer day, in accordance with San Francisco custom, "awkward enough, as people are hard up without the inconvenience of paying notes today that are due tomorrow."

He acknowledged two letters of Turner's dated November 27 and November 30. Mr. Lucas had suffered loss by fire; Sherman understood there was no insurance. "The cares of the rich almost reconcile one to poverty," he commented quizzically.

Once again New Yorkers had prevailed over Turner's attempt to get the contract for government drafts. Both Turner and Sherman used such words as "indignation," "outrageous," and "unjust schemes." James Guthrie, secretary of the treasury, was the special object of Sherman's wrath, for favoring New Yorkers against the West, although he, himself, being from Kentucky, was a Westerner from Sherman's viewpoint. "I don't like to say that Guthrie is bribed but I'll bet my head . . . some clerk at his elbow received a bonus. . . . I think . . . it well to get some Congressman to touch him up on it. Guthrie is so good at accusing others of rascality, it would do him a good turn to reciprocate the compliment."

History is full of subtle ironies. Only five years later, this same James Guthrie—by then the president of the Louisville and

Nashville Railroad—would prove himself one of Sherman's few and badly needed friends. Sherman was then under a cloud because of his wartime experiences around Louisville, and even his sanity was questioned.[1]

This defeat on the matter of the treasury drafts was especially disappointing to Lucas, Turner & Co., because, as Sherman had so often remarked, "for every bill [i.e., exchange draft] we draw . . . we lose money." Sending coin to New York to cover drafts cost the firm from ¼% to ½% more than it received for exchange sold. "I have long since given up . . . hope of making money . . . by exchange business. . . . Only source of profit arises from . . . loans . . . reduced almost to the loan of our own money, for deposits are barely enough to keep in the vault. The profits arising from $150,000 to $200,000 do not more than pay . . . expenses for rent, clerk hire, etc."

Yet in the same paragraph Sherman felt that he could boast, "our reputation and credit here are as good, if not better, than of any of our neighbors." He was sending a trial balance to St. Louis. "Our bills receivable . . . still embraces the $35,000 City debt and some other[s] . . . that may prove bad." In mentioning the very sore subject of the City debt, he said, "I do not despair of that. . . . There is a general conviction that the Legislature, to meet on Monday next, will be compelled to make some legal provision for all these old scores. If there is to be general repudiation, well and good, but I shall watch that no steps are taken to provide for the State debt without carrying with it the city debt."

Reverting to the perennial subject of business conditions, he wrote:

> In San Francisco there has not been two thirds the business of 1853 or 54. . . . San Francisco has been sinking steadily since. . . . It has double the number of people and houses its business requires. . . . Unless emigration can . . . be started, we will continue to enjoy the adversity of the past two years. I suppose you [are convinced] I am a croaker. God grant it may be so.

When Sherman remembered that he had been one of the first to witness the intense excitement over the gold discovery at

Coloma, he may have felt justified in his pessimism. He too had seen the new state emerge so incredibly fast, with such bright promise. The planning, the building, had all been on such a lavish scale, had exhibited such courage and confidence as to rule out failure as unthinkable. How in only seven or eight years could everything have so changed? How explain these statistics in the newspapers he was forwarding to Turner; debts wiped out by bankruptcies—in 1855, $6,000,000; in 1856, $3,000,000? These did not include the liabilities of banks that failed in 1855 or the State and City indebtedness that had been repudiated by the California supreme court. These amounted to another $5,000,000. He had to think property values had declined $10,000,000 in the past year. All in all, he termed what he saw:

> a very pretty kettle of fish for a small town. . . . The money actually sunk in San Francisco in 1855 and 1856 has amounted to about . . . half assessed value of property now, say $15,000,000. I would not pass through the same ordeal again for the prettiest farm in St. Louis County, with an annuity to live on. . . .
>
> Yesterday it was reported that Wm. T. Coleman & Company had failed. . . . This morning it is denied. He owes nothing in San Francisco. . . . If he has failed it must be at New York. Wm. H. Dow,[2] another of our purest and best merchants, a leader in the Church and Vigilantes has failed and compromised with his creditors, also William G. Rudge,[3] a large clothing merchant. . . .
>
> All the notes due today, about $100,000, were paid except one of Cook, Folger & Company,[4] oil . . . merchants . . . endorsed by William F. Hosen.[5] . . . [He] found Cook, Folger & Company in the hands of the sheriff. We . . . demanded the money of Hosen. . . . Up to this moment he has not been able to secure it. Hosen has $37 to his credit . . . and owes us note of $3,800 for which we hold about $4,300 of brandy and butter, not enough to cover both notes. . . . It is . . . impossible to escape these things. . . . Hosen does business with us . . . sold Cook, Folger & Company some turpentine. This note was given in part payment.

The firm's old quarters at Jackson and Montgomery had been occupied by Stone, so the latter's difficulties had created a vacancy there. Sherman had not yet found a tenant to fill it. In studying the problem, he was considering a rather radical solution: "I have a notion to put some person in it, to fill it with stores [i.e., merchandise] and to advance no money on warehouse receipts unless the goods are stored there. That would give us rent and security, for goods in store are the best collateral we can now obtain."

Quite the best news he had been able to report for some time was the word he had received from Meigs of the New York bank that the Russian drafts were about to be paid—principal, interest, and damages. "That will be a good lick as 17% on $64,000 will be a handsome interest . . . and make up something for our exchange account."

The next paragraph dealt with the writer's personal finances: "I am trying to economize. I give Mrs. Sherman . . . $500 a month and she pays all family expenses." Apparently his wife was a good manager for he added: "She saved the last month and gave me today her check for $250, so my account" (i.e., his indebtedness to the bank) "stands so much less than shown on the trial balance. . . . I have sold the horse. When Mrs. Sherman wants, she hires a cab. I foot it. . . . I would like to pay for my house here by the sale of some of my Illinois property."

He gave Turner a list of his Eastern real estate, with the income and taxes of each parcel, and asked his assistance in disposing of it. Even though economy was uppermost in his thinking, Sherman was basically tenderhearted. Three of his Illinois properties yielded some net income, so that he could

> give something to a sister who is poor . . . whose husband is helpless. . . . I would like to sell enough to pay that note . . . in the Lucas & Simonds bank. . . . If you will tell me what it will sell for I will send on a power of attorney.
>
> If I could . . . prevail on Mrs. Sherman to stay here . . . I would be perfectly content to take the chances for I know in time we could do well out here, but encumbered by time, and having the worst part of California's history thrust on my tour of duty makes me . . . somewhat anxious about the result. I will stay until 1860 anyhow and won't ever . . . think of going to New York. If

the St. Louis interests require a branch there, one of you must undertake it.[6]

On January 5, Sherman wrote:

> It has been the tightest steamer day I ever saw. People who had never borrowed before borrowed this time . . . and accounts that always had large credits are now down to cents. . . . The cause . . . is the non receipt of gold from the interior . . . unusually cold in the mountains . . . snow and rain all over the country . . . roads almost impassable . . . good causes for non payment of country debts, making our merchants . . . hard up. . . . They have been forced to look exclusively to the banks. I don't think our discounts are increased . . . but deposits being so low have . . . some effect. . . . The rains will enable the miners . . . to . . . give us that supply of money . . . so much needed to keep the wheels of commerce in motion.

Sherman then remarked that while he had written the details of several serious lawsuits during the past year, he would now describe one "partaking of the comical." It concerned a third-floor tenant at the Jackson and Montgomery building named Dr. Young. He had fallen in arrears in his rent of $17.50 a month. The bank's collector finally reported to Sherman

> that he was satisfied the doctor, who is a man of bad character, used the room not as a sleeping room but as a kind of assignation room for women. I instructed him to enter the room, and if satisfied of the truth of his suspicions, to remove all of the furniture . . . to the basement and let the doctor come to me. . . . He came to the bank and paid his rent for December as though nothing had happened, then discovering the furniture gone, . . . offered police a reward of $25 to find it. They found . . . where it was. . . . He paid the reward and commenced suit against me in a magistrate's court. I did not employ a lawyer but attended in person. . . . The magistrate decided I should restore the furniture . . . and pay . . . a fine of $5 and costs . . . $7 more. I paid it but Dr. Young . . . threatens to appeal and prosecute me for trespass . . . and other heinous things. I admitted I . . . took a summary course to get rid of a bad tenant. The magistrate . . . a friend of mine, advises me to pay the doctor a little more. . . . I am not sure

> . . . what I will do. As the Vigilance Committee principles are now in power, they ought to let me . . . take the Law in my own hands when the Law is too slow in its operations. I confess I have no respect for the Law and the Lawyers here.[7]

By the next steamer day, Sherman wrote that he was going to dine with

> our newly elected United States Senator Broderick[8] at Dr. Bowie's.[9] . . . Notwithstanding the great moral reforms, the old State corrupt politicians, Gwin[10] and Broderick have been elected to the U.S. Senate. . . . The legislature, now in session, as a . . . test question, elected Father Gallagher[11] Chaplain of the Senate and Dr. Scott[12] to the Assembly. These are the ministers who opposed the Vigilance Committee. . . . It . . . appears that that great moral reform is not appreciated by the Legislature. The Vigilantes say . . . the Legislature is not a fair representation of the *decent* people. . . . That old movement is dead and will not turn up again for four years.

Early in January, Sherman received a letter from Turner that drastically changed both his own life and the future of Lucas, Turner & Co. Although the complete text is not available, we know its essential message from a quotation Sherman wrote soon afterward; he quoted Turner verbatim: "Our fixed resolution is to withdraw from the banking business in California, but leave you to accomplish it in such time and manner as will make least sacrifice to the parties in interest."

No wonder that Sherman now replied: "All other things are . . . absorbed in the determination conveyed . . . to break up the California house. This took me by surprise because I supposed you and Mr. Lucas would come out, see for yourselves and then if you saw signs . . . of events such as we have . . ."

There is a break in the manuscript here which leaves his sentence unfinished but the context makes clear that Sherman would have accepted the final decision more willingly if the St. Louis partners had reached their conclusion in San Francisco. Despite all his pessimistic reports, Sherman felt there was a chance that the firm had already experienced its worst vicissitudes, and that a change for the better might not be too far away.

> If you and I were alone [he confided to Turner], we might pitch in and take the chances. . . . Real estate men, moneyed men, bankers, brokers, speculators, contractors . . . have all been swamped . . . merchants . . . pretty well thinned out, and once or twice it was feared Front Street would go in with a crash like the wharves and piling that make our city front, but they bear up manfully, carrying heavy loads of up-country debts . . . paying interest. . . . It is this interest that breaks so many . . . which supports the banks. . . . 2½% a month is not interest alone, it is interest and risk combined.
>
> We think the worst is over. . . . With the coming of gold from the mountains this spring, a new epoch will dawn. . . . If in March and April, it be even partially realized, we can in one steamer's operations put ourselves strong in funds, pay off all and then gradually close the balance of assets and remit. If there be any desire that matters should be hastened, advise me. . . . You will have time after receipt of this to notify me before I make any public demonstration looking like a withdrawal from the country.
>
> It may be that Parrott[13] or some other banker would, in the spring, buy us out, taking our new office. . . . I would shift back to the old bank where there is still one vault . . . fill up the rooms with stores protecting advances, keeping no clerks and using money up to the last moment to advantage.
>
> My . . . opinion . . . is that unless some person would step in present office, we should not refuse to receive cash deposits and discount moderately till . . . say August or September and then wind up promptly, in the meantime doing nothing for Buncombe,[14] selling not a bill of exchange without absolute profit, realizing as fast as consistent with safety, every note and collateral, selling such property as we can so that by fall . . . we can put your funds at your command. The country was never poorer in money than now.

Despite this last pessimistic observation, Sherman noted that the bank's cash balance, after falling to $106,000, had remained at that figure for some days and then built up to $260,000. The steamer day just ahead would certainly reduce this sharply.

All the big merchants [wrote Sherman] have again and again offered us their business if we would promise a line of discount. I would not do it. Our big merchants are all big borrowers . . . and cannot allow money to lie idle in banks. We have very few of their accounts. Those few give more trouble than ten times the number of butchers and shop keepers [Sherman here was distinguishing between "merchants," who were wholesalers and jobbers, and "shop keepers," who had retail establishments].

At this moment, it would not do to draw out of business. It would create a panic and . . . impair value of our securities. . . . I interpret your letter . . . first, perfect security, then to refuse all new business involving time or risk . . . gradually realize on all notes and securities not . . . profitable business.

As to exchange business, which Sherman characterized as "simply outrageous, I propose . . . to notify all the bankers that whether they consent or not, we shall sell no . . . exchange at less than 3½% until freights and insurance are reduced."

Sherman continued,

We have had much rain, more than for many years. . . . In March, April and May, water will be running freely in all the gulches. . . . All agree . . . we are going to have a large quantity [of gold] taken out this spring. If it comes down faster than . . . required to pay Eastern debts, it will accumulate . . . in merchants' and other . . . hands and . . . once more invite speculation . . . or in other words, produce the most favorable state . . . to enable us to draw out safely . . . without loss. . . . This may be more indefinite than you expect, but . . . the most I will now promise.

After a reassuring line as to his health, Sherman admitted he felt concern as to his future: "If safely out of this, I . . . have had too bad a scare to try it again. . . . I fear it is my bad luck to bring misfortune." (This was a theme that we will find recurring in his correspondence in the next few months.)

I won't agree to anything till all these matters are settled. . . . If then I can earn a living at something for which I am qualified . . . I must do it. In meantime all I expect is to keep out of debt, so

> . . . I may start fair in whatever new career may open. . . . As to Nisbet . . . he is entitled to assistance of us all. His habits have been exemplary . . . his qualifications for business . . . well known. . . . If . . . some rich man like Parrott . . . [would] step in as we go out, I would unhesitatingly recommend Nisbet. Parrott is very cautious, acknowledged . . . in confidence, he made no money at his business last year, but as he must live here and must do some business, I believe if Aspinwall[15] in New York could be consulted, he and Parrott would buy us out . . . would simply amount to . . . taking our office and fixtures and some . . . receivables. Then we could recommend the best customers to stay with the new concern. . . . I would shift to our old bank . . . [winding up] at least expense and shortest time. . . . I throw this out as one of the plans but . . . this shall not be determined till we hear from you.

Bowman[16] was going East on the next mail steamer to visit his aged parents. Sherman warned Turner that Bowman knew nothing of the plan to close the California house. If Turner saw him, Bowman was in a good position to discuss the bank's case against the city.[17]

A reader of these letters should realize that many of Sherman's repetitions were deliberate. Because of transportation uncertainties, he frequently sent a long letter on the Panama mail steamer; a few days later another communication, sent by way of the Nicaragua line, highlighted the same news. Therefore, two days after the last letter quoted above had gone aboard the *Golden Gate*, that ship still lay in the harbor; and he wrote a brief note for the *Orizaba*, about to depart. A flare-up of filibuster troubles in Nicaragua made it doubtful that the *Orizaba* would be able to tranship mail and passengers across that harried land, but Sherman chanced it. The *Orizaba* might still prove the tortoise to the *Golden Gate*'s hare.

The *Golden Gate*, he remarked, had "an awful load of passengers, most of them . . . office seekers going to [Buchanan's] inauguration. . . . All suppose a new order . . . is about to open for we have had rains and snows and storms . . . needed to bring out a vast supply of gold. If [we can] keep some of it in this country . . . this city would again feel the revival."

(Sherman, in predicting a revival of business in anticipation of the expected output of gold dust, was only echoing an opinion widespread throughout California where the wish was father to the thought. Actually, production had already passed its peak and, with minor exceptions, each year's volume was on a descending scale that was sometimes precipitous. 1852—that same year that had lured Lucas, Turner & Co. westward—held the all-time record, $81,294,700. Even 1853 had shown a sharp drop to $67,613,487, with a slight increase the next year to $69,433,931. Yet in 1855, a tragic year in banking circles, gold production also plummeted to $55,485,395. 1856 showed a slight recovery to $57,509,411. Then 1857, the year when Sherman and so many others hoped for a revival starting in the mines, produced only $43,628,172.

A distinguished authority on the subject concluded a detailed survey of California's gold production quite aptly when he wrote, "Mining is a good way to pioneer a territory but a poor way to hold it." [18])

On reading Turner's latest letter, Sherman sensed that anxiety about his health had strongly influenced the fateful decision in St. Louis. He protested that his health was "ordinarily good. . . . I have concluded to do nothing sudden but . . . take the full time named in your letter and . . . enable you to reconsider your determination of a discontinuance. . . . In the meantime *Mum* is the word."

In another paragraph he remarked "I agree with Mr. Lucas that there is a great future for this city, and could I reconcile Mrs. Sherman to make this our home for life, and were you willing to trust to chances, I would be most happy to stay here until put under the sod. I feel a reluctance to begin anew elsewhere." [19]

Like many another mortal, Sherman was having poignant second thoughts about the momentous step for which he had long been marshaling arguments. Despite all his grumbling about San Francisco's climate, politics, and business morals, the place clutched at his heart when it seemed he was about to leave it. So he drew back from the edge of the Rubicon.

Two weeks later the rains were still drenching San Francisco. Sherman wrote: "It rained so hard I did not come down to the office last night" (i.e., on the eve of a steamer day) "trusting for time to write . . . before . . . closing the mails at 11: a.m."

Sherman's proposal that all the banks raise their charge for exchange to 3½% had received qualified approval from some. Parrott and Tallant & Wilde were willing if there could be a general agreement. Davidson even proposed a 4% rate; however, Drexel, Sather & Church and Alsop & Co. would not join the movement. Nevertheless, Lucas, Turner & Co. advertised that henceforth every bill sold would be at 3½%. Even though they stood alone, Sherman was surprised to report that they had just sold over $60,000 at the new rate. He was shipping $75,000 in coin and $25,000 in Eastern exchange. Sherman's competitors held to the old rate and McLane of Wells, Fargo & Co. "contends that having no commissions to pay in New York and insurance at 1%, he can afford to ship at 3%, and even offers me to ship our treasure at less but I would not trust them. Their losses here have been awful; by one agent in Sacramento who died or committed suicide, they lost over $175,000 for which they recently received a judgment, but the estate can't refund $20,000."[20]

Sherman was sure the publication of his announcement would immediately reduce all the bank's business. Large purchasers of exchange would certainly not pay 3½% when 3% was available elsewhere, and such purchasers would naturally bank where they bought their Eastern exchange. Even so, he was adamant in his position. "The Legislature talks of taxing the exchange business by . . . a stamp tax. Go ahead! They think 3% clear gain. . . . Half the people . . . think the banks are robbing them of 3% on every dollar they send home."

If business diminished as he anticipated, he could discharge one or more clerks and so begin the retrenchment incident to the bank's ultimate closing. "Heretofore Lucas, Turner & Company were contending partly for present profit, but somewhat for glory . . . to retain a business for the sake of profit at some future indefinite time. . . . This move has caused some stir but not a single customer has left." (Sherman was here referring only to the increase in his exchange rate.) Referring to the large jobbers and importers who were heavy purchasers of New York drafts, Sherman said: "I have conferred with them freely and advise them to buy Alsop's or Parrott's bills or to ship their own coin. . . . I intend to adhere to these rates, to lose none of our good customers if I can help shake off the bad ones, and . . . look to profits until I know your further pleasure."

It is plain that Sherman must still have been hoping that the St. Louis partners would change their minds, or at least hold their decision in abeyance.

> I propose to keep things so arranged that if you really desire to draw out . . . for reasons other than my health that it may be done, but if left to myself, I shall make no open avowal of that purpose till summer or fall, so as to avoid the payment of the next taxes. . . . Business is conducted here at greater risk than anywhere else. . . . Nothing will . . . prove the result but an actual realization of Bills Receivable. It won't do to press ours all now, but in . . . summer and fall . . . with ordinary luck we can realize to good advantage. Our good name . . . is worth something but it is not an article . . . of sale. . . . If you are willing to trust me and my life till 1860, I am willing to stay, but that should . . . be predicated on some successor of your choice. I despair of reconciling Mrs. Sherman to stay here for life. She is willing I should stay my time out, but in the meantime I may send her home. . . . Banking is too sedentary for me . . . yet it troubles me to guess what I *am* fit for. . . . I shall await answers to my last letters and hold things prepared for what you may require.[21]

Strange, is it not, that in this gloomy spring of 1857, as Sherman cast about for a possible place he might adequately fill, the role that was to win him deathless fame was farthest from his thoughts?

29

Early in February, 1857, Sherman took advantage of a spell of fine weather to visit the mining town of Volcano in Amador County, "to look after some securities I hold for a balance due us from Strange," formerly of Murphy's, who was now doing business in Volcano. He had been buying gold dust and shipping it to Lucas, Turner & Co. After he had become well established, Sherman gave him a credit of $5,000,

> but like all the mountain men he ran over his limit. I took security and shut down on him. With interest his balance is $7,000 . . . his security a mortgage of a part of a certain ditch. . . . You remember James King of William's [22] experience, a ditch broke him. They are most tempting for they offer such large returns. . . . Water is absolutely necessary for mining and the miners pay .50 cents for each square inch, taking generally twelve inches for one party.

In writing Turner about this trip, Sherman mentioned only the business that took him to Volcano. We wonder if he found time to admire this picturesque camp in its crater-like setting among the pines. February was a bit too early for the carnival of wild flowers that still deck those hillsides every spring. Naturally his mind was occupied with the debt he had come to collect. Volcano, like a piece of antique sculpture, had to acquire the patina of another century to exert its present charm.

The banker had made an appointment for Strange to meet him but the latter failed to keep it, so Sherman employed his time investigating the ditch. Strange's share was $15,000 of the total cost of $50,000. The owners expected to net about $700 a month from the operation. Their ditch was a tributary of one owned by Pioche & Bayerque [23] of San Francisco, which had cost them more than $200,000. Snow on the ground was preventing the operation of Strange's ditch, so Sherman planned to return in the summer when the water would be running. It was plainly one of the bank's investments that would require close attention. "I found the miners prepared for heavy work and a very large amount of ground ploughed, but the same feeling of doubt and insecurity of the future [as] pervades here. All confidence and hope of California seem at an end."

Sherman's next experience was hardly calculated to change his mood. Returning from Volcano, he wrote Turner that he reached Sacramento "in time to be present at the exposé of the State Treasury. Dr. [Henry] Bates . . . State Treasurer, has evidently for past year had large transactions with Palmer, Cook & Company.[24] . . . He arranged through them for paying the State's interest last July, in which they failed."

Sherman detailed Bates's manipulation of public funds. After Palmer-Cook's failure, the state treasurer arranged with Wells, Fargo & Co. to pay the coupons on the state's bonds in New York, a simple enough operation in itself. However, Wells, Fargo & Co. demanded cash when Bates tried to substitute state warrants and old mortgages of Adams & Co.

Moreover, Bates knew that a committee of the legislature was about to visit the treasury to count its cash. Bates held far less than the books showed he had received as the state's share of taxes. The embarrassed treasurer contrived a way out of his difficulties.

Bates had had a confidential clerk, E. A. Rowe, who in December, 1856, had become president of Pacific Express Company (a concern put together from the fragments of the defunct Adams & Co.). Bates claimed he had paid the missing money to Rowe; Rowe professed to have received it—$124,000 was the tidy amount involved. Rowe, on behalf of his express company, signed a bond to pay the state's coupons. Thus was the shortage in the state treasury covered, according to Messrs. Bates and Rowe and also State Controller G. W. Whitman.

However, the legislature took a dim view of this wheeling and dealing and promptly impeached Bates and Whitman. As Sherman wrote, he expected the momentary indictment of expressman Rowe.

While Sherman probably did not have the whole story when he wrote Turner, we know from other sources that Bates was guilty of many violations of the law. He had juggled funds to finance his own and his cronies' speculation in state warrants and scrip. According to Bancroft, his shortage amounted to at least $272,521—a considerable sum for a state less than seven years old. Coming almost simultaneously with the supreme court's repudiation of California's bonded indebtedness, the blow to public confidence was devastating.[25]

At first Sherman was inclined to feel relieved and said, "In this . . . rascality, we have no interest save in the loss of . . . taxes which will have to be replaced. . . . If we [did not] . . . own real estate . . . I would play my hand so as never to pay another cent of taxes. . . . I'll do all I can to avoid taxation."

On second thought, the banker realized that

> the defalcation of Bates may interest us. From confidence in the man and to secure his brother the post of bookkeeper, John M. Rhodes[26] had gone on Bates' bond for $100,000 along with Edwards and Norris, both good men. I never knew Rhodes was on that bond. . . . He was always so cautious . . . that the moment I learned [it] . . . I saw him . . . and he explained the reasons. We have let him have about $20,000, interest payable monthly. He has always been prompt and . . . kept a large batch of securities in our hands. We have his endorsed [?] note of $4,000, note of Jesse Rhodes for $8,000 secured by mortgage in Sacramento, another by Jesse Rhodes, secured by mortgage on four buildings in Shasta, Yreka, Weaver[ville] and Jackson [four more names to stir the imagination of Gold Rush buffs] Jesse Rhodes is a banker . . . has offices in these . . . places. He borrowed $18,000 of John M.

Rhodes for ten months . . . gave mortgages for security. John M. Rhodes endorsed them . . . to us. I deemed Rhodes so good I inferred securities the same. On these we hold $25,000 of Sacramento County warrants.

On my way to Volcano, I saw Rhodes . . . about the bond of Dr. Bates. . . . He thought no action could be taken on that . . . until the time came to show the July coupons *had not* been paid. On my return from Volcano, I found Rhodes in trouble. His depositors were alarmed from the position taken by the Legislative committee that the simple absence of the money from the . . . Treasury was enough for the State to proceed against Bates' sureties. . . . Rhodes promised to see me . . . that evening but . . . did not. . . . Next morning . . . I saw his doors closed. . . . Suspecting he had failed I . . . telegraphed Nisbet to refuse any checks and endorse any balance on his $4,000 note. I . . . saw [Rhodes] . . . he said the moment it was found he was on the bond, his customers began to draw out and seeing he must ultimately have to pay up on the surety bond of Bates, he concluded to pay . . . as far as his money went and then . . . secure all his private creditors and let the State suffer. . . . He did right. He . . . still enjoys the credit of honesty and fair dealing. . . . He says Uncle Jesse is good for the two notes . . . and the property mortgaged . . . [is] worth more than the debt. I will sell the warrants as soon as possible, wipe out the $4,000 note and hold the overplus until other notes mature. The worst part is that notes of Jesse Rhodes . . . have some eight months to run. No man is wise enough to look ahead eight months in this accursed land. . . . Of all our interior correspondents, I have always thought best of Rhodes. . . . He was so cautious and did his own work . . . always on hand. . . . His fatal error was in going on bond of an official and a California official at that. . . . He assured me he was worth . . . above all private debts . . . $30,000 but . . . he may lose all.

Sherman had set out for Volcano on a fairly routine collection, but en route he had stumbled upon the far more serious defalcation of the state treasurer and the resulting misfortune of his Sacramento correspondent. As he pondered this one fateful misstep of a good man, he may have recalled the adage, "for want of a nail, the kingdom was lost." Just to secure a minor post for his brother, Rhodes had jeopardized and indeed would lose the entire estate he had created, as well as cause serious embarrassment to his uncle.

Sherman's stay in Sacramento afforded him an opportunity to meet a number of the legislators.

> All seem fairly disposed [he informed Turner] to provide for past debts of the State . . . but to be more guarded and economical. . . . The coupons of the State bonds for July next will not be paid, but a bill will . . . probably be passed to enable the city to fund her old warrants. . . . Economy now is practiced by the city authorities . . . the better to pay interest and principal, should we . . . get bonds for our warrants. . . . Our joint interests require that we . . . go on . . . until the fall of this year when if necessary I will be able to close out promptly.

Sherman enclosed a clipping from the *Alta California* quoting "my notions of the general condition of morals and things here." He also sent with his letter the last two statements of Garrison, Morgan, Fretz and Ralston,[27] "they have not a quarter as good a deposit account as we have, though they profess to have double our capital." [28]

Four days later Sherman wrote again. Another heavy rain had drenched the state. At Nevada City, bridges and houses had been carried away, and some of the population had barely escaped with their lives. Miners and farmers were now assured of an abundant supply of water. Some gold dust was beginning to arrive from the mountains, but "not enough to pay off old scores and encourage people once more to indulge in dreams of wealth and speculation."

It seems clear that Sherman was still torn between his doubts about the future of San Francisco and his reluctance to accept defeat; also that he could not yet accept the St. Louis partners' decision as final.

> From the tone of your letters since . . . authorizing me to wind up here, I infer your resolution was based partly on the bad results

of the past year . . . partly from an apprehension that I was going the way of all flesh a little too rapidly. . . . If the last year is an indication of the chronic state of San Francisco, the quicker we get out . . . the better. If it is only one of those periodical stages of depression which overtake all new countries . . . we had better hold on a little longer. . . . It would be idle . . . to expect now to realize the magnificent conceptions we all indulged at the outstart before we got a peep behind the curtains of Page, Bacon & Company, Adams & Company, Meiggs, etc., curtains that concealed as many mysteries as the green baize does to the boy who believes all he sees is real. . . . We now know . . . a great deposit account is out of the question here, that California securities are delusions . . . that 2½ and 3% a month is not all interest but risk insurance. . . . Business here requires unstinting care and study. A knowledge of these facts . . . is something, and I want to try a little longer. . . . I will . . . go on . . . carefully till fall, unless your letters are positive.

Apparently Sherman's frequent proud reference to the high standing of his firm was no idle boast. Even though he was charging more for exchange than any other banker in San Francisco, he had sold $100,000 of Eastern drafts for this latest steamer day. He was shipping $60,000 in bullion and another $60,000 in drafts deposited with Lucas-Turner.

Sherman concluded this letter with a wry quip on the morals of Californians: "I send you a copy of Estill's [29] speech which is a rich production for a state legislator. The legislature has failed to appropriate for the state prison of which he is lessee. . . . He threatens to turn the prisoners loose . . . I don't know as they would much corrupt those outside." [30]

Later in the month Sherman again visited Sacramento

to meet the San Francisco delegation to see if some compromise cannot be agreed upon about the city debt. The finances of city, county and state are all in inextricable confusion. . . . If present legislators do not devise some . . . remedy, this country will be thrown back ten years. . . . I will tell them plainly as long as they keep bad faith with their creditors, they cannot expect moneyed men to pay . . . taxes except when we have visible property.

Unless our warrants are provided for, I shall never pay one cent of taxes save on real estate. . . . This will be a strong argument, for unless the State and city can collect taxes on personal as well as real property, the government cannot be supported.[31]

Another long-time army friend of both Turner and Sherman, Col. Thomas Swords,[32] arrived in San Francisco with his wife on the *Golden Gate* on March 2, 1857. For once Sherman sounded like a California booster. He took Mrs. Swords to his home to see Mrs. Sherman and the children, and noted:

The day was one of those exquisite ones that occur here at this season . . . the flowers of my yard must have pleased Mrs. Swords who was just from the intense cold of New York. The Colonel and Mrs. Swords go to Benicia . . . the headquarters, but all expect the new administration will change it to here, where it ought to be. I told Swords if such were the case . . . I wanted to rent him our building at . . . Jackson and Montgomery . . . [which is] in every way adapted to serve the whole headquarters . . . lower rooms for Quartermaster and Commissary . . . upstairs for rooms and offices. . . . Our present tenants are so uncertain and such bad pay, it amounts to earning the money to collect rents.

Sherman acknowledged two letters of Turner's, dated January 31: "and perceive . . . fully . . . your plans in regard to California." He again summarized the unfavorable features of banking in San Francisco, and admitted:

I am convinced of the truth of those propositions and probably urged them on you and Mr. Lucas with more force than I should have done, but the truth growing stronger and stronger . . . I could not justly withhold it . . . yet having acquired a . . . strong position here in credit and public estimation of my own accord I would not have urged the . . . breaking up of the house, but to content ourselves . . . a year or more with the uncertain chances and be ready to take advantage of the return of fortune which must . . . occur. . . . Your letters . . . show a settled . . . purpose to break up . . . even at some sacrifice and direct your labor in another quarter.

Turner must have outlined plans for the future of the firm elsewhere, for Sherman wrote:

> It is not for me to judge of the wisdom of enlarging the sphere of our operations, or to caution . . . against laying too large a foundation for the future edifice. This was my fault here. . . . I want you to direct, leaving me to execute the part . . . allotted to me. I . . . doubt . . . my powers to cope with the acute operators of New York, and beg you to . . . arrange . . . for at least a year or more, I will have little else to do than . . . act as agent, to fill orders, make collections, etc.

From this it seems clear that Mr. Lucas and his partners in St. Louis had revived the plan for a New York agency proposed by Sherman himself, months before, and that Sherman had been selected to manage it. Apparently now he had told his wife of the decision for he went on:

> Mrs. Sherman is delighted at the prospect of going home and consents to remain in Lancaster and leave me to go anywhere, till I have established myself . . . in New York or wherever within reach my interests call me. I see by John Sherman's letters that he was much gratified at the mere prospect of my going to New York. . . . Mr. Ewing once urged me to the step on the ground that business there was . . . different . . . from here.

Yet the old reluctance to leave San Francisco still asserted itself:

> In spite of asthma, I feel no little regret at quitting this place, where I am somebody and going to be swallowed up in that vast gulf of mankind, where I will be small indeed.
>
> My former letters . . . have explained . . . the abstract proposition of breaking up here. It is perfectly feasible . . . only question is what sacrifice will be made. This winter has been the severest financial one of this country . . . has laid merchants right and left. Fine rains have fallen . . . every prospect of a good year near. . . . [There is] not enough money to supply . . . necessary wants of borrowers. . . . Until April begins to pour down the gold . . . [it is] unpolitic to restrict our customers too much . . . until sales of goods can be made, the merchants have no possible chance of getting along without some assistance. In all May and June how-

ever . . . we can easily draw out, without shock or confusion, and put at least $200,000 in New York in . . . July. I think I ought to make no engagements east till fall. . . . If your subsequent letters evince a desire . . . I should expedite things, it shall be done. Nisbet and I have discussed the subject . . . [and] under . . . absolute secrecy have confided to Mr. Parrott [33] . . . the probability of our winding up here. I spoke to Mr. Parrott . . . whether he would move to our present building and buy our vault and furniture. . . . He is too timid and . . . afraid to undertake a business as large as his and ours joined. . . . He owns so much property on Montgomery Street, it is to his interest to remain. I wish we had not moved. . . . We . . . have about $150,000 of depositors money . . . $100,000 belongs to parties in town who could in ten minutes demand it. Therefore we must proceed with . . . caution. We have about $60,000 of demand notes that could be realized in a week. . . . By refusing all discounts on any one steamer day, we could . . . meet all demands. . . . We generally have from $30,000 to $90,000 in gold in process of mintage. . . . By uniting these sources we feel . . . we can at any opportune moment prepare to wind up. . . . On the other hand, if we shut down suddenly we do injustice to good customers who know not where to look. . . . All our accounts east are more than good. . . . We propose from this to April 5 to curtail discounts with all except our promptest and strongest customers, then to notify our up country customers to change and before the April 20 steamers, to intimate as safely as we can to our strong customers that they must look elsewhere for their accommodation, and at that date, April 20, to shut down, a few days after . . . notify them to draw their . . . balances . . . [and] call in all certificates, assuring ourselves . . . that we can meet all demands. . . . We desire that you strengthen us at the Metropolitan Bank [in New York] . . . to the extent of $50,000 which by the following steamer will more than be made good, and follow up by sending you as fast as the funds are realized. That is the earliest date . . . maybe we may postpone action till, say, May 5 but not later. In either event, we can put . . . at least $200,000 with the Metropolitan Bank by the first or middle of July. . . . In meantime I will send my family home so that I may dispose of my furniture and house. . . . Nisbet may go home so as to return in time to relieve me and close up all that is left, especially the books for which he is, and I am not, qualified. . . . I will try to effect a partition of this property where we are and return to our old building. During this crisis I propose not to send Mr. Lucas his rents, but when we are done, settle with him. . . . When I get east, you can dispose of me as you think proper. . . . You speak of [Nisbet] as an auxiliary to me at New York. I am perfectly willing. [He] has been very proper . . . to my knowledge has not touched a drop and . . . kept good company since his return from home. . . . He may come home with Mrs. Sherman. . . . I propose to offer some of our real estate for sale, if it brings a fair . . . value, to let it slide, if not, hold for better times.

Regardless of the importance of these plans "to break up the California house," Sherman could not allow them to distract his attention from the sore subject of the bank's San Francisco warrants. Toward the end of February he again went to Sacramento. The city's representatives in the legislature were "perfectly willing to pass some refunding bill if they could agree on the details." They were stunned, however, by the supreme court's repudiation of the state's bonds and its further finding that the legislature had no power to levy taxes to pay interest on the bonds. All they might appropriate were funds on hand, and since Bates's defalcation, that was a mere trifle. So pressed for ready cash was the state, that the legislators' own per diem compensation threatened to terminate, "and they may break up in a row," Sherman concluded sardonically.

He had sent some statistics about the indebtedness of other cities and states to William J. Shaw, one of San Francisco's representatives in the state senate. Sherman enclosed Shaw's acknowledgment with his letter to Turner. The senator wrote that California would never repudiate, "it would cost too much to do so. For a vast state like ours, such a debt is . . . trifling . . . when we get a good government, we can pay it without feeling it. It is however the grossest mistake to . . . [pass] an act submitting the question to the people . . . impracticable and most unwise." [34] Senator Shaw told Sherman that California should hold another convention and adopt a new constitution to remedy the debt situation. Many bills had been introduced to increase the state's revenues; one proposal would impose a stamp tax on bills of exchange, bills of lading, notes, and certificates of deposit. "They [the legislators] think the current of gold, flowing from the mountains east, should be taxed. The miners won't pay taxes and . . . all the burdens of government fall on real property. . . . We don't care much but the bill, if it passes, will be exceedingly onerous to banks."

All of the above, written in March, 1857, sounds oddly familiar more than a century later. California has grown beyond the wildest dreams of Sherman's contemporaries; numerous communities scattered all over her broad expanse boast populations larger than that of the entire state at the time he was writing. Yes, the dramatis personae are different in every way, but the central theme—how best to raise more taxes—is as old as the Code of Hammurabi, and will probably be repeated as long as genus Homo inhabits the earth!

> There has been a good deal of talk [Sherman continued] about Wells, Fargo & Company who have agencies all over the country . . . and has been robbed several times. . . . Recently they have been very successful in recovering lost treasure but have had to pay liberal rewards. They still have a banking house in connection with their express business. . . . In my judgment they are inconsistent, the risk attending the express being apt to involve their banking safety.

William Garrison had just called on Sherman and informed him of a defalcation by an employee of Wells, Fargo. On questioning one of the firm's senior officials, Sherman was told the offending bookkeeper had made false entries to the extent of \$5,000. Street rumor gave the amount as \$20,000. All of this made Sherman say: "There appears to be an atmosphere of rascality here that taints everybody, and I hope McLane [head of Wells, Fargo] will punish the fellow. Here, if a man turns rascal, they let him off if he will only clear out and perpetrate new crime somewhere else."

The same letter contained other news of special significance in view of Sherman's stand in favor of adequate exchange charges:

> "Garrison, Morgan & Company [35] have discontinued . . . the exchange business and advertise to confine their business to deposits and discounts. Of the former they have . . . little. . . . Their cash capital is now . . . $500,000, used to be $700,000. I think they are implicated with Walker [the Nicaragua filibuster] . . . ultimately this connection will ruin them. Unless Walker recovers the river boats, I don't see how he can maintain himself. . . . A bad sign . . . is that Crittenden, Randolph . . . and others who profess to be such ardent filibusters have . . . got out of Nicaragua, leaving Walker to do the fighting. Several precious rascals from here are with the Costa Ricans against Walker.[36]

30

On March 19, Sherman was suffering an asthmatic attack so severe that he could not go down to the bank to write his usual steamer-day letter. His mood as he penned a few necessary messages at home was a somber one; "chaos now prevails here in State and City matters." As to the "break up" of Lucas, Turner & Co.,

> it will require careful management on our part to withdraw without shock. We have begun to curtail. You can imagine . . . how many conjectures it gives rise to. I told several . . . customers last week that the repudiation of State and City debt had impaired confidence in this country . . . I would be forced to withhold . . . their usual facilities and today I have carried it out. . . . I shall take all the blame till time develops the reason. . . . A good many people will think I am unreasonable. . . . I think our clerks see some change is designed, but I have . . . remarked that during tight times of winter, I had discounted . . . more liberally than I wanted to. Now that gold was coming down freely was time to haul in, also that repudiation of State debt . . . defalcations, bankruptcies, etc. had . . . shaken your confidence in the country. . . . My instructions were to curtail.
>
> By the April 5th steamer, I propose to have discounts down to $450,000, and on the 20th of next month, we will have more money . . . than is necessary to direct our customers to draw off. I want to keep things quiet so Certificate holders will not take alarm. If I detect any sign of that I may . . . act more summarily and probably lean on the Metropolitan Bank. . . . I hope there will be no necessity for this . . . unless some newspaper ass detects

> our movement and blurts it out. . . . There will be loud regrets at our leaving . . . many think us the top bank of the city. . . .
>
> Gold is coming pretty freely from the mountains and will easily supply any vacuum by our withdrawal. About April 1st we ought to receive answers to our letters of Jan. 20. . . . I feel certain you will reiterate your instructions and we will . . . act with decision. If we force all paper [coming due] between this date and April 20 to be paid, there will be a necessity to act at that date. . . . I propose to advise . . . many of our customers to withdraw their accounts before we give public notice and if possible do the whole thing gradually.

Sherman informed Turner that the legislature seemed disposed to take constructive action on both the state and city indebtedness. Any sincere attempt to recognize these obligations would necessarily require strict economy in government—in itself a very desirable step and calculated to improve the quality of the ultimate legal securities that would be outstanding.

Sherman, however, was not going to be overconfident,

> until the thing is complete. I shall not be sanguine. It is all important . . . to convert our city warrants into bonds before we leave the country. . . . Our State and City governments are in . . . as bad condition as can be. There has been danger . . . of the city and state convicts being turned loose on account of want of means to sustain them. Some of the penitentiary convicts have died of starvation. The public schools are . . . out of funds . . . no alternative to their being closed. . . . The plank streets are in . . . awful condition and some of the wharves have . . . fallen in. The present is as bad as possible . . . whether the future has anything better in store, I don't know.

Sherman wanted his wife to leave with the children as soon as the closing was definitely arranged, but she was anxious to have her husband accompany them. He felt he must have definite word first from the St. Louis interests, whether they wanted him to hasten his departure and leave Nisbet to wind up affairs.

On the personal side, Sherman knew that his early leaving would entail some monetary sacrifice. He could only hope that some of his St. Louis holdings might have appreciated sufficiently to offset such loss.[37]

Two letters went east by this steamer because the *Golden Gate* had to return to her wharf on the 20th of March, a few hours after her departure for Panama. She had struck a rock and had begun to take water immediately, so was forced to put back. This steamer was now at the Navy Yard for repairs. If she proved unable to resume service, the *Sonora* would sail in her place.

Sherman's asthma had kept him confined to his home much of the time. Meanwhile Nisbet was faithfully carrying out the program; discounts were reducing and cash increasing.

> I think our design is suspected but the suspicion is confined to the active merchants who judge quickly from signs. . . . We know there are a great many accounts of persons not resident in the city and a large amount of our certificate [holders] are down the country to buy cattle. . . . I want . . . to move on quietly . . . so long as possible so as never to have . . . the semblance of a run. Our clerks have shown . . . mortification at seeing our shipments fall off . . . to nothing and . . . noticed my refusing loans to . . . good applicants . . . also remarked [that] a friend of mine at my suggestion opened an account at Tallant & Wilde. . . . So this evening after bank closed, I called them all in and told them that . . . since January . . . I had positive orders to break up the California house, . . . and that by the mail before the last I had received . . . fuller directions. . . . I wanted the closest circumspection, to answer no questions save that I was not going to lend money . . . to buy other bankers' exchange because it was a little cheaper than ours, etc. I also notified them . . . we would accomplish enough by the 20th of April to . . . settle all accounts . . . say by May 1, Lucas, Turner & Company would cease to be bankers and they must look elsewhere for employment. Most of these clerks have been with us a long time and are much attached. They . . . can hardly understand how, being so well established in public confidence, we should go away. I explained . . . your intention to convert your house into a big bank with agents at New York and at New Orleans. Poor fellows, they will sleep

badly tonight. If they will be discreet and hold their tongues one week, they may talk as much as they please.

On May 1st I will discharge the whole establishment, excepting Henry for an hour . . . each day to sweep the office. . . . Nisbet and I must do the work. I still have a few mortgage notes. . . . I will sacrifice something to avoid delays and expenses of foreclosure. . . . The gold mines are yielding quite well. . . . By June I think money will be quite plentiful here, in which case we will be better able to realize our notes and securities.

One of Sherman's long-standing responsibilities was the care of General Hitchcock's investments in San Francisco realty and mortgages. With the approaching end of the bank's activities, it was essential that he convert these into cash, as they could not be satisfactorily managed after Sherman left the city. On March 21, he wrote Turner that he had sold some of the properties at auction:

I am afraid the General will be angry with me. . . . I sold the lot on Battery Street, 30 × 67½ feet for $11,500, the lot in the rear, 22½ × 60 for $2,750, making $14,250 for that property, which I was offered $15,000 cash for last year, and which, principal and interest, must stand the General $24,000. I sold the lot on corner of Clay and Mason, 60 × 120 for $2,650. The other two pieces I could get no offers for . . . they bring rent, I think I can make a satisfactory disposition of them . . . tell the General I will report . . . fully next mail. I sold about $10,000 of our bank property at equally unsatisfactory prices. . . . Will . . . wait a couple of months to see if times get better. . . . I think good times for California are a long way off.

We have heard of the Wagon Road [the road long projected from the Missouri River to California]. I saw the Governor and told him the State should . . . provide for a road across the Sierra Nevada. . . . He promised to send in a special message . . . but the State is so flat broke, no contractor will trust her or her bonds. . . . If the mines turn out . . . as rich this year as everybody anticipates, all these things may change. . . . We will then wonder at being so disheartened. I hope so.

I may be absent next steamer day . . . will not leave till I receive your letters about the 1st or 2nd [of April].[38]

Sure enough, Sherman's next communication to Turner was written in Sacramento on April 2. At the top of the sheet, he scribbled "written in haste in Hastings Bank[39] . . . waiting for driver."

He had received all of Turner's letters through February 28; there were no changes in the plans. However, Sherman was surprised to find that as news of the firm's plans leaked out, there was not the rapid withdrawal of accounts he had anticipated. The bank's decision to withdraw "is the source of universal regret . . . our good customers have begged . . . to remain as long as possible."

Nisbet had sent up to Sherman the latest trial balance so that he could enclose it with his letter. Lucas, Turner & Co. now had on hand $313,000 to meet $132,000 certificates and $233,000 deposits. As $50,000 was due depositors now in the interior and a like amount could not be drawn without Sherman's consent, because of various loan arrangements, the bank now held more cash than it needed. On the other hand, they were overdrawn at the Metropolitan Bank some $35,000, but various other credit balances in the East were being sent to the Metropolitan so that situation was a very temporary one.

The Low Brothers' Bank in Marysville was one of the customers who were reluctant to close their accounts. Sherman had had to request them and also Bours of Stockton[40] to transfer their business to another San Francisco correspondent by April 15.

Public notice of the withdrawal was to be made on April 20. On May 1, what was left of the business would be moved back to the old location at Montgomery and Jackson Streets.

Sherman must have smiled grimly when he wrote Turner that Meigs of the Metropolitan had notified him that the insurance companies had reduced their rates on coin and bullion shipments to 1¼%. It must have given him a melancholy satisfaction to advise the New Yorker

> they were too late! For a whole year I had begged and implored it of them. . . . Now they have lost their last treasure policy! . . .

> Every dollar of California treasure is delivered at London, whereby the American firms lose just $500,000 per annum! . . . They persisted in charging us more than the experience of eight years had shown to be the real risk. . . . They will never again receive the business. . . . High freights are . . . turning the shipment of gold to England by Aspinwall. . . . Unless some steps be taken to enable Californians to put their treasure in New York cheaper than now, it will all go to London.

Evidently Turner's latest letter had definitely announced Sherman's selection as Lucas & Simond's representative in New York, for he now wrote Turner:

> As to going to New York . . . I feel . . . complimented and don't care a cent about the share I am to have, so that I can pay expenses. I would rather be associated with you and Mr. Lucas than any persons I know. . . . In New York as your representative if I can have time to study the ground before they have the big smash up, I can serve you well. . . . I have the confidence of everybody out here which together with Mr. Lucas' great wealth, which doesn't lose a cent in my telling, I can in New York, follow your instructions and attract as much business as you may feel disposed to do.
>
> When the first proposition came to me, I feared that Mrs. Sherman or her family had been using undue influence. . . . If such had been the case, I would not have accepted. . . . Mrs. Sherman, of course, doesn't like California . . . would rather see me driving a cart of coal in Ohio than to be Governor of California. . . .
>
> My own ambition . . . [is] to fulfill my duty to my partners. . . . Here I have done everything against my own judgment. I bought a lot and built a good house and have denied Mrs. Sherman nothing. My theory is that nobody can maintain a family in California with Ohio notions of nurses, servants, coal and butler. These things in the West are like the earth, cheap, but here they are like diamonds.

(This is another instance where Sherman regarded California as a land foreign to the United States. In the above sentence he rated Ohio as part of "the West," but California was *not!*)

Nobody of common prudence should have a family here, unless they are of the laboring class, or can board or occupy rooms over a store. It is folly to keep house in the home sense, unless a person is established for life, and has a certain income.

Therefore when I thought I had done so much for my family, and when you had more than seconded me in my efforts to make Mrs. Sherman contented, I did feel a little angry when I thought she had used undue influence to get me away. Mrs. Sherman says she did write you a letter, which she sent to the bank for me to read and forward, but being busy, or not seeing it unsealed, I put it in the . . . mail bag.

Sherman's readiness to accept the blame for the incident of his wife's letter reflects the man's fairness. The same desire to deal punctiliously with his partners is evident in the next paragraph:

What she wrote, I don't know but . . . if any other consideration than business propriety . . . should have entered into this important move, whereby I am drawn away from the protection of valuable property which Mr. Lucas acquired here partly at my instance, I should . . . feel unworthy of further confidence.

I think I shall come east June 5th to Ohio and then to St. Louis for orders. In the meantime I shall labor to forward $200,000 besides making the accounts [i.e., deposits] all good, and will leave Nisbet under light expense to haul in outstanding matters. I am bothered about real estate . . . absolutely no demand. . . . The same reasons that influence you . . . have been at work to cause the withdrawal of all funds possible . . . owned abroad. . . . The consequence is that real estate and securities cannot be forced.

Sherman's driver must have been slow in arriving for we have to read several pages before we find the reason for his presence in Sacramento on that 2nd of April:

I am here to do all I can to get the Legislature to fund the city debt. We have also an interest in the Sacramento County warrants. . . . If these warrants are funded, I can get our Rhodes debt at once, otherwise may have to [wait] till the Jesse Rhodes notes mature in August. I will make no unnecessary sacrifice . . . but if I must will leave these . . . to mature in Nisbet's charge. Up to this moment things have worked . . . smoothly. . . . I . . . anticipate no unnecessary trouble . . . but we have some debts that will require . . . nice management to realize. If the spring and summer develop gold as . . . all . . . believe . . . we will get out of California better than anybody ever did before.

Why don't you go to New York [he continued], get an office and start . . . depend on my taking your place in July or August? If no objection, retain the style of Lucas, Turner & Company . . . name is pretty well known all over the country. . . . Of course it is none of my business, but unless right to issue notes be of very great advantage, I believe with Lucas, Turner & Company in St. Louis as center, New York and New Orleans as wings we could do an exchange business . . . with advances on shipments of produce and discounting a limited amount of good paper, would make the strongest house in the West. I . . . am ignorant of banking in your place but feel certain these houses in the three points . . . with reasonable capital and unlimited public confidence and credit . . . we can do as well as the best.

However, the banker's mind was still centered on California.

I have been here two days. The city [Sacramento] is much improved [since] your day, but same evil is at work here as in San Francisco. Previous extravagance has entailed a debt and consequent taxes. . . . All who have money, prefer to keep it to buying houses and land. I heard a very interesting debate in which it was proven that the mining counties pay little or no taxes. . . . Farms and city property pay enormous amounts. . . . El Dorado County sends four senators to the legislature who represent three millions of taxable property. . . . Santa Clara [County] sends one senator and pays taxes on nine millions. A revenue bill was under discussion. The mining counties having a majority of representation exempt all mining claims from taxation, which have more real value than all the farms in the State. A miner has his claim valued at one, two or ten thousand dollars, has his pockets full of rocks but pays no taxes. . . . The farmer has his lands, houses, fences, animals, plows and gathered grain all taxed from one to four per cent per annum. This . . . must deter prudent men from making . . . improvements. The miners have the power . . . and will keep it.

As to the State bonds . . . it will be left to a vote of the people.

> I believe the people will repudiate. If you have any bonds, get rid of them. . . . Be careful of the issue of the Illinois banks that are based on these bonds. . . . If I can succeed in getting our warrants funded, I'll sell quick and . . . never more trust any California corporation.

(I believe Sherman used "corporation" here in the sense of municipal or public entities—city, county, and the like—as none of his credit problems involved private corporations as we know them today.)

"Nobody feels a fixed interest here, and all are ready to bolt as soon as a good chance offers." Then with the ambivalence we have several times observed, the disillusioned banker abruptly became almost a California Chamber of Commerce enthusiast.

> A wagon road may bring a different character of people, for the country has many advantages, mines of exhaustless gold, a large quantity of fertile land and a good healthful climate. The country is bound to become important and San Francisco is bound to be a great city, but both have got to pass through a severe ordeal. For the present, neither is a fit abode for a person of established fortune or reputation.
>
> There have been a few unimportant failures in the past fortnight. By none . . . are we . . . losers. We hold some unmatured paper, makers of which [have] failed, but the endorsers are good.
>
> It is funny, to see some of these failures. . . . If a man can fail for $1,000 and thereby save $1,500, it is a good commercial transaction. Unless the merchants stamp these failures by their true name of outrageous swindles, they need not talk of stealing office holders or moral reforms. I see no signs of moral reform in California though some Vigilantes see it sticking out in every direction. My opinion is the very nature of the country begets speculation, extravagance, failures and rascality. Everything is chance, everything is gambling, and I shall feel relieved when I am not dependant on the people of California for my repose.[41]

Sherman described his April activities in Sacramento as "the discreditable occupation of logrolling to secure passage of a bill . . . for funding the City debt." By mid-April the assembly had taken favorable action, and he expected affirmation by the senate within a few days when he wrote on the 19th. The proposed step was for San Francisco to issue thirty-year bonds, to bear interest at 1% a year the first year, 2% the second year and so on until the sixth year, when the interest was to be 6% for the balance of the life of the bonds. Sherman described this as "an anomalous kind of bond and an outrage on the City's creditors, but . . . the best we can do."

Sherman had also joined other friends of John M. Rhodes[42] in getting a bill passed to coerce Sacramento County to pay him for a road it had bought from him two years before and "had tried to swindle him out of." Both houses passed this bill and the governor had assured Sherman he would sign it. This would enable Rhodes to pay Lucas, Turner & Co. his debt without waiting for the Jesse Rhodes' notes to mature.

After these dealings with the legislature, Sherman had traveled to Marysville and thence up to Downieville to hasten the collection of two mortgage notes he had taken from Captain Stone.[43] In reporting this trip to another mining camp in the Sierra, his letter makes us sense the different world to which he had climbed. Surrounded by its snow peaks towering above the forks of the brawling North Yuba, Downieville made all visitors aware of its individuality, especially if they lodged at its rambling Saint Charles Hotel. So Sherman wrote: "Downieville is high in the mountains, about 6,000 feet above the plain and though the weather was quite hot in the foothills, I found the snow very deep on the mountains. The miners could not work for the snow."

Sherman found the makers of the mortgages

> men in good standing and good for the notes. . . . I made the best arrangements I could . . . have promises of payment in . . . May, when money will be plentiful in the mining districts. . . . They will have water until September . . . have made preparations . . . to work to the best advantage so I hope in June money will be plentiful in California . . . [which] will facilitate our winding up with as little loss as possible.

Sherman had returned to San Francisco on April 12. He found abundant cash in his bank's vaults, but still the depositors seemed loath "to go away without compulsion," surely a strange experience for a banker! So Sherman concluded to give public notice of the firm's intentions, and he enclosed a copy of the advertisement in his next letter to Turner. He explained its language as having been chosen

> to do as little as possible to increase the distrust of business prospects. . . . So many are "going away," foreigners are drawing out their capital . . . a spark might cause a panic and universal bankruptcy. . . .
>
> A great many have applied to me in strict confidence to know the real secret cause of our withdrawal. I have replied . . . your business in St. Louis is so large . . . you need an agent in New York. . . . Not wanting too many branches you . . . thought proper to break up this establishment *for a time*, and transfer me to New York. I send . . . a newsletter in which the editor gives this version. He . . . said he was compelled to make some allusion to . . . our going out of business. If I would not satisfy him, he might be compelled to guess . . . wrong. Rather than he should make any mistake, I gave him this version. . . . He has expressed it somewhat awkwardly."

Sherman ran his advertisement in three daily newspapers. He "took it for granted deposits would be drawn instanter. Not so, as we gave till the 20th, many still cling to us."

On the previous day these "clinging" deposits still totaled about $135,000. In addition, some $35,000 was held in the various trust funds Sherman was carrying for several investors. Against this, the bank's cash totaled $219,352, of which roundly $50,000 consisted of good Eastern exchange, which Sherman was sending by the next steamer to the Metropolitan Bank, "so you see we keep things snug."

He planned to send Lucas & Simonds $200,000 very shortly, "then leave Nisbet to manage the balance, to loan a little, pay expenses and . . . realize the William Lucas [trust fund] account."

A man by the name of Dominick Gann had just proposed an

exchange of several lots in St. Louis for some of the bank's San Francisco real estate. Sherman planned to investigate this as soon as he reached St. Louis. In the meantime, he suggested that Turner also examine Gann's property.

> I would like to part with our San Francisco property for many reasons. All agencies here are unsafe . . . charge ruinous commissions, and so help me Moses, I don't know a lawyer here whom I can absolutely trust. . . . For this reason . . . Nisbet should stay here the rest of this year. He is bound to us by self interest, is honest . . . his youthful vanity less dangerous than positive dishonesty. I shall give him an earnest warning about wine or brandy . . . he has abstained ever since his return. . . .
>
> You will observe . . . we give notice of our intention to buy Eastern exchange. . . . The object . . . is to transfer our money East as cheap as possible. Having money on steamer day, we thus buy 30 and 60 day bills at about par and sight bills from 1½ to 2. To ship coin would cost us full 3 per cent. . . . The notice is evidence of strength . . . we not only have plenty of money to pay off our depositors but to buy exchange and even leave a little on Time certificates.
>
> The credit of Lucas, Turner and Company stands higher this day . . . than ever. Should in the lapse of time, it become prudent to revive this business here, it will have the benefit of this good will. I shall make no sacrifice of vaults, counters or locks but put everything away, so you may be prepared . . . three or five years hence, when things here assume something like a permanent value, to reestablish the business.

Soon after his journey to Downieville, a similar collection problem had taken Sherman to Sonoma. There he had met that most famous of all Spanish Californians of the day, General Mariano G. Vallejo. En route he had stopped at Benicia and called on Colonel and Mrs. Swords.[44] He had tried to enlist the former's aid in leasing the Lucas-Turner building to the army for its Pacific headquarters or at least to house the quartermaster's department. "Swords is so conscientious," Sherman wrote, "that he fears to treat with a friend on business, but he promised . . . to give it favorable consideration. . . . Headquarters will not come to the city until General Clarke [45] arrives here." After berating the low quality of the building's present tenants—especially as tardy rent payers, he declared "No city can boast of such a poor set of fellows as San Francisco. If the Quarter Master will take the whole building except the U.S. Land Office and one or two other good paying tenants, I will leave here with a clearer conscience . . ."

Nisbet would assume general charge of the building, and Sherman was employing a "young man named Thibault to collect rents and keep his eye on the other property."

Rumor had it that another banker was leaving San Francisco:

> It is said Drexel of Drexel, Sather & Church [46] is going out of the concern. If so, they won't last long. Garrison [47] is doing little or nothing. Most of our business has gone to Parrott and Tallant & Wilde.[48] I think a new concern will attempt a . . . savings bank of which Bainbridge, our cashier, is to take charge. Bainbridge has been faithful and industrious. I would . . . recommend him to that extent.

(It seems quite probable that the new savings bank mentioned by Sherman was the Savings and Loan Society that was organized on July 23, 1857, although the absence of Bainbridge's name among its first officers justifies some doubt. However, the Savings and Loan Society's record was so remarkable in some respects, and in such shining contrast to the many unstable financial institutions of the 1850's as to merit brief mention here. At the end of the first six months of its existence, deposits totaled $21,522. It paid a monthly dividend of 1½%. Over a period of fifty-three years from organization until its merger with the San Francisco Savings Union in 1910, it paid an average rate of 7.4% interest on savings deposits! The highest rate paid was 19⅓% for the half year ending July 21, 1858; the lowest 3⅛% from January 1, 1901, to July 1, 1902.[49]

Sherman closed his April 19 letter, "I might leave May 20th but think June 5 [will be] the time." [50]

By May 4, 1857, Lucas, Turner & Co., now reduced to a skeleton force, was back at the old location, which had been built with such bright hopes. Anyhow, Sherman was for once

> free . . . of the importunities and troubles of steamer day. I have just taken a turn on Front Street and recognize . . . the look of the merchants and so help me, Moses, I would rather be a second lieutenant of foot [i.e., infantry] than be an Arrington or Brewster or Castle.[51] Their . . . stores full of goods are tempting baits to up-country buyers who make good promises of payment, but find themselves short and force the merchant to raise his balance, somehow, anyhow, on steamer day.
>
> We will be able to put in New York about $75,000 this steamer besides the insurance scrip now at the bank, by the next steamer $25,000 to $50,000 more. . . . I trust to have $200,000 in July. I have concluded to come home next steamer, May 20 in the *Sonora* . . . reach New York June 14 . . . St. Louis by June 20. . . .
>
> We keep out $40,000 in Mint certificates . . . the only securities in which I now feel absolute reliance. . . . The legislature broke up in a row before they reached the funding bill, so we have to hold over the warrants another year. They passed a bill which gives us $20,000 Sacramento County Bonds, 10% as additional security for Rhodes' debt. . . . I made two trips to Sacramento on that. . . . My personal influence with the Governor secured his approval but the failure of the funding bill is a serious affair to us. We cannot sell the warrants . . . must hold them.

Sherman reiterated the impossibility of selling any real estate and of collecting debts involved in realty. However, the failure to accomplish any recovery on those long-standing Powell Street paving warrants was undoubtedly one of the worst blows he sustained in the bank's closing days. It even overshadowed his failure to dispose of his own home on Harrison Street with its furnishings.

> I think I can . . . rent it for something, furnished. . . . There are several applicants, among them Major Mackall[52] . . . who is Adjutant General. . . . Headquarters are to come down from Benicia this week.

Swords was down. . . . I waylaid him and tried . . . to get him to say he would rent the south half of the bank building . . . showed him through it. . . . He admitted it was admirably adapted to the purpose, but he hopes to be exchanged with Colonel Cross,[53] who is still here, then Cross would choose the old office over Parrott's. Swords has it in his power to benefit us materially. . . . If he don't do it, I will never . . . do a man in the Army a favor again. I have done a great deal for . . . officers . . . without a cent of charge, if now the first time . . . I have asked a reciprocal favor, they do not confer it, I will remember it always. General Clarke likes our building, so do all the officers, but Swords talks offish. . . . At parting he said . . . he would come down and select offices for the General Headquarters, Quarter Master's and Pay Master's offices.

From Sherman's viewpoint, this last legislature had dealt the banking business a serious blow by passing a stamp tax that would become effective July 1. All bills of exchange, drafts, notes, mortgages, and deeds must bear stamps or not be recognized in the California courts. This measure would increase an average bank's expenses some $500 a month, besides the vexatious attention to the stamps and the large amount of them of every denomination that must be kept on hand. This provoked an angry observation by Sherman: "Legislation in this state . . . has been all against capital ever since we have been here . . . an additional reason, if any were needed, for us to draw out."

He confirmed his earlier report that Drexel, "the only rich man in the concern," was going to retire from the house and return to the East in June.

This house has done more to ruin business . . . than any other. When freights raised . . . all but they were willing to increase rates. Whenever the other bankers proposed to change . . . commissions they stood in the way. If there were other good banks here they would lose the bulk of business.

Mr. Moss[54] tells me his house, Pioche, Bayerque & Company, have returned to France 800,000 of their capital [francs or dollars?] Schwarbe [?] & Company, a Hamburg house, who controlled much money, have gone out of business, drawing their money as we are doing. . . . The general mistrust pervades all classes . . . soon the cash system must prevail in business.

Even on the eve of his departure, Sherman's underlying reluctance to terminate the venture continues to manifest itself. Qualifying phrases such as "for the time being," "re-establish this business," "to revive this business," seem unerring indicators of his sentiments. The following paragraph from his May 4 letter repeats the theme:

Were we to resume tomorrow, we could recover all our old business and more too, but I think best to conclude as we began, and if some years hence, when the business of the country assumes a more tangible and certain state, you can send a person here with Nisbet, with all the signs, counters, vaults, and paraphernalia of business, with the good will and confidence now felt throughout the country.

And again, in the concluding lines of the last letter written before he boarded the steamer, he had to add: "When we have our office in New York, this business can if necessary be resumed with better prospects."

On the domestic side, he reported: "Mrs. Sherman is so happy at the thought of going East . . . will agree to anything I propose. I shall insist on her staying home and economizing till I can repair the expenses . . . I incurred here in extra efforts to make her comfortable and contented."

A postscript late the same evening detailed some last-minute instructions to Nisbet and concluding letters sent Eastern correspondents. He also enclosed a press clipping about the money stringency in California. "The *World* supposes," he ended on a sardonic note, "we are drawing half a million dollars from circulation. I don't deny it, as it does no harm to let them deceive themselves." [55]

Although the affairs of the bank later brought Sherman back to San Francisco, the signing of this last report to St. Louis figuratively locked the doors of Lucas, Turner & Co. as bankers in California. Sherman recalled the bright hopes when the doors had opened in 1853, the ordeals that the partners had survived, and the gradual dimming of those hopes under an assault of forces too great to be withstood. Nevertheless, Sherman's head and shoulders were carried proudly as he walked away from Montgomery and Jackson Streets, because the initial ideals of the partners had never been sullied. All men who had trusted their house had been paid in full. The signs over the doors had come down with honor, as does the flag over a military post when the bugle sounds "Retreat."

Part Six:
The After-Glow

31

When the *Sonora* bore Sherman and his family away from California on May 5, 1857, he believed he was entering upon a new career. It promised to be as permanent as the move to San Francisco had seemed four years earlier. Since this narrative is concerned only with the Gold Rush period of Sherman's life, many details contained in his Eastern letters to Henry Turner will be omitted. At the outset there was little of importance to discuss from New York, so his letters sound like echoes of earlier communications, dealing largely with men and affairs in California. They reveal a disillusioned man much inclined to blame himself for everything that had gone wrong—with Lucas, Turner & Co., as well as with his own destiny.

The Shermans reached the Ewing home in Lancaster, Ohio, in due course. Sherman proceeded in a few days to St. Louis, where he found some changes. Mr. Lucas had bought out his partner, Captain Simonds. The firm's name had been changed to James H. Lucas & Co. Lucas, Turner, and Sherman agreed to meet in New York soon after July 4 to complete the plans for opening their agency.[1]

In the meantime, Sherman returned to Ohio on July 1 and found an accumulation of mail from Mr. and Mrs. Bowman and Nisbet. Some of their news irritated Sherman. When he left San Francisco, Nisbet had just moved into one of the rooms in the bank building and was boarding at restaurants. The Bowman letters informed him that his assistant had made a housekeeping arrangement with two other young men, "a piece of extravagance," Sherman wrote Turner, "that the circumstances don't warrant." But more alarming was the comment that Nisbet was seeing a great deal of a Miss Thornton; "my opinion is that he should defer any matrimonial plans until the future . . . will justify such a step. . . . The Thorntons are extravagant and aristocratic, and supposing him a banker, would draw him out on his weakest point—vanity." Sherman proposed to admonish the junior partner on these matters; hopefully he wrote: "he generally defers promptly to my advice."

From the very beginning of the New York venture, Sherman repeatedly expressed the opinion that the firm could not hope for any profit during the first year's operations. Sherman liked the new name of the St. Louis firm and recommended its use in New York but on this point he was outnumbered and the business was started under the San Francisco style of Lucas, Turner & Co.

Consistent with his cautious view of the outlook in New York, Sherman had decided to leave his family with the Ewings, where they were welcome, until he could be more certain as to the prospects of the business. Both Lucas and Turner favored his taking them to New York, but chafing at the debts already facing him, he chose the most economical course. One of his letters requested Turner that both he and his wife, in writing Mrs. Sherman, refrain from bright predictions or any urgings that the family join the husband.[2]

By late July, the quarters at 12 Wall Street were being cleaned and painted, and signs installed. Sherman was busy mailing out circulars announcing the opening and inviting accounts. He wrote many personal letters to old army friends and various business acquaintances.

On his arrival in New York, he registered at the Metropolitan Hotel, a house patronized by many visitors from St. Louis and the West. He wrote Turner that he had "a room in which I can manage to open the door and window at the same time, but a close fit." A little later he moved to 100 Prince Street, in the same building with his old friend Major Barnard[3] at $13 a week, and breakfasts at $2 a week. He planned "to dine on the town," at various restaurants.[4]

Presently Turner sent him articles of co-partnership of the new banking firm for his signature. Sherman had a few suggestions about these, but again caution and uncertainty of profits were uppermost in his mind.

> If you will insure my being as well off in 1860 as when I sailed from New Orleans I will . . . deed you . . . every foot of land I own in this little sphere. What the St. Louis business is, I don't know . . . and don't . . . build any calculations. Here our profits are likely to be on the wrong side of the ledger the first year, but may in . . . five or six years begin to be valuable.

Despite his own pessimism, he wrote Turner that "everybody says we are going to do a fine, smashing business . . . I am willing to try my best."[5]

Nisbet reported that almost all of the certificate holders had been paid off. Also that a decision favorable to Lucas-Turner had been announced in its case against the City of San Francisco. However, with monotonous regularity came word of loans that were not being collected because the debtors could not sell any property. "The whole country [California] seems bankrupt," Sherman commented grimly. His greatest worry was the unliquidated trust accounts. Even though not legally liable for them, the moral obligation was continually on his mind.

Possibly such gloomy reflections influenced Sherman as he set about familiarizing himself with conditions on the East Coast, for he wrote Turner: "I have no faith in banking, unless we can have the privilege like our neighbors of breaking occasionally. That seems the most profitable part of the business save when it is done after a long, slow, patient and frugal term of probation. . . . I already see that competition has brought down the range of profit to a very narrow limit. I hope however that I may be wrong."

Sherman instinctively applied the same conservative principles that, despite his savage self-castigation, had largely guided him in San Francisco. It was better that the firm invest its funds in St. Louis rather than send them to him, as he was "afraid yet of loaning on call or paper." He found it was customary in New York to lend call money at 7%; much higher rates could be obtained on commercial loans for a term. Yet accidental overdrafts were charged only 7%. This seemed inconsistent to Sherman; why would a businessman pay higher rates on a term loan when he had to pay only 7% on his overdrafts?

At first Sherman employed no assistants; he could do all the work for the time being, although this meant he had to remain in the bank from ten o'clock till three in order to pay and sign checks.

In August, he again chafed at the slow progress Nisbet was making. "I haven't the heart to blame him," Sherman admitted, "as all accounts present everything in the blackest colors. All credit to California is refused by merchants here." While there was no present need for the money in New York, it grieved Sherman that his confident promise of a remittance there of $200,000 from San Francisco in July had not been fulfilled. Again the note of self-accusation was uppermost: "I ought to have stayed there [in California] and finished up, but Mrs. Sherman would not come home and leave me. She could not appreciate the importance of it." [6]

On one weekend, he enjoyed a change of scene and companionship when he dined aboard ship with Henry Turner's two older brothers, Thomas and Charles, both naval officers, on the craft commanded by the latter. "Charles strongly resembled Henry," remarked Sherman.[7]

Very quickly his mind reverted to business. "The signs are bad," he told Turner, "bidding for customers and paying dearly for them. Gebhard [of the firm of Schuchardt & Gebhard] whose ideas are like mine, says 'Charge fair rates and never mind, business will come in due time.' Your Nisbet is like B. R. Nisbet, Jr., he believes in sound; anybody who sounds high is A No 1." [8]

One reference to California was worded so breezily that it is too good to omit. Quite unconsciously, it again reveals the deep attraction the land had for Sherman. "California is now and always has been a riddle to me. I don't like it and yet I do. I would no more trust money there than throw candy among a parcel of school boys and expect to recover it, and yet I don't believe theoretically they are more dishonest than here."

Evidently Sherman had overestimated his influence on Nisbet, especially when it was exerted from across the continent, and on such a personal plane as affairs of the heart.

> Unless Nisbet hurries up, he will not fulfill my promises and expectations. Instead of giving the subject his concentrated attention he is fooling away about that young Miss—has engaged himself. . . . I could not be astonished if you . . . hear of the most elegant party and presents of the age. Whilst I feel too poor to buy a new shirt, he writes to Mrs. Sherman that he expects a present from her. . . . Present forsooth! I have not felt able to make a present for six years. I'll give him a present—remind him that even on the most favorable settlement in California, he will be in debt to the House."

As to himself, Sherman reiterated his resolve

> to practice absolute economy and leave my family in Ohio. Mrs. Sherman is like most ladies who think bankers are made of gold and that it is a piece of my usual folly to be preaching economy, but I think she is now satisfied of my determination . . . and will content herself at home if I keep well. If I can put these matters . . . so that I have nothing on my mind but the business of the house, it will contribute to my health. . . . You can . . . understand the dependence of the one on the other.

If the last lines indicate that Sherman was a practical psychologist, a later reference in the same letter suggests that he was a shrewd judge of the Eastern money market.

> The business of selling railroad bonds and stocks has been overdone. . . . All the sales made now are by brokers, shifting from one to the other their present loads. There are few bonafide sales to new parties. This is Mr. Meigs' opinion and . . . many

others with whom I have conversed. . . . I have now over a hundred thousand that should be out on call but call loans on A 1 stock are not so plenty.

Sherman was a solitary stranger amid alien scenes, separated from family and friends. No wonder that he closed this letter: "Barnard is away. It is raining hard and I am lonely. . . . If I get the Blues [and he capitalized the word!] no human being save you or Mrs. Sherman shall know it." [9]

One of the San Francisco accounts that gave Sherman the most concern was Captain Clary's endorsement of the note of his son-in-law, Captain Stone, for $25,000. Stone's collapse had forced the bank to look to Clary. He had secured $5,000 by pledging some of his St. Louis property. The balance had run on for what Sherman felt was an unreasonable time. His excuse was one that the bank had grown tired of hearing—his inability to sell his San Francisco real estate. The exasperated Sherman commented:

If anybody offered me all Montgomery Street for $50,000, even if I had it, I would be afraid to take him up. . . . Clary, like most men in prosperity, can boast of their liberality to their children and their great wealth, but when adversity catches them, they quickly shield themselves behind their wives. I dread the day when the rest of our country is subjected to the same test as California a great deal more than I do the day of judgment.[10]

Sherman's old bête noire, McKee, was another of the delinquent debtors whose recalcitrancy was especially infuriating. "You see McKee's tone, he is a most consummate hypocrite and liar. Dr. Scott may preach to him til Doomsday and won't save him. . . . He had a mortgage on a saw mill and gold mill at Nevada [City] which I looked at but preferred to keep the debt unsecured. . . . I ought to have attached when his store was full of goods."

In mid-August Sherman received a letter from Nisbet that convinced him that one reason collections were proceeding so slowly in San Francisco was that Nisbet hoped that the St. Louis owners would soon reopen the California house. Here again, Sherman shouldered much of the blame. He himself had frequently voiced the expectation this would eventually happen. At the same time, Sherman believed that any reopening would be initiated only under "a safe, prudent *and* adventurous man sent out there in my stead." Evidently, however, word had been written Nisbet while Sherman was in St. Louis that no such plan was contemplated. Because of the slowness of the mails, Nisbet had not yet received this advice and was evidently indulging in dreams that would be rudely shattered. Sherman hoped that would at least spur him to renewed attack on the collections, "to pitch in and show no mercy."

Nisbet, with the same letter, sent Sherman a printed copy of the supreme court's decision in the suit against the City of San Francisco. He thought "the decision final and unassailable, and San Francisco cannot shift the debt." He rather expected a proposal to compromise the claim.

As to the New York office, Sherman wrote on August 13: "We pick up accounts slowly. . . . I suppose you are anxious to see things growing as fast as a cottonwood tree—better imitate the oak, slow and sure." [11] A few days later he wrote indignantly about a proposal that had been made to him by an ostensibly responsible businessman. It involved Lucas, Turner & Co.'s assuming considerable risk, doing a lot of collecting and accounting, then paying a high rate of interest on whatever balance this new depositor might leave in his account! Sherman wished to refuse the proposition but submitted it to St. Louis. If he was being too conservative, he wanted Turner to correct him. Meanwhile, he concluded: "We keep picking up a little money on other terms and are willing to bide our time." [12]

Turner's next letter evidently drove New York details from Sherman's mind. His reply informs us of what the St. Louis partners were thinking:

The subject has occupied my waking and sleeping thoughts. . . . I am very glad . . . you think as I do . . . that I would have to return to California for a while. . . . I am perfectly willing. . . . Nisbet only knows . . . books . . . cannot see things as they are. . . . If other big bankers were going right to destruction, he would go along. I don't think he can manage that city case, the real estate and other . . . interests remaining in California. . . . I don't apprehend that Nisbet will use the firm name in any dangerous way, but he will consider a Bill Receivable as cash long after it has ceased to be worth [anything]. . . . I on the contrary . . . give up a debt too easy when it appears hopeless. . . . I can make more than he can by management.

Reading between the lines it is plain that Turner was now contemplating relieving Sherman in New York, when the latter returned to California. Sherman proposed that matters be left in *status quo*

until about Christmas. When you can come here . . . after a short visit to Lancaster, I can go to California [send Nisbet home] and remain there until spring. I can be there during the session of the legislature when I feel satisfied . . . we can make the City fund the debt at a fair rate. . . . We can use [the bonds] as collateral . . . until California securities rise in the market, when we can sell.

Sherman also felt his own expenses in California would be far less than when he had his family there. Evidently thought had been given to Turner himself going to San Francisco. Sherman opposed this because "you would be discouraged by seeing too great change in affairs. . . . Here you can do as well if not better than I, for the only risks are loans and discounts which . . . I am afraid of, and you knowing better the condition of affairs, could operate better than I can." [18]

The above reads like a sound, carefully devised plan to solve several practical problems. Like so many blueprints of the future, it did not take into account a force already poised to exert a crushing influence on American finance and financiers.

Sherman's next letter, written on August 24, apparently gave him the melancholy satisfaction of a Cassandra:

> It feels quite natural, but by no means agreeable, to see one's predictions of misfortune so soon realized. The Ohio Life and Trust Company failed today . . . will occasion great loss to your Western friends. They are the sort of bankers who promise so much, coax people to confide in them, and at a moment of least preparation . . . break, pocket the profits, get the sympathies of the public and swindle all fair dealing men. I am not going to croak for you'll abuse me and say it is my nature, but I believe in mathematics and cannot help growling when I know there is a leak.

(The reference to interest rates which follows sounds curiously familiar today!)

> I call it a leak to pay 5% for money and get only 7%, but we are in for it. . . . You must remember I . . . am not responsible. The way to make credit is to deserve it. . . . We must . . . shake off all 5% customers and come down to 4% and nothing. Call loans which were all the go two weeks ago are no go now. Stocks which could be sold twice a day within a fraction of a cent of quotations are now doubtful of a bid.

With grim satisfaction, Sherman recounted a recent offer of business which he had lost because the terms he had quoted were not as liberal as those of the Ohio Life and Trust Company! "Of course," he wrote, "a bank that intends to grab the principal, can afford for a while to pay large interest."

Sometime in those early weeks after opening the New York agency, Sherman must have employed one or more assistants, for in August Mr. Lucas wrote to urge that he authorize someone to sign checks in his absence. Sherman agreed to arrange this; he admitted "it is necessary that I . . . go about more in business." On the score of his health, he made a curious observation: "I am now very well, having had asthma only twice—once at your house, and once at Uncle Charles' at Norwalk. At both places trees grow close to the house . . . vegetation gives off carbonic acid at night. It must be this acts more quickly on my lungs than yours. . . . In this city without vegetation . . . I find a solution for all my asthma."

By a curious coincidence, a few days after quoting excerpts

from this letter, my attention was called to an article on allergies by the well-known medical commentator, Dr. Walter Alvarez. He told of a woman patient who suffered from asthma in the homes of certain relatives but was quite free from it in other houses. Investigation showed that the houses that were "bad" for her contained considerable pressed board, while there was none in the "good" houses. Paint and varnish applied to the pressed board resulted in nonrecurrence of her spells of asthma.

A physician or psychiatrist could better speculate about Sherman's carbonic acid theory and correlate his observations of more than a century ago with the incident reported by Dr. Alvarez.

Reverting to the business scene, Sherman wrote: "Times . . . are not inviting. . . . It may be well . . . to feel our way cautiously. . . . We can do best by keeping our discounts for the benefit of St. Louis merchants. *You look out for yourselves.* If I don't *make* money . . . I'll try to lose as little as possible." [14]

A few days later he wrote:

> The money panic . . . seems to be subsiding. The banks have not broken but they are badly scared. Had one gone [i.e., failed] and specie been demanded of others . . . we would have had a suspension of specie payments, and . . . universal alarm. . . . By their own showing they have only $10,000,000 of specie to meet a full hundred millions of *demand*. . . . All the banks are curtailing as fast as possible and won't accommodate their best customers. A good deal of specie has been drawn for export and safety. Yet . . . everybody says the panic is over and that the banks are safe. In view of the threatening aspect . . . I loaned . . . on three days and ten days call $130,000 . . . have reduced our balance at the Metropolitan Bank below $50,000 and . . . deposited $50,000 at the Bank of America, a regular old fogey. [The Bank of America referred to here was in New York and not in any way related to the present Bank of America NTSA, headquartered in San Francisco.] The deposit account is light save yours which is heavy.

In Sherman's state of mind, he thought longingly of the strong vault he had installed in the San Francisco bank.

> Our vaults here are not safe enough to entrust money. All stocks are flat, Missouri 6% [apparently a bond] 74½, Illinois Central fallen from 125 to 99 since we have been here—nearly 100% for the [former] was on $30 paid in. They now call for $10 a share more. Gebhard [15] looks as though he had been through the mill. . . . When in the midst of life we are in death. At a time of greatest prosperity we should be most alert to danger.[16]

For once Sherman's gloomy views were too optimistic. The panic grew worse. A letter from Mr. Lucas in mid-September, 1857, indicated that he was very apprehensive about both national conditions and business affairs in St. Louis. Sherman had implicit confidence in Mr. Lucas, and the greatest respect for his views. If, with all his wealth and prestige, he was worried, then Sherman had to fear the worst. In writing Turner, he drew on his own hard experience in meeting a bank run in San Francisco and ventured suggestions as to precautionary steps: "Preparation beforehand is better than to be caught napping." He suggested that if timid depositors in St. Louis wanted their money, they might be persuaded to take over some of the bank's sound loans and investments in lieu of cash. That had worked for Sherman in February, 1855, and was worth trying again. Most of all, Sherman wanted Mr. Lucas to conserve his own estate even if the firm had to curtail its business and forego profits. He believed the St. Louis public would approve any conservative course the bank might adopt in a panic, because "the interest of everybody is to sustain some good private bankers, and yours is certainly the best of any in St. Louis." [17]

Sherman must have been reminded of his San Francisco days when, late in September: "the best paper commands 3% a month." Turner had asked him to write daily during this hectic period and "communicate the most minute events." These largely consisted of discounts refused and drafts protested.[18]

Presently it was St. Louis rather than New York or even San Francisco that caused Sherman the most acute worry. He was doing his best to succor the firm's home office as demands upon them increased. "It is an awful time," he sadly confessed, "and

. . . will make many change their minds as to the profits and comforts of a banker's life."

By September 29, 1857, the New York agency still had roughly $109,000 in its two depositories, as well as about $200,000 of St. Louis and Missouri state bonds. Evidently the Lucas bank in St. Louis was experiencing a serious run, for Sherman wrote: "Today in St. Louis will tell the tale. If your depositors have not made a sweep today, I shall consider ourselves out of the woods."[19]

Several more failures both in St. Louis and New York during the next few days made him write:

> [These] afford a good excuse for doubting the credit of everybody. . . . Whilst we must meet every obligation instanter, nobody pays us. This is exactly my notion of banking. Ever since I have had my eyes opened to its chances, I have regarded the Faro Bank about as safe as the Bank as conducted in America. . . . The Metropolitan Bank is hard up. . . . All who have money are paralyzed. Worse and worse all the time.

Perhaps in retrospect banking on the West Coast did not now seem so beyond the pale to Sherman!

Just as Sherman felt that the whole world was crashing about his head, his wife wrote that she and her mother were coming to New York the following week, "giving me hardly time to interpose." Small wonder that the distraught banker added: "Ladies have no reason, and always do things at the wrong time. If Mrs. Sherman does come, she will only bring the baby and stay a short time . . . promises distinctly not to object to my returning to California if I say . . . I should do so." [20]

Three days later the blow fell. On October 6, 1857, he wrote Turner:

> I cannot say I was much surprised when my cousin came into my bedroom this morning to announce that all the city papers contained a telegraphic notice of the closing of J. H. Lucas and Company. . . . I hurried down but no dispatch from you . . . did

not get it till near 3: p.m. I have paid . . . all checks save . . . yours for $5,000 thinking it best to wipe out the smaller checks. . . . I will sell all my receivables at any sacrifice and protect all our depositors so as to make your liabilities all at home. . . . I advise most unhesitatingly the immediate breaking up of this house and liquidation of yours. . . . Have an auction . . . of property . . . most readily spared, taking all [of] mine save the Morgan Street lots which Mrs. Sherman won't sell, it being a present from her father. . . . I want to get at something else as soon as possible as I have a family and will not have a cent when I quit here, a result I have seen so long in prospect that I am not even surprised at its occurrence.

I will write to Nisbet . . . telling him he must *now* make a full settlement. There is no longer any necessity of my going out. . . . I fully relinquish all interest, present and prospective, and throw in my little estate, thankful at so easy an escape from such a disaster.

Tell Mr. Lucas I sympathize with him deeply. . . . I hope he will clean out and never again undertake so disreputable a business as banking.[21]

He expanded these thoughts in his next letter, adding:

I assure you, (and Mr. Lucas), [that] among all men [there] is but one feeling, not of reproach or of blame but of alarm. When such houses as yours fail, what about the prospect in the future? I believe there will be a universal suspension. I am anxious to pay off every cent before the banks break. . . . The . . . condition of things is attained which I so much feared . . . the mere prospect of which gave me those feelings . . . you always called the blues. An acquaintance says you are not blue in St. Louis, but *black!*

After detailing some more unpaid receivables, accompanied by bitter moralizing, he wrote:

What a fearful load of bad debts must these (New York) banks carry! It is a sad lesson to us all, but we know . . . too late, that we ought not to be bankers, most of all Mr. Lucas, who has to pay his debts. Nisbet and I have little to lose . . . and thank God it is no worse. I felt . . . the principles on which we as well as others were operating, were not mathematical . . . [and] must in the end prove disastrous. . . . I gave till 1860 for that event. I save two years . . . during which . . . I must learn some better trade.

I think . . . next week I can square our matters here and . . . transfer our collections to any bank, if still any stands, and come to St. Louis. . . . Don't attempt to resume. This is no temporary thing but a proof that banking is and must be disastrous. . . . The sacrifice may be . . . terrible . . . but the sooner made, the better, and *before* property becomes *valueless*. . . . This would make my return to California mortifying and will impair my influence.[22]

The next day Sherman wrote:

Some fellow last night attached . . . our funds at Bank of America. For a time I was flurried but I stopped everything with a certificate of deposit. . . . Have closed nearly every account and have over $5,000 cash locked up in a friend's vault. . . . I will discharge all hands, make some disposition of our rent and furniture. . . . I may get through next week. . . . I now feel a great desire to see my family. . . . If on arriving at Lancaster, I should find an invitation to bring [Mrs. Sherman] out to your house, I should be tempted. I now think I will settle at St. Louis if I see a chance of getting work as a surveyor, engineer or land agent. I can work as long as anybody and I used to draw pretty well.

This letter closed with the remark that he and a friend planned that evening "to witness an intellectual exhibition of a ballet." We can hope that perhaps for a few hours, the music and grace of the ballet supplanted the gloomy news of the panic and the forebodings about the future.[23]

On October 13, 1857, his letter began: "Well, all hell has broken loose. . . . There is a run on every bank of the city, many of which have gone in. I see no reason why all must not succumb. Of all excitement heretofore, this exceeds by ten fold."

Sherman planned to leave for the West upon the arrival of some collections from New Orleans on which he was counting. Before this letter could reach Turner, Sherman was certain that St. Louis had learned by telegraph of the closing of virtually all the New York banks. In the midst of this general collapse, he added, "Mrs. Sherman telegraphs that her mother must come to New York. If she [Mrs. Sherman] comes along, I can leave her at Lancaster on my way out. Thank God, she and the children have a good home for this winter. . . . Better that everybody should break and then interchange debts." [24]

32

His *Memoirs* tell us that Sherman reached St. Louis on October 17, 1857, taking with him the firm's portable assets. Prior to leaving New York, he had transferred the bank's remaining accounts to other institutions. Again, as in San Francisco, he walked away from a project disappointing to its owners, but with the satisfaction of having settled fully and fairly with every creditor. Small wonder that in these days he wrote his brother, John: "I am the Jonah of banking; wherever I go, there is a break down."

In St. Louis, liquidation was proceeding rapidly. Mr. Lucas paid his creditors in full without too great a sacrifice. He assumed all the firm's liabilities, so that the other partners would not have to pay any part of the indebtedness. This materially lightened Sherman's worries. Nisbet was on his way east with his bride. He left behind in San Francisco much uncollected paper and considerable real estate not yet sold, so Mr. Lucas requested Sherman to return to San Francisco to complete the liquidation.

Sherman left St. Louis on December 7, reaching Lancaster on the 10th, and remained with his family until after Christmas.

His next letter to Turner, a long one, was written from the Metropolitan Hotel in New York on January 3, 1858 (although he made the mistake so common in the first few days in January and wrote 1857). He had arrived in New York on New Year's morning after brief stops en route to visit his brothers and sisters.

He wrote that despite the windy day, New York "was all

agog. I joined the crowd and made some New Year's calls."

Turner had asked for a detailed statement of all unpaid balances remaining in the so called "trust accounts." Sherman made a complete list, even including his own investments in San Francisco real estate to house his family. Before he had finished, he had recapitulated most of the successive crises and also the misfortunes of both Lucas, Turner & Co. and William T. Sherman from 1853 through 1857.

He had engaged passage on the *Moses Taylor* to sail from New York on January 5 for Aspinwall. Of his errand, he wrote:

> It is going to be a task of no common difficulty . . . may take six months . . . or more, during which time I waive all claim to compensation save actual expenses. . . . I know I return to California now as representative of a broken bank. . . . In worldly estimation my influence will be much lessened. . . . Still I must try to hurry up that city case. . . . If in lieu of warrants, I judge city bonds better I will try for a funding bill. In all other matters I will compromise when the sacrifice is not too great.

He informed Turner that he had applied to the adjutant general for any field officer commission available. He had asked his brother John to assist in this matter but had scant faith in any success. He hoped his wife could sell some of her own property to assure her expense money, and ended this portion of the letter in a somber vein:

> If I can't earn a living, the quicker I am disposed of the better. You and I were brought up with . . . ideas of honor utterly out of date. We think it wrong to lie, to cheat, to borrow or steal of a friend. I fear . . . we are too old to learn anew, but until we do learn that, we are not fit to cope with modern bankers, brokers, land agents. . . . I would prefer to be associated with you in business than any man of my acquaintance. . . . If you can learn to lie without blushing, to borrow of your friend without feeling uncomfortable, charging a hundred per cent for collecting money, etc., during my sojourn in California, we will on my return try something.

However, he followed this jibe by a truly eloquent tribute to his friend's "high, chivalrous feeling of integrity that pervades every act of your life." [25]

A short letter written just before he boarded the steamer summed up a lot: "Don't trouble yourself about me. When this business is done, *done;* then will be time enough. I will be a charge to no one, will not touch a cent not worked for honestly. You will hear from me minutely . . . more than you will have patience to read. Goodbye." [26]

After an uneventful voyage to the Isthmus, Sherman left Panama on the *Golden Gate* on January 15 and reached San Francisco on January 28, 1858. The Nisbets, bound for St. Louis, passed him on the high seas. The Lucas-Turner ledgers and books had been taken east by Nisbet, but he had left schedules of notes and other records with attorney Bowman, who gave them to Sherman.

He wrote Turner within a few days:

> Since my arrival, I have had a real levee. All our friends and customers have been here in quick succession, all wondering why, now that there is a complete breakdown among the bankers, we don't start again. . . . As to Mr. Lucas being broke, the St. Louis people laughed at the idea. Still . . . nothing on earth would induce me again to attempt anything like it. . . . Thank God, no new liabilities can be created. . . . I have only to collect as fast as I can . . . wipe out the trust accounts and remit to you. I send you today $1,700. . . . If I had no family and could stay here all my life, I believe I could in time collect the bulk of the notes and make good disposition of the property, but . . . my family are now dependent. . . . After I get through here I must learn a new calling. . . . furthermore Mrs. Sherman thinks every week I stay . . . is a . . . nail in my coffin. If I stay too long she will just as leave start alone to attend me.

Since his former home was now rented to William Blanding,[27] an attorney, Sherman described his new bachelor quarters: "I have taken the back room second story north side of the bank for a sleeping room and office . . . will take my meals at a restaurant unless some one invites me to dinner . . . thereby saving 50 or 75 cents."

A few weeks later he wrote in greater detail about his living arrangements. "[I] board at Miss Griffin's at $8 a week out of rent of the Meiggs House" (this property at the northeast corner of Montgomery and Broadway had been acquired by Lucas, Turner & Co. at foreclosure following the flight of "Honest Harry" Meiggs) "so my outlay will be not more than $20 or $25 a month." He sent a jocular message to H. L. Patterson, one of the St. Louis partners:

> Tell him I invite him to dine with me at Miss Griffin's, but can't promise him much in the way of roast beef as I ain't [*sic*] very particular myself, but Miss Griffin's roast beef may be mule or anything else in that line for all I know or care. My friends here laugh at this idea of my eating out of rent, but I tell them that is the most certain way of collecting and least troublesome.

In the first letter written after his arrival in San Francisco, Sherman said:

> All tell me it is no use to try to sell, that property will bring nothing. . . . Property here [is] lower in price than any village in Missouri whilst here is a seaport, a population of 60,000, with exports of $50,000,000 of gold. . . . I can get $6,000 for my dwelling house, but want $7,000, cost $10,000 . . . if times don't mend, will take $6,000 very soon.
>
> I am afraid to write to Mr. Lucas, his rents keep falling. . . . The big bank room is still vacant.

Sherman even hoped to interest the federal government in buying the building for a new mint or the city, for a hall of records. In the meantime, he was going after the tenants, many of whom were in arrears for rent. "Dr. Bowie tells me that where he used to get $2,500 a month, he now gets scarcely $600. Parrott tells me two-thirds of his property is vacant." Sherman reported that relatively speaking, property in other parts of California was faring better.

On January 24, Sherman published notice of the dissolution of co-partnership of the firm of Lucas, Turner & Co. All its debtors were notified to pay their obligations immediately, failing which same would be sold at auction. He also advertised the sale of all the real estate in which the bank had an interest. This included the bank building, the Meiggs House, Sherman's former residence on Harrison Street, and various other parcels, totaling fifteen or more.

The City of San Francisco scrip was the largest remaining asset of the firm.

> I thought [wrote Sherman] the decision of the Supreme Court in our case amounted to a judgment against the City, but Bowman tells me they still fear a trial, and advise a funding bill if possible. . . . I hear a bill favorable to the scrip holders is before the legislature and may be passed with the assistance of a contribution of scrip. . . . I will . . . contribute if necessary.

Sherman had detached the January 1, 1858, coupons from the Sacramento County bonds taken on Rhodes' debt and sent them for collection. They were returned with the notation "No funds." "Outrageous," stormed the ex-banker. He was sending the bonds ($17,400) to Meigs in New York to sell for whatever they would bring and remit to St. Louis. This was a heavy blow to Sherman's hopes of a speedy liquidation, as the Rhodes debt was one of the firm's largest assets, and he had always regarded the Sacramento bonds as the best collateral pledged on it. The remaining mortgages were on upcountry properties of small value.

Captain Stone was one of the first of his San Francisco friends to call upon him. He was about ready to set sail in a schooner on an expedition to Sonora, Mexico, where he and some associates were planning a colonization scheme. "Stone looks badly and is much fallen," Sherman wrote. "I esteem him as an honorable, honest man, who like myself undertook what he was not qualified to do." He was pessimistic about the Sonora venture.[28]

"The whole town is for sale and there are no buyers," he wrote in mid-February. "Everybody seems broke, worse by far than I had apprehended."

Sherman had stayed away from Sacramento, even though a bill to fund the city scrip with bonds bearing 6% interest was then pending before the legislature. Lucas, Turner & Co. owned about $50,000 of the scrip. Sherman contributed $1,500 of this to a fund for procuring passage of the bill; "all the best people here have contributed in like proportion . . . It is deemed prudent not to go up [to Sacramento] as our presence might be misconstrued. . . . I know however I do not now possess the influence I did last year and . . . must take a back seat in the congregation."

In this same letter he reported that a bill had been introduced in the legislature

> to charter savings banks that might attract deposits from their . . . hidden places. In Page & Bacon's time, the deposits in this city could not have been less than $5 or $6,000,000. Now . . . they do not reach $1,000,000. Tallant & Wilde have nothing, Parrott's books look . . . like ours. I have seen them. His deposit account may be half a million. Davidson has the Jewish accounts . . . the other bankers, Tallant & Wilde, Fretz & Ralston, and Wells, Fargo & Company, have nothing worth having. Their rooms are silent and deserted."

The letter continued, "There have been good rains, so the miners and farmers will have a good year. . . . Why San Francisco should remain thus, I can't conceive."

Sherman had already sold one house and lot for about half its worth; "it does seem a pity. . . . I must clear myself of this trust account for the owners . . . are clamoring. I shall send Myers $3,000 tomorrow and . . . Barnard and Ruff $5,000 just as quickly as possible."

Turner had evidently written that James H. Lucas & Co. might resume business in St. Louis. Despite Sherman's recent outbursts against banking, it is apparent that calmer second thoughts had modified his aversion, for he now wrote: "If you can [resume] I believe you will regain . . . considerable deposits and . . . get money cheaper than you now pay, viz 10%." (This must have been the rate Lucas was paying on the loan he had negotiated in Philadelphia to pay off the creditors in the 1857 crash.)

> . . . It would be judicious but I hope . . . you will remodel the house. Let nobody be members, but Mr. Lucas, Patterson and yourself . . . leave me out. I won't engage in the business. I am flat broke and utterly disqualified, so is Nisbet. There is no use minding matters. . . . The supposed success of Page & Bacon blinded us all, and we are all . . . to blame, but I will not recommit the same error. . . . In any new move, leave my name out.
>
> I see Colonel and Mrs. Swords [29] very often [he told Turner]. They have rooms in the International Hotel,[30] close by our building. I have no doubts the Colonel . . . regrets he did not rent a part of this house. . . . It is . . . preferable to the one they now use for Army offices. I don't know that he would be a good tenant as Uncle Sam is among the non-payers now. Swords pays all bills against the Department in drafts on the Quarter Master General payable when the Deficiency Bill passes, when . . . he does not know. He thinks the Quarter Master's Department will require about $5,000,000 to pay up arrearages on this year. I think Congress will soon get tired of the cost of our new territorial acquisitions, though it is said Mr. Buchanan is trying to buy Sonora and Lower California—about as poor a part of the world as could be picked out.

Another paragraph asked,

> I want to know what Nisbet proposes to do for himself. He is very unpopular here. . . . I'm told was on a spree *after* he was married. I hope it was not true. Still he needs the restraint of his family. . . . I suggest you let him fix his own career. . . . He gave out the idea that his father was very wealthy and that the suspension of your house embarrassed his family. No doubt—but not in the sense he meant. I am satisfied his father and brother have for years been feeding his vanity.

Slow collections and impecunious debtors were not Sherman's only source of worry and discouragement. "I have had asthma every night since my return," he said in a February letter. "This

I expected. . . . In daytime I . . . get around and chase up our debts . . . innumerable promises . . . slow of execution. Rents have declined to a mere nothing and . . . hard to collect. . . . I suppose I have gone fifty times to some tenants. . . . Suicides are very common."

The letters in this period are a mixture of negative business reports and anecdotes of the city around him—some droll, some scandalous—followed by sardonic reflections like the following: "The worst mistake I made is . . . not getting drowned on my first arrival or getting knocked on the head in some of the rows of the country; my reputation in history would have been better."

On the night of one steamer day, he wrote in the same vein:

> [It is] raining like blazes . . . my room looking cheerful with its tallow candles . . . as lonely I sit [and] think of the pleasant group . . . in your country place, Mrs. Turner and her children . . . and that fairy little baby. . . . Then again my thoughts turn on McKee . . . or some other of the scoundrels that have our money and take things easy. . . . Then [in] spite of myself, my thoughts turn to my poor children, asking each day if papa won't come home next Sunday, and my poor wife answering with fear that I am gasping for life and she so far away—But, I won't think of these things . . .

One of Sherman's greatest worries was that his wife might become so alarmed about his health that she would impulsively and without notice rush to his side: "That would be a $1,000 useless expense and . . . the last stroke to my financial existence." [31]

Mr. Ewing, Mrs. Sherman's father, had proposed that Sherman and Ewing's youngest son, Charles, take charge of some coal fields and salt wells that he owned in Ohio. These were presently being managed by an agent, and Mr. Ewing thought the brothers-in-law could make a decent living from these properties. Sherman's reply had been that he could not possibly finish his work in California until the fall; then he would "be absolutely dependent and must take anything that will promise a decent support to my family. . . . A tent and ration would be preferable to a palace with the desperate chances of a banker."

He continued to request that he be omitted from any reorganization in St. Louis, so apparently some suggestion that he be included had been made. "Joint stock banks, beginning small and gradually enlarging, covering hundreds of years, may do well, but private bankers rarely do."

Since Lucas-Turner's withdrawal from San Francisco, another small banking firm had entered the field—Haight and Bainbridge.[32] In February, Sherman reported their failure, "after a short career, just long enough for bad debts and expenses to eat up their small capital. Bainbridge has shown me the books, which look . . . so natural. . . . Bainbridge owes us $4,000 secured by property which at the time was considered ample but is now inadequate." Subsequently Sherman reported that Bainbridge "in desperation has fled. . . . One half of a lot and hotel on North Beach is mortgaged to us, the other half is liable for $1,500 [to an Eastern lien holder]. Before departing [Bainbridge] deeded it to Bowman for us, so we have title without necessity of foreclosure." The tenant had been splitting profits with Bainbridge in lieu of rent. Sherman was trying to get him to agree to a fixed rent. "Four years ago the property was worth $10,000, now . . . may be worth from nothing up to $4,000. . . . It cannot be sold for any price."

"Tomorrow," he reported in his March 4, 1858, letter, "two steamers sail for Panama, the *Golden Age* and the *Orizaba* in opposition, to connect with one of Vanderbilt's steamers on the [Atlantic] side . . . the first show of opposition since Walker reached Nicaragua."

Another paragraph in the same letter helped to explain the depressed realty market in California. "All the agents for foreign money are foreclosing, selling, collecting and straining every effort to send money away. . . . Their orders are sell, sell. I know them from Paris, Hamburg and Switzerland, and from our own states. . . . We can't sell till somebody will buy . . . there is no speculation." [33]

A little later Sherman forwarded to Turner a proposed settlement of one of the trust accounts that had annoyed him considerably:

> I send . . . through you to Major Ruff, a statement of his affairs. . . . Ruff is an ugly customer who wants the highest rate of interest without risk. I have settled with him on a fair basis . . . $1,754 in money, and turn over to him a good secured note of $3,990. This note should have been paid. . . . I do not know why [the maker] did not come to time. I do not think we are bound to guarantee every transaction. I loaned Ruff's money with as much security as I could and don't care if he growls. He will get his money and interest in time . . . can better afford to wait than I can.[34]

On March 21, Sherman was able to report the passage of the funding bill in one branch of the legislature, with the probability it would soon become law despite some opposition.

Turner had written of better conditions prevailing in the money market in both Europe and the East. Since it seemed likely that the Lucas Bank would resume business in St. Louis, Sherman wished its proprietors "all success and waive for a time my opinion. I have been croaking so long that I know my letters are of doubtful welcome. I wish to God I could be the harbinger of better news but the time is not yet."

In the workout of Captain Stone's indebtedness to the bank, Sherman had taken two mortgage notes, one for $5,000 and the other for $12,500, both supposedly well secured. The smaller note had matured and Sherman heard indirectly that it had been paid. Before he had gone east, he had left these loans with a firm of Downieville attorneys, Spear and Thornton. He had written to W. S. Spear, who had the matter in charge, but received no reply. In March, Spear came to San Francisco but was very ill with typhus fever. His brother, who was well known to Sherman, would not let him interview the sick man. The other partner, Thornton, who was the brother of Nisbet's wife, was also in San Francisco and promised to go to Downieville to investigate the matter and report to Sherman. Thornton had not previously had anything to do with these loans, but he also believed the $5,000 note had been settled in some fashion and that foreclosure had been commenced on the $12,500 loan. Unless the matter was soon cleared up, Sherman proposed to visit Downieville to press a settlement.

He was glad to inform Turner that Captain Stone, despite all his misfortunes, had paid up nearly all of the Clary debt, through sales of Clary's properties "at ruinous sacrifice." Only a small balance remained which Sherman expected to collect shortly.

Stone himself had now sailed for Sonora on what Sherman called "a desperate expedition." He had promised that in the event of success of this Mexican adventure, he would pay up every cent he owed, and Lucas, Turner & Co. would be first on the list of his creditors.

Mrs. Sherman's deep concern for her husband's health made him anxious to return to Ohio by fall. He still feared she might in desperation come back to California from a mistaken sense of duty. He discussed with Turner several possible substitutes to take his place; but he was unable to make a practical suggestion.

In this connection, he pointed out how much more cheaply a liquidating agent might now subsist in San Francisco: "$100 a month will now go further than $600 did three years ago." Were it not for his family, Sherman would be willing to stay on and eventually get into some other line of business. He admitted it was "mere dreaming" but he thought of running a warehouse and lending on goods stored there, also of turning the large banking room into a family grocery store.

The "man on the street" still believed Lucas, Turner & Co. would soon reopen, and Sherman was kept busy denying this. During these days he met Henry D. Bacon,[35] just arrived on the *Sonora* from St. Louis. His appearance in San Francisco prompted

> the universal inquiry . . . what does it mean? There is a belief here that they own, covered up, a good deal of property, that their building in the hands of Haight . . . still belongs to them. I, myself, am . . . puzzled to see the object of his [Bacon's] coming . . . hardly . . . idle curiosity . . . in seeing the wrecks of his once world renowned bank. Haight is still here but he is really down by Bainbridge's failure. . . . Some even think they [Page & Bacon] want to resume but of course that is absurd.

In March Sherman went to Stockton and pressured his old friend Hammond [36] to negotiate a loan elsewhere on his property which was under lien to Lucas-Turner. "Stockton seemed to me very prosperous . . . they say the whole interior of California is quite prosperous whilst the city remains depressed. The real reason . . . is . . . 9/10 of property here was mortgaged at ruinous interest and has passed under control of foreigners . . . who would take any price for it." He listed several of these as agents of French, German, and Swiss bankers, all hard up with not a dollar to lend; "they send their money away as fast as they collect, so Mr. Moss says." [37]

33

California had been experiencing a cold spring with little rain, but by early April Sherman was glad to write of "magnificent rains which promise large crops of grain and gold and may revive trade . . . stimulate enterprise and speculation . . . but the immediate effect of the rain has been to wash down part of the rock on which the Meiggs House stands, carrying away plumbing that will cost $75—a month's rent—to replace."

Soon afterward the bank building developed plumbing troubles caused by the heavy rainfall. Mud and sand had filled the Jackson Street sewer until it flooded the basement. Sherman had to have it pumped out and the floor raised.

By mid-April, the funding bill became law, with an added provision that action under it must be submitted to the electorate for approval at the polls, provided five hundred property owners petitioned to that effect. It meant one more delay, one more uncertainty, and Sherman in exasperation wrote: "I doubt if anybody will take the trouble to get up such a petition. If they do, I think the people will vote to pay, as they did in the case of the State debt. All promise to pay—but to pay is a different matter."

The same logic influenced his recommendation that Turner accept Meigs's offer of 60 cents on the dollar on the defaulted Sacramento County bonds. "I doubt the ability of Sacramento County to pay interest or principal. I doubt their intention to pay. . . . Let Meigs make a sale . . . so I can state the account with Rhodes." [38]

The Downieville collections entrusted to Spear & Thornton had now reached an acute stage. Sherman had repeatedly discussed it with Judge Thornton,[39] father of Spear's partner,

> who admits fully the liability but at present is unable to help his son. He thinks Spear actually insane. I think not. No doubt he feels bad enough and it is the highest compliment I can offer him, that he has sensibility enough to go crazy, after having so basely betrayed his trust. Spear was so highly esteemed in his county that he would have been elected District Judge this year. He is a stranger in this city but resembles his brother the auctioneer so much that I will have no trouble in having the steamer watched so that he shall not go off.[40]
>
> I will be there myself tomorrow and . . . give . . . notice to the police officer who . . . remains on board till the steamer clears herself of stowaways. A steamer ticket is the cheapest mode of paying debts here. . . .
>
> I would have gone to Downieville at once but the mountain is impassable. . . . I can do no good until May 1 when the note of $3,050 matures. I want Thornton to nail it even if he must pay Spear's note of $400 for which ours is collateral. I am satisfied Thornton is honest, though God alone knows.

His bad experience with these Downieville lawyers made Sherman reluctant to assign San Francisco collections to others:

> I say without hesitation that if I leave here and entrust any lawyer with the collection of notes and management of real estate, I will not be responsible for the consequences. I will stay here as far into the year as I can keep Mrs. Sherman quiet. . . . Beyond all hope there must remain much valuable outstanding business after fall or winter.[41]

By mid-April, the self-proclaimed insane Spear had returned to Downieville with his wife. Sherman followed in an attempt to retrieve the bank's note for $2,000, which Spear had pledged for $400.

The next letter to Turner was written from Downieville on May 1, 1858. He had just attended the trial of Nisbet's suit, on behalf of the bank, to obtain possession of the note of one

McHutton for $3,053, which Attorney Spear had pledged for the $400 loaned him by one Freehill. McHutton had already paid $800 in interest and $2,100 in principal, which Spear had appropriated to his own use. Both McHutton, who lived a few miles from Downieville, and an endorser on the note, were reported as being responsible parties.

In addition to this loan, Spear had held for Lucas-Turner a note of Green & Purdy for $12,000 and interest. He had sued upon it and obtained a judgment of $15,000, on which he had collected $1,600. He had also levied in Nisbet's name on several pieces of property, real and personal. Some of this Sherman hoped to sell very shortly. The rest he would have to leave in the hands of other lawyers in the mountain town "who may serve us the same trick as Spear. . . . Young Thornton is liable to us for all moneys collected and misapplied by his partner. He is District Attorney for a term of two years." [42]

On Sherman's arrival in Downieville, he learned that Spear and his wife had sold their furniture and other effects and were evidently preparing to leave town.

> I waited some days to see if Thornton was going to be swindled in that way. . . . He had a good deal of feeling for his . . . partner, more especially for his wife whom all admit to be an excellent lady. . . . Without his advice I lodged a criminal complaint against Spear . . . now under bond to await . . . the next Grand Jury on charge of grand larceny, for the law makes the conversion of funds collected by a lawyer the same as if stolen. Spear still affects insanity. . . . No one pretends he was insane in November when he stole the moneys.

While he waited for the mountain wheels of justice to grind out the fate of Mr. Spear and the loans, Sherman wrote Turner about some dealings with other lawyers. Bowman, who had for a long time represented the bank, owed it $3,000 secured by mortgage. This loan was one of the investments in the "trust account" that had for so long plagued Sherman. He asked the attorney to pay the debt.

Bowman has no money [the letter said]. To sell his property would be a hard sacrifice. . . . I told him either he or I would have to sacrifice, and of the two, he ought. I was not . . . satisfied with his conclusion. . . . He has several times applied for reduced rents [his law office was in the Lucas-Turner Building] his rent now being lower than in any Eastern village. . . . I thought he ought to make allowances for the past advantages he has derived from the connection with us. He has recently formed a new co-partnership with a Judge Sloan [43] and wanted me to vacate for them the two rooms long occupied by the Russian River Company, our best paying tenants. I would not do it. . . . He informed me he could get three large rooms directly opposite in the Wright building for $40 a month. I . . . advised him to take them and told him . . . his room . . . [would be] vacant from May 1st. . . . I . . . made arrangements with William Blanding, Esq.[44] to take [two] rooms at $35 a month. . . . When I return I shall consider Bowman as a stranger save in . . . business still in suit. . . . Should I leave before all is settled, which seems inevitable, I shall entrust [all new business] to Mr. Blanding . . . because I regard him as more reliable.

From these incidents, Sherman went on to moralize generally on a man's reliability and frailties and on the important influence a wife, whether provident or extravagant, could have upon his behavior:

No man should have a wife in California. . . . Unless she be a working woman, no man can by his own labor support her. Trying to keep my family in California has ruined me. It will ruin Bowman and was in my judgment the cause of Spear's downfall. He had the largest and most lucrative practice here, but no amount of money can maintain a family when servants are from $35 to $60 a month, wood, coal, and washing in proportion. Spear is not a drinking man . . . did not gamble . . . no other cause to which I can attribute . . . the expenditure of our $3,700 but the accumulated expense of his family. When in November he heard of the failures in the East, he thought we had gone in like Page & Bacon and other banks, and flattered himself we would not miss the money. In January and February, finding out his mistake, it . . . preyed on his mind till it made him reckless. . . . Now he affects insanity . . . he is no more insane than any other man who was fool enough to attempt to live in California with a family. This is my interpretation of the matter. Had Spear come out, acknowledged it, and pitched in to help Thornton earn the money, I would not have preferred a criminal charge. . . . I regarded his foolish effort to play . . . insane . . . and throw on his . . . partner all the burden as criminal . . . [I] stopped his going away. Were his friends here to come forward and undertake to pay this money or any considerable part . . . I might relent, but I have no hope of this. People here are generous with the money of others . . . but not their own.

After this long and extremely misogamic outburst, Sherman resumed the more congenial role of the observing visitor with an engineering background:

This is an extremely rich mineral country. The placer deposits are nearly worked out. That is the reason why the canal, ditches, mills, etc., on which we have a lien for the Green and Purdy note are unsaleable, but the quartz ledges are being worked to great profit . . . with considerable economy. They have the advantage of roads already made, and of water ditches constructed at great expense . . . now of comparatively little value. . . . Labor is now $4 a day or $70 a month and found. I have been in innumerable mills and tunnels some of which are doing very well, but the mass of people and miners are very poor . . . would gladly escape the toils and exposure of a miner's life. I was quite reduced in strength when I left San Francisco but here I am much better. I walked to the top of Monte Christo,[45] one of the highest peaks of the Sierra Nevada, about five miles of steep ascent from this mountain gorge. I would much prefer to live up here to San Francisco, but I am doomed to the cursed place. When in due course of human events, I exchange it for purgatory, I will not be much worsted.[46]

In a few days the judge sitting in the Downieville court ruled that the McHutton note belonged to Lucas, Turner & Co., that Freehill had full knowledge of that fact when he loaned Spear $400 and accepted a pledge of the McHutton note. The latter had been paid in the interim; and as Freehill was appealing, the judge ordered that $466 be lodged with the court pending the outcome of the appeal and the balance of the money be paid to Lucas, Turner & Co. Sherman had offered to pay Freehill $100 if he would dismiss his appeal but he demanded $200, which Sherman refused to pay. He brought back to San Francisco $3,100, the balance of the paid note.

> My criminal charge [wrote Sherman] brought him [Spear] to his senses somewhat, though he still professes not to remember any of the circumstances . . . would not say what had become of the money. After much crimination and recrimination, I agreed to allow $100 for costs of court, $500 for [illegible] and settled upon $3,400 as due us from collections made. . . . I tried to get his friends to pay me $1,000 cash and I would look to Thornton for the balance, but they could not raise the money. . . . I agreed to divide the amount into five parts, . . . $680 each, one . . . to be paid yesterday . . . the balance in 6, 12, 18 and 24 months with interest at 10% per annum, secured and guaranteed. . . . My reasons . . . I was in their power; to sue would entail expense. . . . Thornton is District Attorney and has great delicacy in prosecuting his old partner. . . . In that shape, I would get some money . . . the balance . . . most likely to be paid. When a man falls among thieves he is at their mercy. I will know whether the $680 was paid . . . in a day or so. If so I will not push the criminal charge. If . . . not, I must make up my mind whether . . . to go to Downieville again at the next term of the Criminal Court. . . .
>
> At Downieville, I sold a lot for $300 cash . . . put rest of property bid in with Ladd & Co.[47] for sale . . . balance of judgment with other lawyers, Van Clief and Stewart,[48] to watch Green & Purdy, and Langton, both of whom are liable. Have beyond doubt property . . . covered up, and who ultimately must pay. They are the most enterprising men of Downieville . . . one of the richest mining localities in the state.
>
> Things in this country seem more unsettled than ever. The Nevada stage was robbed of $20,000 almost in sight of town. . . . I begin to fear I was robbed of my carpet bag . . . in it some shirts, etc., and . . . many specimens of auriferous quartz which I had picked up . . . in different claims. The mule train was to start at 2: p.m. I carried my bag, marked with my name . . . told the agent . . . to put it on the pack mule and a Judge McCann [49] and I started ahead, probably a half hour. We rode to Camptonville,

> where the next morning we took the stage for Marysville. When the express got to Camptonville, my bag was missing. After searching . . . at the stable and office . . . came to conclusion it had been over-looked . . . at Downieville . . . wrote back to have it forwarded next day . . . should have reached me last night, but . . . did not come. I fear some fool supposed I had money in it and sneaked it out. . . . Of course I had the money about my person . . . it is here . . . safe. . . . If stolen, my loss is only some clothing which I need, my quartz specimens and papers of the Downieville case, which are of no value. . . . I hope, finding that out, they will have the politeness to forward it, as the Robbers generally profess great respect for private property.

On his return to San Francisco, Sherman learned that in his absence, a nephew of Henry Turner's, Lt. Elwyn Turner,[50] had visited his office. The young man was en route to his post in Humboldt County. A letter from Henry Turner and Mr. Lucas also awaited him, giving cheering news of the revival of business in St. Louis. Another letter from banker Strange at Murphy's caused Sherman to plan to go there. Before leaving he filed the necessary claim with the funding board on the $46,000 of City of San Francisco warrants.[51]

On May 13, Sherman was served with a summons to appear before the grand jury in Downieville on May 18, 1858, in the case of Spear. He also received a letter from Spear himself; the latter had now dropped his feigned insanity and pleaded for mercy for his wife's sake. Spear and his friends had *not* made the initial payment of $680 and Sherman decided to appear before the grand jury, then await the court hearing. He wrote:

> I can see the game they are playing to . . . bluff me . . . by putting me to the expense . . . of these journeys. . . . I am . . . aware . . . it is quixotic in . . . trying . . . to *reform* California lawyers, but when I go we must trust them and . . . impress them . . . that if they do rob us, we will sting back. Spear is ruined beyond hope and must . . . quit the country, but I am not . . . certain that he may not have to go to the penitentiary.

He was still smarting about the missing carpetbag: "Those d____d rascals stole my carpetbag, and . . . got some shirts I cannot well spare. I'll be after the express company . . . they got $11 for transporting me and my baggage to Marysville, and allowed some of their servants to get the rags. They are *liable*, but will they pay?"

Apparently someone in St. Louis had suggested that H. L. Patterson, one of the partners, come out to relieve Sherman of his liquidation duties. This prompted him to reply:

> [I] feel disposed to . . . laugh at Patterson's coming through the steaming tropics cooped up with . . . women . . . then boarding at Miss Griffin's, chasing bad debts over mountains, through dust and miners' camps. I rather guess he would see us all in Jericho first. You and I got them into this scrape and must see them out. When bad debts and worse mistakes were made, I must bear the burden. . . . These things will haunt me long after I am stuck under ground.
>
> Mr. Ewing has cut out some work for me beginning in September, so I must come East then, but as times have so mended with you, I do not think it worth while for any one to come out immediately, unless William Lucas comes for life, or unless some acquaintance comes out to live here. I will take time to realize both property and debts . . . gradually as opportunities offer. To force sales would be ruinous. . . . I sometimes conclude that property is of *no value* . . . that San Francisco is a mere dream and delusion.
>
> Bowman has moved . . . and William Blanding is in his place. . . . When I do go, I . . . feel confident he will not *steal*. . . . I knew him and his family in Charleston. . . .
>
> Mr. Lucas instructs me not to push matters here *to a sacrifice* . . . times may mend here. It cannot be till there be some means for people to come here. There is no doubt about the great wealth of the mines . . . export of $2,000,000 every fortnight proves that. . . . Also . . . there is no place for a city from Puget Sound to Acapulco but this. . . . Sometime this must be a great city. . . . The mountains look far more prosperous than the towns, all of them look old and flat. St. Louis . . . is the place. . . . You stick to it.[52]

On the afternoon of May 17, Sherman again arrived in Downieville. For once it is evident that he felt the charm of the mountains for he wrote: "Weather superbly beautiful, and it would repay the trip just to breathe the air and drink the water. Were it not for the inhabitants, Downieville would, like the Big Trees, be a charming spot."

His slighting reference to the local residents undoubtedly reflected his reaction not only to W. S. Spear's embezzlement but also to the failure of Spear's friends to assist in righting the wrong, as they had so recently promised to do. Spear himself in writing his pleading letter had bitterly commented: "rats desert a sinking ship." Even his own small debtors had not paid what they owed. When Spear's wife returned from Nevada City for the trial, Sherman expected "some melting scenes, either addressed to me or the jury. I perceive a strong disinclination to prosecute on the part of the lawyers. They all have a fellow feeling."

Sherman did not relish his role as the hard-hearted banker demanding his pound of flesh, "but it strikes me that to submit to such a villainous robbery could invite others to repeat the game. . . . I will be forced to leave behind, both here and San Francisco, important interests in the hands of lawyers. If they cheat us, they will have at least the fear of exposure such as now overwhelms Spear."

At Camptonville, on his return trip, Sherman learned that a man had handed the stage driver some papers he said he had found on a log. They proved to be his missing file on the Spear case, but the carpetbag and remaining contents had vanished.[53] Sherman's letters are silent as to the outcome of the criminal charges against W. S. Spear. The last-quoted communication from Downieville dated May 17, 1858, is the final letter in the Fitch Collection bearing a California dateline.

Sherman's own *Memoirs* tell us:

> I managed to save something out of Spear and more out of his partner Thornton. . . . I remained in San Francisco till July 3rd,

> when having collected and remitted every cent that I could raise. . . . I put all the papers with a full letter of instructions and power of attorney in the hands of William Blanding, Esq., and took passage on the . . . *Golden Gate* for Panama. . . . I reached Lancaster on July 28, 1858, and found all the family well.[54]

A few references to unfinished California business are to be found in letters Sherman wrote Turner from Fort Leavenworth in September, 1858, and from St. Louis in October, 1859. The San Francisco warrants were still a sore problem. This was some of the "old" business retained by Bowman and his partner Baldwin after Sherman changed lawyers. The following is characteristic of his bitter mood toward both San Francisco and himself: "The City and every man in San Francisco will avoid a debt created before 1855 on the ground that everybody there was *non compos mentis*—about true." [55]

The St. Louis letter was written while Sherman was waiting to board a steamboat for New Orleans. (He had accepted an offer to act as superintendent of a new military academy in Louisiana.) He had hoped to see Major Turner but had missed him by a few hours. He had had a very satisfactory interview with Mr. Lucas. The letter refers inconclusively to the litigation with the city of San Francisco. Evidently some compromise was about to be effected.

On another score, this stopover in St. Louis proved a very pleasant surprise. Sherman had long before deeded his Harrison Street home in San Francisco to Turner to secure his indebtedness to the Lucas firm. The St. Louis firm had just received an offer for its purchase that would net the seller about $5,600. Mr. Lucas favored the sale but insisted that the proceeds were equitably due Sherman. He stoutly resisted but Lucas was equally firm and quoted Turner as being of the same opinion. So Sherman wrote in his saturnine way: "I still would prefer that Mr. Lucas should take that money . . . but as he says he wants me to have it and as you are so ugly and stubborn, I must submit. I propose to place that money with Mrs. Sherman to place with her brother Phil to be by him lent . . . to good farmers on mortgages at 10%." [56]

Thus closed a turbulent and melodramatic chapter in the life of William Tecumseh Sherman. Some weeks before his final departure from San Francisco, he had written about it to Henry Turner:

> I certainly have had bad luck. Hardly had we got fairly under weigh here, when smash went all the banks, and ever since matters are getting worse and where or when it is to stop, no one can tell. Same in New York, but as soon as I leave, up she bounds again. Though the most consummate folly to suppose it, it does look as though I carry misfortune in my train and I yearn to escape.[57]

As so often occurs on the human scene, a few more years would cause this tense and tragic period to seem but an episode, a curtain raiser, before the earthshaking events that would fill a far wider stage on which Sherman would loom as one of the leading actors of his time.

Appendixes

Notes

ABBREVIATIONS USED IN THE NOTES

ANNALS–Frank Soulé, John H. Gihon, M.D., and James Nisbet, *The Annals of San Francisco* (New York: D. Appleton & Company, 1855).

BACON–Letters and other papers of Henry D. Bacon (of Page & Bacon and Page, Bacon & Co.) in the Huntington Library, San Marino, California.

BANCAL–Hubert Howe Bancroft, *History of California* (San Francisco: The History Company, 7 vols., being Vols. XVIII through XXIV of Bancroft's *Works,* 1888).

BL–The Bancroft Library, University of California, Berkeley, California.

CALLAHAN–Edward W. Callahan, *List of Officers of the Navy of the United States, etc. from 1775 to 1900* (New York: L. R. Hammersby, 1901).

CHS–California Historical Society, San Francisco, California.

CHSQ–California Historical Society *Quarterly.*

CROSS–Ira B. Cross, *Financing an Empire, History of Banking in California* (Chicago, San Francisco and Los Angeles: S. J. Clarke Publishing Company, 5 vols., 1927).

ELDREDGE–Zoeth Skinner Eldredge, *The Beginnings of San Francisco* (San Francisco, 2 vols., 1912).

FITCH–Eleanor Sherman Fitch Collection of Letters, of more than two hundred in number, mostly unpublished, from William T. Sherman, nearly all to Major Henry Smith Turner of St. Louis. Copies of originals were deposited in the New York Public Library by Miss Eleanor Sherman Fitch, a granddaughter of W. T. Sherman.

HARDIE–James Allen Hardie Papers in the Library of Congress, Washington, D.C.

HEITMAN–Francis B. Heitman, *Historical Register and Dictionary of United States Army* (Washington, D.C.: Government Printing Office, 1903).

HL–Huntington Library, San Marino, California.

HSSCQ–Historical Society of Southern California *Quarterly*.

LEWIS–Lloyd Lewis, *Sherman, Fighting Prophet* (New York: Harcourt, Brace & Company, 1958).

LUCAS–James H. Lucas Papers in Missouri Historical Society, St. Louis.

MEMOIRS–William Tecumseh Sherman, *Memoirs* (New York: D. Appleton & Company, 2 vols., 1875).

MHS–Missouri Historical Society, St. Louis, Missouri.

PIONEER–Hubert Howe Bancroft, *Pioneer Register and Index, 1542–1848*, at the ends of Volumes II, III, IV, and V of Bancroft's *History of California*, described above (Vols. XIX, XX, XXI, and XXII of Bancroft's *Works*).

POPULAR–Hubert Howe Bancroft, *Popular Tribunals* (San Francisco, The History Company, 2 vols., being Vols. XXXVI and XXXVII of his *Works*, 1887).

SHUCK–Oscar T. Shuck, *History of the Bench and Bar of California* (Los Angeles: Commercial Printing House, 1901).

SIERRA–*History of Plumas, Lassen and Sierra Counties, California* (San Francisco: Fariss & Smith, 1882).

TURNER–*Original Journals of Henry Smith Turner, with Stephen Watts Kearny to New Mexico & California 1846*, edited and with introduction by Dwight L. Clarke (Norman, Okla.: University of Oklahoma Press, 1966).

Notes for Part One

1. For authorities on population of San Francisco during its pioneer period, see ANNALS, pp. 173, 200, 226, 246, 413, and 488; also BANCAL, Vol. VI, p. 195, n. 38 (quoting Bayard Taylor, *El Dorado,* 3d ed. [New York: Putnam, 1850], i, 59, 203) and p. 168, n. 11; also MEMOIRS, Vol. I, p. 33.
2. For authorities on population of California during the 1840's and 1850's, see BANCAL, Vol. V, p. 643, and Vol. VI, p. 159; also ANNALS, p. 485. However, Bancroft (BANCAL, Vol. VI, p. 305) estimated California's population as of the date of adoption of the constitution (Nov. 13, 1849) at 107,000.
3. Carl I. Wheat, *The Maps of the California Gold Region 1848–1857* (San Francisco: The Grabhorn Press, 1942), p. xiv.
4. PIONEER, Vol. II, pp. 683–795; Vol. III, pp. 733–792; Vol. IV, pp. 688–786; Vol. V, pp. 687–784. ANNALS, pp. 718–804. Also membership registers of Society of California Pioneers at Society's headquarters, 456 McAlister St., San Francisco.
5. ANNALS, p. 512.
6. Andrew F. Rolle, *California: A History* (New York: Thomas Y. Crowell Company, 1963), pp. 291–294.
7. CROSS, Vol. I, pp. 44, 47, 48, and 51.
8. ANNALS, p. 512. Naglee and Sinton's "Exchange and Deposit Office" was on Kearny Street, facing Portsmouth Plaza, in a building known as the Parker House. Sinton soon retired from the firm, and the business was continued by Henry M. Naglee until its failure on Sept. 7, 1850. Another authority states: "[Henry M.] Naglee established the first bank in San Francisco, January 9, 1849, under the firm name of Naglee and Sinton. His partner was Richard H. Sinton who came on the line-of-battle ship Ohio in 1848 with Commodore Jones, as acting paymaster" (ELDREDGE, Vol. II, pp. 553–554).
9. ANNALS, p. 254. Wright and Company must have found either

brokerage or banking highly profitable, as they are reported to have paid a yearly rent of $75,000 for their quarters in 1849.

10. ANNALS, p. 513.
11. J. Ross Browne, *Report on the Debates in the Convention of California on the Formation of the State Constitution* (Washington: John T. Towers, Printer, 1850), pp. 108–120 and 124–136.
12. *Ibid.*, Section 34 of Constitution.
13. *Ibid.*, Section 35 of Constitution.
14. BANCAL, Vol. VI, pp. 286–288.
15. Browne, *Report on Debates, op. cit.*, p. 478, lists Manuel Dominguez, one of the delegates from Los Angeles, with the occupation of banker. In Robert Gillingham's *The Rancho San Pedro, the Story of a Famous Rancho and of Its Owners, the Dominguez Family* (Los Angeles: The Dominguez Estate Company, 1961), pp. 143–150 and 152–154, Manuel Dominguez' activities are detailed with no indication that he had ever had any connection with banking. On p. 153, the author notes that at the constitutional convention Dominguez "opposed liberal provisions for banks." Correspondence with Dr. Gillingham (his letter to the author, dated Dec. 17, 1965) states that he had never found any evidence to substantiate the occupation assigned to Dominguez by Browne. Dr. Gillingham believed Browne either erred inadvertently or in transcribing his notes, mistook "rancher" or "ranchero" for "banker."
16. Paul Mason (compiler), *Constitution of the State of California and of the United States and Other Documents* (Sacramento: State Printing Office, 1929), p. 37.
17. ANNALS, p. 289.
18. *Ibid.*, p. 353.
19. For text of King's editorial, see CROSS, Vol. I, p. 202.
20. SIMONDS' name is spelled "Simmonds" in the advertisements of Lucas, Turner & Co. that appeared in the *San Francisco Herald* (e.g., issues of Mar. 23, 1853, Apr. 10, 1853, and many others). Both Sherman and Turner in their correspondence wrote it "Simonds," but Sherman in his *Memoirs* sometimes spelled it "Symonds" (e.g., pp. 92 and 134). I have followed the spelling "Simonds." Mrs. Frances Stadler, archivist of MHS, has informed me that most of the manuscript and printed references in their files so spell it.

    H. D. Bacon, writing from New York to one of his partners in St. Louis, said: "the letters of our house [i.e., Page, Bacon & Company in San Francisco] to American Exchange Bank and Duncan, Sherman & Co. . . . speak of the opening of a house at San Francisco by Lucas & Simons [*sic*] . . . they are making their boast of how they are going to end [?] up our business." (BACON, letter of H. D. Bacon to D. D. Page dated New York, Mar. 31, 1853.)
21. JAMES H. LUCAS was the son of John Baptiste Charles Lucas and his wife Anne Seben, natives of France who arrived in Philadelphia, May 23, 1784, and settled near Pittsburgh. John B. C. Lucas was a judge of the Court of Common Pleas and also served in the Pennsyl-

vania legislature and as a member of Congress. President Thomas Jefferson appointed him a judge of the territorial supreme court and land commissioner for the newly acquired Territory of Upper Louisiana in 1805. Lucas and his family moved to St. Louis in June of that year. James H. Lucas was born near Pittsburgh, probably not very long before the family moved to St. Louis. He died in that city in November, 1873. (Information supplied me by Mrs. Joseph C. Colquitt of Washington, D.C., a granddaughter of Henry Smith Turner. Mrs. Colquitt's data were taken from an unpublished Notebook of her mother, Mrs. Delphine Heyl, a daughter of Turner.)

BENJAMIN R. NISBET was the son of William Nisbet, who had two other sons, Robert N. and Henry A., and a daughter, Mary Spotswood. The father, William Nisbet, of Scottish ancestry, was cashier of the Kentucky Bank in Louisville. He had come there from Petersburg, Va. The record is not clear as to whether his children were born in Kentucky or Virginia. Mary Spotswood Nisbet was born in 1839. Robert N. Nisbet, also a St. Louis banker, died Nov. 7, 1878. These are the only vital statistics my research has uncovered. Benjamin's granddaughter, Miss Gertrude C. Creswell, wrote in 1968 that "he died many years ago in either Arizona or New Mexico." The above information supplied by MHS, Miss Creswell, Miss Lillian Cabell Maben of Blackstone, Va., and William N. Chambers, Professor of History at Washington University, St. Louis. The last two are descended from Nisbet forebears. Professor Chambers cited Leonard Matthews, *A Long Life in Review* (St. Louis: *privately printed*, 1928), pp. 3, 88, 121, and 122. Leonard Matthews married Mary Spotswood Nisbet, above mentioned; they were Professor Chambers' grandparents.

22. HENRY SMITH TURNER, the son of Thomas Turner and his wife Eliza Carter Randolph, was born Apr. 1, 1811, in King George County, Va. He graduated from the United States Military Academy at West Point in the class of 1834. He married Julia Mary Hunt on Feb. 1, 1841. They were the parents of seventeen children. Henry Smith Turner died in St. Louis on Dec. 16, 1881. For further details of his career, see biographical chapter in TURNER.
23. Unpublished letter, H. S. Turner to Capt. Wm. T. Sherman, dated New York, Jan. 19, 1853, in files of MHS.
24. For Sherman's account of Lucas and Turner's negotiations with him, see MEMOIRS, Vol. I, pp. 92–93.

WILLIAM TECUMSEH SHERMAN, son of Charles R. Sherman and his wife Mary Hoyt, was born Feb. 8, 1820, in New Lancaster, Ohio. He graduated from the United States Military Academy at West Point in the class of 1840. He married Ellen Ewing on May 1, 1850. Histories and biographies of Sherman, detailing his great military career, are so numerous that it is unnecessary to list them here. Sherman died Feb. 14, 1891, in New York City.

25. RICHARD BARNES MASON: born in Fairfax County, Va., in 1797; commissioned 1st Lieutenant, Sept. 25, 1817; Captain, 1st Dragoons,

July 31, 1819; Major, 1st Dragoons, Mar. 4, 1833; Lieutenant Colonel, July 4, 1836; Colonel, June 30, 1846; brevetted Brigadier General, May 30, 1848, for meritorious conduct; succeeded Brig. Gen. Stephen Watts Kearny as military governor of California, May 31, 1847, serving as such until Apr. 13, 1849; died July 25, 1850. (HEITMAN, Vol. I, p. 695.)

26. See MEMOIRS, Vol. I, pp. 40, 41, 46, and 81 for Sherman's experiences from 1848 to 1850.
27. In *The California Gold Fields in 1848* (printed for Frederick W. Beinecke, Christmas 1964) there are two letters from Lt. W. T. Sherman, U.S.A.: (1) dated Oct. 28, 1848, Camp on American Fork near Sutters, from W. T. Sherman to Lt. E. O. C. Ord and (2) dated Nov. 14, 1848, same place from same to same.
28. Letter of Lt. W. T. Sherman, reporting on conditions in California in 1848, from original in the collection of Thos. W. Norris, Carmel, Calif., printed at the Grabhorn Press, San Francisco, 1947: dated Aug. 5, 1848, Monterey, Calif., from W. T. Sherman, 1st Lt., etc., to Gen. Geo. Gibson, Com. Gen. Subs., Washington City, D.C.; also William Rich Hutton, *Glances at California 1847–1853* (San Marino, Calif.: Huntington Library, 1942), pp. 85–86: letter of William Rich Hutton, Paymaster U.S.A., dated Oct. 23, 1848, Monterey, Calif., to George N. Towson, Paymaster General, U.S.A., Washington, describing the difficulties the Pacific Squadron experienced in retaining crews and the desertions sustained by the 1st Dragoons and the 3rd Artillery.
29. Rachel Sherman Thorndike (ed.), *The Sherman Letters* (between General and Senator Sherman) (New York: Charles Scribner's Sons, 1894), p. 44.
30. There were nineteen banking firms doing business in San Francisco in 1853, "of which more than one half are extensive establishments of the highest credit" (ANNALS, p. 492). The same authority (p. 513) lists twelve banks in operation in April, 1854: BURGOYNE & CO.; B. DAVIDSON; JAMES KING OF WILLIAM; TALLANT & WILDE; PAGE, BACON & CO., ADAMS & CO.; PALMER, COOK & CO.; DREXEL, SATHER & CHURCH; ROBINSON & CO. (savings bank); SANDERS & BRENHAM; CAROTHERS, ANDERSON & CO.; LUCAS, TURNER & CO. The *San Francisco Daily Herald* of Mar. 23, 1853, under the heading "Banking Houses," lists Lucas, Turner & Co. Bankers at 104 Montgomery Street. Four partners are named in the advertisement: James H. Lucas and John Simonds of St. Louis and Henry S. Turner and Benjamin R. Nisbet of San Francisco. The advertisement also lists correspondents of the new bank in seven Eastern cities, and closes with the information, "Gold Dust, Bullion and Exchange purchased at best market rates."

In October, 1852, F. A. Bonnard printed at the Despatch Office, corner of Commercial and Leidesdorff Streets, a *Register of First Class Business Houses in San Francisco* (a copy is in the Library of CHS). Under "Banking and Exchange" are listed ADAMS & CO.;

ARGENTI & Co.; BURGOYNE & Co.; S. BRANNAN; B. DAVIDSON; DREXEL, SATHER & CHURCH; TALLANT & WILDE; JAMES KING OF WILLIAM; McNULTY, CAROTHERS & Co.; PAGE, BACON & Co.; ROBINSON & Co.; SANDERS & BRENHAM; SMITH, G. F.; WELLS, FARGO & Co. (a total of fourteen). Four other firms appear under "Banking and Commission": COLLINS, CUSHMAN & Co.; GODEFFROY, SILLEM & Co.; GUY, ABEL; RISING, CASELLI & Co. As evidence of the shadowy line that then divided banks from other enterprises, it is noted that PALMER, COOK & Co. are not listed with the banks in Bonnard's *Register* but under "Real Estate and Stocks."

31. ETHAN ALLEN HITCHCOCK: native of Vermont; entered United States Military Academy, Oct. 11, 1814; commissioned 3rd Lieutenant, July 17, 1817; brevetted Brigadier General, Sept. 8, 1847; resigned, Oct. 18, 1855; Major General of Volunteers, Feb. 10, 1862; honorably mustered out, Oct. 1, 1867; died, Aug. 5, 1870. (HEITMAN, Vol. I, p. 532.)
32. Sherman in his *Memoirs* (Vol. I, p. 97), gives the name of this reef as Duckworth's, but the United States Geological Survey and other modern maps show the promontory of which the reef is an extension as Duxbury Point. The bay, the nearby town, and the lagoon are called Bolinas, but the adjacent Mexican land grant appears in the records as Rancho Baulenas. The *San Francisco Daily Herald* of Apr. 10, 1853, reported the wreck in detail.
33. MEMOIRS, Vol. I, pp. 93–101.
34. Rachel Sherman Thorndike (ed.), *The Sherman Letters* (between General and Senator Sherman) (New York: Charles Scribner's Sons, 1894), pp. 52–53: letter, W. T. Sherman to John Sherman, dated San Francisco, June 3, 1853.
35. LUCAS, unpublished letter of Henry S. Turner to James H. Lucas, dated San Francisco, Cal., July 31, 1853.
36. MEMOIRS, Vol. I, pp. 101–102, and 107; also Anna McAllister, *Ellen Ewing, Wife of General Sherman* (New York: Benziger Bros., Inc., 1936), pp. 94–97, 105, and 144.
37. A few weeks after James Lick arrived in San Francisco on Jan. 7, 1848, he purchased a fifty-*vara* lot at the northeast corner of Jackson and Montgomery Streets for $3,000 from one S. J. Ellis. An adobe house stood on the lot, which Lick occupied. Soon afterward, he bought several other parcels of San Francisco real estate, but the $3,000 purchase from Ellis was the highest price Lick paid for any of them. Six years later, Sherman purchased *one half* of this lot from Lick for $31,000 (the adobe had been destroyed by fire in the interval). Lick's $3,000 in six years had grown to $31,000, to say nothing of the one half of the lot not included in Sherman's purchase. In *A Generous Miser* (Los Angeles, The Ward Ritchie Press, 1967), pp. 33–34, Miss Rosemary Lick states that the price paid to Lick was $32,000. Sherman in his *Memoirs* (Vol. I, p. 104) written twenty-one years later, also gave the price as $32,000; but in his report made to Turner, immediately after the transaction, he

stated that the purchase had been made for $31,000. Miss Lick is incorrect in naming Duncan, Sherman & Co. as the buyer; doubtless she confused W. T. Sherman's name with this firm although they were not related. Duncan, Sherman & Co. was a banking firm in New York City and a correspondent of Page, Bacon & Co. with whom W. T. Sherman declined to do business. They could not have had anything to do with the Jackson and Montgomery Streets purchase.

The Halleck Building was the famous MONTGOMERY BLOCK completed late in 1853 and owned by the law firm of Halleck, Peachy, Billings and Parke. It fronted 122 feet on the east side of Montgomery Street, bounded on the north by Washington and on the south by Merchant Street, with a depth of 138 feet. It was four stories in height and contained more than 150 rooms. The Block withstood the severe earthquake of 1868 and, in its old age, survived the far greater catastrophe of Apr. 18, 1906, when the flames swept nearly everything around it. After the vicissitudes of more than a century, it finally succumbed to wreckers and bulldozers in 1959; the site became just another parking lot. Idwal Jones, in *Ark of Empire* (Garden City, N.Y.: Doubleday & Company, Inc., 1951), gives the building's picturesque history. See also ANNALS, pp. 483 and 489.

38. ANNALS, pp. 517–518. This improvement was installed by the San Francisco Gas Company, forerunner of Pacific Gas and Electric Company. A few street lamps fueled by oil had been installed as a private venture in 1850.

39. The mail steamships of the Panama line docked at the Pacific Street Wharf; the opposition vessels, plying to and from San Juan del Sur in Nicaragua, used the Jackson Street Wharf (ANNALS, p. 630).

40. Regular mail service via steamships (usually on the Panama run but on occasion via Nicaragua) began very early in the Gold Rush. The mail steamers departed from San Francisco on the 1st and 16th of each month. Not only eastern and foreign mails but also express, banking, trade, and commerce quickly adjusted all transactions to meet these deadlines. Bills and open accounts were payable just long enough in advance of steamer day to permit debtors, importers, and bankers to make remittances via the mail steamers. Long after the completion of the transcontinental railroad had changed mail routes, most business firms continued to observe steamer day as a time for collections and balancing accounts. (ANNALS, pp. 626–638.)

41. FITCH, unpublished letter of W. T. Sherman to Maj. H. S. Turner, dated San Francisco, Feb. 25, 1854, with additions on Feb. 27 and 28.

42. HENRY A. MEIGGS, often referred to as "Honest Harry" Meiggs, arrived in San Francisco in July, 1849. He occupied various aldermanic and municipal posts in the city from 1851 to 1853, was active as a lumber merchant and sawmill operator, and built a wharf at North Beach, which bore his name for many years. (ANNALS, pp. 326, 350, 432, 461, 664, and 823; also BANCAL, Vol. VI, p. 765.) He

had a finger in all manner of speculative undertakings, which made him a heavy and continual borrower and eventually brought his San Francisco career to the violent climax described in later chapters hereof.

43. The two original partners of PALMER, COOK & CO. JOSEPH C. PALMER and CHARLES W. COOK, were natives of Nantucket, Mass. They came to California soon after word of Marshall's discovery of gold reached the East. Ambitious and enterprising men, they soon made a fabulous profit from a schooner load of lumber. With this nest egg, they purchased the banking business of Thompson & Co. in San Francisco in 1849. EDWARD JONES was Thompson's clerk. In the deal, the seller stipulated that Jones should be retained as a partner. Palmer became a very close friend and financial backer of John C. Frémont. From this time, Palmer, Cook & Co. busied itself with politics. Palmer had a falling-out with Senator William M. Gwin and espoused the cause of David C. Broderick, who sought to succeed Gwin in the United States Senate. The Frémont connection also caused the firm to involve itself in the tangled affairs of the Mariposa Grant. Palmer, Cook & Co. early made profitable investments in San Francisco real estate and eventually were large purchasers of beach and water lots located in the original cove between Rincon and Clark Points. All of these activities possessed political overtones so that Palmer, Cook & Co. for some years were the principal bondsmen for local officials. Their bank was largely favored as a depository for very substantial sums of municipal and state funds. Charges of the misapplication of these funds, both for the firm's own profit and to advance the senatorial ambitions of David C. Broderick, eventually brought about Palmer, Cook & Co.'s downfall, as Sherman forecast in his letter to Turner quoted above. (Henry R. Wagner, "Edward Bosqui, Printer and Man of Affairs," CHSQ, Vol. XXI [December, 1942], 323–327; also Robert P. Hastings, "Rufus Allen Lockwood," CHSQ, Vol. XXXIV [December, 1955], 333; also BANCAL, Vol. VI, p. 618, and Vol. VII, pp. 177–180.)

44. DAVID C. BRODERICK, according to Bancroft, was born in Kilkenny, Ireland, in 1820. Brought to New York in his youth, he came to California in the spring of 1849. Another authority states he was a native of Washington, D.C. He was active in politics in both New York and San Francisco, serving in the California state senate. The allusion to him in Sherman's letter had to do with the attempt Broderick made early in 1854 to have the legislature elect him to succeed William M. Gwin as United States senator from California. Gwin's term did not expire until 1855, and the attempt failed. However, Broderick was elected to the United States Senate in 1857 and while so serving was slain in a duel by David S. Terry on Sept. 13, 1859. (BANCAL, Vol. VI, pp. 659–662; Vol. VII, pp. 731–732; also A. Russell Buchanan, *David S. Terry of California, Dueling Judge* [San Marino, Calif.: Huntington Library, 1956] p. 84.) Ban-

croft (BANCAL, Vol. VI, pp. 616–618), fully substantiates Sherman's report about the misapplication of the state's interest fund by Palmer, Cook & Co., adding the very discreditable detail that the bankers deliberately withheld payment of interest so as to depress the market for the bonds in which they were speculating. Bancroft further charges similar wrongful withholding of such interest by Palmer, Cook & Co. in 1856. This time they refused payment because they had applied the funds elsewhere, and this caused the failure of the firm.

45. Sherman sent Turner his own drawing of the proposed building, and a photostat of the drawing is among the letters of FITCH. It is a draftsman-like elevation of the Montgomery Street front, roughly to scale. The pediment over the upstairs entrance is identical with the existing doorway (1969). Windows on first floor, while not detailed by Sherman, are the same in number and spacing as the present structure. On the other hand, the second-story windows on the Jackson Street side are fewer and farther apart than those in Sherman's drawing and in photographs made prior to April, 1906. The present building has only two stories, although Sherman drew and built three. A photograph taken on Mar. 31, 1906, shows three stories in good condition. While proof is lacking, the present writer thinks it probable that the upper stories were damaged by the 1906 earthquake, requiring the removal of the top and perhaps of the second-story walls. Mrs. Helen S. Giffin, Librarian of the Society of California Pioneers, agrees with this opinion (her letter to author, May 20, 1964). Certainly the building did not burn in the conflagration, as today's granite front is identical with that of March, 1906. Also, very old beams and stonework in the basement show no evidence of fire.

The present owner (1969), James A. Lawrence, an artist and photographer living in Nevada, purchased the property in 1946. The following are excerpts from his interesting comments furnished the author through the courtesy of Miss Irene Simpson, Director of the Wells Fargo Bank's History Room: "After the demise of the bank, 802 Montgomery Street was . . . many things to many people. It sheltered . . . among others, a house of ill fame, a Chinese garment factory, a soybean factory and one of the great old French restaurants of San Francisco, the Tour Eiffel." Mr. Lawrence said the structure was only slightly damaged in the 1906 quake but that the third story was shortly thereafter removed. He extensively remodeled the building, "taking care to preserve that quality given by the 24″ walls . . . of brick made in China . . . deep set windows and pillars made of ship's masts. . . . Later sandblasting of countless layers of paint off the base of the building revealed the fine old granite of the first floor. . . . Careful chipping uncovered the warm old brick, still strong . . . and very beautiful." In this remodeling, many layers of wallpaper and spatterings of soybean sauce were removed—mute evidence of the building's varied and lurid past. "On January 17, 1950, the Society of California Pioneers dedicated a plaque [which] marks Sherman's Bank as one of San Francisco's historical landmarks."

Today the building seems well maintained and is fully tenanted. In February, 1969, a linen shop occupied the bank corner. A wholesale print shop was on the Jackson Street front to the east and in part of the basement. A fabrics, furniture, and wallpaper shop occupied the north side of the Montgomery Street frontage and the north half of the basement. A public relations firm, certified public accountants, advertisers, and interior decorators occupied several offices on the second floor. The basement walls and foundations are quite massive for a building of this size, and several large stones brought as ballast by early-day ships are visible. Apparently, at one time Gold Street's grade was considerably lower than today, as there are bricked-up windows in the north and west walls of the basement that are now below the surface of the street.

46. JOHN E. WOOL: native of New York; commissioned Captain of Infantry, Apr. 14, 1812; Brigadier General, Jan. 25, 1841; Major General, May 16, 1862; retired, Aug. 1, 1863; died, November 10, 1869. (HEITMAN, Vol. I, p. 1059.)
47. FITCH, unpublished letters dated Mar. 15 and Apr. 1, 1854.
48. FITCH, unpublished letters dated Mar. 29 and Apr. 1, 1854.
49. FITCH, unpublished letter dated Apr. 12, 1854.
50. For a detailed discussion of this mercantile distress, see ANNALS, pp. 519 and 543.
51. See ANNALS, p. 540 concerning these squatter activities. Sherman's mention of "commissioners" refers to the United States Land Commission established under the act of March 1851 to pass upon titles to land in California. The "four leagues" relates to the Mexican law that a pueblo held title to four square leagues of land around it. San Francisco's municipal authorities and public opinion contended that San Francisco came within the definition of a "pueblo" in this connection.
52. See ANNALS, p. 548 about the agitation to extend San Francisco's waterfront.
53. See ANNALS, pp. 536–537 for the controversy over the so-called Hoadley street grades, which would have included the destruction of most of Telegraph Hill. The problem had not been finally settled when Sherman wrote Turner on May 29, 1854. (FITCH, unpublished letter dated May 29, 1854.)

    The Major Hardie mentioned was JAMES ALLEN HARDIE, native of New York, Cadet at the United States Military Academy, class of 1839; brevetted 2nd Lieutenant, 1st Artillery, July 1, 1843; 2nd Lieutenant, 3rd Artillery, May 28, 1846; Major, 1st New York Infantry, Aug. 1, 1846 to Oct. 26, 1848; 1st Lieutenant, 3rd Artillery, Mar. 3, 1847; regimental adjutant, Nov. 1, 1851 to Dec. 1, 1853 and May 3, 1855 to Oct. 5, 1857; Captain, Oct. 5, 1857; transferred to 5th Artillery, May 14, 1861; Brigadier General, Volunteers, Nov. 29,

1862; Major General, Mar. 13, 1865, for faithful and meritorious service in Inspector General Department; died Dec. 14, 1876. (HEITMAN, Vol. I, p. 499.) While a major of the New York Volunteers, Hardie in March, 1847, was in command of the garrison (of two companies) at the San Francisco Presidio. (ELDREDGE, Vol. II, pp. 553 and 723.) Hardie was one of Sherman's closest army friends. There is a considerable file of his letters to Hardie in the James Allen Hardie Papers in the Library of Congress. A very interesting one is dated New York City, Apr. 12, 1850, in which the writer says he is about to go to Washington "to redeem a promise made a certain young lady some time ago"—his way of announcing his approaching marriage (May 1, 1850) to Miss Ellen Boyle Ewing and of inviting Hardie to serve as his best man.

54. FITCH, unpublished letter dated Apr. 15, 1854.
55. FITCH, unpublished letters, dated Apr. 28 and 29, 1854.
56. Page, Bacon & Co. opened an express office in 1849. They soon engaged in a banking business; and although generally considered a local concern, the firm was really a branch of Page & Bacon of St. Louis. The San Francisco partners were Daniel D. Page and Henry D. Bacon of St. Louis, David Chambers and Henry Haight of San Francisco, and Francis W. Page of Sacramento. Haight served as governor of California from 1867 to 1871. (CROSS, Vol. I, p. 71.)
57. ANNALS, p. 545. John Gross Barnard: native of Massachusetts; second in the class that entered the United States Military Academy in July, 1829; brevet 2nd Lieutenant of Engineers, July 1, 1833; brevet Lieutenant, May 15, 1835; Captain, July 7, 1838; Brigadier General of Volunteers, Sept. 23, 1861; retired Jan. 2, 1881; died May 14, 1882. (HEITMAN, Vol. I, p. 191.) Since Sherman gives no Christian name for this Major Turner, it is impossible to identify him.
58. FITCH, unpublished letter dated Apr. 29, 1854.
59. Thomas Swords: native of New York state; Cadet United States Military Academy class, July 1, 1825; 2nd Lieutenant, 4th Infantry, July 1, 1829; 1st Lieutenant, 1st Dragoons, Mar. 4, 1833; Captain, Mar. 3, 1837 to Apr. 21, 1846; assistant quartermaster, July 7, 1838; Major and quartermaster, Apr. 21, 1846; Lieutenant Colonel and deputy quartermaster general, Aug. 1, 1856; Colonel and assistant quartermaster general, Aug. 3, 1861; brevetted Brigadier General and Major General, Mar. 13, 1865; retired Feb. 22, 1869; died, Mar. 20, 1886. (HEITMAN, Vol. I, p. 941.) Swords served as quartermaster to the Army of the West under Brigadier General Kearny, 1846–1847.
60. For the affair Steinberger, see FITCH, unpublished letter dated May 29, 1854; also MEMOIRS, Vol. I, pp. 68–69, and 196; also ELDREDGE, Vol. II, pp. 576–577.
61. Charles L. Wilson in 1850 was granted a franchise to build a plank toll road from Portsmouth Square to the Mission Dolores. The original road was very sandy and difficult to travel, and the city was

financially unable to improve it. Wilson's franchise was soon transferred to a stock company. The plank road, built in the winter of 1850–1851, was two and a quarter miles in length and ran from California Street south on Kearny Street to Third Street, thence to Mission Street and to the Mission Dolores. It cost $90,000 and paid nearly 8% a month in dividends for some time. Tolls charged were 25 cents for a *caballero*, 75 cents for a two-horse wagon, $1 for a four-horse team. The plank road was bridged over a marsh from Sixth to Eighth Streets. Some years after it was opened, Robert B. Woodward built his famous resort, Woodward's Gardens, on Mission Street where the plank road crossed 14th Street. (ANNALS, p. 296; also ELDREDGE, Vol. II, pp. 617–618; also BANCAL, Vol. VII, p. 143, n. 31.)

62. FITCH, unpublished letter May 29, 1854. This was probably the JAMES C. FALL who in 1858 was the first president of the California Central Railroad, which was projected to run from Folsom to Marysville but was completed only to Lincoln; the railroad was purchased by Central Pacific Railroad in 1863. BANCAL, Vol. VII, p. 586, n. 40.
63. FITCH, unpublished postscript dated June 1, 1854.
64. MEMOIRS, Vol. I, p. 348.
65. FITCH, unpublished letter dated June 15, 1854.
66. *Ibid.* Sherman actually wrote "15th of May," but letter continues to discuss matters mentioned in the preceding letter of June 15th.
67. JAMES KING OF WILLIAM was born at Georgetown, District of Columbia, in January, 1822, the son of a William King, an Irishman. To distinguish himself from a number of other James Kings, he followed an old custom of his people by writing his name James King of William. After being employed in the post office and a Washington bank, he came west in 1848. He first settled in Sacramento and moved to San Francisco in 1849. (POPULAR, Vol. II, p. 22.)
68. FITCH, unpublished letter dated June 30, 1854. The reference to cleaning the bar for the passage of these boats must have referred to San Antonio Creek, which was the route used by the ferries prior to the construction of the Oakland Mole.
69. This was undoubtedly WILLIAM LUCAS, a brother of James Lucas. A family notebook lent to the author by Mrs. Joseph C. Colquitt of Washington, D.C., mentions William Lucas as a brother of James, who graduated from the Yale Law School about 1818 and successfully practiced law in St. Louis for many years.
70. FITCH, unpublished letter dated July 1, 1854.

Notes for Part Two

1. The *America* was a wooden, side-wheel steamer with two decks and three masts, that measured 201 feet by 31 feet by 18 feet, 8 inches. She was launched in New York in April, 1853, by builder and owner William H. Brown. She sailed for Aspinwall with passengers Oct. 20, 1853, and continued thence around South America to San Francisco, where she entered coastwise service to Humboldt Bay, Crescent City, Port Orford, and the Umpqua River. In June, 1855, while the *America* was landing troops at Crescent City for duty in the Indian Wars, the soldiers set fire to the vessel, whether intentionally is not recorded. Passengers were all taken off and the fire was extinguished, but only after upper deck and staterooms had been destroyed. Two weeks later, the hull was towed to San Francisco for repairs; but rough weather was encountered, the towing hawser parted, and the hulk foundered. Also see Note 25, Part Two, hereof. (Above information supplied author by Dr. John Haskell Kemble of Pomona College, Claremont, Calif., in his letter of Oct. 13, 1966.)
2. Cornelius K. Garrison, a native of the state of New York, was connected with the shipping industry from youth. In 1849, he established a banking and mercantile house in Panama. In 1852, he became manager of the Pacific Agency of Nicaragua Steamship Company with headquarters in San Francisco, where he arrived in March, 1853. In September, 1853, he was elected mayor of San Francisco. After acquiring large fortune, he returned to New York in 1859. (ANNALS, pp. 744–747; BANCAL, Vol. VI, p. 766.)
3. This was undoubtedly Col. Jonathan Drake Stevenson, who arrived in San Francisco, Mar. 15, 1847, in command of the 7th Regiment of New York Volunteers (later renamed the 1st Regiment). He died in San Francisco Feb. 14, 1894.
4. James Gadsden, United States minister to Mexico, concluded a treaty on Dec. 30, 1853, whereby the United States acquired all of modern Arizona south of the Gila River for $10 million. Sherman's

opinion of the worthlessness of the Gadsden Purchase as here expressed was in sharp contrast to the recommendations that Brig. Gen. Stephen Watts Kearny had made as early as December, 1846, that the United States should own the level land south of the Gila. (Hubert Howe Bancroft, *History of Arizona and New Mexico, 1530–1888* [Albuquerque, N.M.: Horn and Wallace, 1962], pp. 491 ff.; also letter of Brigadier General Kearny to the adjutant general, Washington, D.C., dated San Diego, Upper California, Dec. 13, 1846, Exec. Doc. No. 11, 30th Cong., 1st Sess., pp. 513–516.)

5. Samuel Millard Bowman, listed in the 1856 *San Francisco Directory* as an attorney with office in Lucas, Turner & Co.'s building and residing on Harrison Street between Fremont and First Streets. A native of Pennsylvania, he was commissioned Major, 4th Illinois Cavalry, Sept. 5, 1861; Colonel, 84th Pennsylvania Infantry, Jan. 21, 1862; brevetted Brigadier General of Volunteers, Mar. 13, 1865, for gallant and meritorious service during the war; honorably mustered out, May 15, 1865; died June 4, 1885. (HEITMAN, Vol. I, p. 235.) With Lt. Col. R. B. Irwin, Colonel Bowman was author of *Sherman and His Campaigns* (New York: Charles B. Richardson, 1865).
6. FITCH, unpublished letters dated July 31, 1854, and Aug. 15, 1854.
7. FITCH, unpublished letters dated July 14, 1854, and Aug. 15, 1854.
8. FITCH, unpublished letter dated Aug. 31, 1854.
9. FITCH, unpublished letter dated Sept. 15, 1854.
10. See Note 61, Part One.
11. This must have been Thomas H. Stevens: passed Midshipman, July 1, 1842; Master, July 25, 1842; Lieutenant, May 10, 1849; Commander, July 16, 1862; Rear Admiral, Oct. 27, 1879; died May 15, 1896. (CALLAHAN.) The list of navy officers does not show any Captain Taney or any other officer with that surname whose dates would be relevant. Senator William M. Gwin introduced a bill in January, 1852, to establish a navy yard in the San Francisco Bay Area. Mare Island was selected as the site, for which the government paid $50,000. Active construction began in September, 1852.
12. Donaldson's identity is somewhat uncertain. In 1846, an A. C. Donaldson was a member of Company C of the 1st Dragoons (PIONEER, Vol. II, p. 763). Both Turner and Sherman had had ample opportunities to know the members of this unit. On the other hand, Sherman's letter links Donaldson to the quartermaster department, so it seems probable that the reference was to James Lowry Donaldson: native of Maryland; Cadet at the United States Military Academy, class of 1832; 2nd Lieutenant, 3rd Artillery, July 1, 1836; transferred to 1st Artillery, May 25, 1837; 1st Lieutenant, July 7, 1838; brevetted Captain, Sept. 23, 1846; brevetted Major, Feb. 23, 1847; Captain in quartermaster department, August 20, 1847; served in Civil War and brevetted Brigadier General, Sept. 17, 1864; resigned Jan. 1, 1874; died Nov. 4, 1885. (HEITMAN, Vol. I, p. 378.)
13. This was probably Lt. Col. Benjamin Lloyd Beall of the 1st

Dragoons, who on the death in San Francisco of Brig. Gen. Newman S. Clarke of the 6th Infantry on Oct. 17, 1860, succeeded to the command of the Department of the Pacific. (BANCAL, Vol. VII, p. 472, n. 17.) Benjamin Lloyd Beall: Cadet at United States Military Academy from the District of Columbia, Jan. 1, 1814, until Oct. 15, 1818; Captain, Washington City Volunteers in Florida War, June 1, 1836; Major, 1st Dragoons, Feb. 16, 1847; Lieutenant Colonel, Mar. 3, 1855; Colonel, May 13, 1861; retired Feb. 15, 1862; died Aug. 16, 1863. (HEITMAN, Vol. I, p. 202.)

14. DR. JOHN STROTHER GRIFFIN, born in Virginia in 1816, was graduated as Doctor of Medicine from University of Pennsylvania in 1837. In 1846–1847, he was medical officer of Army of the West under Brig. Gen. Stephen Watts Kearny. He resigned his commission in 1854, settled in Los Angeles, and soon afterward became superintendent of schools. He was elected first president of Los Angeles County Medical Association in 1871. He died in Los Angeles on Aug. 23, 1898. (Arthur Woodward, "Lances at San Pascual," CHSQ, Vol. XXV [December, 1946], 305; Viola Lockhart Warren, ed., "Dr. John S. Griffin's Mail, 1846–53," CHSQ, Vol. XXXIII [June, 1954], 97.)
15. FITCH, unpublished letter dated Sept. 15, 1854.
16. "Minnie" was Maria Sherman, the eldest child of the family, who was born in Lancaster, Ohio, Jan. 28, 1851. When her mother and father went to California, they left her with Mrs. Sherman's parents. She married Thomas W. Fitch on Oct. 1, 1874.
17. SCHUYLER HAMILTON: born in New York; Cadet at United States Military Academy, Class of 1837; 2nd Lieutenant, 1st Infantry, July 1, 1841; regimental quartermaster, Apr. 19, 1847; 1st Lieutenant, Mar. 5, 1848; brevetted Captain, Aug. 13, 1847, for gallant conduct; resigned Mar. 31, 1855; served in Civil War, Brigadier General of Volunteers, Nov. 12, 1861; Major General of Volunteers, Sept. 17, 1862; resigned Feb. 27, 1863; died, Mar. 18, 1903. (HEITMAN, Vol. I, p. 494.)
18. FITCH, unpublished letter Sept. 29, 1854.
19. FITCH, unpublished letter Sept. 30, 1854.
20. GEORGE HASKET DERBY ("John Phoenix"): native of Massachusetts; Cadet at United States Military Academy, class of 1842; brevetted 2nd Lieutenant of Ordnance, July 1, 1846; transferred to Topographical Engineers, Aug. 12, 1846; 2nd Lieutenant, Aug. 4, 1851; 1st Lieutenant, Oct. 2, 1855; brevetted Captain, July 1, 1860, for gallant conduct at Battle of Cerro Gordo, Mexico; died May 15, 1861. (HEITMAN, Vol. I, p. 368.)
21. The TEHAMA HOUSE was built on piles in 1850 by Capt. J. L. Folsom at northwest corner of Sansome and California Streets and was the rendezvous of army officers and wealthy rancheros. In 1864, to make way for the Bank of California, the building was moved to the corner of Montgomery and Broadway, where it stood until de-

stroyed in the conflagration of April, 1906. (ELDREDGE, Vol. II, p. 576.)

22. FITCH, unpublished letter of Sept. 30, 1854.
23. JOSEPH LIBBEY FOLSOM: born in New Hampshire, 1817; Cadet at United States Military Academy, class of 1836; brevetted 2nd Lieutenant, 8th Infantry, July 1, 1840; 2nd Lieutenant, 5th Infantry, Nov. 3, 1840; 1st Lieutenant, June 29, 1846; Captain and assistant quartermaster, Sept. 10, 1846. (HEITMAN, Vol. I, p. 427.) After graduating from West Point, Folsom was for some time an instructor there. He came to California in 1847 with Colonel Stevenson's regiment of New York Volunteers, of which he was a staff officer. For a time, he served as collector of the port of San Francisco. By orders of Colonel Mason, Captain Folsom laid out the military reservations for the United States Army at the Presidio and at Black Point. Shortly thereafter, he purchased the estate of William A. Leidesdorff (who had died in 1848) from his heirs. This included the house built several years before at southwest corner of Montgomery and California Streets (later site of the Clunie Building). Folsom died in Mission San Jose on July 19, 1855, leaving a very substantial estate. (ELDREDGE, Vol. II, pp. 456, 519, 553, and 725.) If Sherman's statement that Folsom was engaged to a daughter of Senator Gwin was correct, it must not have resulted in marriage. Folsom's will, probated soon after his death, names as legatees only his mother, his sister, and a nephew. ("An Irishman in the Gold Rush. The Journal of Thomas Kerr," CHSQ, Vol. VIII [September, 1929], 269–270.)

    The Ord mentioned must have been Sherman's very good friend and fellow 1st Lieutenant of Company C of the 3rd Artillery, who arrived at Monterey with Sherman Jan. 28, 1847, EDWARD OTHO CRESAP ORD. He was briefly a partner with Sherman and Colonel Mason in a mercantile venture at Coloma. Fort Ord, the military reservation in Monterey County, bears his name. Immediately after the Mexican War, Ord augmented his slender income as a junior officer (quite inadequate for California's scale of living costs) by many land surveys. The most famous of these was the one he made for the Pueblo of Los Angeles in 1849. Ord was one of the army friends whose money Sherman was willing to accept for investment in what he termed his "trust funds." He wrote Captain Ord on Dec. 31, 1853, acknowledging receipt of $500, which he agreed to invest for his friend. On Oct. 14, 1854, in San Francisco, Captain Ord married Mary Mercer Thompson. Two sons and a daughter were the issue of that marriage. (*HSSCQ*, Vol. XVII, p. 139.) The bride may have been the daughter of Augustus Thompson, one of the United States land commissioners appointed by President Millard Fillmore under the act of 1851. (Franklin Tuthill, *History of California* [San Francisco: H. W. Bancroft & Company, 1866], p. 535.) Edward Otho Cresap Ord; Cadet at the United States Military

Academy, class of 1835; 2nd Lieutenant, 3rd Artillery, July 1, 1839; 1st Lieutenant, July 1, 1841; Captain, Sept. 7, 1850; Major, 4th Artillery, Nov. 21, 1861; Major General of Volunteers, May 2, 1862; honorably mustered out of volunteer service, Sept. 1, 1866; retired with rank of Major General, Jan. 28, 1881; died, July 22, 1883. (HEITMAN, Vol. I, p. 759.) Edward O. C. Ord was reliably reported to be a cousin of Queen Victoria. His father, James Ord, was said to have been the son of George IV by his morganatic marriage with Mrs. Maria Anne Fitzherbert. James Ord was brought up by the Ord family of Baltimore and took their name. Edward Ord and others of his family bore a strong resemblance to members of the House of Hanover (Amelia Ransome Neville, *The Fantastic City* [Boston: Houghton, Mifflin & Co., 1932], pp. 225–226.)

The Keyes mentioned was probably ERASMUS DARWIN KEYES: native of Massachusetts; Cadet at the United States Military Academy, July, 1828; brevetted 2nd Lieutenant, 3rd Artillery, July 1, 1832; 2nd Lieutenant, Aug. 1, 1833; 1st Lieutenant, Sept. 16, 1836; Captain and assistant adjutant general, July 7 to Nov. 16, 1838; Captain, 3rd Artillery, Nov. 30, 1841; brevetted Brigadier General, May 31, 1862; resigned, May 6, 1864; died Oct. 14, 1895. (HEITMAN, Vol. I, p. 596.) Capt. E. D. Keyes, in command of Co. M of the 3rd Artillery, is mentioned as parading at Captain Folsom's funeral and at the Admission Day celebration on Sept. 10, 1855. ("Continuation of the Annals of San Francisco," CHSQ, Vol. XV [December 1936], 373; *Ibid.*, Vol. XVI [March 1937], 82.)

24. The wreck of the *Yankee Blade* was reported in the San Francisco papers on October 9, 1854. Also see "Continuation of the Annals of San Francisco," CHSQ, Vol. XV (June, 1936), 173–176, 178, and 179.

25. See Part One, p. 24, and Note 42, Part One. Meiggs and his family fled from San Francisco in a small sailing ship, a bark named *America.* Now, note a strange coincidence. At the instigation of his many creditors, the authorities dispatched the steamer *America* to overhaul the bark and to return the fugitives to the jurisdiction of the California courts. The vessel selected to make this chase was the steamer in whose financial troubles Lucas, Turner & Co. had been involved. (See Chapter 7, pp. 49 ff., hereof, and Note 1, Part Two.) According to an article that appeared in the *San Francisco Bulletin* on Aug. 15, 1887, friends of Harry Meiggs gave the captain of the pursuit ship $500 to delay its departure. While preparing to leave San Francisco, the captain deliberately made a rough landing at one of the wharves and so damaged his craft that the necessary repairs delayed it for forty hours, thus giving Meiggs time for a perfect getaway. The brief career of the steamer *America* was so stormy that superstitious mariners may well have considered her a hoodoo craft. (Above information supplied to author by Dr. John Haskell Kemble of Pomona College, Claremont, Calif., in his letter of Oct. 13, 1966.)

Either a variation of the above story or the tale of another group that was foiled in their pursuit of the fugitive Meiggs appears in "Continuation of the Annals of San Francisco" (CHSQ, Vol. XV, [June, 1936], 177). This item reads: "Oct. 8 1854 New developments about Meiggs' forgeries, increased the excitement. Adams & Co., in connection with other gentlemen interested, chartered the steamship *Active*, to go in search of Meiggs in the bark *America*, but when attempting to come alongside a hulk to coal, she stove in her wheel-house and was thus prevented from leaving the harbor."

26. The *vara* is the Spanish linear measure, thirty-three inches in length. In the original survey of San Francisco, the area north of Market Street was laid off in lots fifty *varas* in depth (or 137½ feet). In real estate circles, it came to be known as the fifty-*vara* district. The surveys later made on the southeast side of Market Street, generally referred to as "South of Market," were laid off in lots one hundred *varas* deep (275 feet).
27. FITCH, unpublished letter dated Saturday, Oct. 15, 1854.
28. While Sherman spelled this name "De Russy," it appears as "Derussey" in BANCAL, Vol. V, p. 456. RENE EDWARD DE RUSSY (Heitman's spelling agrees with Sherman's): native of the West Indies; Cadet at United States Military Academy, Mar. 20, 1807; 2nd Lieutenant, Engineers, June 10, 1812; 1st Lieutenant, July 6, 1812; Captain, Feb. 9, 1815; Major, Dec. 22, 1830; Lieutenant Colonel, Dec. 7, 1838; Colonel, Mar. 3, 1863; Brigadier General, Mar. 13, 1865; died Nov. 30, 1865. (HEITMAN, Vol. I, p. 369.) This officer was one of the members of the court-martial that tried Lt. Col. John C. Frémont in 1847–1848.

    MAJOR J. G. BARNARD is mentioned in Chapter 5 herein and Note 57, Part One, in connection with the construction of the fortifications defending San Francisco Bay.

    MRS. HARDIE was undoubtedly the wife of the MAJOR HARDIE mentioned in Note 53, Part One.

    GENERAL PERSIFER SMITH made Sonoma the headquarters of the Pacific Department of the Army but transferred it to Benicia in 1851. The legislature made Benicia the state capital on May 18, 1853 but countermanded the action the following March.
29. FITCH, unpublished letter dated Sunday, Oct. 15, 1854. Note that both the Saturday letter (see Note 27 above) and this Sunday letter are dated Oct. 15, 1854.
30. It is not clear to which customhouse Sherman was referring. In November, 1853, the customhouse was moved to the southeast corner of Sansome and Sacramento Streets (ANNALS, p. 473 and on p. 14 a picture of "Custom House now being erected on Battery Street"; in BANCAL, Vol. VII, p. 140, n. 26, Bancroft speaks of a permanent customhouse and appraisers store erected in 1854.) Probably Sherman referred to the new location at Jackson and Battery Streets. Burgoyne's bank was at the southwest corner of Washington and Montgomery Streets. (BANCAL, Vol. VI, p. 204.)

31. FITCH, unpublished letter dated Oct. 23, 1854.
32. JACOB R. SNYDER was born in Philadelphia about 1813, according to Bancroft. He came overland to California in 1845. His military title is due to his participation in the Bear Flag Revolt in which he served as quartermaster. He held the same post in Frémont's California Battalion, organized its artillery corps, and served in the campaign that resulted in the surrender of the Californios at Cahuenga. He was a delegate from Sacramento County to the constitutional convention in 1849. In 1852–1853, he served as state senator from San Francisco and was a partner in the banking firm of James King of William. He was United States subtreasurer for the Pacific Coast from 1853 to 1860. See BANCAL, Vol. VI, pp. 286, 288, and 669. ANNALS (p. 19) states he was president of the Society of California Pioneers in July, 1854, when William T. Sherman was its treasurer. Snyder was a man of distinguished appearance and most highly esteemed. He died in Sonoma, California, in 1878. For biographical details, see the *Quarterly* of the Society of California Pioneers, Vol. VIII (December 1931), 203–219.
33. In August, 1850, SATHER & CHURCH commenced business. They had been money brokers in New York. In May, 1851, the name was changed to DREXEL, SATHER & CHURCH; Francis Drexel of Philadelphia had become a partner. Their bank was at northeast corner of Montgomery and Commercial Streets. Drexel retired from the firm in 1859, and it again became Sather & Church. It was incorporated in 1887 as Sather Banking Company, reorganized as the San Francisco National Bank on Dec. 10, 1897, and in July, 1910, was absorbed into the Bank of California N. A. It was the only San Francisco bank dating from 1850 that continued actively in business into the twentieth century. (CROSS, Vol. I, pp. 64 and 65.)
34. BANCAL, Vol. VII, pp. 160 and 168. Also "Hides and Tallow," CHSQ, Vol. VI (September, 1927), 257; "Continuation of the Annals of San Francisco, June 1854," CHSQ, Vol. XV (June, 1936), 177; William Henry Ellison (ed.), "Memoirs of Hon. William M. Gwin," CHSQ, Vol. XIX (September, 1940), 260; "News of the Society: Gifts Received by the Society," CHSQ, Vol. XXIV (June, 1945), 182 and 183; J. N. Bowman, "The Question of Sainsevain's Signature," CHSQ, Vol. XXVIII (December, 1940), 361, 365, 369 (n. 113). Also CROSS, Vol. I, pp. 121 and 123.
35. I am unable to identify the Ray mentioned. Judge Parsons was doubtless LEVI PARSONS, elected by the first legislature of California as a district judge for the 4th, or San Francisco, district. He acquired considerable notoriety for his clash with the press in 1851. He imprisoned William Walker, the future filibuster, who as an editor of the *San Francisco Herald* criticized Judge Parson's leniency toward criminals. The uproar that followed culminated in an unsuccessful attempt to impeach Parsons. His judicial career was brief. In 1860, he headed a movement by private interests to reclaim much of the San Francisco waterfront. The very unpopular Bulk-

head Bill was passed by the legislature but was vetoed by Gov. John G. Downey. Parsons lived for many years on California Street near Grace Episcopal Church. He left California in 1866 for New York, where he died Oct. 23, 1887. (SHUCK, p. 476.)

36. FITCH, unpublished letter dated Oct. 31, 1854.
37. I am unable to identify COLONEL STEWART. Sherman's reference plainly indicates that he was well known both to Turner and himself, presumably through their army connections. Yet none of the Stewarts, Stuarts, or Steuarts listed in HEITMAN fits the dates, title, etc., nor does he appear in Bancroft's PIONEER, ANNALS, or several other sources checked. Mr. James de T. Abajian, Librarian of CHS, called to my attention two Stewarts with military titles in the California records of the period: (1) Col. Franklin Stewart, Butte County, 1853, is mentioned on p. 12 of Edward Eberstadt *Catalogue*, No. 159, 1962; and (2) *San Jose Pioneer*, Oct. 30, 1880 (p. 2, col. 2), has an obituary for Col. James M. Stewart, who was Tuolumne County sheriff in 1855. I have not researched the source of their titles. As the Colonel Stewart who was Sherman's friend was en route to army headquarters at Benicia, it seems less likely that an officer with militia or volunteer units could have been the man mentioned.
38. FITCH, unpublished letter dated Nov. 8, 1854.
39. FITCH, unpublished letter dated Nov. 15, 1854.
40. FITCH, second unpublished letter dated Nov. 15, 1854.
41. FITCH, unpublished letter dated Nov. 24, 1854.
42. DUNCAN, SHERMAN & Co., a private banking firm in New York City, who were Page, Bacon & Co.'s correspondent. In BACON several references to this firm are critical of its business operations and ethics. Letter from Henry D. Bacon dated New York City, Apr. 3, 1854, reflects on Duncan, Sherman & Co.'s dealings with Palmer, Cook & Co. concerning the payment of the interest on the state of California bonds. Again on Apr. 4, 1855, Henry D. Bacon wrote D. D. Page from New York: "Between Watts Sherman [apparently a partner of Duncan, Sherman & Co.] and Henry Haight our slaughter seems almost complete."
43. FITCH, unpublished letter dated Nov. 30, 1854.
44. MEMOIRS, Vol. I, p. 109.
45. FITCH, unpublished letter dated Dec. 8, 1854.
46. FITCH, unpublished letter dated Dec. 2, 1854.
47. FITCH, unpublished letter dated Dec. 23, 1854.
48. FITCH, unpublished letter dated Dec. 2, 1854.
49. FITCH, unpublished letter dated Dec. 31, 1854.
50. CHARLES POMROY STONE: native of Massachusetts; Cadet Military Academy, 7th in class graduating July 1, 1845; brevetted 2nd Lieutenant of Ordnance, 2nd Lieutenant, Mar. 3, 1847; brevetted 1st Lieutenant, for gallantry at Battle of Molino del Rey, May, 1847; brevetted Captain, for gallantry at Battle of Chapultepec, Sept. 13, 1847; resigned Nov. 17, 1856, and became banker in San Francisco;

Colonel of Volunteers, Apr. 16, 1861; Brigadier General of Volunteers, May 17, 1861; honorably mustered out of service Apr. 4, 1864; died Jan. 24, 1887. (HEITMAN, Vol. I, pp. 928–929.) Brigadier General Stone was in command of Union forces at Battle of Ball's Bluff, Va., Oct. 21, 1861, when Col. Edward D. Baker (also United States senator from Oregon) was killed. A bitter controversy followed, partly because of Baker's fame and popularity. Stone was charged with negligence, incompetence, and even worse. The case against him became a *cause célèbre*. He was relieved of his command and confined in prison for several months. Despite his earnest request to be heard in his own defense, he was not brought to trial. Although eventually released, he was never again given any military assignment. (Russell Buchanan, "James A. McDougall—A Forgotten Senator," CHSQ, Vol. XV [September, 1936], 207; Milton H. Shutes, "Colonel E. D. Baker," CHSQ, Vol. XVII [December, 1938], 320; Paul Fatout, "The California Regiment, Colonel Baker, and Ball's Bluff," CHSQ, Vol. XXXI [September, 1952], 233–237.)

51. FITCH, unpublished letter dated Jan. 8, 1855.
52. William Hooper, commissioner of funded debt. (ANNALS, p. 373.)
53. FITCH, unpublished letter dated Jan. 8, 1855.
54. FITCH, unpublished letter dated Jan. 15, 1855.
55. FITCH, unpublished letters dated Jan. 23, 1855, and Jan. 31, 1855.
56. This was the first railroad actually built in California. It was proposed to run from Sacramento along the foothills, branching north and south in Placer and Sutter Counties to Mountain City in Yuba County—a distance of forty miles. Grading commenced in February, 1855, under the competent engineering direction of Theodore D. Judah, who later projected the Central Pacific Railroad across the Sierra Nevada. Formal opening of the road to Folsom, twenty-two miles from Sacramento, occurred Feb. 22, 1856. The road cost a little less than $60,000 a mile. Its early operation was profitable because of the heavy tonnage of freight from river-borne transportation to the mines. In 1864, it earned $500,000 and was purchased the following year by representatives of the Central Pacific Railroad. (BANCAL, Vol. VII, pp. 537–539.)
57. FITCH, unpublished letter dated Jan. 31, 1855.
58. For census figures of the 1850's, see ANNALS, pp. 286, 300, 357, 411, 413, 484, and 546.
59. FITCH, unpublished letter dated Feb. 8, 1855.
60. For *Pearl* boiler explosion, see "Continuation of the Annals of San Francisco, Dec. 5, 1854 to June 3, 1855," CHSQ, Vol. XV (September, 1936), 271.
61. FITCH, unpublished letter dated Feb. 15, 1855.

Notes for Part Three

1. JOHN PARROTT, born in Virginia in 1810, came to California in 1845. He was for some years prior to that time engaged in trade on the west coast of Mexico and served as United States consul at Mazatlán. Shortly after the gold discovery, he moved with his family to San Francisco, where he was a shipping merchant, banker, and capitalist. On Sept. 10, 1855, Parrott, in partnership with Walter B. Comstock, opened a bank in San Francisco under the name of Parrott & Co. This merged with the London and San Francisco Bank Ltd. on Jan. 1, 1871. The latter was in turn absorbed by the Bank of California in 1905. Parrott died Mar. 30, 1884 (PIONEER, Vol. IV, pp. 767–768; also CROSS, Vol. I, p. 211.)

   THOMAS O. LARKIN was the former United States consul at Monterey. He was born in Massachusetts in 1802 and came to California in 1832. He died in San Francisco in 1858. Since much has been published about Larkin, one of the most famous pioneer Californians, it seems unnecessary to detail his many activities here. (PIONEER, Vol. IV, pp. 706–707; ANNALS, pp. 758–764.)

   JOHN G. DOWNEY, a native of Ireland, came to California in 1849. He opened a drugstore in Los Angeles in 1850, then later engaged in stock raising and real estate investments in Southern California, thereby accumulating a large fortune. He was elected lieutenant-governor of California in 1859 and became governor in 1860, a few days after Milton S. Latham was inaugurated as governor, when Latham resigned to become United States senator. (BANCAL, Vol. VII, p. 279, n. 6.)

   It is uncertain which Paine (or Payne) was the man referred to by Sherman; there were several of that name in San Francisco in early days. It is probable that the reference is to THEODORE PAYNE, born in New York City in 1816. He came to California in 1849 and was active as both an auctioneer and a real estate agent and in 1851 was elected a street commissioner. (ANNALS, pp. 799–804.) For Capt. Joseph L. Folsom, see Note 23 of Part Two.

2. While Sherman sent Turner a copy of the offensive circular issued by Page, Bacon & Co., there is no copy of it in the file of Sherman's letters to which reference is being made; nor have I been able to locate a copy. From the references made to it, the circular apparently predicted that if Page, Bacon & Co. was forced to close, every other bank in San Francisco would also fail. Letters in BACON contain repeated evidence of antagonism on part of Page, Bacon & Co. toward both Lucas & Simonds and Lucas, Turner & Co.; e.g., letter from R. Whitney (evidently an employee of Page, Bacon & Co. in San Francisco) to Henry D. Bacon, dated San Francisco, May 27, 1853; also letter from H. D. Bacon to D. D. Page, dated New York, Jan. 27, 1855, saying: "Lucas & Simonds are taking great credit to themselves for manner in which they sustained the run . . . but for the card of O'Fallon and others guaranteeing their depositors against loss . . . they could not have sustained themselves one hour on Monday morning"; also letter from H. D. Bacon dated New York, Mar. 11, 1855, to Page, Bacon & Co., San Francisco, in which he says: "Lucas & Simonds have been very industrious in circulating doubts as to your liability to sustain yourselves. It has not seemed improbable to us they would not suffer as much in California as you but time will show." Again on Apr. 11, 1855, Bacon wrote Page from New York, commenting on the adverse rumors circulated by a Mr. Badt [?], a particular friend of James H. Lucas.
3. Sherman's listing of the bank's assets and liabilities both before and after the run differ in several instances from the figures recited in his *Memoirs* (Vol. I, p. 113). Also on subsequent pages of the *Memoirs*, his accounts of raising funds to meet the run vary in details from the report of these efforts that he wrote to Turner.
4. While Sherman was properly grateful for the aid extended him by Palmer, Cook & Co. in February, 1855, its general record during this period was far from exemplary. See Note 43 of Part One.
5. This was undoubtedly the partner in the private assay firm of KELLOGG, HEWSTON AND COMPANY, mentioned in BANCAL, Vol. VII, p. 176.
6. This was MAJ. RICHARD PINDELL HAMMOND: native of Maryland; entered the Military Academy at West Point, July 1, 1837; brevetted 2nd Lieutenant, 3rd Artillery, July 1, 1841; brevetted Captain, Apr. 18, 1847, for gallant conduct at Battle of Cerro Gordo; brevetted Major, Aug. 20, 1847, for gallant conduct at Battles of Contreras and Churubusco; resigned, May 26, 1851; died, Nov. 28, 1891. (HEITMAN, Vol. I, p. 495.) Major Hammond married Sarah E. Hays, sister of Col. John Coffey Hays, first sheriff of San Francisco, and they were the parents of John Hays Hammond (1855–1936), the famous mining engineer. (Ernest A. Wiltsee, "In Memoriam—John Hays Hammond, 1855–1936," CHSQ, Vol. XV [September, 1936], 290–291.) In 1848, Charles M. Weber employed Hammond to lay

out the town of Stockton. In 1849, Colonel Stevenson employed him as well as William T. Sherman to survey the site of the town of New York at the mouth of the San Joaquin River. In 1852, Hammond was a member of the state assembly of California. (BANCAL, Vol. VI, p. 674; also Theodore H. Hittel, *History of California* [San Francisco: L. J. Stone & Company, 1897], Vol. II, p. 734, and Vol. IV, p. 98; also MEMOIRS, Vol. I, p. 73.)

7. ADAMS & Co. began as an express company in 1849 and soon added banking to their activities, setting up branches in every promising town and mining camp. News of the runs on various San Francisco banks in February, 1855, became quickly known throughout the state. The panic spread to the local centers, forcing most of the branches of the beleaguered city banks to close. (CROSS, Vol. I, p. 184; also BANCAL, Vol. VII, pp. 149–150, 161, and 174.)

   In HL there is a large collection of papers and correspondence (750 pieces) dealing with the attempts to settle the tangled affairs of Adams & Co., including the activities of Albert A. Cohen, its first receiver. Also, Card Am 131, Palmer, Cook & Co. at HL contains account of Messrs. Richard Roman, Alfred A. Cohen, and Edward Jones, assignees of Adams & Co.

8. See Note 17 of Part Two.
9. See Note 28 of Part Two.
10. FITCH, unpublished letter dated Feb. 25, 1855.
11. Unpublished letter from H. S. Turner to W. T. Sherman, dated St. Louis, Feb. 26, 1855, in the William T. Sherman Papers, Library of Congress, Washington, D.C.
12. FITCH, unpublished letter dated Feb. 28, 1855.
13. CROSS, Vol. I, pp. 188–190; also Milton H. Shutes, "Henry Douglas Bacon (1813–1893)," CHSQ, Vol. XXVI (September, 1947), 194.
14. Edwin A. Sherman, "Sherman Was There," CHSQ, Vol. XXIV (June, 1945), 179, n. 2.
15. BANCAL, Vol. VII, p. 180 (footnote).
16. CROSS, Vol. I, p. 190.
17. Nineteen is the number stated in CROSS, p. 165, but a review of its pages descriptive of early day banking suggests that an exact enumeration would be difficult. Firms and individuals slipped in and out of the banking business quite casually in the 1850's. One day a concern called itself a brokerage or exchange office, or the like; the next day it might be described as a bank, and vice versa. Regardless of the exact number, it must be remembered that the actual banking business done in many cases was quite small. Not more than twelve or fourteen houses did the bulk of what we regard as banking.
18. FITCH, unpublished letter dated Mar. 1, 1855.
19. This was probably DR. ALEXANDER J. BOWIE, a retired navy surgeon. He was a San Francisco alderman in 1852. According to one authority, he lived for many years in a house surrounded by a beautiful garden at the northwest corner of Sutter and Stockton

Streets. Another authority shows him living at South Park. As no dates are stated, it is possible he lived at both locations at different periods. (ANNALS, p. 407; Amelia Ransome Neville, *Fantastic City* [Boston: Houghton, Mifflin & Company, 1932], p. 134; and ELDREDGE, Vol. II, p. 617.)

20. FITCH, unpublished letter dated Mar. 8, 1855.
21. FITCH, unpublished letter dated Mar. 15, 1855.
22. FITCH, unpublished letter dated Mar. 23, 1855.
23. FITCH, two unpublished letters dated Mar. 31, 1855.
24. JOHN FITZGERALD LEE: native of Virginia; Cadet at United States Military Academy, class of July 1, 1830; brevetted 2nd Lieutenant, 1st Artillery, July 1, 1834; 1st Lieutenant, Ordnance, July 9, 1838; Captain, Mar. 3, 1847; judge advocate general, brevetted Major, judge advocate department, Mar. 2, 1849; resigned Sept. 4, 1862; died, June 17, 1884. (HEITMAN, Vol. I, p. 625.) Captain Lee was the judge advocate at the court-martial of Lt. Col. John C. Frémont, Nov. 2, 1847 to Jan 31, 1848.
25. FITCH, unpublished letter dated Mar. 31, 1855.
26. WILLIAM H. ASPINWALL, JOHN L. STEPHENS, and HENRY CHAUNCEY had the government contract to carry the mails from New York to the Pacific Coast via Panama. Aspinwall in 1848 had contracted for a new line of side-wheel steamers to run from Panama City to San Francisco and a few years later started surveys for a railroad across the Isthmus to connect with the two steamer lines. He was the moving spirit in the organization of the Pacific Mail Steamship Company. (BANCAL, Vol. VI, pp. 121–129, and Vol. VII, p. 522; also Milton H. Shutes, "Colonel E. D. Baker," CHSQ, Vol. XVII [December, 1938], 308.)
27. This was the famous NEW ALMADEN MINE, a few miles southwest of San Jose.
28. FITCH, unpublished letter dated Apr. 8, 1855.
29. C. K. Garrison. See Note 2 of Part Two.
30. FITCH, unpublished letter dated Apr. 13, 1855.
31. "Southern mines" and "northern mines" have always been terms loosely applied. Originally, the area directly tributary to Sacramento was called the northern mines, that more convenient to Stockton, the southern mines. In a general sense by Sherman's time, the regions south of the Mokelumne River were termed the southern mines, those north of it the northern. (Rodman W. Paul, *California Gold* [Cambridge, Mass.: Harvard University Press, 1947], pp. 91–92.)
32. Horner was very probably either JOHN HORNER, one of the Mormon colonists who arrived in California from New Jersey in 1846, or his brother (name not recorded) who joined him in 1849 or 1850. John engaged in farming near Mission San Jose, with some mining experiences in 1848. The brothers were active in Alameda County and by trade in farm produce and land speculation became wealthy. They engaged in real estate speculation on the San Francisco penin-

sula. They lost their property in 1854 and continued to live in Alameda County until 1880 when they went to the Sandwich Islands. (PIONEER, Vol. III, p. 788.)

Peter Smith was probably the DR. PETER SMITH who in 1849–1850 contracted to erect a hospital in San Francisco. In January, 1850, his bill was $6,600; in April of that year, $13,000. This hospital burned down in September, 1850. (BANCAL, Vol. VI, p. 215.) His name appears a little later as the city physician (BANCAL, Vol. VI, p. 676), and he contracted to care for the destitute sick at $4.00 per diem. By 1851–1852 his claim for this service totaled $64,431. He refused to accept scrip in settlement, sued, and obtained judgment against the city. He attached beach and water lots belonging to the city; these were sold, but the sale was generally considered invalid. (BANCAL, Vol. VI, p. 773 and n. 37.) I am unable to identify Beard.

33. BANCAL, Vol. VI, p. 766, n. 23.
34. FITCH, unpublished letter dated Apr. 23, 1855.
35. Andrew F. Rolle, *California: A History* (New York: Thomas Y. Crowell Company, 1963), pp. 346 and 347.
36. FITCH, unpublished letter dated Apr. 30, 1855.
37. Sherman was referring here to the *second* closing of Page & Bacon in St. Louis, news of which was brought to San Francisco on May 1, 1855, by the S.S. *Sonora*. See Chapter 13 hereof, p. 117.
38. See Appendix hereof, p. 420, for references to A. A. COHEN, both as a defendant in suit brought by Page, Bacon & Co., and in his capacity as receiver of the bankrupt firm of Adams & Co. He was born in London in 1829, and came to California in 1850. He was at first a commission merchant but later studied law and was admitted to the bar in 1857. He was active in building railroads in Alameda County and built and operated some of the early ferryboats. Later he was an attorney for the Central Pacific Railroad. He died in 1887. (BANCAL, Vol. VII, pp. 178–179, n. 48.) See Note 7 (2nd paragraph thereof) of Part Three for references to Cohen's receivership of Adams & Co.
39. This was LT. THOMAS H. STEVENS, U.S.N., referred to in Note 11 of Part Two.
40. FITCH, first unpublished letter dated May 8, 1855.
41. WILLIAM TELL COLEMAN was born in Kentucky in 1824. In 1849, he came to California where he started a commission and shipping business in 1850 under the name W. T. Coleman & Co. When the Vigilance Committee of 1851 was organized, Coleman was its second in command. He became the leader of the Second Vigilance Committee of 1856. He died in 1893. See James A. B. Scherer, *The Lion of the Vigilantes* (New York: Bobbs, Merrill Company, 1939) for his biography.
42. FITCH, second unpublished letter dated May 8, 1855.
43. I have found no clue to G.'s identity.
44. FITCH, third unpublished letter dated May 8, 1855.

45. FELIX ARGENTI started a banking business in June 1850 under name F. Argenti & Co. and was supposed to have prospered. He was a member of the Vigilance Committee of 1851 and was the defendant in a famous suit, *Metcalf* vs. *Argenti*, involving that committee. He was also the plaintiff in a suit against the City of San Francisco, in 1854 and 1855, involving the title to the city slip lots that he had purchased. These were the same lots for whose sale C. K. Garrison had been criticized, as mentioned in pp. 131 ff. hereof. ("Continuation of the Annals of San Francisco," CHSQ, Vol. XV [June, 1936], 186; *Ibid.* [September, 1936], 282; *Ibid.* [December, 1936], 366, 367, 370; *Ibid.*, Vol. XVI [March, 1937], p. 82; "Continuation of the Annals of San Francisco," compiled by Dorothy H. Huggins, CHSQ, Vol. XVI [June, 1937], 182; *Ibid.*, Vol. XVII [June, 1938], 174; "Preliminary Listing of Manuscripts: Collection of Personal Papers in Library of California Historical Society," compiled by James De T. Abajian, CHSQ, Vol. XXXIII [December 1954], 372; and Robert P. Hastings, "Rufus Allen Lockwood," CHSQ, Vol. XXXIV [September, 1955], 243, 244, 248, and 249.) Notwithstanding Sherman's unfavorable opinion, Argenti did succeed in opening another bank on Sept. 3, 1855, under name of Argenti, Cavallier & Co.
46. FITCH, unpublished letter dated May 14, 1855.
47. On Apr. 29, 1855, while a short distance north of Panama, the *Golden Age* struck a sunken reef and at once began to fill with water. Commodore J. T. Watkins, who was on deck at the time, ordered full speed ahead to a nearby island. The vessel grounded gently on a beach just at the last revolution of the wheels, and all the passengers were safely landed. With nearly a thousand persons on board, only the officer's prompt action had prevented a great loss of life. (MEMOIRS, Vol. I, p. 117.)
48. FITCH, unpublished letter dated May 16, 1855.
49. Today we think of Contra Costa as the county to the north and east of Alameda County. Sherman was here using the term in its original meaning, which was formerly quite common, i.e., "the opposite coast, or shore"—the land to the east and south across the waters of San Francisco, San Pablo, and Suisun Bays.
50. FITCH, unpublished letter dated May 31, 1855; also see Anna McAllister, *Ellen Ewing, Wife of General Sherman* (New York: Benziger Brothers, Inc., 1936), p. 133.
51. For the BOLTON AND BARRON CLAIM, see Note 94 of Part Four; for LAS MARIPOSAS RANCHO CASE, see "Continuation of the Annals of San Francisco," CHSQ, Vol. XV (September, 1936), 275.
52. Probably one of the Horner Brothers mentioned in Note 32 of Part Three.
53. FITCH, unpublished letter dated June 15, 1855.
54. JOSEPH LIBBEY FOLSOM. See Note 23 of Part Two.
55. HENRY WAGER HALLECK and ARCHIBALD CAREY PEACHY were members of the well-known law firm of Halleck, Peachy, Billings and

Parke, with offices in the Montgomery Block, which it owned. (See Note 37 of Part One.) P. WARREN VAN WINKLE was an employee of Captain Folsom and was to become a pilot commissioner of the port of San Francisco in 1860.

56. Sherman was of course figuring the distance by sea via Panama or Nicaragua.
57. The reference here is to the KNOW NOTHING political party, quite active in the 1850's. Orthodox partisans of other parties were inclined to impute moral turpitude to its members.
58. EDWARD JENNER STEPTOE: native of Virginia; Cadet at the Military Academy at West Point, entering July 1, 1833; 2nd Lieutenant, 3rd Artillery, July 1, 1837; Captain, Mar. 3, 1847; Major, 9th Infantry, Mar. 3, 1855; Lieutenant Colonel, 10th Infantry, Sept. 9, 1861; brevetted Major, Apr. 13, 1847, for gallant conduct at Battle of Chapultepec; resigned Nov. 1, 1861; died April 1, 1865. (HEITMAN, Vol. I, p. 921.) Colonel Steptoe commanded the riflemen sent in pursuit of the Indians who murdered Captain Gunnison and his party in Utah in 1853. (Jacob H. Schiel, "Journey through the Rocky Mountains and the Humboldt Mountains to the Pacific Ocean," translated and edited by Thos. N. Bronner [Norman, Okla.: University of Oklahoma Press, 1959], cited in CHSQ, Vol. XXXVIII [March, 1959], 82.) He also commanded an army detachment defeated by Indians in eastern Washington in May, 1858. (Fred B. Rogers, "Early Military Posts of Mendocino County," CHSQ, Vol. XXVII [September, 1948], 217.)
59. FITCH, unpublished letter dated July 31, 1855.
60. "Continuation of the Annals of San Francisco," CHSQ, Vol. XVI (March, 1937), 83.
61. SANDERS & BRENHAM were running a bank at least as early as 1852. (BANCAL, Vol. VII, p. 161.)
62. For DREXEL, SATHER & CHURCH, see Note 33 of Part Two. Wells Fargo & Co. was incorporated in New York in 1851–1852 as an express company. It soon extended its operations to California and by 1852 had added banking to its express business. (BANCAL, Vol. VII, pp. 150–151 and 161.) For Palmer, Cook & Co. see Note 43 of Part One.
63. EDWARD JONES was the clerk of Thompson & Co. who sold out to Palmer, Cook & Co. in 1849. The sellers stipulated that Jones should be retained as a partner in the firm. Although a junior partner, he remained quite active in Palmer-Cook's management until its failure. With Richard Roman and A. A. Cohen (see Note 38 of Part Three), he became one of three assignees of Adams & Co. after its failure in February, 1855. This position involved Jones in an interminable succession of law suits and legal entanglements. (BANCAL, Vol. VII, p. 177; also Henry R. Wagner, "Edward Bosqui, Printer and Man of Affairs," CHSQ, Vol. XXI [December, 1942], 323–324.)
64. FITCH, unpublished letter dated Nov. 4, 1855.
65. FITCH, unpublished letter dated Nov. 5, 1855.

66. DRURY J. TALLANT started a bank at the corner of Clay and Montgomery Streets in February, 1850. In the spring of 1851, Judge J. W. Wilde became a partner and the name was changed to TALLANT & WILDE. In 1891, the firm was incorporated as the Tallant Banking Company. In 1898, it was absorbed by the Crocker Woolworth National Bank, later the Crocker National Bank. (BANCAL, Vol. VII, p. 161; also CROSS, Vol. I, p. 64.)
67. JAMES KING OF WILLIAM, see Notes 30 and 67 of Part One.
68. CASTLE BROTHERS appear in Joseph Baggett & Company's 1856 *San Francisco Directory* as importers and dealers in groceries and provisions at 82–84 Front Street, corner of Clay. Schloss Brothers appear in Samuel Colville's *San Francisco Directory* for 1856–1857 as importers of clothing and dry goods at 7 California Block, southeast corner of California and Battery Streets. McKee was probably REDICK MCKEE of R. MCKEE & Co. who appear in Colville's *Directory*, *op. cit.*, as jobbers and wholesale merchants at 48 Front Street. This firm was established in February, 1853.
69. HOLLAND, LITTLE and MORGAN were apparently clerks recently employed, perhaps while Turner was in San Francisco, as I have not previously noticed their names in Sherman's letters.
70. The reference must be to WILLIAM F. BABCOCK, born in Massachusetts in 1820, who came to California in 1852 as representative of New York shipping interests. With A. B. Forbes, he established the agency of the Pacific Mail Steamship Company in San Francisco. In 1864, he became president of the Spring Valley Water Company. He died in 1885. (BANCAL, Vol. VII, p. 186.)
71. This was ROBERT NISBET, who is named in Sherman's letter of Jan. 5, 1856 (FITCH). This is the first mention of him that I have found in Sherman's correspondence. Various references to him suggest that Robert Nisbet was either an employee of James H. Lucas & Co. in St. Louis or in some manner connected with the firm.
72. WILLIAM H. RICHARDSON was active in the Democratic Party and in March, 1853, had been appointed United States marshal for the Northern District of California. He was usually called General Richardson because of an office he had held in the California state militia. His apparently premeditated murder by the gambler Charles E. Cora inflamed San Francisco even more than Sherman indicated in his first report of the crime. This feeling was intensified by the trial, which dragged on for several months, and repeated charges made by James King of William and others of jury tampering by Cora's friends. This indignation was rekindled by the assassination a few months later of King himself by James Casey. This precipitated the creation of the Second Vigilance Committee and a long train of stirring events. ("Continuation of the Annals of San Francisco," compiled by Dorothy H. Huggins, CHSQ, Vol. XVI [December, 1937], 344–347.)
73. FITCH, unpublished letter dated Nov. 18, 1855.

74. For Castle Brothers, see Note 68 of Part Three. I do not find Harold Randall & Co. in the directories of the period but there was the firm of A. G. Randall & Co. in Samuel Colville's *San Francisco Directory* for 1856, listed as real estate agents and stock auctioneers at 100 Merchant Street. J. H. Bosworth was a partner of Bosworth, Masten & Co., listed in Colville's *Directory*, *op. cit.*, as wholesale merchants at 69 Front Street.
75. Castle Brothers Overdrafts. The "notices" published by Castle Brothers protested the refusal by Lucas, Turner & Co. to pay checks of said Castle Brothers that would have overdrawn their account with the bank. Other references indicate that the first such "notice" appeared in the *Herald* of Wednesday morning, Nov. 21, 1855. There is nothing novel about a bank depositor becoming angered under such circumstances, but this writer has never heard of a depositor advertising his displeasure in the newspapers! Therefore, I made a careful search for the protesting "notice." The BL has the *Herald* of this date on microfilm. The California State Library at Sacramento also has a file of this journal for this period. Unfortunately, my search proved unsuccessful. However, BL has a complete file of the *Daily California Chronicle*. In its issues of Nov. 21, 22, 23, and 24, 1855, appear four articles, too long for inclusion here, setting forth both Castle Brothers' contention and Lucas, Turner & Co.'s rebuttal. In form these are interviews by the newspaper's commercial reporter, and resemble present-day "letters to the editor." Castle Brothers claimed the overdraft privilege had been long in use and that they had not been informed of its termination. Sherman replied that he had published notices in all the newspapers for one month that such overdrafts would no longer be permitted. He closed: "We think money is at least worth asking for and we insist upon being consulted before advancing it."
76. W. C. Annan & Co. appears in Colville's *Directory*, *op. cit.*, as commission merchants and importers at 89 Front Street. The firm had been established as Annan, Lord & Co., later became W. C. Annan & Co., then changed to Annan, Talmadge & Co. They advertised in the *Directory* as agents for Virginia tobacco manufacturers and cognac brandy. J. H. Coghill appears in the Colville *Directory* as a dealer in groceries and provisions at 137 Front Street.
77. McCreery was probably Andrew B. McCreery, listed in Henry G. Langley's *San Francisco Directory* for 1858 as a merchant at 39 California Street.
78. Brewster was doubtless R. E. Brewster & Co., listed in Joseph Baggett & Co.'s *San Francisco Directory* for 1856 as wholesale grocers at 85 Front Street, corner of Clay.
79. Arrington & Co. are listed in Baggett's *Directory* for 1856 as wholesale grocers at 55 Front Street, corner of Richmond. William T. Coleman & Co. appear in Colville's *San Francisco Direc-*

tory for 1856–1857 as commission and shipping merchants at northwest corner of California and Front Streets. See also Note 41 of Part Three.

80. GARRISON, MORGAN, FRETZ AND RALSTON. C. K. Garrison has been mentioned several times in these pages. Charles Morgan was a New York partner, doing business there as Charles Morgan & Co. He had started his career as a Mississippi River steamboat captain. For W. C. RALSTON, see Note 3 of Appendix, "The Page-Bacon Failures . . ." The new bank opened on New Year's Day, 1856, at the corner of Clay and Montgomery Streets, subsequently moving to the southwest corner of Washington and Battery Streets. On July 14, 1857, the partnership was dissolved and a new one started under the name FRETZ & RALSTON. On December 1, 1860, the firm was joined by Eugene Kelly and Joseph A. Donohoe. The next year the name was changed to DONOHOE, RALSTON & CO. On June 30, 1864, this partnership was terminated when Ralston assumed a leading role in the organization of the Bank of California, as detailed in Note 3 of Appendix, "The Page-Bacon Failures . . ." Donohoe and Kelly opened their own banking house, which continued for many years at the northeast corner of Sutter and Montgomery Streets as DONOHOE, KELLY & CO. or the DONOHOE KELLY BANKING COMPANY. Their "temporary" quarters, erected immediately after the 1906 conflagration, were razed only a few years ago when the Equitable Life Assurance Society Building was constructed on the site. (CROSS, Vol. I, p. 214.)

81. Sherman seems to have misspelled the name of the head of Wells, Fargo & Co. in 1855. All other references I have found show him as LOUIS W. MCLANE (sometimes with "Jr." added). He became a midshipman in the United States Navy at the age of 16 and came to California on the U.S.S. *Savannah* during the Mexican War. While a passed midshipman on the U.S.S. *Levant*, he volunteered for and became a lieutenant of a company of dragoons raised by Commodore John D. Sloat's orders, and later served under John C. Frémont in the California Battalion, in which he commanded an artillery company. He was one of the American peace commissioners for the Cahuenga Capitulation. He resigned from the navy in 1850 and entered the express business, becoming head of Wells, Fargo & Co.'s Pacific Coast express business in 1855. He was one of the original incorporators of the Bank of California. In the heyday of the Comstock Lode, he became associated with James C. Flood in the establishment of the Nevada Bank of San Francisco, which he managed for some time. ("Continuation of the Annals of San Francisco," CHSQ, Vol. XV [December, 1936], 373; Anson S. Blake, "Letters of Charles T. Blake: Working for Wells Fargo—1860–1863," CHSQ, Vol. XVI [March, 1937], 40; Susan Mitchell Hall, "The Diary of a Trip from Ione to Nevada in 1859," CHSQ, Vol. XVII [March, 1938], 79, n. 13; "Continuation of the Annals of San Francisco," compiled by Dorothy H. Huggins, CHSQ, Vol.

XVII [June, 1938], 169 and 179; "San Francisco Society," from the *Elite Directory of 1879*, with introduction by Dorothy Harriet Huggins, CHSQ, Vol. XIX [September, 1940], 232; George Walcott Ames, Jr., ed., "A Doctor Comes to California: The Diary of John S. Griffin, Assistant Surgeon with Kearny's Dragoons, 1846–1847," CHSQ, Vol. XXII [March, 1943], 64, n. 105; Fred B. Rogers, "Bear Flag Lieutenant, The Life Story of Henry L. Ford (1822–1860): IV. With Frémont's Battalion," CHSQ, Vol. XXX [March, 1951], 53.) For JOHN PARROTT, see Note 1 of Part Three. SAMUEL W. INGE had emigrated to California from Alabama about 1853. He had served several terms as a member of the United States House of Representatives from Alabama. He soon formed a partnership with Parker Crittenden, an eminent member of the San Francisco bar, and a little later was appointed United States district attorney. (William Henry Ellison, ed., "Memoirs of Hon. William M. Gwin," CHSQ, XIX [September, 1940], 256.)

82. FITCH, unpublished letter dated Dec. 3, 1855.
83. See Note 59 of Part One.
84. FITCH, unpublished letter dated Dec. 19, 1855.
85. For SCHUYLER HAMILTON, see Note 17 of Part Two.
86. See p. 159 hereof and Note 71 of Part Three.
87. This refers to CHARLES POMROY STONE. See p. 93 hereof and Note 50 of Part Two.
88. See p. 167 hereof and Note 80 of Part Three about this new bank.
89. GEN. ETHAN ALLEN HITCHCOCK. See Note 31 of Part One.
90. FITCH, unpublished letter dated Jan. 5, 1856.
91. FITCH, unpublished letter dated Jan. 18, 1856.
92. Henry G. Langley's 1858 *San Francisco Directory* lists WILLIAM PICKETT as jobber and wholesale groceries and provisions at 61 Front Street.
93. HUSSEY, BOND & HALL. Samuel Colville's *San Francisco Directory* for 1856 lists BOND & HALL, commission merchants, at 59 & 61 Sansome Street, established 1849, as Hussey, Bond & Hall, changed to Bond & Hall, January, 1856.
94. FITCH, unpublished letter dated Jan. 19, 1856.
95. WILLIAM DAVIS MERRY HOWARD was born May 2, 1819, in Boston, Mass. He came to California in 1838 (his granddaughter's account, noted below, says 1839), was active both as a merchant and a public official and died in San Francisco Jan. 19, 1856. Howard Street in San Francisco was named for him. (ANNALS, pp. 779–780; also Gertrude Howard Whitwell, "William Davis Merry Howard," CHSQ, Vol. XXVII [June, 1948], 105–112; [September, 1948], 249–255; and [December, 1948], 319–332.)
96. FITCH, unpublished letter dated Jan. 21, 1856.
97. For example, Stephen E. Ambrose's interesting article: "William T. Sherman: a Reappraisal" in the January, 1967, issue of *American History Illustrated*.
98. JOSÉ YVES LIMANTOUR on Feb. 5, 1853, filed a claim with the United

States Land Commission based on alleged grants by the Mexican Governor, Manuel Micheltorena in 1843. They purported to cover some 600,000 acres of land in California, the Farallon Islands, Alcatraz and Yerba Buena Islands in San Francisco Bay, and various other parcels. Four square leagues of the land covered much of San Francisco itself. The land commission rejected the 600,000-acre grant but confirmed Limantour's claim to the islands and the four square leagues of San Francisco real estate. The United States government appealed the case, and ultimately the United States district court pronounced the alleged grants forgeries, declaring "proofs of fraud are . . . conclusive and irresistible." Limantour was a captain in the French navy who resided and traded in Mexico City in the 1840's. Innumerable property owners in San Francisco paid him considerable sums for quitclaim deeds to their holdings before the fraud was discovered. There is a considerable volume of authorities on this famous case. (BANCAL, Vol. VII, pp. 243–244; ELDREDGE, pp. 569–571. Perhaps the latest and quite exhaustive account may be found in Kenneth M. Johnson, *Limantour vs. the United States* [Los Angeles: Dawson's Book Shop, 1961].)

99. This was possibly JUDGE EDWARD NORTON of the 12th Judicial District Court, who is frequently mentioned in San Francisco litigation of the period. ("Continuation of the Annals of San Francisco," CHSQ, Vol. XV [June, 1936], 183; *Ibid.* [September, 1936], 271 and 274; *Ibid.* [December, 1936], 372; "Continuation of the Annals of San Francisco," compiled by Dorothy H. Huggins, CHSQ, Vol. XVI [December, 1937], 340; *Ibid.*, Vol. XVII [June, 1938], 182.) But there was also a JUDGE MYRON NORTON on the bench at the same time. He had come to California in 1848 as an officer of the New York Volunteers, was a justice of the peace and a member of the constitutional convention in 1849, and was prominent in legal and governmental circles in both San Francisco and Los Angeles. (BANCAL, Vol. IV, p. 775. Also ANNALS, pp. 218–220, 559, and 703. Also "Continuation of the Annals of San Francisco," CHSQ, Vol. XV [December, 1936], 369; *Ibid.*, Vol. XVI [March, 1937], 81; "Bound for the Land of Canaan, Ho! The Diary of Levi Stowell, 1849," with introduction and notes by Marco G. Thorne, CHSQ, Vol. XXVII [September, 1948], 266, n. 93; J. M. Scammell, "Military Units in Southern California, 1853–1862," CHSQ, Vol. XXIX [September, 1950], 245 and 246, n. 19; Dello G. Dayton, "Polished Boot and Bran New Suit: The California Militia in Community Affairs," CHSQ, Vol. XXXVII [December, 1958], 360.)

100. See p. 25 hereof and Note 43 of Part One. Naglee was one of the receivers of Adams & Co. and the Naglee referred to on p. 131 hereof.

101. See p. 70 hereof.

102. FITCH, unpublished letter dated Feb. 4, 1856.

103. John Sherman was born in Lancaster, Ohio, May 10, 1823. He studied law and was admitted to the bar in 1844. In 1854 he was elected to Congress and in 1855 was active in organizing the new

Republican Party. He became a United States senator in 1861 and retained this position until 1877, when he was appointed secretary of the treasury by President Rutherford B. Hayes. In 1881, he returned to the Senate, where he remained until 1897, when he was appointed secretary of state by President William McKinley, a position that he resigned in 1898. He died in Washington, D.C., on Oct. 22, 1900. Senator John Sherman was an early leader in the anti-trust movement, and the Sherman Anti-Trust Act of 1890 bears his name.

104. RICHARD STODDERT EWELL: born in Virginia; Cadet at West Point Military Academy, July 1, 1836; brevetted 2nd Lieutenant, 1st Dragoons, July 1, 1840; 2nd Lieutenant, Nov. 1, 1840; 1st Lieutenant, Sept. 18, 1845; Captain, Aug. 4, 1849; resigned May 7, 1861; Lieutenant General, Confederate States of America, 1861–1865; died, January 25, 1872. (HEITMAN, Vol. I, p. 410.)

105. Unpublished letter dated Mar. 31, 1856, from Henry S. Turner to W. T. Sherman in Sherman Collection, Library of Congress.

106. The reference is to JOHN T. DOYLE of the law firm of Janes, Doyle, Barber and Boyd, attorneys for the closed bank of Adams & Co. and for the receivers thereof. ("Continuation of the Annals of San Francisco," compiled by Dorothy H. Huggins, CHSQ, Vol. XVII [June, 1938], 171 and 172.)

107. FITCH, second unpublished letter dated Feb. 19, 1856.

108. This was JAMES SMILEY, the contractor who built the new customhouse. Lucas, Turner & Co. loaned him $36,000 to use in this construction, taking as collateral two acceptances for $20,000 each of Maj. R. P. Hammond, collector of the port. This loan was involved in Sherman's heroic efforts to raise cash during the run on the bank on February 23, 1855 (see p. 111 hereof). On completion of the building, a dispute arose between Smiley and Hammond as to the accounts, and the contractor sued Lucas, Turner & Co. for the $40,000 covered by these same acceptances but lost his case. (MEMOIRS, Vol. I, p. 116. See also pp. 188–191 hereof.)

109. This was the SACRAMENTO VALLEY RAILROAD, which ran from Sacramento to Folsom; the first railroad in California. See also Note 56 of Part Two.

110. FITCH, unpublished letter dated Mar. 4, 1856.

111. WADSWORTH AND MEISAGAES are listed in Colville's *San Francisco Directory* for 1856–1857 as commission merchants at 65 Clay Street.

112. FITCH, unpublished letter dated Mar. 19, 1856.

113. There are several references to EDWARD STANLY practicing law in San Francisco in the 1850's; one mention is made of his law partnership with William Hayes. He was active in Whig politics and later in the new Republican Party. He was frequently a public speaker and delivered the eulogy at the funeral of Col. Edward D. Baker on Dec. 11, 1861. ("Continuation of the Annals of San Francisco," compiled by Dorothy H. Huggins, CHSQ, Vol. XVI [March, 1937], 81–82; Milton H. Shutes, "Colonel E. D. Baker," CHSQ, Vol.

XVII [December, 1938], 309, 320, and 321; Paul Fatout, "The California Regiment, Colonel Baker and Ball's Bluff," CHSQ, Vol. XXXI [September, 1952], 236.) He was an unsuccessful candidate for the state senate in 1855 and in 1857 was the Republican nominee for governor, receiving 21,040 votes as against 53,122 for the winner, John B. Weller; a third candidate received 19,471. (Peyton Hurt, "The Rise and Fall of the 'Know Nothings' in California," CHSQ, Vol. IX [June, 1930], 113; Milton H. Shutes, "Colonel E. D. Baker," CHSQ, Vol. XVII [December, 1938], 309.) Another authority says that he ran for the United States Senate in 1857. (Theodore H. Hittel, *History of California* [San Francisco: L. J. Stone & Company, 1897], Vol. IV, pp. 202 and 215.) I particularly noted Sherman's statement that the Smiley case was "*referred* to Edward Stanly, the best *reference*, etc." Since I found no evidence that Stanly was actually a judge, I made inquiry of my good friend, William W. Clary, eminent both as an attorney and historian. He informed me that as early as 1851 a California statute authorized a trial court to refer a case to a referee. In researching the question, I found that on Sept. 2, 1855, one F. J. Lippitt, Esq., was appointed referee by the Fourth District Court to report on the priorities of the creditors of Adams & Co. ("Continuation of the Annals of San Francisco," compiled by Dorothy H. Huggins, CHSQ, Vol. XVI [March, 1937], 82.)

114. See p. 111 hereof.

115. For PALMER, COOK & Co., see Note 43 of Part One, Note 4 of Part Three, and also Note 63 of Part Three concerning Jones.

116. The ORLEANS HOTEL on Second Street, Sacramento.

117. JAMES VAN NESS, born in Burlington, Vt., in 1808, son of a governor of that state; mayor of San Francisco, 1855 and 1856; in 1871, state senator from San Luis Obispo and Santa Barbara Counties; died in San Luis Obispo, Dec. 28, 1872. (BANCAL, Vol. VI, p. 767, n. 26.)

118. For details of Smiley suit, see FITCH, unpublished letters dated Mar. 19, Apr. 4, and Apr. 17, 1856; also MEMOIRS, pp. 114–116.

119. FITCH, unpublished letter dated Mar. 20, 1856.

120. See Note 3 of Appendix, "The Page-Bacon Failures . . ." and Note 80 of Part Three.

121. This was the JAMES P. CASEY, who a short time later assassinated James King of William, the murder that triggered formation of the Second Vigilance Committee of 1856 and all the stormy events narrated in Chapter 22 hereof (pp. 203 ff.). In writing his *Memoirs* (Vol. I, p. 119) nearly twenty years later, Sherman's memory enlarged on this incident. He then wrote that he had threatened to have Casey and his press thrown out of the windows, if he did not mend his ways.

122. See Note 28 of Part Two.

123. FITCH, unpublished letter dated Apr. 4, 1856.

124. JOHN NUGENT, editor of the *San Francisco Herald*, was noted for

his extreme views and caustic editorials. He fought several duels as a result of his stormy editorship.

125. The present Humboldt River in Nevada.

126. FITCH, unpublished letter dated Apr. 5, 1856.

127. Major Hammond's predecessor as collector of the port was BEVERLEY C. SANDERS, who served in that capacity in 1852 and 1853. On retiring from that position, he became a partner in the banking firm of Sanders & Brenham, mentioned on pp. 153 ff. hereof.

128. This was COL. JOHN COFFEY HAYS, first sheriff of San Francisco and brother of Major Hammond's wife. See Note 6 of Part Three.

129. JOHANN AUGUSTUS SUTTER, a native of Switzerland, born in 1805, settled in 1839 on a grant obtained from the Mexican government. The fortification and other buildings he erected were called by him Nueva Helvetia but soon became known as Sutter's Fort—today within the city limits of Sacramento. He employed a large staff of Indians, Hawaiians, and Mexicans to cultivate his extensive land holdings. During this development he hired James Marshall to build a sawmill at Coloma, forty miles east of Sutter's Fort. In the course of its construction, on Jan. 24, 1848, Marshall discovered gold dust in the millrace. This event changed the whole course of history, and incidentally disrupted Sutter's dream of an agricultural empire. Hock Farm, mentioned by Sherman, was a valuable holding on the Feather River, which Sutter retained for a time. He eventually lost most of his once princely acreage and died in Washington, D.C., in 1880, in comparative poverty.

130. FITCH, unpublished letter dated Apr. 17, 1856.

131. See Note 45 of Part Three.

132. This was LT. GEORGE H. DERBY, who wrote under the pen name JOHN PHOENIX. See Note 20 of Part Two.

133. The first San Francisco Mint had opened Apr. 3, 1854, on Commercial Street between Montgomery and Kearny Streets. (ANNALS, pp. 525–526.)

134. See Note 24 of Part Three.

135. This was THOMAS EWING, Mrs. Sherman's father: born 1789; United States senator from Ohio, 1831–1837; secretary of the treasury for a few months in 1841; first secretary of the interior, 1849–1850; again a United States senator, 1850–1851; died Oct. 26, 1871.

136. FITCH, unpublished letter dated May 4, 1856.

Notes for Part Four

1. POPULAR, Vol. II, pp. 38 ff.
2. Original letter in possession of MHS.
3. See p. 193 hereof and Note 121 of Part Three.
4. J. Neely Johnson, a native of Southern Indiana, came to California overland in 1849, studying and practicing law in Sacramento, where he became both city attorney and district attorney. In 1855, he was the successful candidate of the Know Nothing party for the governorship. After serving one term as governor of California, he moved to Carson City, Nevada, and eventually became a superior judge in that state. He died in Salt Lake City in August, 1872. (BANCAL, Vol. VI, p. 695, n. 21.)
5. It is difficult to identify these men, although from the context they must have been prominent citizens. It is possible that Beall was Lt. Col. Benjamin Lloyd Beall described in Note 13 of Part Two. Since only Woodworth's surname is given, he may have been one of several men of that name who resided in San Francisco at the time (e.g., Selim E., Frederick A., W. A.). Selim E. Woodworth was prominent as a member and an officer of the Vigilance Committee in 1851, 1852, and 1853. (POPULAR, Vol. I, pp. 210, 218, 247–248, 384 and 394; Vol. II, p. 19.) Frederick A. Woodworth and W. A. Woodworth were also members of the earlier committee. The first named, Selim E. Woodworth, native of New York, born in 1815, became a midshipman in the United States navy and arrived in San Francisco in 1846 or 1847. He was elected to the state senate from Monterey in 1849. He died in 1871. Frederick A. Woodworth was his brother; they were sons of the poet, Samuel Woodworth, author of "The Old Oaken Bucket." (ELDREDGE, Vol. II, p. 707.)
6. Col. Joseph R. West came to California in July, 1849. He had been a United States senator from Louisiana. In 1853 he was an assistant alderman of San Francisco. (POPULAR, Vol. II, pp. 163 and 390; also ANNALS, pp. 461 and 823.) It is difficult to identify the Major Johnson mentioned. There were several of that name in San Fran-

cisco at the time. He could have been an officer of one of the private military companies.

7. For JUDGE MYRON NORTON, see Note 99 of Part Three. In 1851, when a Vigilance Committee had been created because of outrages perpetrated by the Hounds, or Regulators, Norton was appointed to defend some of the accused. At the time of King's assassination, Norton was serving as a district judge in San Francisco. King in one of his editorials expressed confidence in Judge Norton's integrity. He was a candidate for the supreme court in 1855 and 1865. He died between 1867 and 1871. (PIONEER, Vol. IV, p. 755; also ANNALS, pp. 220, 222, 229, and 559; also POPULAR, Vol. I, p. 100; Vol. II, p. 31; also BANCAL, Vol. VI, pp. 279 and 295; Vol. VII, p. 454.)

   JAMES DABNEY THORNTON was active in the group of citizens that tried to serve as a moderating influence between the Vigilance Committee and the Law and Order Party. In this capacity, he was part of the delegation that waited on Gov. J. Neely Johnson at Benicia in June, 1856. He was elected a judge of the supreme court of California in 1880 and served as such for a number of years. (POPULAR, Vol. II, pp. 290, 307 and 405; also BANCAL, Vol. VII, pp. 409–735.)

   A. C. PEACHY and FREDERICK BILLINGS were members of the law firm of Halleck, Peachy, Billings and Parke, that owned the Montgomery Block. HALL MCALISTER (usually spelled McAllister) was born in Georgia in 1826, graduated from Yale, and arrived in California on the *Panama* on June 4, 1849. General Bennett Riley, military governor, appointed him attorney for the San Francisco District in September, 1849. He took an active part as counsel for both prosecution and defense in the movement to cleanse the city of the lawless actions of the Hounds. McAllister Street in San Francisco is named for him. (ELDREDGE, Vol. II, pp. 458, 599, 600, and 737; also ANNALS, pp. 318, 558, 559, and 703.) BALDWIN may have been the attorney mentioned on p. 190 hereof as being associated with Samuel M. Bowman in the defense of the suit brought against Lucas, Turner & Co. by Smiley. This Baldwin is also mentioned on p. 96 hereof, but I have not found any reference to his full name. There was also a Joseph G. Baldwin, appointed a justice of the supreme court of California in 1857. (BANCAL, Vol. VII, p. 221.) Sherman's reference in the letter may have been to this man; Bowman's associate and the future supreme court justice may have been the same person.

8. CORNELIUS K. GARRISON; see Note 2 of Part Two.

9. WILLIAM T. COLEMAN, see Notes 41 and 79 of Part Three; ARRINGTON BROTHERS, see Note 79 of Part Three. JAMES P. FLINT was a well-known merchant of Boston who came to California in October, 1849, and soon founded the San Francisco firm of Flint, Peabody & Co., commission merchants. He died Mar. 8, 1873. ("Marginalia," CHSQ, Vol. XXXIII [December, 1954], 381.)

10. For JOHN PARROTT, see Note 1 of Part Three; for WILLIAM C. RALSTON, see Note 3 of Appendix, "The Page-Bacon Failures . . ." and Note 80 of Part Three. For DREXEL, SATHER & CHURCH, see Note 33 of Part Two.
11. ANNALS, p. 699, lists an H. C. BEALS as one of the trustees of a chapel at Sacramento and Stockton Streets, dedicated June 4, 1854, for the Chinese residents of the city. I have not found any other mention of the name.
12. MIERS F. TRUETT was one of William T. Coleman's principal aides during the activities of the 1856 Vigilance Committee and was a member of its executive committee. In the committee's trials of both Charles Cora and Judge David Terry, he served as counsel for the defendants. In the winter of 1856–1857, while traveling in the East, he was several times arrested and also was sued at the instigation of some of the victims of the Vigilance Committee. (POPULAR, Vol. II, pp. 113, 178, 188–191, 226, 230–232, 382, 436, 473–474, 611, and 612–616.)
13. For CASTLE, see Note 68 of Part Three.
14. ABEL GUY is listed in Henry G. Langley's *San Francisco Directory* of 1862 as a commission merchant and banker at 411 Washington Street. (André Chavanne, "The Burning of the Golden Gate in July 1862," CHSQ, Vol. XIX [March, 1940], 42, n. 4.) He owned San Francisco real estate, as well as mining interests in the vicinity of Grass Valley. He committed suicide in Paris, France, in 1891.
15. See Anna McAllister, *Ellen Ewing, Wife of General Sherman* (New York: Benziger Brothers, Inc., 1936), pp. 145–150.
16. For THOMAS EWING, see Note 135 of Part Three.
17. MEMOIRS, Vol. I, pp. 118–132.
18. LONE MOUNTAIN CEMETERY was formally dedicated May 30, 1854, on a 160-acre tract. (ANNALS, p. 239.) It eventually was divided into several cemeteries: Laurel Hill, Calvary, Odd Fellows, and Masonic. They extended from California to Geary Streets, running west several blocks from Presidio Avenue. Over a number of years in the forepart of this century, all tombs and monuments were razed and the bodies removed for reburial in San Mateo County, the entire area becoming part of the residential developments around it.
19. DAVID S. TERRY was born in Kentucky, Mar. 8, 1823, moved to Texas in early youth, was a Texas Ranger, and served in the Mexican War. He also studied law and was admitted to the bar in Texas. In 1849, he came to California. After brief mining experience in Calaveras County, he practiced law in Stockton. Originally a Democrat, he joined the Know Nothing Party in or before 1855. It nominated him for judge of the supreme court in 1855 and he was elected. In 1859, he killed Sen. David C. Broderick in the most famous duel in the history of California. This caused his resignation from the bench; and he resumed the practice of law, which he followed for the balance of his life, except for service as a Confederate officer in Texas during the Civil War. In the 1880's, he

became embroiled with Judge Stephen J. Field of the United States Supreme Court. At Lathrop, Calif., on Aug. 14, 1889, a bodyguard of Justice Field shot and killed Terry because he feared Terry was about to assault Field. (A. Russell Buchanan, *David S. Terry of California, Dueling Judge* [San Marino, Calif.: The Huntington Library, 1956].)

20. VOLNEY E. HOWARD was born in Maine in 1809, became a lawyer, and went to Mississippi, where he was elected to the United States House of Representatives. He came to California in 1853. (BANCAL, Vol. VII, pp. 374–375, n. 5; for his activities during Vigilance Committee period, see POPULAR, Vol. II, pp. 306–310, 393–396, 404, and 456–465.)
21. JOHN L. DURKEE was a San Francisco policeman at the time Casey shot James King of William. Two weeks later, he resigned from the force, joined the committee's police, and shortly became its deputy director. Soon after the Vigilance Committee disbanded, he was made city fire marshal. Bancroft eulogized his energy and comprehension and credited the man with saving Bancroft's own valuable library from a dangerous fire. Durkee stood trial on the piracy charge but the jury found him not guilty. (POPULAR, Vol. II, pp. 282, 373–376, and 501–506.)
22. JOHN G. PHILLIPS, JAMES R. MALONEY and JAMES MCNAB (or McNabb). Maloney had chartered the *Julia* to transport the munitions being sent to General Howard by order of the governor. With him were J. G. Phillips and James McNab. In July, 1856, Maloney, by order of the Vigilance Committee, departed for Panama on the *John L. Stephens*. He later instigated actions, both criminal and civil, in New York against William T. Coleman and other members of the Vigilance Committee who chanced to be in New York. While these proceedings were pending, Maloney died. (POPULAR, Vol. II, pp. 375–376, 385, 400–407, 591, 607, and 612–615.)
23. STERLING A. HOPKINS, native of Maine, by occupation an artesian well-borer, aged about thirty-three. He was an active member of the Vigilance Committee and was described by Bancroft as "a man of great pertinacity, good at obeying orders" and courageous. He served as executioner of Casey and Cora. (POPULAR, Vol. II, pp. 235–236, 376–379, 398–399, 428–429, and 569.)
24. DR. RICHARD PORTER ASHE was a Texan. He and Judge Terry had been fellow privates in Bellow's company of mounted Texas Rangers in 1846. The two men remained close friends until Terry's death. Ashe was sheriff of San Joaquin County from 1850 to 1853. He then went to San Francisco to become United States naval agent. His office was over Palmer, Cook & Co.'s bank at the northeast corner of Kearny and Washington Streets. Politically, Ashe was a leader in the "Chivalry" or Southern wing of the Democratic Party. Ashe was captain of Company A of the California militia and in command of its armory. After he and Terry were arrested by the Vigilance Committee, Commander Boutwell of the United States

navy in a letter urged the committee to release Ashe as a federal official. I have found no explanation for his title of "Doctor." (POPULAR, Vol. II, pp. 377, 378, 383–385, 405, 422, and 495; also Buchanan, *Terry, Dueling Judge, op. cit.*, pp. 11 n, 13, 14, 28 n, 35–40, 47, 57, 59, 154, and 210.)

25. SOLOMON HEYDENFELT was the first elected judge to succeed S. C. Hastings when the latter's term expired in 1852. He served until 1857, when he resigned. Hugh C. Murray, who had been appointed to fill a vacancy in 1851, then elected in 1852, claimed that by seniority he was chief justice. Heydenfelt, whose election had occurred in 1851, was entitled to the place, but to avoid a quarrel, yielded his right to the post. (BANCAL, Vol. VII, pp. 220–221.)
26. The reference here is to the pending suit of Lucas, Turner & Co. against the City of San Francisco, growing out of the defaulted city warrants for the Powell Street paving contract, described in pp. 69 ff. hereof.
27. JUDGE HUGH C. MURRAY, mentioned in Note 25 above. At the general election of 1852, he had been chosen to fill the unexpired term of Nathaniel Bennett. In 1855, he was reelected to a full term but died before his term expired. Murray was born in St. Louis of Scottish ancestry, served under General Winfield Scott in the Mexican War, emerging from it a lieutenant. He came to California in 1849. (BANCAL, Vol. VII, pp. 220, 221, and 224.)
28. This was Sherman's involved way of saying that Judge Heydenfelt was a strong Southern Democrat and follower of Sen. John C. Calhoun of South Carolina.
29. FITCH, letter dated July 2, 1856 (partially published by *Century Magazine* in 1891, as explained in text).
30. SEN. JOHN SHERMAN, see Note 103 of Part Three.
31. FRANKLIN PIERCE (1804–1869), fourteenth president of the United States, 1853–1857.
32. CHARLES POMROY STONE, see Note 50 of Part Two.
33. FITCH, unpublished letter dated July 3, 1856.
34. I am not sure I understand this expletive. It is plain from the context that Sherman used it because of his opposition to the Vigilance Committee. Vigilantism in California in 1856 was not primarily a partisan movement, nor did it draw a line between pro- and anti-slavery forces. The Republican Party, organized only in 1854, was started in opposition to the extension of slavery. Its first national convention, held on June 17, 1856, nominated John C. Frémont and William Dayton for President and Vice-President. Sherman never admired Frémont, and in an earlier chapter we read of his opposition to the Abolitionists. Of nearly equal importance to the Republicans' opposition to slavery at that first convention, was their endorsement of the bill to construct the Pacific railroad. Sherman must have approved of this action. In 1856, "red" did not possess the connotation we attach to it today. In one of his letters about the Vigilance Committee, Sherman likened it to the excesses

of the French Revolution. I am inclined to believe that he used "Red Republican" in that sense.

35. EDWARD B. BOUTWELL: passed midshipman, Mar. 3, 1819; Lieutenant, May 15, 1828; Commander, June 2, 1860; dismissed, July 31, 1861. (CALLAHAN, p. 68.)
36. See p. 193 hereof.
37. Sherman's bracketing of Drexel and Garrison did not mean that this was the name of a new banking firm, merely that the two firms of Drexel, Sather & Church and Garrison, Morgan, Fretz and Ralston now had their respective banking houses on Battery Street. See Note 33 of Part Two for the former, and Note 80 of Part Three for the latter.
38. FITCH, unpublished letter dated Aug. 18, 1856.
39. Sherman's letter is not very legible here—probably, debtor is Kuhtman & Co., which appears in Charles P. Kimball's *San Francisco Directory* for 1850 as general commission merchants, Montgomery Street between California and Pine Streets.
40. GEN. ETHAN ALLEN HITCHCOCK; see Note 31 of Part One.
41. JUDGE MATTHEW HALL MCALLISTER was born in Savannah, Georgia, in 1800. He attended Princeton College, then practiced law in his native city for twenty-nine years. He was United States attorney for southern district of Georgia. He served as the first and only judge of the United States Circuit Court at San Francisco, resigning in 1862, three years before his death in San Francisco in 1865. His son Hall McAllister was an eminent lawyer of pioneer San Francisco. (BANCAL, Vol. VII, p. 237.)
42. FITCH, unpublished letter dated Sept. 4, 1856.
43. *The Daily Sun* was started May 19, 1853. In 1854, R. B. Quayle and J. C. Cremony were editors. Later, J. C. Lawrence bought the paper. Subsequently, A. S. Gould and W. Bausman became its proprietors. *The Daily Sun* originally was independent in politics, but in 1855 it became the organ of the Democratic Party. When James King of William was assassinated, *The Sun* wavered, then came out against the Vigilance Committee—"with all the venom, malignancy and abuse that the wrath of man could devise." During the campaign of 1856, it was edited by C. H. Hempstead. In 1857, J. C. Cremony was again editor. In the fall of same year, the *Sun* died. (Edward C. Kemble, *A History of California Newspapers, 1846–1858*, reprinted from *Supplement to Sacramento Union*, Dec. 25, 1858, edited by Helen Harding Bretnor [Los Gatos, Calif.: Talisman Press, 1962], p. 113.)

    The Sept. 6, 1856, issue of the *Daily Evening Bulletin* reported the impaneling of the grand jury by the Court of Sessions and the swearing in of William T. Sherman as its foreman. The newspaper commented that there was considerable curiosity as to what action the grand jury might take concerning an investigation of the affairs of the Vigilance Committee. However, no further mention of the grand jury's activities appeared until the issue of Sept. 26, which reported several indictments not related to the Vigilance Committee or to our narrative. The *Daily Evening Bulletin* of Sept. 30 (p. 3) reported the indictment of Francis A. Bonnard, editor of the *Sun,* for libel against Augustus H. Heslep. Sherman's statement that the editor and printer of the *Sunday Times* was indicted "for numerous offenses" is at variance with the report in the *Daily Evening Bulletin* just mentioned. Here the name of the paper is given as the *Sunday Varieties,* the indicted proprietors being James W. Walsh, Jacob C. Young, and Joseph H. Josselyn for libel against Dr. Czapkay (?), apparently two separate instances of libel.

44. *The Weekly Sunday Times* was established by James P. Casey on Dec. 24, 1855. Nominally, Casey was editor and proprietor, but J. C. Cremony was actual editor. Upon Casey's execution, *The Times* died. (Kemble, *History of California Newspapers, op. cit.,* p. 123.) See Note 43 above for Sherman's confusion of the names *Sunday Times* and *Sunday Varieties.*

45. SISTERS OF CHARITY. The *Alta California,* Apr. 3, 1851, noted that the French Sisters of Charity were working in San Francisco. (Julia Cooley Altrocchi, "Paradox Town, San Francisco in 1851," CHSQ, Vol. XXVIII [March, 1949], 33.) There were apparently two Sisterhoods ministering to the indigent sick. The Board of Supervisors of San Francisco had also appropriated funds for the same purpose, to the SISTERS OF MERCY. It seems likely that the Sisters of Charity were the ones attacked by the *Bulletin.* ("Continuation of the Annals of San Francisco," compiled by Dorothy H. Huggins, CHSQ, Vol. XVI [June, 1937], 183.)

46. The Board of Supervisors on May 22, 1855, ordered the purchase, for $24,000, of a brick building on Greenwich Street near Jones Street. This must have been the COUNTY HOSPITAL. ("Continuation of the Annals of San Francisco," compiled by Dorothy H. Huggins, CHSQ, Vol. XV [September, 1936], 280; *Ibid.,* Vol. XVI [September, 1937], 283; *Ibid.,* Vol. XVI [December, 1937], 337.)

47. JAMES KING OF WILLIAM started the *Daily Evening Bulletin* on Oct. 8, 1855, and was its editor until his death on May 20, 1856. Business manager was Christian O. Gerberding, apparently a half owner from the beginning. King's interest passed to his brother, Thomas Sim King (see Note 48, following). He became editor, the *Bulletin* prospered. On Jan. 17, 1859, Thomas King sold his half interest to Gerberding, who soon made James W. Simonton editor. Three months later, George Kenyon Fitch, a well-known journalist, purchased a quarter interest. Gerberding sold out to Fitch and Simonton in January, 1861. In January, 1895, Fremont Older purchased the paper at an auction sale. (John Denton Carter, "George Kenyon Fitch, Pioneer California Journalist," CHSQ, Vol. XX [December, 1941], 336 and 337; see also Kemble, *History of California Newspapers, op. cit.,* pp. 115–116.)

48. THOMAS SIM KING was born in the District of Columbia, Dec. 29, 1823. He served in the Mexican War and arrived in California in

March, 1853. Sherman's reference to "my clerk" probably refers to T. S. King's service in the army under Sherman. King's biographer says King traveled from Fort Leavenworth to Kansas City in Sherman's company. Sherman was stationed in St. Louis from September, 1850, to September, 1852, and in his *Memoirs* mentions a trip he made to Fort Leavenworth in 1851. King may well have been Sherman's clerk on this trip because in his editorial in the *Evening Bulletin* on June 4, 1856, he wrote "some five years since we were in the employ of General Sherman at St. Louis and have always entertained the most friendly feelings towards him." Through his brother's influence, King secured a lucrative clerkship in the San Francisco customhouse. Adams & Co.'s bank failure in February, 1855, deprived James King of William of his position and left him and his large family without means of subsistence. Thomas King supported them for some six months. Then he gave his brother part of the money needed to start the *Daily Evening Bulletin*, in partnership with C. O. Gerberding. When James King of William was assassinated, Thomas King became a most vigorous supporter of the Vigilance Committee in the seizure and execution of his brother's murderer. On May 28, 1856, he became editor of the *Bulletin* and was soon a real force in the community—an extremist in his opposition to the Law and Order Party. He denounced the executive committee of the Vigilantes when he thought them unduly moderate in their reforms. However, he built his newspaper into a prosperous enterprise. Selling his interest in the *Bulletin* to his partner, Gerberding, on Jan. 17, 1859, he left California and never returned. After the Civil War, he settled in Buffalo, New York, where he was a police judge for many years. He died in Buffalo Apr. 10, 1911. (John Denton Carter, "Thomas Sim King, Vigilante Editor," CHSQ, Vol. XXI [March, 1942], 23–38 [portrait of King opposite p. 23]. In the opinion of Mr. Carter and some others, Hubert Howe Bancroft, most biased in favor of the Vigilance Committee of 1856, deals harshly with T. S. King. [POPULAR, Vol. II, pp. 36 and 59.])

49. William T. Sherman was definitely not a Catholic—his wife was a devout one. He occasionally joked with her about it, but he always respected his wife's faith and treated priests and nuns with great consideration. His children were reared as Catholics. At the time of General Sherman's death, the press reported that a priest was present and administered extreme unction. (LEWIS, p. 108 for the anecdote, pp. 650–651 for the deathbed rites.)

50. The Abell of this firm was probably ALEX G. ABELL listed in Samuel Colville's *San Francisco Directory* of 1856–1857 as "commissioner of immigrants" and grand secretary of Grand Lodge F. & A. M. of California, office southeast corner Washington and Battery Streets. Stevens was probably the WILLIAM H. STEVENS listed in James M. Parker's *San Francisco Directory* for 1852 as commission merchant at 110 Battery Street.

51. JOHN PARROTT, see Note 1 of Part Three. SAMUEL BRANNAN was one of the best-known, most picturesque figures of pioneer San Francisco. He was born in Saco, Maine, on Mar. 2, 1819, moved to Ohio in his youth and learned the printer's trade. In 1842, he became a zealous Mormon. He led a colony of 238 fellow parishioners who sailed for California on the ship *Brooklyn* in 1846, bringing with them his printing press, stock of paper, flour-mill machinery, and agricultural implements. The *Brooklyn* arrived in San Francisco July 31, 1846, and the colony prepared to receive the main Mormon exodus. Meanwhile, Brannan started the *California Star,* the second newspaper to be published in California.

When Brigham Young decided not to come to the Coast but settled his followers in Utah, Brannan was greatly disappointed. He had become a preacher, a politician and a merchant, active in San Francisco, Sacramento, Mormon Island, and Coloma. Later he abandoned the Mormon faith. He continued to amass wealth in a variety of enterprises and was soon rated the richest man in the new state. He supported both the Vigilante movements actively. Becoming a heavy drinker in his later years, he lived a more and more irregular life. For his zealous support of the native Mexicans struggling against the Emperor Maximilian, he was rewarded with a large grant of lands in the state of Sonora, which he planned to colonize. The scheme did not thrive—his old-time energy was gone. When he died in Escondido, Mexico, May 5, 1889, nearly all his vast wealth had disappeared. (See ELDREDGE for a fair summary of his colorful life [Vol. II, pp. 709–711]. Brannan's name appears frequently in Bancroft's *History of California* and occasionally in his *Popular Tribunals.* Bancroft dealt harshly with this man's complex and baffling personality, overstressed its more unfavorable sides. See also ANNALS, pp. 748–753 [Brannan's portrait on p. 748].)

52. HENRY MORRIS NAGLEE. See p. 130 hereof for earlier mention of this difficulty. Naglee was born in Texas in 1815 (Bancroft gives Texas, but Heitman states Pennsylvania). Entered United States Military Academy as Cadet, July 1, 1830; Brevet 2nd Lieutenant, 5th Infantry, July 1, 1835; resigned Dec. 31, 1835; Captain, 1st New York Infantry, Aug. 15, 1846; honorably mustered out, Oct. 26, 1848; Lieutenant Colonel, 16th U.S. Infantry, May 14, 1861; resigned Jan. 10, 1862; Brigadier General of Volunteers, Feb. 4, 1862; honorably mustered out Apr. 4, 1864. (HEITMAN, Vol. I, p. 740.) While serving in Baja California during the Mexican War, Captain Naglee was severely censured by his commanding officer for causing two prisoners to be shot. Colonel Mason ordered Naglee's arrest, reported the facts to the Adjutant General for action by the President. The end of War and the mustering out of his regiment prevented further proceedings. (ELDREDGE, Vol. II, pp. 480, 553–554.)

The first military unit created in California under American rule was the 1st California Guard. Naglee was commissioned captain of same by Gen. Bennett Riley, military governor of California in 1849, and was also a partner of the banking firm Naglee and Sinton, established in 1849. He was appointed receiver of the defunct banking and express firm, Adams & Co., as successor to A. A. Cohen, the original receiver; litigation between the two receivers and others was extended and vexatious. Naglee purchased large tracts around San Jose in 1852 and after his Civil War service made his home there. He became an extensive vineyardist and a manufacturer of brandy. William T. Sherman employed unusually harsh terms about Naglee, as is evident both here and on p. 131. Since Sherman was Colonel Mason's adjutant general at the time of Naglee's arrest, perhaps the enmity of the two men had its origin in that affair. Naglee died Mar. 5, 1886 (according to Heitman; Eldredge gives year of death as 1885).

53. See p. 26 hereof where Brown & Keyser were referred to as "St. Louis contractors" who built the building at Montgomery and Jackson Streets for Lucas, Turner & Co.
54. FITCH, unpublished letter dated Oct. 5, 1856.
55. See p. 71 hereof for story of acquisition of the Meiggs property.
56. The ORIENTAL HOTEL was built in 1851 at the intersection of Bush, Battery, and Market Streets. For the next several years it was the center for many formal banquets and receptions. It is pictured on p. 639 of ANNALS.
57. The "overcheck game," or what we today call overdrafts, refers to a series of incidents in November, 1855, which are detailed in Chapter 18 (pp. 161 ff.).
58. DAVID OLCOTT SHATTUCK, was born in Colchester, Conn., on March 21, 1800. He moved to the South in 1820, taught school, and was a Methodist preacher. In 1827, he married Elizabeth Ann Saunders; they had seven sons and three daughters. He practiced law in Tennessee and in Mississippi. He was elected district judge in 1837; and in Mississippi he was unsuccessful candidate for governor. He taught law, became president of a college, then resigned in 1849 to go to California, arriving in San Francisco in April, 1850. He was soon elected one of the first three superior judges in San Francisco, resigned, but was re-elected on the ticket of the Know Nothing Party in 1854. He resigned again in 1857. During the disorders of 1851, Shattuck was appointed as one of counsel to defend numerous prisoners charged with various crimes. Shattuck was a moderate in the contentions of the Vigilance Committee of 1856 with the Law and Order Party. In 1862, he and his family moved to Sonoma County, where he had purchased an estate in 1850. Mrs. Shattuck died in 1875, the Judge in 1892. (*History of Sonoma County* [San Francisco: Alley, Bowen & Company, 1880], p. 682; portrait of Judge Shattuck opposite p. 64. Also ANNALS, pp. 314–318 and 701. Also Peyton Hurt, "The Rise and Fall of the 'Know Nothings' in California," CHSQ, Vol. IX [March, 1930], 29; "Continuation of the Annals of San Francisco," compiled by Dorothy H. Huggins,

CHSQ, Vol. XVI [September, 1937], 284. Also POPULAR, Vol. II, pp. 339 and 430. Also index cards in Library of CHS. Date of Judge Shattuck's death was furnished by his great-granddaughter, Mrs. Janet Dakan of Sonoma, Calif.)

59. See Notes 19, 25, and 27 of Part Four.
60. Samuel Millard Bowman; see Note 5 of Part Two.
61. Referring to the great American statesman Henry Clay (1777–1852) of Kentucky and to his speeches in support of the compromise of 1850, generally credited with having postponed the Civil War for a decade.
62. Reference is to a heavy influx of German immigrants to St. Louis, following the revolutionary year 1848 in Europe. The failure of various liberal uprisings caused a great exodus to the United States of freedom-loving Germans, many of whom settled in St. Louis. Because of bitter experiences in the Old World, to a man they were devoted to Free Soil and Abolitionist principles and formed a powerful pro-Union bloc in St. Louis during the stormy years ahead.
63. Sherman referred here to the election of Republican Francis Preston Blair, Jr., (1821–1875) as Congressman from Missouri.
64. Thomas Ewing Sherman. His father later was greatly disappointed when his son decided to become a Jesuit; he hoped Thomas would follow a career in the law or in engineering.
65. FITCH, unpublished letter dated Oct. 19, 1856.
66. James Allen Hardie, see Note 53 of Part One.
67. For Sherman's differences with General Wool, see p. 221 hereof.
68. HARDIE, unpublished letter from William T. Sherman, dated Oct. 22, 1856.
69. Langton & Co., the banking and express firm described on pp. 231 ff.
70. In Peter J. Delay's *History of Yuba and Sutter Counties* (Los Angeles: Historic Record Company, 1924), p. 155, Macy & Lowe (*sic*) & Company appear as "bankers" in a list of early business firms in Marysville, but no date is given as to its start. Frederick F. Low, born in 1828 in Maine, came to San Francisco and Sacramento in 1849. After working as a miner, in 1850 he went with two brothers to Marysville and established Low Bros. Company which took over local business of Adams & Co. when it failed. (CROSS, Vol. I, p. 212, gives 1855 as date of Frederick Low's arrival in Marysville.) After Macy's retirement, the firm became Low Brothers & Company and continued until 1861 when it became part of Rideout & Smith Bank. Low moved to San Francisco and served one term as congressman-at-large from California. He was governor of California from 1863 to 1867 and later served as United States minister to China from 1869 to 1873. From 1874 to 1892, he was manager of the Anglo California Bank in San Francisco. He died there on July 21, 1894. (H. Brett Melendy and Benjamin F. Gilbert, *Governors of California* [Georgetown, Calif.: Talisman Press, 1965], p. 129; also see BANCAL, Vol. VII. p. 306.)

In some of the earlier published histories (e.g., Delay, cited above) Low's name, as well as the banking firm's, is spelled "Lowe." BANCAL as well as CROSS give it as "Low," as does Andrew F. Rolle in *California, A History* (New York: Thomas Y. Crowell Company, 1963), pp. 321 and 411. The carefully edited *Index* to CHSQ Vols. I–XL at p. 255 carries many listings of Governor Low's name under "Low." Sherman in his letters to Turner spelled it "Low."

71. For Banker Rhodes of Sacramento, see pp. 39 and 112 hereof; also CROSS, Vol. I, pp. 77 and 165.
72. For Governor Johnson's message to the legislature on this subject, see POPULAR Vol. II, pp. 577–581.
73. E. P. FLINT was a member of the merchandise firm of Flint, Peabody & Co. and a member of the executive committee of the 1856 Vigilance Committee. (POPULAR, Vol. II, pp. 80 and 113; see also Note 9 of Part Four, where the name is given as *James* P. Flint, as given in "Marginalia," CHSQ, Vol. XXXIII [December, 1954], 381. Since the same firm of merchants is mentioned by both authorities, possibly there was more than one Flint in the firm.) CLANCEY J. DEMPSTER, a native of New York, arrived in California in 1849. He too was a member of the executive committee of the Vigilance Committee and was the first named of the several vice-presidents listed by Bancroft (POPULAR, Vol. II, p. 113); highly eulogized by Bancroft (*Ibid.*, pp. 121–125).
74. THOMAS W. FREELON was elected county judge in San Francisco, Sept. 7, 1853. (ANNALS, p. 461.)
75. The text of GOVERNOR JOHNSON'S PROCLAMATION of Nov. 3, 1856, is given in POPULAR, Vol. II, p. 577.
76. The reference is to CAPT. CHARLES POMROY STONE, several times mentioned in earlier chapters, especially in Note 50 of Part Two.
77. The reference is probably to ROBERT EMMET CLARY: native of Massachusetts; Cadet at United States Military Academy, class of 1823; brevetted 2nd Lieutenant, Infantry, July 1, 1828; 1st Lieutenant, Apr. 1, 1836; Captain, Apr. 3, 1839; Major and quartermaster, May 17, 1861; Colonel and additional aide de camp, July 5, 1862; honorably mustered out of volunteer service, May 31, 1866; died, Jan. 19, 1890 (HEITMAN, Vol. I, p. 308.)
78. From the context, this man was almost certainly a merchant; he may have been R. MCKEE, who appears in a list of merchants at the time of the Vigilante excitement, in POPULAR, Vol. II, p. 80.
79. FITCH, unpublished letter dated Nov. 4, 1856.
80. FITCH, unpublished postscript dated Nov. 5, 1856.
81. FITCH, unpublished letter dated Nov. 19, 1856.
82. FITCH, unpublished letter dated Nov. 20, 1856.
83. HARDIE, unpublished letter from W. T. Sherman dated Nov. 28, 1856.
84. The reference is to the HONORABLE THOMAS EWING, Mrs. Sherman's father, mentioned in Note 135 of Part Three.

85. FITCH, unpublished letter dated Dec. 4, 1856.
86. For the failure of PAGE, BACON & Co., see pp. 107 ff. hereof.
87. For FRANK W. PAGE, see Appendix, "The Page-Bacon Failures . . ." particularly Note 1 thereof.
88. For JOHN PARROTT, see Note 1 of Part Three.
89. FITCH, unpublished letter dated Dec. 5, 1856.
90. BANCAL, Vol. VI, pp. 619–620; also letter, Alex D. Steinkamp, deputy state treasurer, to Wallace H. Meyer, vice-president, Crocker-Citizens National Bank, dated Aug. 17, 1967.
91. For details of the POWELL STREET WARRANTS, see pp. 69, 176, 187, and 235 hereof.
92. For TALLANT & WILDE, see Note 66 of Part Three.
93. For the LIMANTOUR CLAIM, see Note 98 of Part Three.
94. For BOLTON AND BARRON CLAIM, see "Continuation of the Annals of San Francisco," compiled by Dorothy H. Huggins, CHSQ, Vol. XV (December, 1936), 364; also ELDREDGE, Vol. II, p. 571. This claim, sometimes known as the SANTILLAN CLAIM (the name of the priest who allegedly received the original Mexican patent) was approved by the United States Land Commission in 1855. On an appeal by the government, the Supreme Court in 1860 rejected it as based on fraud. At that time, the claim was owned by an eastern association, which continued, as late as 1886, to seek some compensation from Congress. (BANCAL, Vol. VI, p. 561; also Elliott Evans, ed., "Some Letters of William Jewett, California Artist," CHSQ, Vol. XXIII [September, 1944], 229 and 245.)
95. FITCH, unpublished letter dated Dec. 18, 1856.
96. HARDIE, unpublished letter dated Dec. 27, 1856, W. T. Sherman to Lt. James Allen Hardie.
97. HARDIE, unpublished letter dated Dec. 30, 1856, W. T. Sherman to Lt. James Allen Hardie.

Notes for Part Five

1. For Sherman's relations with Guthrie during the Civil War, see LEWIS, pp. 206–207, 352, 396–398, and 410–411; also MEMOIRS, Vol. I, pp. 197–198, 200–202, and 213.
2. WILLIAM H. DOW appears in A. W. Morgan & Company's *San Francisco Directory* for 1852—groceries and provisions at 41 Battery Street. ANNALS, p. 697, mentions him as trustee of Howard Street Presbyterian Church in February, 1851. He was elected assistant alderman in June, 1855. (Peyton Hurt, "The Rise and Fall of the 'Know Nothings' in California," CHSQ, Vol. IX [June, 1930], 109; "Continuation of the Annals of San Francisco," compiled by Dorothy H. Huggins, CHSQ, Vol. XV [September, 1936], 280; *Ibid.* [December, 1936], 364.)
3. I have been unable to locate this name in the directories of the period.
4. COOK, FOLGER & COMPANY appears in LeCount & Strong's *1854 Directory*—oil works at 114 Broadway near Dupont.
5. I have been unable to locate this name in the directories of the period. Both in this case and the one referred to in Note 3 above, Sherman's penmanship may have been at fault.
6. FITCH, unpublished letter dated Jan. 3, 1857.
7. FITCH, unpublished letter dated Jan. 5, 1857.
8. SENATOR DAVID C. BRODERICK; see Note 44 of Part One.
9. Undoubtedly this was DR. ALEXANDER J. BOWIE; see Note 19 of Part Three.
10. SENATOR WILLIAM MCKENDREE GWIN, born Oct. 9, 1805, in Tennessee, was educated both in medicine and the law and was admitted to the bar. He served as congressman-at-large for state of Mississippi. A few hours after his arrival in San Francisco on June 4, 1849, he was appointed one of two judges to assist Alcalde Leavenworth in trying numerous prisoners who had been arrested because of the disorders of the Hounds, or Regulators. He was a member of San Francisco's delegation to the 1849 constitutional convention in

Monterey. In December, 1849, he was elected one of the first two United States senators from California, to serve as soon as the state was admitted. Gwin drew the long term of six years, Frémont the short term. Gwin was reelected and served a second term. He died in New York, Sept. 3, 1885. (See William Henry Ellison, ed., "Memoirs of Hon. William M. Gwin," CHSQ, Vol. XIX [March, 1940], 1–26; *Ibid.* [June, 1940], 157–184; *Ibid.* [September, 1940], 256–277; *Ibid.* [December, 1940], 344–367 for especial reference to his early career and senatorial service; also ANNALS, pp. 137, 229, 237, 558, 559, and 790–793; also ELDREDGE, pp. 458, 487, and 600; also *Dictionary of American Biography*, 1932 edition, Vol. 8, pp. 64–65.)

11. There were two Gallagher brothers, both priests in San Francisco at this time. Father Hugh (1815–1882) and Father Joseph (1821–1887). The (California) *Senate Journal* for Jan. 6, 1857, reported the election of "Rev. Mr. Gallagher [as Chaplain] on the second roll call." On p. 92 of the *Senate Journal* of 1857 is letter of Joseph A. Gallagher, Assistant Pastor of St. Mary's Cathedral, San Francisco, expressing regret that he is unable to accept his election as Chaplain. (Letter of W. N. Davis, Jr., chief of archives, state of California, dated Sept. 14, 1967, to the author.) According to another authority, Rev. Hugh Gallagher was Pastor of St. Mary's Cathedral during this period. (Thomas Denis McSweeney, *Cathedral on California Street* [Fresno, Calif.: Academy of California Church History, 1952] pp. 15, 21, and 22.) According to H. H. Bancroft (POPULAR, Vol. II, p. 235), "Father Gallagher and Bishop Alemany" attended Cora and Casey immediately prior to their execution by the Vigilance Committee. Since the two brothers were pastor and assistant pastor of the Cathedral, it is not certain which one is meant. It is equally uncertain which priest baptized Sherman's son, Thomas Ewing, born in San Francisco. In the letter quoted on p. 250 hereof, Sherman merely stated that he was baptized by "Mr. Gallagher."
12. REVEREND WILLIAM ANDERSON SCOTT, pastor of Calvary Presbyterian Church, San Francisco, 1854–1861. As stated by Sherman, Scott vigorously opposed the Vigilance Committee and was hanged in effigy for his attitude. In a recently published biography (Clifford Merrill Drury, *William Andrew Scott, No Ordinary Man,* [Glendale, Calif.: The Arthur H. Clarke Company, 1967], pp. 194–195), is a letter written to the Rev. Mr. Scott by W. T. Sherman, dated Nov. 17, 1856, praising him for his courage. Author Drury, however, in reporting the episode makes two errors: he describes Sherman as a "Roman Catholic soldier turned merchant."
13. JOHN PARROTT, see Note 1 of Part Three.
14. BUNCOMBE. Sherman used an idiom that originated in politics. Early in the nineteenth century, Congressman Felix Walker of North Carolina delivered a speech in the House that was full of florid rhetoric and extravagant proposals. To colleagues who remonstrated with him that he could not expect the Congress to take

his expressions seriously, he replied that he had not spoken to impress the House but merely for the edification of his constituents back home in Buncombe County. Ever since, such perfervid oratory has been termed "buncombe."

15. WILLIAM H. ASPINWALL, see Note 26 of Part Three.
16. SAMUEL MILLARD BOWMAN, see Note 5 of Part Two.
17. FITCH, unpublished letter dated Jan. 18, 1857.
18. For California's gold production, see Rodman W. Paul, *California Gold* (Cambridge, Mass.: Harvard University Press, 1947), pp. 118, 241, 262, and 345–346.
19. FITCH, unpublished letter dated Jan. 20, 1857.
20. For LOUIS W. McLANE, president of WELLS, FARGO & CO. EXPRESS, see Note 81 of Part Three.
21. FITCH, unpublished letter dated Feb. 5, 1857.
22. JAMES KING OF WILLIAM, see pp. 43–44 hereof, Note 67 of Part One, and Note 47 of Part Four.
23. A. HUGHES, F. L. A. PIOCHE, and J. B. BAYERQUE were prominent San Francisco merchants in early years following the Gold Rush, located on the south side of Clay Street facing Leidesdorff. They did a slight amount of banking about 1850 but did not advertise as bankers until April, 1851. A little later, their office was at the southeast corner of Montgomery and Jackson Streets. Hughes retired from the firm in March, 1850; thereafter, the firm was PIOCHE & BAYERQUE and became most active in organizing some of the more important public utilities. The firm dissolved in February, 1873. (CROSS, Vol. I, pp. 66 and 230.)
24. PALMER, COOK & CO. closed its doors on July 29, 1856. (CROSS, Vol. I, p. 208; see also Note 43 of Part One.)

    HL index cards: AM 130 shows "letter to John Cook dated May 31, 1855"; also AM 131 "account of Richard Roman, Alfred A. Cohen and Edward Jones, assignees of Adams & Company, 1 volume 8vo 1855–56."
25. BANCAL, Vol. VI, pp. 617–619.
26. For JOHN M. RHODES, see pp. 39, 112, and 252 hereof.
27. GARRISON, MORGAN, FRETZ AND RALSTON, see Note 80 of Part Three and Note 3 of Appendix, "The Page-Bacon Failures . . ."
28. FITCH, unpublished letter dated Feb. 15, 1857.
29. This refers to STATE SENATOR JAMES M. ESTILL of Placer County. (BANCAL, Vol. VI, p. 656.)
30. FITCH, second unpublished letter dated Feb. 19, 1857.
31. FITCH, unpublished letter dated Feb. 26, 1857.
32. COLONEL THOMAS SWORDS, see Note 59 of Part One.
33. JOHN PARROTT, see Note 1 of Part Three.
34. STATE SENATOR WILLIAM J. SHAW arrived in San Francisco in June, 1849. He was elected state senator from San Francisco on the Democratic ticket at the election in September, 1855. (ANNALS, p. 824; also "Continuation of the Annals of San Francisco," compiled by Dorothy H. Huggins, CHSQ, Vol. XVI [March, 1937], 80 and

84.) This letter to Sherman, dated Sacramento, Mar. 3, 1857, about the repudiation of the state's bonds, is in FITCH. In it, he addresses Sherman as "Dear General," because of his briefly held militia rank.

35. See Note 80 of Part Three.
36. FITCH, unpublished letter dated Mar. 4, 1857.
37. FITCH, unpublished letter dated Mar. 19, 1857.
38. FITCH, unpublished letter dated Mar. 21, 1857.
39. HASTINGS BANK. B. F. Hastings & Co. were operating a bank in Sacramento as early as 1850. In the panic of September of that year, they made an assignment for the benefit of creditors but later reopened. The firm failed in 1871, with liabilities of $160,000 and assets of approximately $100,000. (CROSS, Vol. I, pp. 92 and 387.)
40. For LOW BROTHERS, see Note 70 of Part Four; for ROBINSON BOURS & Co., see p. 112 hereof.
41. FITCH, unpublished letter dated Sacramento, California, Apr. 2, 1857.
42. For references to JOHN M. RHODES, see pp. 39, 112, 252, and 287 hereof.
43. For CHARLES POMROY STONE, see Note 50 of Part Two and pp. 230 ff. hereof.
44. COLONEL THOMAS SWORDS, see Note 59 of Part One.
45. BRIGADIER GENERAL NEWMAN S. CLARKE: native of Connecticut; Ensign in the 11th Infantry, Mar. 12, 1812; 2nd Lieutenant, Mar. 13, 1813; Captain, Oct. 1, 1814; Major, July 21, 1824; Lieutenant Colonel, 8th Infantry, July 7, 1838; Colonel, 6th Infantry, June 29, 1846; Brigadier General, Mar. 29, 1847, for gallantry at Siege of Vera Cruz; succeeded Col. Thomas T. Fauntleroy, 1st Dragoons, in command of Department of the Pacific. General Clarke transferred headquarters of the Department of the Pacific to San Francisco. Its designation was changed to Department of California in October, 1858. General Clarke died in San Francisco, Oct. 17, 1860, and was succeeded in command of the department by Lt. Col. Benjamin L. Beall. (HEITMAN, Vol. I, p. 307; also BANCAL, Vol. VII, p. 472.)
46. For DREXEL, SATHER & CHURCH, see Note 33 of Part Two and several subsequent references. Both Sherman and "rumor" were inaccurate here. Drexel did not retire from the firm until 1859; and as shown in Note 33 of Part Two above cited, the firm, despite his withdrawal, survived into the twentieth century.
47. The reference is to the firm of GARRISON, MORGAN, FRETZ AND RALSTON, for which see Note 80 of Part Three and Note 3 of Appendix, "The Page-Bacon Failures . . ."
48. For TALLANT & WILDE, see Note 30 of Part One.
49. THE SAVINGS AND LOAN SOCIETY's first officers were E. W. Burr, president; John Archbald, vice-president; and William Herrick, secretary. Its first office was on the second floor of a building on Washington near Montgomery Street. It later occupied its own brick building on Clay Street. In 1890, it erected new quarters at the northwest corner of Sutter and Montgomery Streets. On Apr. 17,

1910, it consolidated with the San Francisco Savings Union (incorporated in 1862). The name was soon changed to Savings Union Bank of San Francisco, later Savings Union Bank and Trust Company, which was absorbed by Mercantile Trust Company of San Francisco, July 5, 1920. The latter merged with the American Bank of San Francisco in 1927 to form the American Trust Company. Some years ago, the last named institution was merged into the present Wells Fargo Bank. (CROSS, Vol. I, pp. 221–223; also *Savings Union Service* [a house organ of the Savings Union Bank and Trust Company] for April, 1913, Vol. II, No. 1, p. 7.)

50. FITCH, unpublished letter dated Apr. 19, 1857.
51. For ARRINGTON, see Note 79 of Part Three; for BREWSTER, see Note 78 of Part Three; for CASTLE, see Note 68 of Part Three.
52. MAJOR WILLIAM WHANN MACKALL: native of the District of Columbia; appointed to United States Military Academy from Maryland, July, 1833; 2nd Lieutenant, 1st Artillery, July 1, 1837; 1st Lieutenant, July 9, 1838; regimental adjutant, Jan. 20, 1840; Captain, August 20, 1847; brevetted Major, Aug. 5, 1853; resigned, July 3, 1861; Brigadier General, Confederate States of America, 1861–1865; died, Aug. 19, 1891. (HEITMAN, Vol. I, p. 670.)
53. COLONEL OSBORN CROSS: native of Maryland; entered United States Military Academy, July 1, 1820; 2nd Lieutenant, 1st Infantry, July 1, 1825; 1st Lieutenant, Dec. 31, 1831; Captain and assistant quartermaster, July 7, 1838; Major and quartermaster, July 24, 1847; Lieutenant Colonel and deputy quartermaster general, Feb. 26, 1863; Colonel, July 29, 1866; retired, July 29, 1866; died, July 15, 1876. (HEITMAN, Vol. I, p. 341.)
54. SAMUEL MOSS, JR., in July, 1850, was admitted as a partner to Pioche, Bayerque & Co. but retired before the dissolution of the firm. In 1851, he was a member of the first Vigilance Committee. (ANNALS, p. 575; also CROSS, Vol. I, p. 66.)
55. FITCH, unpublished letter dated May 4, 1857.

Notes for Part Six

1. MEMOIRS, Vol. I, pp. 134–135.
2. FITCH, unpublished letter dated Lancaster, Ohio, July 1, 1857.
3. MAJOR JOHN G. BARNARD, see Note 57 of Part One.
4. FITCH, unpublished letters dated New York, July 20 and 21, 1857.
5. FITCH, unpublished letter dated New York, July 29, 1857.
6. FITCH, unpublished letter dated New York, July 30, 1857.
7. CHARLES C. TURNER and THOMAS TURNER. Charles Turner (an elder brother of Henry Smith Turner): Midshipman, May 10, 1820; Lieutenant, May 17, 1828; Commander, July 20, 1851; died March 4, 1861. (CALLAHAN, p. 553; also several references to him in TURNER.) Thomas Turner (another older brother of Henry Smith Turner): Midshipman, Apr. 21, 1825; passed Midshipman, June 4, 1831; Lieutenant, Dec. 22, 1835; Commander, Sept. 14, 1850; Captain, July 16, 1862; Commodore, Dec. 13, 1862; Rear Admiral, May 27, 1868; retired Apr. 21, 1870; died Mar. 24, 1883. (CALLAHAN, p. 554; also several references to him in TURNER, including his command of U.S.S. *Ironsides*. In TURNER [p. 10], it is stated from family notes that Thomas Turner was the eldest brother of Henry. However, the above record shows Charles was his senior in the various ranks attained by both, through the rank of Commander.)
8. FITCH, unpublished letters dated New York, Aug. 7 and 10, 1857.
9. FITCH, second unpublished letter dated New York, Aug. 10, 1857.
10. FITCH, unpublished letters dated New York, Aug. 11 and 12, 1857.
11. FITCH, unpublished letter dated New York, Aug. 13, 1857.
12. FITCH, unpublished letter dated New York, Aug. 18, 1857.
13. FITCH, unpublished letter dated New York, Aug. 21, 1857.
14. FITCH, unpublished letter dated New York, Aug. 24, 1857.
15. Gebhard was a member of the banking firm of SCHUCHARDT & GEBHARD, New York, a correspondent of Lucas, Turner & Co. while in San Francisco, and mentioned several times in earlier chapters.
16. FITCH, unpublished letter dated New York, Aug. 28, 1857.

17. FITCH, unpublished letter dated New York, Sept. 17, 1857.
18. FITCH, unpublished letter dated New York, Sept. 22, 1857.
19. FITCH, unpublished letter dated New York, Sept. 29, 1857.
20. FITCH, unpublished letter dated New York, Oct. 3, 1857.
21. FITCH, unpublished letter dated New York, Oct. 6, 1857.
22. FITCH, unpublished letter dated New York, Oct. 9, 1857.
23. FITCH, unpublished letter dated New York, Oct. 10, 1857.
24. FITCH, unpublished letter dated New York, Oct. 13, 1857.
25. FITCH, unpublished letter dated Metropolitan Hotel, New York, Jan. 3, 1858.
26. FITCH, unpublished letter dated New York, Jan. 5, 1858.
27. WILLIAM BLANDING, of English and French lineage, was born in South Carolina in 1818, son of a distinguished lawyer. William Blanding was admitted to the bar in 1840. In 1846, he raised a company in Charleston, S.C., which served in the War with Mexico, Blanding being elected its Captain. He came to San Francisco in 1854, his family following a year later. In 1855, he was appointed United States district attorney for the northern district of California, serving about two years. He held various other public and corporate positions. He died in San Francisco, Oct. 25, 1882. His son, Gordon Blanding, was a prominent San Francisco attorney. (SHUCK, p. 550.)
28. CAPTAIN CHARLES POMROY STONE, see Note 50 of Part Two. FITCH, unpublished letter dated San Francisco, Feb. 4, 1858.
29. COLONEL THOMAS SWORDS, see Note 59 of Part One.
30. INTERNATIONAL HOTEL, a five-story structure, was opened in 1854 on the south side of Jackson Street, between Kearny and Montgomery Streets. (ANNALS, pp. 650–651, including its picture.)
31. FITCH, unpublished letter dated San Francisco, Feb. 18, 1858.
32. HAIGHT AND BAINBRIDGE. HENRY HAIGHT had been a partner in the now-defunct firm of PAGE, BACON & CO. HENRY BAINBRIDGE was a former employee of Lucas, Turner & Co. Langley's 1858 *San Francisco Directory* gives their address as southwest corner of Merchant and Montgomery Streets.
33. FITCH, unpublished letter dated San Francisco, Mar. 4, 1858.
34. MAJOR CHARLES FREDERICK RUFF: native, state of Pennsylvania; Cadet at United States Military Academy, Sept. 1, 1834; 2nd Lieutenant, 1st Dragoons, July 1, 1838; resigned, Dec. 31, 1842; Lieutenant Colonel, 1st Missouri Volunteers, June 18, 1846; Captain, Mounted Rifles, July 7, 1846; Major, Dec. 30, 1856; Lieutenant Colonel, June 19, 1861; 3rd Cavalry, Aug. 3, 1861; retired, Mar. 30, 1864; died, Oct. 1, 1885. (HEITMAN, Vol. I, p. 850.)
35. HENRY D. BACON was born in Massachusetts in 1813. He moved to St. Louis, married Julia Ann Page, daughter of David D. Page. He became a partner in Page & Bacon of St. Louis and in Page, Bacon & Co. of San Francisco. He died on Feb. 19, 1893. (Milton H. Shutes, "Henry Douglas Bacon (1813–1893)," CHSQ, Vol. XXVI [Sept. 1947], 193–200.) Four boxes of Bacon papers are in HL. Many

of these are letters from Henry D. Bacon to D. D. Page and others; also some from D. D. Page, as well as correspondence of other parties. Most of the collection deals with the failures of Page & Bacon, and of Page, Bacon & Co., as well as with the affairs of the Ohio and Mississippi Railroad.

36. Major Richard Pindell Hammond, see Note 6 of Part Three.
37. FITCH, unpublished letter dated San Francisco, Mar. 21, 1858. The reference is to Samuel Moss, Jr., mentioned in Note 54 of Part Five.
38. FITCH, unpublished letters dated San Francisco, Apr. 4 and 18, 1858.
39. The reference here is to Harry I. Thornton, who arrived in California Jan. 1, 1852, having already been appointed a United States land commissioner. He died in San Francisco in January, 1861. It is easy to become confused about the Thornton lawyers in California during the 1850's. James Dabney Thornton, no relative of the aforesaid Harry I. Thornton, married the latter's daughter, Sarah. James Dabney Thornton arrived in San Francisco June 14, 1854, and soon became a member of the firm of Thornton, Williams and Thornton, the other Thornton being Harry I., just mentioned, the father of James's wife. James D. Thornton in 1879 became an associate justice of the California supreme court and served eleven years in this capacity. Harry I. Thornton had a son, Harry I. Thornton, Jr., also a lawyer, mentioned in Note 42 below. (SHUCK, p. 751. Also "The Law and Order View of the San Francisco Vigilance Committee of 1856," arranged by Herbert C. Florcken from the correspondence of Gov. J. Neely Johnson, CHSQ, Vol. XIV [December, 1935], 364; Carl I. Wheat, ed., "California's Bantam Cock: The Journals of Charles E. De Long, 1854–1863," CHSQ, Vol. X [September, 1931], 262, 274, and 289; Henry R. Wagner, "Albert Little Bancroft: His Diaries, Account Books, etc.," CHSQ, Vol. XXIX [June, 1950], 108. Also BANCAL, Vol. VII, pp. 409 and 735.)
40. Edward S. Spear, furniture auctioneer, is listed in Langley's 1858 *San Francisco Directory* at 131 California Street.
41. FITCH, unpublished letter dated San Francisco, Apr. 18, 1858.
42. Harry I. Thornton, Jr., was district attorney of Sierra County, 1858, 1859, 1860; state senator, Sierra County, 1860. (SIERRA, pp. 431, 432, and 435.) W. S. Spear appears on a list of attorneys admitted to the bar of Sierra County, under date of 1852 (SIERRA, p. 431). Of other Sierra County names mentioned in immediately preceding paragraphs, Thaddeus Purdy appears as having been admitted to the local bar in 1852 and as addressing the grand jury in the same year. Benjamin Green is listed as county treasurer of Sierra County in 1856 and 1857. (SIERRA, pp. 428, 429, and 433.)
43. This was undoubtedly Judge E. W. F. Sloan, who appears in Langley's 1858 *San Francisco Directory* with office in the Lucas-Turner Building. He was also for a time a law partner of William

Henry Rhodes, well known in early San Francisco as a poet, playwright, and author who wrote under the pen name Caxton. (Carl I. Wheat, ed., "California's Bantam Cock: The Journals of Charles E. De Long, 1854–1863," CHSQ, Vol. X [September, 1931], 266.)

44. See Note 27 above.
45. Opposite p. 208 of SIERRA, there is a picture of the Camp of the Monte Cristo Gold Mining Company, giving its altitude as 6,350 feet.
46. FITCH, unpublished letter dated Downieville, May 1, 1858.
47. CROSS states that W. H. LADD & Co. "engaged in banking in Downieville," no date mentioned (Vol. I, p. 243).
48. VAN CLIEF AND STEWART. A. VAN CLIEF is listed as having been admitted to the Sierra County bar Nov. 19, 1855. W. M. STEWART also appears as a member of local bar, no date given. Stewart, a few years after Sherman's visit to Downieville, moved to Nevada and became quite wealthy from fortunate investments or speculation on the Comstock Lode. He eventually achieved considerable fame from his service as a United States senator from Nevada. (SIERRA, p. 431.)
49. In all probability this was JUDGE FERDINAND J. MCCANN, who became judge of the court of sessions, Aug. 19, 1852. He was of Irish and Spanish descent and a resident of Kentucky before coming to California in 1850. He practiced law briefly in Marysville and went to Downieville in 1851. In a few years, he resigned from the bench, returned to Kentucky, and married. He later settled in Santa Cruz, Calif. (SIERRA, pp. 428 and 429.)
50. THOMAS ELWYN TURNER: native of Pennsylvania; 2nd Lieutenant, Artillery, May 20, 1857; transferred to 4th Infantry, Mar. 7, 1858; 1st Lieutenant, May 14, 1861; Captain, Nov. 25, 1861; brevetted Major, June 27, 1862, for gallant conduct at Battle of Gaines Mill, Va.; died Aug. 18, 1862. (HEITMAN, Vol. I, p. 975.)

    Henry Turner may have had more than one nephew named Elwyn. In view of the military rank attained by the above named in May, 1857, it seems unlikely that he was the Elwyn Turner who became an employee of Lucas, Turner & Co. in the forepart of 1855, as mentioned in an earlier chapter. *That* Elwyn wrote to his uncle from San Francisco on July 30, 1855 (letter in LUCAS). The letter contains an interesting comment on the bank's personnel: "I wish for your arrival. . . . I want somebody that can advise me. . . . No person could be kinder to me than Captain S. has been but . . . I do not like to trouble him. . . . He has always something to do, either at his house or in the bank, and for Mr. Nisbet, I only wish to talk to *him* on business matters."

51. FITCH, unpublished letter dated San Francisco, May 9, 1858.
52. FITCH, unpublished letter dated San Francisco, May 13, 1858.
53. FITCH, unpublished letter dated Downieville, May 17, 1858.

54. MEMOIRS, Vol. I, p. 139.
55. FITCH, unpublished letter dated Fort Leavenworth, Sept. 20, 1858.
56. FITCH, unpublished letter dated St. Louis, Mo., Oct. 1, 1859; also LEWIS, p. 116.
57. FITCH, unpublished letter dated San Francisco, Apr. 18, 1858.

Sherman's Banking Terminology

Every business employs words and phrases intelligible to its own members but less clear to the uninitiated. Banking is no exception, so the lay reader may appreciate an explanation of some of the terms encountered in Sherman's correspondence.

"Discounts," "drafts," "acceptances," and "exchange" are continually mentioned with no elaboration because they were so well understood by both Sherman and his St. Louis partners.

When California business houses ordered goods from Eastern wholesalers or manufacturers, they sometimes remitted cash (i.e., bank drafts) with their orders but far more frequently sought some form of credit in making payment. On rare occasions, the seller opened an account on his books in the name of the purchaser and charged the shipment to it. Not many firms in the new, far-western frontier boasted sufficient standing to merit such liberal treatment. Usually, the goods were shipped with a draft attached to the bill of lading, which had to be paid before the buyer could obtain delivery. If the full amount of the purchase was not paid upon delivery, the buyer sometimes executed time drafts for part or all of the amount due the seller. These drafts were made payable in whatever number of days had been agreed upon—usually thirty days or sixty days. The purchaser's endorsement on such time drafts was his acceptance of the terms stipulated by the seller.

Usually, the seller's own financial situation made it inconvenient for him to hold these accepted drafts until they came due. He would therefore endorse them over to a bank which gave him the cash immediately. As the price for the immediate cashing of such a time draft, the bank deducted a charge known as a "discount." That was its compensation for cashing the paper ahead of its maturity. The bank ordinarily termed all such obligations as its "discounts." Frequently on a bank's own statement of condition, all such discounted drafts as well as all promissory notes in its assets were lumped under the title of "discounts" or "loans and discounts."

The principal source of earnings of the banks was the interest collected on loans it had made and the discounts from drafts it had purchased. These commonly ranged in the Gold Rush from 2½% to 5% a month.

Sometimes the San Francisco banks discounted the drafts held by Eastern shippers. Frequently, local buyers of merchandise, who were jobbers or wholesalers, sold portions of the goods involved to third parties. In these cases, more drafts were executed and discounted in the selling process.

Commerce in California was a one-way street. Virtually all necessities and luxuries were imported from elsewhere. The state's one sizable export was gold. Much gold dust and bullion were shipped East, but the bulk of settlements due Eastern shippers was drafts drawn by California banks on their Eastern correspondents. Before the days of the short-lived Pony Express and the first transcontinental railroad, all such mail transfers had to be made by the long, slow steamer routes by way of Panama or Nicaragua. Such bank drafts necessarily remained outstanding for several weeks after they were purchased in San Francisco. Money, or gold dust and bullion, had to be shipped East by the same cumbersome method, to be credited to the California bank that sold its drafts on Eastern banks. From this arose the "exchange" problem about which Sherman complained so bitterly. The transfer of coin, gold, and bank drafts entailed shipping charges made by the steamship companies, cost of insuring such shipments, loss of interest (always at a high rate), and incidental costs.

Initially, most of the banks and express companies thought they could profitably sell exchange on New York at 3%. That meant they charged a customer $103 for a $100 draft on New York. Sherman seems to have been one of the first to realize that his bank could not break even at 3% for such transactions, because actual costs exceeded 3%.

In several letters, Sherman referred to bids for, or purchases of, transfer drafts or treasury drafts. This must have referred to drafts sent by the federal government to the treasurer in San Francisco involving transfer of government funds to the Pacific Coast to cover disbursements made there to pay for goods or services, such as the erection of public buildings and the fortifications on San Francisco Bay. Since these drafts were payable in the East, any local bank cashing them had to have the cash in San Francisco to do so. If it bid, say ¼% or ½% less than the face amount, such discount was compensation for providing actual cash on the spot for a piece of paper payable in New York or Washington.

The Page-Bacon Failures as Viewed by F.W. Page

Sherman was not the only one to blame Henry Haight for much of Page, Bacon & Co.'s troubles.[1] The failures of its banks in both St. Louis and San Francisco is a tale of the long ago retold many times in histories. Yet even at this late day, added light is thrown upon the disaster by a hitherto unpublished diary of one of the firm's partners.

In 1849, when Page, Bacon & Co. opened their express office in San Francisco, Francis W. Page, son of Daniel Page, head of the house, was placed in charge. In June, 1850, it grew into a bank; Henry Haight and Judge David Chambers became partners and managed the San Francisco office, while the third partner on the Coast, F. W. Page, went to Sacramento to head the branch started there. He remained active in the firm's affairs until the failure in the spring of 1855.

On May 30, 1855, three trustees were appointed to conserve and liquidate the assets of Page, Bacon & Co. for the benefit of creditors. These were John Parrott, A. A. Ritchie, and Ira P. Rankin.[2] The partners also gave powers of attorney to F. W. Page to take the necessary steps to protect the creditors. His diary from July to September, 1855, reveals the ill feeling among the partners. Henry Haight threatened to revoke the power of attorney he had given Page and seems generally to have hampered the work being done for the creditors. The huge remittance of coin to New York made just before the failure was still a matter of bitter recrimination. Bacon,

[1] See p. 423.
[2] See p. 423.

one of the senior partners, had desperately pleaded for that money to save the St. Louis house. Haight challenged Bacon's right to give orders about the remittance. He threatened to sue the steamship company and all others concerned for not delivering the shipment to the New York correspondent of Page, Bacon & Co. F. W. Page confessed to his diary on July 8, "I'll not be surprised if Haight causes us trouble. I'll watch him." In the "watching" process, he was frequently a passenger on the Sacramento river boats. Several times, surprisingly enough, Page was Haight's companion at meals and social journeyings to and from San Mateo. D. O. Mills, John Parrott, W. C. Ralston, and A. J. Easton [3] and their families were frequently present; so was another Page, Bacon & Co. partner, Judge Chambers. Frank Page's opinion of the latter gentleman was also mixed: "Chambers talks of going to the States on the 16th. I think will cause trouble." Other friends of the rival partners were Ben Holladay and C. K. Garrison.[4]

One of the more picturesque incidents of the liquidation was a suit brought in July, 1855, by Page, Bacon & Co. against I. C. Woods and A. A. Cohen. (Cohen had recently been made receiver of Adams & Co.) The plaintiffs charged that some time before the failure of Page, Bacon & Co., Woods and Cohen had run inferior gold dust from the northern mines through some kind of a machine to make it appear to be dust of greater value from the southern mines. Agents of the defendants so represented it to the bank, and Page said Woods and Cohen had profited some $100,000 by the deception. His diary described this as part of a conspiracy as Woods said "to break down that d——d Pike County Bank" (a reference doubtless to Page-Bacon's Missouri origin). Haight had at first urged Page and Chambers to "do something in the matter, then after we had gotten so far . . . , that we could not retrace, he (Haight) wished to withdraw the suit and not do anything in the case."

Apparently because of Page's refusal to abandon the suit, Haight revoked the power of attorney he had given Page, and published notice of such revocation in the press. "I certainly told him he had treated me very unjustly," Page noted in his diary. Later, Haight and Chambers called at Page's room in San Francisco and the former said that he had reconsidered and taken the offensive notice out of

---

[3] See p. 423.

[4] See p. 424.

the *Herald.* He asked Page to return the revocation notice, which he destroyed. Haight explained his conduct as due to his resentment at the hard things Henry Bacon had reportedly said about him. According to the reports that had reached Haight, Bacon "laid all the blame of the failures on him (Haight)."

About the same time C. K. Garrison told Page that Haight's real object was to force the dismissal of the suit against Woods and Cohen, because these defendants and Palmer, Cook & Co. "hold something over Haight which he fears they will expose." Page declared in his diary: "I think the time has come now for me to pitch into the whole Haight family."

Another informant told Page that while Haight was a passenger on the S.S. *Uncle Sam* with William Ruxton (whom Page, Bacon & Co. had employed shortly before its first closing), Haight proposed to Ruxton "that he and Ruxton should break the house of Page Bacon and Company, and build themselves up on the ruins of the house." Page also noted in his diary: "A. J. Easton says Haight is one to Ruxton "that he and Ruxton should break the house of Page, with the details of a quarrel he himself had had with Haight. Easton said he had offered to lend Henry Haight, his brother Samuel Haight, and a third party $7,000 if the three would sign a bond to pay the Protestant Orphan Asylum $1,000 if any one of them drank any ardent spirits, wines, or beer in the next twelve months. Easton declared that both Haight brothers violated this bond within two days, and that Henry Haight had been in Sacramento a short time previously and gotten so drunk that he had to be put to bed. Page concluded this edifying anecdote by observing: "Henry Haight gets so drunk now every day or so that he is foolish. I think he begins to find he has fallen from the esteem of this people and drinks to drown his feelings not conscience as I don't believe he has . . . any soul."

One drunken partner was not enough; presently the diary notes: "Judge Chambers is said to [have] had a spree the night before last; was off with some of the Bhoys [*sic*], he did not get to bed until 4:A.M."

Altogether this summer of 1855 was a very hectic one for F. W. Page. Incidental to the liquidation of assets for the creditors, his Sacramento dwelling was sold by the Sheriff in July for $2,950. Two months later, ranch property he owned was sold for $100, over and above an attachment against it for $900. In addition, the firm's

Napa farm was sold for $1,350; it had cost the partnership $10,000.

In the midst of all of this, Page wrote in his diary that he watched the funeral procession of Sherman's friend, Capt. Joseph Folsom, which took eleven minutes to pass before his window on Montgomery Street.

NOTES

1. Sources for this appendix include particularly the unpublished diary of F. W. Page, July 1 through Sept. 6, 1855, in the F. W. Page Papers in the CHS Library; also "Continuation of the Annals of San Francisco," compiled by Dorothy H. Huggins, CHSQ, Vol. XV (September, 1936), 273, 275, 278, and 280–281; *Ibid.* (December, 1936), 370 and 377; *Ibid.*, Vol. XVI (September, 1937), 282 and 283.
   F. W. Page was a member of the executive committee of the Vigilance Committee of 1856. (POPULAR, Vol. II, p. 113.)
   Several letters in BACON express serious doubts not only of Henry Haight's honesty but also of his loyalty to the firm. They placed chief responsibility for the failure on Haight's not having sent forward remittances as promised (letters, H. D. Bacon dated Jan. 11, 1855, to D. D. Page; also same to same, Feb. 28, 1855; also same to same, Apr. 11, 1855). D. D. Page in letter to Francis Page, June 10, 1855, voiced similar unfavorable opinions.
2. For JOHN PARROTT, see Note 1 of Part Three. A. A. RITCHIE was probably ARCHIBALD A. RITCHIE of the San Francisco firm of Ritchie, Osgood and Co. He was a sea captain who arrived in California in 1848, bought land in Solano County, and was later successful claimant for several ranches. (BANCAL, Vol. IV, pp. 671 and 674.) He died in 1856, leaving a family. (PIONEER, Vol. V, p. 696.) IRA P. RANKIN was collector of the port of San Francisco. (Henry R. Wagner, "Edward Bosqui, Printer and Man of Affairs," CHSQ, Vol. XXI [December, 1942], 327.)
3. DARIUS OGDEN MILLS was born in North Salem, N.Y., Sept. 5, 1825. He early entered the banking business in Buffalo. He came to California in 1848, according to Bancroft (another authority says in 1849), engaging in trade in Sacramento. With $40,000 profits, which he quickly made, he started his own bank in Sacramento. In the early 1850's, he invested heavily in real estate on the San Francisco peninsula, acquiring among other holdings nearly 1,500 acres in the vicinity of present-day Burlingame and Millbrae. He was one of the organizers of the Bank of California in 1864 and was its first

president, holding that office until 1873. On its reorganization in 1875, Mills again became president of the bank, which he remained until May, 1878. He died in 1910. (BANCAL, Vol. VII, p. 183, n. 53; also Frank M. Stanger, "A California Rancho under Three Flags: A History of Rancho Buri Buri in San Mateo County," CHSQ, Vol. XVII [September, 1938], 254–257; also Neill C. Wilson, *400 California Street* [San Francisco: Bank of California N.A., 1964], pp. 19, 22, 41, 48, and 49.)

William C. Ralston was born in Ohio in 1826. As a young man clerking on a Mississippi River boat, he soon entered into a partnership with some steamboatmen to engage in trade and shipping at Panama. This brought him in close touch with the Gold Rush, and he arrived in San Francisco in August, 1854. He and a partner became agents for the Morgan steamers *Yankee Blade* and *Uncle Sam*. On Jan. 1, 1856, the firm of Garrison, Morgan, Fretz and Ralston opened a banking office in San Francisco. Ralston's bold imagination and tireless energy helped this and some successor banks to prosper. These qualities aided him in organizing the Bank of California in 1864, the first incorporated bank in the state. He became its first cashier and, on D. O. Mills's retirement, its second president. Ralston made the Bank of California the dominant force in the development of the great Comstock Lode. While this brought it much prosperity, various speculations and the effects of the Panic of 1873 finally forced it to suspend payment on Aug. 26, 1875. The next day, Ralston, whose habit it was to swim almost daily, died in the waters of the Bay off the foot of Hyde Street. (Wilson, *400 California Street, op. cit.*, pp. 2, 3, 4, 8, 13, 17, 19, 28, 43, 45, and 46.)

A. J. Easton evidently owned considerable real estate in or near San Francisco, as well as an interest in the plank road to the Presidio. He seems to have been a business associate of D. O. Mills. There are indications that the Mills and Easton families were well acquainted and possibly related. (F. W. Page, unpublished diary, *op. cit.*)

4. Ben Holladay was one of the most successful operators of mail, stage coach, and freight in the West. He built this into such a large and profitable system that on June 1, 1866, Wells Fargo & Co. purchased it "for a large fortune." (E. A. Wiltsee, "The Emigrant's Dream," CHSQ, Vol. XV [December, 1936], 328.) Later, he had extensive railroad interests and also silver mines in the Mexican state of San Luis Potosi. (Kenneth M. Johnson, "Frederic Hall," CHSQ, Vol. XXXVIII [March, 1959], 52.) For Cornelius K. Garrison, see Note 2 of Part Two.

Bibliography

Armstrong, Leroy, and J. O. Denny. *Financial California.* San Francisco: Coast Banker Publishing Company, 1916.

Athearn, Robert G. *William Tecumseh Sherman and the Settlement of the West.* Norman, Okla.: University of Oklahoma Press, 1956.

Atherton, Gertrude. *California: An Intimate History.* New York: Harper & Brothers, 1914.

Bailey, Paul. *Sam Brannan and the California Mormons.* Los Angeles: Western-lore Press, 1943.

Bancroft, Hubert Howe. *History of Arizona and New Mexico 1530–1888.* Albuquerque, N.M.: Horn and Wallace, 1962.

———. *History of California.* 7 vols. (Vols. XVIII to XXIV of Bancroft's *Works*). San Francisco: The History Company, 1888.

———. *Popular Tribunals.* 2 vols. (Vols. XXXVI and XXXVII of Bancroft's *Works*). San Francisco: The History Company, 1887.

Bowman, Samuel Millard, and R. B. Irwin. *Sherman and His Campaigns.* New York: Charles B. Richardson, 1865.

Browne, J. Ross. *Muleback to the Convention.* San Francisco: Book Club of California, 1950.

———. *Report on the Debates in the Convention of California on the Formation of the State Constitution.* Washington, D.C.: John T. Towers, Printer, 1850.

Buchanan, A. Russell. *David S. Terry of California, Dueling Judge.* San Marino, Calif.: Huntington Library, 1956.

Callahan, Edward W. *List of Officers of the Navy of the United States, etc., from 1775 to 1900.* New York: L. R. Hammersby, 1901.

Caughey, John Walton. *Gold Is the Cornerstone.* Berkeley and Los Angeles: University of California Press, 1948.

Clarke, Dwight L. (ed.). *Original Journals of Henry Smith Turner, with Stephen Watts Kearny to New Mexico and California 1846.*

With an introductory and biographical chapter by the editor. Norman, Okla.: University of Oklahoma Press, 1966.

CLELAND, ROBERT GLASS. *From Wilderness to Empire: A History of California 1542–1900.* New York: Alfred A. Knopf, 1944.

CROSS, IRA B. *Financing an Empire: History of Banking in California.* 5 vols. Chicago, San Francisco and Los Angeles: S. J. Clarke Publishing Company, 1927.

DELAY, PETER J. *History of Yuba and Sutter Counties.* Los Angeles: Historic Record Company, 1924.

DODGE, GRENVILLE M. *Personal Recollections of President Abraham Lincoln, General Ulysses Grant and General Sherman.* Council Bluffs, Iowa: Monarch Printing Company, 1914.

DRURY, CLIFFORD MERRILL. *William Andrew Scott, No Ordinary Man.* Glendale, Calif.: The Arthur H. Clark Company, 1967.

ELDREDGE, ZOETH SKINNER. *Beginnings of San Francisco.* 2 vols. San Francisco: 1912.

FLEMING, W. L. (ed.). *General William T. Sherman as College President.* A collection of letters, documents and other material, and the like. Cleveland, Ohio: Clark, 1912.

FORCE, MANNING FERGUSON. *General Sherman 1820–1891.* New York: D. Appleton & Company, 1899.

GILLINGHAM, ROBERT. *The Rancho San Pedro: The Story of a Famous Rancho and of Its Owners.* Los Angeles: The Dominguez Estate Company, 1961.

HEADLEY, PHINEAS CAMP. *Life and Military Career of Major General William Tecumseh Sherman.* New York: Leavitt, 1868.

HEITMAN, FRANCIS B. *Historical Register and Dictionary of United States Army.* 2 vols. Washington, D.C.: Government Printing Office, 1903.

History of Plumas, Lassen and Sierra Counties, California. San Francisco: Fariss & Smith, 1882.

History of Sonoma County. San Francisco: Alley, Brown & Company, 1880.

HITTELL, THEODORE H. *History of California.* 4 vols. San Francisco: L. J. Stone & Company, 1897.

HOWE, M. A. DE WOLFE (ed.). *Home Letters of General Sherman.* New York: Charles Scribner's Sons, 1909.

HUTTON, WILLIAM RICH. *Glances at California 1847–1853.* San Marino, Calif.: Huntington Library, 1942.

JACOBSON, PAULINE. *City of the Golden Fifties.* Berkeley and Los Angeles: University of California Press, 1941.

JOHNSON, KENNETH M. *Limantour vs. the United States.* Los Angeles: Dawson's Book Shop, 1961.

JOHNSON, WILLIS FLETCHER. *Life of William Tecumseh Sherman.* Philadelphia: Edgewood Publishing Company, 1891.

JONES, IDWAL. *Ark of Empire.* Garden City, N.Y.: Doubleday & Company, 1951.

KEMBLE, EDWARD C. *History of California Newspapers 1846–1858.* Edited by HELEN HARDING BRETNOR. Los Gatos: Talisman Press, 1962.

LEWIS, LLOYD. *Sherman, Fighting Prophet.* New York: Harcourt, Brace & Company, 1932.

LICK, ROSEMARY. *A Generous Miser.* Los Angeles: The Ward Ritchie Press, 1967.

LIDDELL-HART, BASIL HENRY. *Sherman: Soldier, Realist, American.* New York: Dodd, Mead & Company, 1929.

Life and Reminiscences of General William T. Sherman (by various distinguished men of his time). Baltimore: Woodward, 1891.

MASON, PAUL (compiler). *Constitution of the State of California and of the United States and Other Documents.* Sacramento, Calif.: State Printing Office, 1929.

MATTHEWS, LEONARD. *A Long Life in Review.* St. Louis: (privately printed), 1928.

MCALLISTER, ANNA. *Ellen Ewing, Wife of General Sherman.* New York: Benziger Brothers, Inc., 1936.

MCSWEENEY, THOMAS DENIS. *Cathedral on California Street.* Fresno, Calif.: Academy of California Church History, 1952.

MELENDY, H. BRETT, and BENJAMIN F. GILBERT. *Governors of California.* Georgetown, Calif.: Talisman Press, 1965.

MIERS, EARL SCHENCK. *The General Who Marched to Hell and His March to Fame and Infamy.* New York: Alfred A. Knopf, 1951.

NEVILLE, AMELIA RANSOME. *The Fantastic City.* Boston: Houghton, Mifflin & Company, 1932.

NORTHROP, HENRY DAVENPORT. *Life and Deeds of General Sherman.* Philadelphia: International, 1891.

PAUL, RODMAN W. *California Gold.* Cambridge, Mass.: Harvard University Press, 1947.

———. *The California Gold Discovery.* Georgetown, Calif.: Talisman Press, 1966.

PHILLIPS, CATHERINE COFFIN. *Portsmouth Plaza, The Cradle of San Francisco.* San Francisco: John Henry Nash, 1932.

PHOENIX, JOHN (alias JOHN P. SQUIBOB, or in fact, Lieut. GEORGE H. DERBY, U.S.A.). *Phoenixiana.* San Francisco: The Grabhorn Press, 1937.

ROLLE, ANDREW F. *California: A History.* New York: Thomas Y. Crowell Company, 1963.

SCHERER, JAMES A. B. *The Lion of the Vigilantes.* New York: Bobbs Merrill Company, 1939.

SENOUR, FAUNT LEROY. *Major General William T. Sherman and His Campaigns.* Chicago: Sherwood, 1865.

SHERMAN, WILLIAM T. *Memoirs.* 2 vols. New York: D. Appleton & Company, 1875.

———. *Recollections of California 1846–1861.* Edited by JOSEPH A. SULLIVAN. Oakland, Calif.: Biobooks, 1945.

SHUCK, OSCAR T. *History of the Bench and Bar of California.* Originally published in 1888. Los Angeles: Commercial Printing House, 1901.

SOULÉ, FRANK, JOHN H. GIHON, M.D., and JAMES NISBET. *Annals of San Francisco.* New York: Appleton & Company, 1855.

TAYLOR, BAYARD. *El Dorado, or Adventures in the Path of Empire, etc.* 3d ed. New York: Putnam, 1850.

THORNDIKE, RACHEL SHERMAN (ed.). *The Sherman Letters* (between General and Senator Sherman). New York: Charles Scribner's Sons, 1894.

TUTHILL, FRANKLIN. *History of California.* San Francisco: H. W. Bancroft & Company, 1866.

WHEAT, CARL I. *The Maps of the California Gold Region 1848–1857.* San Francisco: The Grabhorn Press, 1942.

WILSON, NEILL C. *400 California Street.* San Francisco: Bank of California N.A., 1964.

Index

H

L

M

N

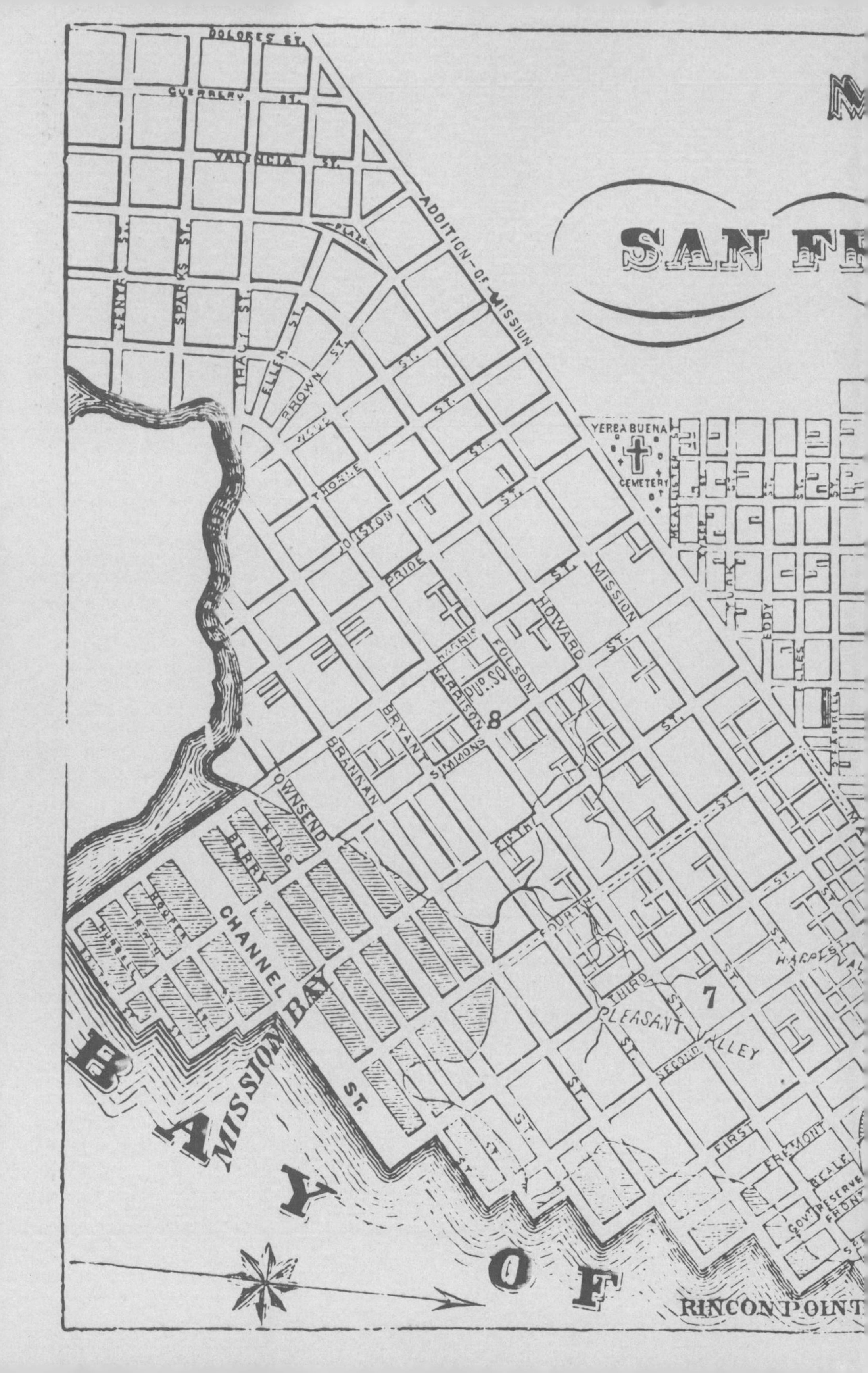

SAN FR
DOLORES ST.
VALENCIA ST.
ADDITION OF MISSION
YERBA BUENA
CEMETERY
MISSION
HOWARD
FOLSON
HARRISON
BRYANT
BRANNAN
TOWNSEND
KING
BERRY
CHANNEL
MISSION BAY
SIMMONS
FIFTH
FOURTH
THIRD
SECOND
FIRST
FREMONT
BEALE
PLEASANT
ALLEY
EDDY
HARPER ST.
BAY
OF
RINCON POINT
8
7